The City, Revisited

The City, Revisited

Urban Theory from Chicago, Los Angeles, and New York

■■■■■

Dennis R. Judd and Dick Simpson, Editors

University of Minnesota Press
Minneapolis • London

An earlier version of chapter 4 was published as Michael Dear and Nicholas Dahmann, "Urban Politics and the Los Angeles School of Urbanism," *Urban Affairs Review* 44, no. 2 (November 2008). Portions of chapter 6 were published as Steven P. Erie and Scott A. MacKenzie, "The L.A. School and Politics *Noir:* Bringing the Local State Back In," *Journal of Urban Affairs* 31 (2009); reproduced with permission of Blackwell Publishing. An earlier version of chapter 10 was published as Dick Simpson and Tom Kelly, "The New Chicago School of Urbanism and the New Daley Machine," *Urban Affairs Review* 44, no. 2 (November 2008).

Published by the University of Minnesota Press
111 Third Avenue South, Suite 290
Minneapolis, MN 55401-2520
http://www.upress.umn.edu

Library of Congress Cataloging-in-Publication Data

The city, revisited: urban theory from Chicago, Los Angeles, and New York / Dennis R. Judd and Dick Simpson, editors.
p. cm.
Includes bibliographical references and index.
ISBN: 978-0-8166-6575-4 (hc : alk. paper)
ISBN: 978-0-8166-6576-1 (pb : alk. paper)
1. Sociology, Urban—United States—Case studies. 2. Metropolitan government—United States—Case studies. 3. Sustainable development—United States—Case studies. I. Judd, Dennis R. II. Simpson, Dick W.
HT123.C4978 2011
307.760973—dc22
2010019700

Printed in the United States of America on acid-free paper

The University of Minnesota is an equal-opportunity educator and employer.

18 17 16 15 14 13 12 11   10 9 8 7 6 5 4 3 2 1

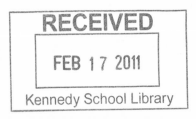

Contents

Part I

Revisiting Urban Theory

1

Theorizing the City

■ Dennis R. Judd

In 1925, a group of sociologists from the University of Chicago published a book that became a foundational work for generations of urban scholars. In *The City: Suggestions for Investigation of Human Behavior in the Urban Environment,*[1] Robert Park, Ernest Burgess, Roderick McKenzie, and some of their colleagues proposed an elegant, sweeping version of social Darwinism to explain the dynamics of urban spatial and social structure (the first footnote of the book's introduction is to Oswald Spengler). The "Chicago School" scholars interpreted cities as constantly evolving organisms subject to the processes of growth and decay, interdependence, competition and cooperation, health, and disease. This ecological language and logic perfectly reflected the social and cultural preoccupations of the day, but the ideas proved to have an enduring influence that continues to reverberate almost a century later.

The Chicago School had its detractors from time to time, but an alternative explanation for the processes of urban change did not emerge until the late 1980s, when the Los Angeles school of urbanism made its appearance. The foundational text of the L.A. School had been published a couple of decades earlier, in 1967, when Robert Fogelson published *The Fragmented Metropolis: Los Angeles, 1850–1930*. Fogelson asserted that the fragmented Los Angeles conurbation is "the archetype, for better or worse, of the contemporary American metropolis."[2] The scholars later identified with the L.A. School, however much some of them might protest that they are not members,[3] helped to turn Fogelson's idea into a conventional wisdom that is now ubiquitously present in urban scholarship.

Any paradigm so eagerly accepted cries out for rebuttal. In his book *New York and Los Angeles (2003),* David Halle has contested the premise that the modern metropolis is becoming sprawled, centerless, and fragmented. Halle asserts that a New York School, "as distinctive as . . . the Los Angeles school," evolved in the years after World War II, and that its members reached different conclusions about the spatial geography of the modern metropolis. [4] The writers he names as members of the school shared "a fascination with contemporary New York City, especially with Manhattan, and a belief, in some cases passionate, in the superiority of city life over suburban life."[5] He mines their admittedly disparate work as a way of demonstrating that a unique urban culture, nurtured by the densely packed neighborhoods of New York, continued to thrive in the late twentieth century despite the postwar flight to the suburbs. The several contributors to his volume provide ample documentation to support the idea that the metropolitan center, at least in New York, continues to be vibrant.

When Halle and Andrew Beveridge revisit this thesis in chapter 7 of this volume, they offer an interesting revisionist statement. They marshall a great deal of data to support the argument that the revitalization of the metropolitan center not only characterizes New York but Los Angeles as well. Noting that the differences between the urban core and periphery may be gradually disappearing, Halle and Beveridge question whether the L.A. or New York School is still a useful metaphor because neither of them adequately describes the complex spatial form of the modern metropolis.

A second rejoinder to the L.A. School has been articulated by an eclectic collection of Chicago-area scholars. The diverse multidisciplinary literature produced by this group calls into question the paradigms identified with both the original Chicago School and the L.A. School. Although they disagree about many matters, the Chicago scholars generally agree that the approach most helpful for understanding Chicago pivots around the idea that politics, as an expression of human agency, is the primary shaper of the spatial and social dynamics of cities and metropolitan regions. The implication is that there is likely to be no singular urban form, but many, each reflecting the influence of local political culture and institutional dynamics.

The essays in this volume address several interrelated questions: Are the theories of the original Chicago School still relevant? Does the L.A. School provide an accurate model for understanding contemporary urban development?

What do the theoretical premises of the New York School contribute to our understanding of cities? Is a new Chicago School emerging with its own distinctive voice? Finally, is the concept of "schools" a useful language device for understanding metropolitan development in the twenty-first century?

The Chicago School

The Chicago School of the 1920s offered an elegant theory of the city that fit comfortably within the gestalt of the time. The social Darwinists had, by then, already applied Darwin's theory of evolution to social and economic relations. For the members of the school, the concept of ecological change could be regarded as a perfect metaphor for the urban processes they saw unfolding all around them. As Edward Soja has noted, the idea that the city could be understood as a "pseudo-biological organism" became the foundation for the Chicago School's theories about the geographic patterning of the city.[6] Ernest Burgess, for example, wrote that, "as in plant communities successions are the products of invasion, so also in the human community the formations, segregations, and associations that appear constitute the outcome of a series of invasions . . . The general effect . . . is to give to the developed community well-defined areas."[7] This kind of evocative language became the vehicle for a sweeping and powerful narrative of urban change.

Burgess famously proposed that urban areas revolved around a dense core surrounded by concentric rings of progressively less densely settled zones; each performed a necessary function for the organism that was the city. The map of Chicago developed by Burgess placed the Loop at the center; it was encircled (from near to far) by a "factory zone," "zone in transition," "zone of workingmen's homes," "residential zone," and "commuters zone." As Chicago—or any city—grew, a process of succession unfolded marked by "the tendency of each zone to extend its area by the invasion of the next outer zone."[8]

Burgess and Park were convinced that meticulous fieldwork would confirm their theories about the processes of urban change. Their stress on empirical work and detailed case studies became a hallmark of the school, and it laid the foundation for twentieth-century sociology. An outpouring of studies of hobos, the homeless, "taxi-dance" halls, gangs, prostitutes, ethnic and racial ghettos, and other groups and lifestyles documented the human behavior nurtured within the "ecological crucible" of Chicago.[9] Any one of the studies might have seemed merely descriptive and studiously empirical, but for the Chicago researchers a larger picture emerged that revealed the deleterious effects of urban life. Park wrote that "the slum areas that invariably grow up just on the edge of the business areas of great cities, areas of deteriorated housing, vice, and crime, are areas of social junk."[10] He was convinced that social breakdown was the norm rather than the exception in industrial cities, an impression confirmed over and over by the legions of graduate students who took to the field.

It is difficult to overestimate the influence of the Chicago School on generations of urban scholars. Over the years, literally dozens of urban sociology programs sprang up, inspired by the Chicago School's theoretical premises and its model for empirical social science scholarship. The idea that there was a distinct human ecology became thoroughly incorporated into popular and scholarly discourse on the city. In her classic work *The Death and Life of American Cities,* Jane Jacobs compared urban environments to ecosystems; as in nature, the measure of a neighborhood's health was to be found in the diversity that it nurtured.[11] The ecological perspective was refined and elaborated in the work of Amos Hawley in the 1950s and Gerald Suttles in the 1960s and 1970s. In 1956, Hawley published *Human Ecology: A Theory of Urban Structure.* Suttles asserted that the behavior of both gangs and suburban homeowners reflected a moral order arising from geographical proximity.[12] The ecological perspective continued to inform the work of urban geographers and scholars in economics and regional science. In 1977, for example, Brian J. L. Berry and John Kasarda published *Contemporary Urban Ecology,* which used factorial methods and other statistical techniques to map the land-use patterns of urban regions.[13]

The L.A. School

Michael Dear may be regarded as the official historian and voice of the L.A. School. In the opening pages of what has become the school's main text, *From Chicago to L.A.,* Dear and Steve Flusty trace the formal

PART B. Mapping Stock and Flow Networks

A manufacturing plant such as an oil refinery or assembly line has many thousands of machines and tools that require maintenance. The goal of maintenance is to maximize equipment availability (up time) while keeping maintenance costs low. Consider all the pumps in a chemical manufacturing plant. A typical plant might have several thousand pumps. Pumps are either running, in working condition and available to run if needed, broken down and awaiting repair, under repair, or taken down for preventive maintenance. Map the stock and flow structure relating these various states.

PART D. Modeling Goal-Seeking Processes

HVAC system maintains constant temperature of the room. At some point in time, due to the peak load in the grid, the electricity goes out and the temperature in the room starts rising until it reaches the outside level. Consider for simplicity that outside temperature is record the temperature in the room.

Time after electricity went out, hr	Temperature inside the room, F
0	70
10	80
20	85

What information can you get from this table? Hint: think about half-life.

1) Build a simple Vensim model simulating the process of increasing temperature in the room following exponential decay process.

2) Using the same model, predict what would happen to the same room in wintertime if the heating were broken. Assume initial room temperature is 70F and the outside temperature is constant and is 30F. In how many hours would the room temperature reach 50F?

beginning of the school to a gathering of nine southern California scholars at Lake Arrowhead in the San Bernardino Mountains. Following that October 1987 meeting, the L.A. School quickly became identified with the idea that Los Angeles was the paradigmatic city of the late twentieth century, the harbinger of what cities are today or are destined to become. As vividly summarized by Soja a couple of years after the group's mountain retreat, "Los Angeles is the place where 'it all comes together'... One might call the sprawling urban region . . . a prototopos, a paradigmatic place"; he has added elsewhere that Los Angeles "insistently presents itself as one of the most informative palimpsests and paradigms of twentieth-century urban development and popular consciousness."[14]

The thrust of the L.A. School's argument is the assertion that urban regions have morphed from geographic landscapes revolving around a central nucleus to centerless, sprawled urban agglomerations inexorably enveloping everything in their path. Soja invented the term "postmetropolis" to denote the spatial form—or formlessness—of what he calls the "postmodern city." The chapter titles and subheadings of *Postmetropolis* give some feel for the texture of the postmodern landscape: outer cities; post-suburbia; Exopolis; fractal city; the ethnic mosaic; the carceral archipelago; simcities; re-imagining Cityspace: Travels in Hyperreality; Off-the-edge cities.[15] Dear and his collaborators have elaborated on the themes of an indefinite and plastic urban form in which "time and space define two axes of a 'fabric' (or 'tapestry') upon which are inscribed the processes and patterns of human existence, including political, socio-cultural, and economic activities."[16] Mike Davis meant his title *City of Quartz* to signify the refraction of light through a prism, and he brilliantly dissects Los Angeles through the lens of the archaeological layering of history, culture, and space.[17] Dear treats the project of theorizing postmodern geographies as a very serious enterprise but also encourages a spirit of playfulness by beginning his coedited book, *The Spaces of Postmodernity,* with a Calvin and Hobbes cartoon and a disquisition on Lewis Carroll. All this is put in the service of his view that postmodernism is "an ontology of radical but principled uncertainty."[18]

A relentlessly noir interpretation of the urban condition informs the L.A. School's literary canon. The fracturing of the urban landscape is treated, variously, as a theoretical statement, a description, and a condemnation.

The latter view comes into play in the treatment of enclaves as a means of protecting white middle-class privilege. Thus, the L.A. School appropriated or invented an entire lexicon composed of such terms as "global latifundia," "privatopia," "cyber-geoisie," "protosurps," "holsteinization," "praedatorianism," and many more.[19] Soja devotes a chapter of *Postmetropolis* to the subject of "carceral archipelagos," which are the spatial manifestation of social welfare, the destruction of urban space, policing, imprisonment, gated communities, and insular lifestyles. He concludes his chapter with a "Beyond *Bladerunner* scenario."[20]

What does Los Angeles reveal about the future? That the stark inequalities of the Third World are being exported, and that these are written on urban landscapes in a patchwork of prosperity and despair. Dear has eloquently captured the mood when he observes, "The luxury compound atop a matrix of impoverished misery, the self-contained secure community, and the fortified home can be found first in places such as Manila and São Paolo."[21] Among the L.A. School authors, Davis writes in an inflamed rhetoric about a coming environmental Armageddon, an "ecology of evil"[22] foretold by balls of rattlesnakes washed up on the beaches of Los Angeles, "pentecostal earthquakes," "dead cities," and the question, "Who killed L.A.?"[23]

Such a noir interpretation conveys an inescapable impression of human helplessness in the face of inexorable, overwhelming forces. Dear, Soja, Davis, and several other scholars have dealt with the critical issue of whether a politics may emerge capable of forestalling the dire future the L.A. School writers foresee. Their answer seems to be a decisive no: their consistent appraisal is that L.A. and its region is so politically fractured into a patchwork of local governments and privatized enclaves that effective governance is nearly impossible. As summarized by Jennifer Wolch and Michael Dear, "social heterogeneity, geographic sprawl, and economic vitality have encouraged an intense and effective localization of politics, work, personal life, and culture. One important consequence is the difficulty of formal governance . . . As the urbanized area continues to expand geographically, local government becomes increasingly remote and less able to respond to grass-roots concerns."[24]

By Dear's account, the L.A. School might seem less a school of thought than a mélange of various perspectives. He asserts that the L.A. School is as fragmented as Los Angeles itself; that it is "pathologically antileadership"; that its focus is "fractured, incoherent, and idiosyncratic"; that it began to fragment soon after the Lake Arrowhead gathering.[25] Almost no one admits to being a member.[26] Even so, it is widely acknowledged that an L.A. School exists. It does so because whatever their disagreements, the diverse group of scholars now and in the past who have been swept into its orbit have produced a remarkable body of literature identified by a coherent, encompassing, and rhetorically powerful theory of metropolitan development. The powerful narrative that runs through much of this work can now be found in a broad range of urban scholarship that spans the disciplines.

The New York School

In *New York and Los Angeles,* Halle, a scholar who works in Los Angeles but lives in New York, suggests that a New York School of literature emerged in the 1950s, with its roots in the work of Jane Jacobs and her contemporaries. Halle drew a sharp contrast between the New York School's focus on the urban center and the L.A. School's preoccupation with fragmentation and the urban periphery. In his account, these two schools of scholarship appropriately reflected their respective metropolitan regions: Los Angeles, with its "multiple clusters of economic and social activity," and New York, which "represented renewed interest in the central city as a place to work and live."[27]

The collection of writers making up the New York School is ambiguous, but Halle's brief (and rather casual) list includes Jacobs, Sharon Zukin, Kenneth Jackson, Robert Stern, William H. Whyte, and Richard Sennett as the "key figures."[28] These scholars constitute a remarkably diverse lot hailing from different times and various disciplines; presumably, all of them would be surprised to find themselves lumped together under any label at all. Nevertheless, despite the polyglot membership of the school, it does seem as if its writers drew from a common well: a unique urban culture that acted as a glue binding together the diverse neighborhoods of Manhattan and its boroughs.

Halle's book appeared at a critical juncture, at a time when urban scholars began documenting a remarkable and unexpected renaissance of the urban core. Since the 1980s, most American central cities have experienced at least some degree of downtown development and neighborhood gentrification. From 1990 to 2000, downtown populations increased in eighteen of twenty-four cities studied by the Fannie Mae Foundation and the Brookings Institution.[29] Although the number of new downtown residents was quite small in some cities, even modest growth represented a historic turnaround. Some cities that had been losing population since the 1950s gained in the 1990s, and even the few that continued to lose population did so at a reduced rate.[30] Something extraordinary was happening, and urban scholars were scrambling to account for a phenomenon none of them had predicted.

An economic restructuring brought about by globalization has been identified as a leading factor in the revival. Particularly in the largest global cities, downtowns have been revitalized for the simple reason that some kinds of business firms find it advantageous to be located next to one another. High-level professional operations and information industries have become clustered into "strategic nodes with a hyperconcentration of activities"[31] supporting layer upon layer of highly educated, technologically sophisticated professionals offering specialized services: corporate managers, management consultants, legal experts, accountants, computer specialists, financial analysts, media and public relations consultants, and the like.

The professional workers in these sectors have flocked to downtown areas and nearby neighborhoods. But a purely economic explanation is not sufficient to account for the move to the urban center, in part because it does not explain why the renewal of the core is occurring even in smaller cities that cannot be counted among the global elite. Something is going on that cannot be explained by economics; it fits better under the heading of social and cultural change. It is in this arena where the most significant disagreements have broken out among scholars. Richard Florida has identified the rise of "the creative class" to explain the downtown renaissance.[32] Though his thesis has come under vigorous attack, the critics have not, in general, offered an alternative convincing explanation of their own.

Probably the answer is to be found in an appreciation that urban dynamics of long standing are changing. Urban scholars have been slow to appreciate that the fundamental dynamic driving the post–World War II urban crisis has all but disappeared. The decline of the cities is no longer associated with suburban growth.[33] Central cities may be gaining population, but this phenomenon appears to have little to do with the extent of urban sprawl in those same regions. As Halle and Beveridge note in chapter 7, the dynamics that scholars have associated with Los Angeles and New York are now being played out almost everywhere. Are today's metropolitan regions like L.A., or like New York? They are both, which is why previous paradigms must be reconsidered, or at least modified.

A Second Chicago School?

In the fall of 2001, a dozen urban scholars from several campuses in the Chicago region met in Terry Nicholls Clark's apartment in Bronzeville, on the near south side of the city. For a couple of years, we had presented our work to one another, discussed literature, and argued about the theoretical approaches that defined our field. Sometimes, it seemed, we disagreed about almost everything. But on two points there seemed to be a clear consensus. First, the theories of the original Chicago School no longer described the Chicago region's development (if they ever did). All of us came to the conclusion that it would not be useful to resurrect a refined version of Homer Hoyt's concentric rings, and the ecological metaphors employed in an earlier generation provided no useful guide. Second, we reached an agreement that the ideas of the L.A. School were equally deficient for understanding Chicago's contemporary development. Although Chicago is a sprawled region, it retains a vital center, and its suburban development is far from formless.

In the interpretation of the L.A. School scholars, globalization has exerted three main effects on cities: post-Fordist, service-based economies have dispersed economic activities and people from the urban core; demographic decentralization has fragmented and weakened urban governance and strengthened privatized responses to social problems; and massive immigration has fomented racial and ethnic animosities. The overall picture that emerges from these trends is the ungovernable metropolis, one characterized by spatial, political, and social disorganization and disorder.

In its meetings, the Chicago group considered the question: Does the Chicago metropolitan region fit such a description?

Is Chicago helpless before the forces of globalization?

Globalization is not a great leveler sweeping all differences among cities aside and replacing them with uniform copies of one another. Janet Abu-Lughod has convincingly argued in her path-breaking book *New York, Chicago, Los Angeles* that the impact of globalization on the three cities reflects "the preexisting legacies of the built environment and the traditions of governance." As a result, globalization has had different effects, and these can only be understood by studying the historical development that has made each city unique.[34]

Even before the nineteenth century, New York's borough system (brought together into one city by the charter reform of 1898) and aldermanic form of government institutionalized a style of governance that brokered the differences among the multitude of ethnic groups that made up the city's population. In the twentieth century, the several boroughs of the city were kept together by a politics of constant negotiation that persists to the present day. At the same time, the dominance of Manhattan was preserved by a subway system and then an integrated regional transit system. Finally, the region's growth was guided by a remarkable degree of regional planning presided over by the several special authorities run for decades by Robert Moses. Strong government formed New York. It still does in the global era.

By contrast, in the first decades of the twentieth century, Los Angeles took on a fragmented metropolitan form. Early in the twentieth century, entrepreneurs and land speculators pushed development to the urban periphery. Local governments were founded to promote growth, and they managed to fight off attempts by the city of Los Angeles to force a degree of governmental consolidation. Against this background, it should come as no surprise that in the era of globalization, massive population growth and immigration has produced an extremely balkanized spatial geography.

Chicago has taken its own distinct path. The city developed as an industrial powerhouse and a key destination for waves of foreign workers.

Its immigrants developed homogeneous neighborhoods, and though the groups moving to the city are different in global Chicago than in its industrial past, its neighborhoods retain a strong ethnic identity. The Great Migration brought thousands of blacks into the city's south side, and by World War I a sprawling black belt had formed. There was a growing fear among whites that blacks would invade their neighborhoods. Realtors imposed restrictive covenants throughout much of the city, but violence became an equally effective weapon for enforcing segregation. The 1919 race riots left a legacy of racial tension that festered for decades, and the racial antagonisms were further inflamed when waves of southern blacks poured into the city after World War II. And yet Chicago's political system adapted to these tensions with remarkable dexterity, incorporating blacks into the machine as early as the 1920s — earlier than any other northern city.

Despite decades of suburbanization and the deindustrialization of the 1970s, the city of Chicago has remained the anchor for the region, in part because the machine became Chicago's unique version of a strong state. Mayor Richard J. Daley, who served from 1955 to 1976, forged a powerful civic alliance dedicated to the cause of protecting the Loop. In the 1960s he brought more federal dollars per capita than any other city. Under the second Mayor Daley, Richard M., who was first elected in 1989, the city has fought hard to keep major businesses and corporations downtown and has invested massively in an infrastructure of culture, entertainment, and tourism. Globalization has changed Chicago, but the city has not become more like New York or Los Angeles. The three cities have retained their distinct geographies, social structures, and political styles.

Is Chicago becoming ungovernable?

The scholars of the L.A. School have described Los Angeles as a region fractured by a privatized politics that renders governments almost powerless. Michael Dear and Steven Flusty have written that edge cities, private gated communities, and fortified enclaves are substitutes for democratic governance; they are, in their description, "essentially a plutocratic alternative to normal politics"; in place of governments that broker among contending interests, these privatized arrangements "are responsive primarily to wealth (as opposed to voters)."[35] The forces of the marketplace overwhelm most public efforts to shape metropolitan development.

Such a view manifestly does not apply to Chicago.[36] As in virtually all metropolitan regions, condominium towers, townhouse developments, and gated communities have proliferated in the city of Chicago and its suburbs. But it would betray a remarkable misunderstanding of Chicago's politics to think that privatized developments have eclipsed public governments in significance or political authority. Volumes have been written about the party machines that centralized power in the city's past. In the postwar period, Chicago remained an oft-noted anomaly because of the resurrection of machine politics under Richard J. Daley. His son arguably wields even a firmer hand than his father did. In his book tracing the history of Chicago's politics, Dick Simpson asserts that Daley has built a "new machine" perfectly adapted to the global era. Whereas his father ran campaigns through aldermen and precinct captains, the second Daley overwhelms his opponents with direct mail and television ads crafted by political consultants, a political style that has seeped down from national politics. The new style of politics has proven congenial for Daley, who has been able to maintain at least as much control over a "rubber-stamp" city council as did his father.[37]

As a consequence, City Hall remains firmly in control of all important policy matters. Mayor Daley has proven adept at brokering among blacks, Latinos, and other ethnic groups. But this is in the city, leaving open the question of whether the region might have gone in the direction of Los Angeles, with its patchwork of suburban governments and privatized enclaves. This is definitely not the case. The Democratic Party extends its authority well beyond the city through the party's Central Committee, which is made up of committeemen from each of the city's fifty wards and the thirty suburban townships. The collar counties, too, are filled with local governments capable of guiding their own destinies. Bonnie Lindstrom's research has demonstrated that mayors in suburban municipalities have been able to come together on important regional matters and that they have learned to cooperate with Mayor Daley on a variety of common projects.[38] The impact of rapid growth has become a major concern; in response, suburban governments have taken measures to preserve open space and regulate new development (as they have, as well, throughout Southern California). This makes the absence of formal regional governance a somewhat moot point. The Chicago Metropolitan Area Planning (CMAP) agency is empowered to do little more than facilitate communication among the governments making up the metropolitan region and has virtually no authority to force compliance with its plans. This does not mean, however, that there is little capacity to mobilize significant governmental resources to achieve regional goals. As in metropolitan areas across the United States, several metropolitan-wide authorities provide important services, such as regional transportation, sewage disposal, and water provision.

Is urbane public culture disappearing?

The construction of monumental corporate fortresses and the prolifera-tion of defended residential enclaves constitute the most compelling images from Davis's *City of Quartz*. Davis's L.A. is an urban landscape fractured into fortified, privatized cells of affluence, malls and gated communities inhab-ited by the affluent middle class. Within this urban nightmare, downtown Los Angeles continues to exist only as a walled citadel, its few public spaces subject to close surveillance and intense law enforcement. Urban culture has been so fractured that it is scarcely possible to think of what it might be; instead, there are many warring cultures, each expressing a specific racial or ethnic identity or a retreat into protected sanctuary.

The city of Chicago, by contrast, is rapidly evolving into a mature global city of public spaces and vital urban culture. In Chicago, as in cities nearly everywhere, the leading industry is now tourism and entertainment. A high level of cultural amenities has become a central feature of the city's strategy for economic growth.[39] But the emphasis on tourism, urban amenities, culture, and entertainment goes far beyond an economic calculus. Terry Nicholls Clark's research shows that the demand for amenities is part of what he calls a globalized new political culture.[40] The spread of such a culture, which Clark defines as a demand for public amenities, more public space, and an open city, serves as a convincing rebuttal to the idea that a distinctive urban culture is being lost to a featureless urban sprawl. Instead, urbane culture is becoming as rich as it has ever been, albeit different than in the past.

In recent decades, almost all big cities have become magnets for tourists and cultural events. In Chicago's case, its status as a regional playground and global tourist city is rooted in a historical development that goes back more than a century. Edward Bennett and Daniel Burnham's Chicago Plan and the subsequent improvements to Grant Park created a unique landscape that continues to distinguish Chicago from most other American cities. The park is nearly two miles deep, north to south, and more than a half-mile wide. It keeps the densely built environment of the city from encroaching on the lakefront. The park contains Buckingham Fountain, completed in 1926; the Art Institute of Chicago; flower gardens, ball fields, tennis courts, and sweeping expanses of trees and lawns. Its location has made it the logical location for community gatherings of every kind– among many others, the Taste of Chicago; the jazz, blues, gospel, and country music festivals; Fourth of July fireworks; and an endless schedule of ethnic parades.

The activities in Grant Park and along the lakefront attract extraordinarily diverse audiences. People using the lakefront have direct access to the rest of the city. Following in the tradition of Burnham, there is public access to all three miles of the city's lakefront. Along its entire length, it is seamlessly connected with nearby neighborhoods. Users of Grant Park trade back and forth from the Loop, Michigan Avenue's Miracle Mile, and the residential neighborhoods on all sides of the park. Navy Pier and Millennium Park have free entry; the museums sponsor admission-free days. Even if the Chicago lakefront has become mostly a playground, it has remained remarkably open. Millions of suburbanites pour into the city each year to mingle with city residents and tourists; in this sense, they have retained "the urban habit." The Chicago region may be sprawled, but the city is the cultural heart of the metropolitan region, whatever one may think of its entertainments.

Conclusion

Urban theory is contested terrain. One must acknowledge the limitation of any single story line that proposes to interpret the "urban." It pays to be modest. It must be recognized that cities in Europe, Latin America, and Asia offer sharp contrasts to the paradigms developed on the basis of studying U.S. cities. The absence of a direct national role in urban land-use planning and political development is unique to the United States. The political fragmentation and the degree of sprawl of U.S. metropolitan regions should be treated as an anomaly, and not the norm. In the United States, municipalities have substantial control over land-use policy, and national governments play only an indirect role in housing provision. The result is that residential housing patterns tend to mirror political fragmentation: by contrast, in some European and Asian cities, rich and poor live in close proximity, while in others, like Paris, the usual U.S. housing pattern is reversed, with the poor living in suburban slums and the wealthy in the urban center. Patterns of residential development in Latin America contrast sharply with the U.S. model as well. In the United States, gated communities are associated with rising levels of residential segregation and the withdrawal of their residents from the public realm. As Rodrigo Salcedo and Francisco Sabatini demonstrate in chapter 15, in Santiago, Chile, and other Latin American cities, gating has had the effect of reducing large-scale patterns of segregation and making it possible for the poor to live close to the wealthy, with better access to jobs, urban services, and urban amenities.

Another difference is that the spatial patterning of cities with a history of protracted religious and ethnic violence is also likely to be different from the U.S. model. In chapter 14, Frank Gaffikin, David Perry, and Ratoola Kundu argue that in such contested landscapes, religious and ethnic groups have participated in generations of often bloody conflict. Belfast and Kolkata are two examples. In contested cities, urban space becomes a means of asserting overt legal, political, administrative, and cultural domination. The formal negotiations and overt debates about the segmentation of urban space have no analogue in the U.S. context. The conclusion one can draw from these cases is that spatial theories about metropolitan development are very likely to be culturally specific, and it is especially dangerous to generalize from the U.S. experience.

The search for an all-encompassing theory of the city is irresistible, but one must suspect that goal is impossible to achieve. No theory plausibly can explain all of the spatial and social dynamics that govern cities and metropolitan regions. Conceiving of intellectual schools is useful for clarifying the conceptual choices to be made in thinking about cities. In her essay, Abu-Lughod maintains that "our job is to engage in a dialectical and almost mystical process in which we ask questions about some problematic, studying the real world but through multiple theoretical lenses. Theories suggest a variety of things to look at, but they do not tell us what we will find or how to interpret what we find." We believe the essays in this book provide the multiple narratives she has in mind.

Notes

1. Ernest Burgess, in Robert E. Park, Ernest Burgess, and Roderick D. McKenzie, *The City: Suggestions for Investigation of Human Behavior in the Urban Environment* (Chicago: University of Chicago Press, 1925; reprint, 1967).

2. Robert M. Fogelson, quoted in David Halle, ed., *New York and Los Angeles: Politics, Society, and Culture—A Comparative View* (Chicago: University of Chicago Press, 2003), 8. See Robert M. Fogelson, *The Fragmented Metropolis: Los Angeles, 1850–1930* (Berkeley: University of California Press, 1967). Halle should be credited with calling Fogelson's book the "founding text" of the L.A. School.

3. Edward Soja, for example, is generally thought to be one of the most prominent members of the L.A. School, but in conversations he vehemently denies it.

4. Halle, *New York and Los Angeles*, 15.

5. Ibid.

6. Edward W. Soja, *Postmetropolis: Critical Studies of Cities and Regions* (New York: Blackwell, 2000), 86.

7. Ibid., 74.

8. Burgess, in *The City: Suggestions for Investigation of Human Behavior*, 58.

9. Soja, *Postmetropolis*, 87.

10. Park, in *The City: Suggestions for Investigation of Human Behavior*, 109.

11. Jane Jacobs, *The Death and Life of Great American Cities* (New York: Vintage, 1961), 428–35.

12. Soja, *Postmetropolis*, 89–92; cf. Amos Hawley, *Human Ecology: A Theory of Social Structure* (New York: Ronald Press, 1950); Gerald D. Suttles, *The Social Order of the Slum* (Chicago: University of Chicago Press, 1968); Gerald D. Suttles, *The Social Construction of Communities* (Chicago: University of Chicago Press, 1972).

13. Soja, *Postmetropolis*, 91–92; cf. Brian J. L. Berry and John D. Kasarda, Contemporary Urban Ecology (New York: Macmillan, 1977).

14. Edward W. Soja, *Postmodern Geographies: The Reassertion of Space in Critical Social Theory* (New York: Verso, 1989), 191, 248. It should be noted that in a volume edited in 1996 with Allen J. Scott, the editors treat the question of whether Los Angeles is typical as still

subject to debate when they ask if the "scattered collection of towns and villages" that makes up the Los Angeles urban agglomeration is "an exceptional case, a persistently peculiar and unreproducible type of city, or . . . an exemplary, if not paradigmatic, illustration of the essential and generalizable features of late-twentieth-century urbanization." See Allen J. Scott and Edward W. Soja, *The City: Los Angeles and Urban Theory at the End of the Twentieth Century* (Berkeley: University of California Press, 1996), 1.

15. Soja, *Postmodern Geographies.*

16. Michael J. Dear and Steven Flusty, eds., *The Spaces of Postmodernity: Readings in Human Geography* (New York: Blackwell, 2002).

17. Mike Davis, *City of Quartz: Excavating the Future of Los Angeles* (New York: Verso, 1990).

18. Dear and Flusty, *The Spaces of Postmodernity,* xi.

19. This list of terms was compiled by Halle in *New York and Los Angeles,* 13.

20. Soja, *Postmodern Geographies,* 298–322.

21. Michael J. Dear and Steven Flusty, "The Resistible Rise of the L.A. School," in Michael J. Dear, ed., *From Chicago to L.A.: Making Sense of Urban Theory* (Thousand Oaks, Calif: SAGE Publications, 2002), 14.

22. Mike Davis, *City of Quartz: Excavating the Future of Los Angeles* (New York: Verso, 1990), 3.

23. Mike Davis, *The Ecology of Fear: Los Angeles and the Imagination of Disaster* (New York: Metropolitan Books, 1998); *Dead Cities and Other Tales* (New York: The New Press, 2002).

24. Jennifer Wolch and Michael Dear, *Malign Neglect: Homelessness in an American City* (San Francisco: Jossey-Bass, 1993), xxiii.

25. Dear and Flusty, "The Resistible Rise of the LA. School," 11–13.

26. Remarkably, over the years our colleagues and we have never encountered anyone except Michael Dear who professes to be in the L.A. School and have met many scholars who emphatically insist that they are not.

27. Halle, *New York and Los Angeles,* 1.

28. Ibid., 15.

29. Rebecca R. Sohmer and Robert E. Lang, *Downtown Rebound* (Washington, D.C.: Fannie Mae Foundation and Brookings Institution Press, 2003), 1–4.

30. Patrick A. Simmons and Robert E. Lang, "The Urban Turnaround," in *Redefining Urban and Suburban America: Evidence from Census 2000,* ed. Bruce Katz and Robert E. Lang (Washington, D.C.: Brookings Institution Press, 2004), 56–58.

31. Saskia Sassen, *Cities in a World Economy* (Thousand Oaks, Calif.: Pine Forge Press, 2001).

32. Richard Florida, *The Rise of the Creative Class: And How It's Transforming Work, Leisure, Community, and Everyday Life* (New York: Basic Books, 2003).

33. Robert Beauregard, *When America Became Suburban* (New York: Columbia University Press, 2005).

34. Janet Abu-Lughod, *New York, Chicago, Los Angeles: America's Global Cities* (Minneapolis: University of Minnesota Press, 1999), 7.

35. Dear and Flusty, "Los Angeles as a Postmodern Urbanism," in *From Chicago to L.A.*, 64.

36. We should note that it may not even accurately describe Los Angeles. The development of Los Angeles has been guided by the actions of powerful governments and public leaders. Robert Fogelson's book, which Halle has called "the founding text" of the L.A. School, is based on a closely textured history describing how Los Angeles has been shaped by powerful entrepreneurs and government action (see Fogelson, *The Fragmented Metropolis*). More recently, Steve Erie has shown that the region has been molded in almost every respect by large public bureaucracies. See Steven P. Erie, *Globalizing L.A.* (Stanford, Calif.: Stanford University Press, 2004).

37. Dick Simpson, *Rogues, Rebels, and Rubber Stamps: The Politics of the Chicago City Council from 1863 to the Present* (Boulder, Colo.: Westview Press, 2001).

38. Bonnie Lindstrom, "The Metropolitan Mayors Caucus: Political Fragmentation, Global Competition, and Regional Cooperation" (paper presented at the annual meeting of the Midwest Political Science Association, Chicago, April 10, 2005).

39. See especially Terry Nichols Clark, *The City as an Entertainment Machine* (New York: JAI Press, 2003).

40. Terry Nichols Clark and Vincent Hoffmann-Martinot, eds., *The New Political Culture* (Boulder, Colo.: Westview Press, 1998).

2

Grounded Theory
Not Abstract Words but Tools of Analysis
■ Janet Abu-Lughod

Is our question really about the trinity of urban theory: one or many? At the insistence of my children, I have begun to write my "intellectual memoirs" (a compromise with the more salacious account they perhaps hoped for). This may be why my memories of being a seventeen-year-old, starting in Hutchins College of the University of Chicago more than sixty years ago, led me back to vacuous medieval debates about the number of angels on the head of a pin.

Having been so early imprinted, I shall always be a member of the Chicago School, but I think we are all descended from it, albeit critical of its limitations, expanding beyond its provincialism, updating it to take into account real changes in cities, and constantly enriching it through perspectives widened by the comparative and historical study of urban forms and city life.

From the start, I confess that I am not a theorist—obvious to anyone who has read my work; some readers, indeed, have criticized me severely for failing to spin general theories. Even worse, I have a jaded view of theory, probably intensified by my exposure to Theory as it was enshrined at the New School, which I dismissed as words about words. I routinely admonished my students that the only theories worth having are theories in action, in use, for the purpose of understanding and explaining real things. I also told them that they would need a lot of them in their toolkits, drawn not only from urban studies but from psychology, economics, sociology, political science, geography, and history.

At the start, one must distinguish clearly between generalizations about places and theories about general processes of urban formation and change for the purpose of explaining something that is going on in a given place at a given time. That something, whatever it is, has to be treated as problematic. The utility of comparative and historical studies of cities is that they expand our ability to identify significant problematics and to place them in the context of time, space, and culture.

Our goals, therefore, are to apply theories to construct credible narratives about enormously complex ongoing processes in the real world that, if we understood them in advance, would not require any research. Unfortunately, then, we would end with words about words. On the other hand, theories in use are the tools we deploy on the object until it makes sense to us. Our job is to engage in a dialectical and almost mystical process in which we ask questions about some problematic, studying the real world but through multiple theoretical lenses. Theories suggest a variety of things to look at, but they do not tell us what we will find or how to interpret what we find.

In the long empirical process of investigation, we come to find some theories more fertile than others.[1] This evaluation of their relative utility helps us to select what to keep and what to ballast, in our search for answers to the particular questions we are posing. We need this testing for relative explanatory power because our job is not to reproduce reality (an impossible task), but to simplify it. I can illustrate this point by my favorite quote. It comes from Argentine novelist Jorge Luis Borges's *El Hacedor,* and its message is simple—and bitingly satirical.

> In the Empire, the Art of Cartography reached such Perfection that the map of a single Province occupied a whole City, and the map of the Empire, a whole Province. In time, these Enormous Maps no longer sufficed and the Colleges of Cartographers raised a Map of the Empire that was the same size of the Empire and coincided with it exactly . . . The following generations understood that the expanded Map was Useless and . . . relinquished it to the inclemencies of the Sun and . . . Winters.[2]

Theories are indispensable as guides that help us select from this big booming world ways to make our maps more usable.

Being an urbanist is not an easy life. But it is a most exciting and challenging one and we have chosen it. Obviously, no two cities are alike, and each city is a composite of many moving parts and tiny enclaves that nestle within larger patterns. Every city has its unique ecological setting, its environmental resources and constraints that shift with technology, as does its strategic location in the larger changing systems of region, nation, and world. Each has it own history of development within these changing parameters, its own racial/ethnic and cultural mixes, its own evolving and disappearing economic bases and their associated power and class systems. Each has its multiple ways of being and models for interaction, its ideologies and its institutional structures. Each city not only has its own changing reality, but also its own continuities. But certainly one does not need a different theory for each city—not if one acknowledges that theories are about processes of urban formation and change, not about the ephemeral (temporary but not final) product at any one time or expanse.

I suggest that these are the theoretical assumptions we urbanists have in common, and it is remarkable to think that this basic approach was conceived in Chicago. The names of Park and Burgess[3] are always invoked together, but they were seeking different theories. Park was fixated on interrelationships among variables at different levels and with their dialectical interplay;[4] Burgess became fixated on discovering how urban patterns were formed, prematurely generalizing the object in a given time and place. Park's approach was basically in the right direction. Burgess was somewhat off the mark, although we owe him a debt of gratitude for his sensitivity to the spatial dimension of city growth.[5]

I mentioned the dialectic. There are not three theoretical schools appropriate for New York, Chicago, and Los Angeles, or even a school for every city at every stage of its development. There is theory (or rather, theories) and the objects that must be dissected, in order to understand or explain them, and there are even different techniques for dissection that are more or less appropriate for each city. I know. I've worked in all three cities, not only following different leads but forced to follow different method-ologies.[6] True, different schools develop because scholars studying a given place communicate with one another and are influenced by the findings of fellow researchers. That should come as no surprise, nor should it worry us. Of course, schools grow up among scholars working in the same city. Colleagues are important in the search for scientific validation: "Do you see what I see?" This is their strength but also their weakness. Strength comes from the ability to build on the work of others, but paradigm changes come only when someone or something wrenches one out of the collective consensus. For many of us, exposure to a variety of urban places serves as just such a wrenching experience.[7]

Perhaps the reason Michael Dear has had trouble assigning me to a school[8] is that I've always been a bit of an itinerant freelancer. I get inter-ested in (get stuck in) a given place and start asking questions about many aspects of it. Relatively isolated from local colleagues, I follow a method I later found described in an obscure monograph by Kurt Wolff called *Surrender and Catch: Experience and Inquiry Today.*[9] It might also be described as induction: learn everything you can about everything by as many methods as possible—books, statistical studies, ethnographic expo-sure, living there, exploring with eyes, ears, and nose—trying to figure out how different places work and why. Out of this, with enough theories to offer possible explanations, some problematic catches you, and then, once caught, 90 percent of what you've learned recedes as the specific landscape takes on perspective, begins to make sense. Out of this theoretically informed per-spective, one begins to concentrate on a specific problematic—a question.

I know that this sounds romantic and very unscientific, but I think we all do this more or less, although it is embarrassing to admit it. *I con-sider the most exciting development in our field in the past decade or so the generation of new problematics arising from controlled comparisons, whether at the international, country, or regional levels.* If I may, I am once again going to draw on another powerful theory foreshadowed in the Chicago School, albeit applied by Park and W. I. Thomas to the immigrant experience and given the ungainly name of "apperception mass," a concept borrowed from psychology. Explaining that the meaning/interpretation of new experience is always affected by the background of prior (and variable) experience against which it is compared, they suggest that immigrants living in two cultures may, if not "mentally mobile," another of Thomas's favorite terms, derive the meaning of the new in rigid fashion from the old known. However, such dual or multiple experiences have at least the potential to widen and deepen interpretations in the mentally mobile.[10]

I am about to make an outrageous parallel. Urbanists studying more than one city are like (smart) immigrants, forced to test and possibly question or integrate what they see against the apperception mass built up in the mini-community or school that created the universe of discourse they learned to see and speak in their place of origin. This is the main payoff for itinerants like myself, and I recommend it strongly as a method for transcending place-specific tunnel vision.

There is a second important paradigm change I sense happening in urban studies, and that is recognition of the limitations of statistical positivism (an approach that disaggregates variables and hypothesizes similar causal chains) in favor of a more historical and holistic approach. The latter uses a far more inductive (and apparently less scientific) method, comparing patterns, configurations, and structural systems of process, often focused on a problematic.

Let me illustrate from my newest book, *Race, Space, and Riots in Chicago, New York, and Los Angeles.*[11] This book looks systematically at pairs of the most serious twentieth-century race riots in each city. In Chicago it was easy to single out the lethal white-on-black riot of 1919 and the black rebellion triggered by the assassination of Martin Luther King Jr. in 1968. In New York, which had a longer and more diverse history of shorter but less lethal racially-charged incidents, I focused on the very similar riots that occurred in Harlem in 1935 and 1943, contrasting these with the lengthier and more geographically dispersed Harlem–Bedford Stuyvesant riot of 1964. In Los Angeles, the Watts riot of 1965 and its reignition in the so-called South Central (the same foyer) riot of 1992 were the obvious choices. My aim was to trace differences, continuities, and local changes by controlled comparisons.

Detailed research into the dynamics of each riot yielded a set of inductively established conclusions that had to be explained. Eventually, I homed in on a basic problematic, asking why, in a generally racist country where most whites live in a bubble of inattention at best and aggressive, fearful defensiveness at worst, twentieth- century race riots in Chicago, New York, and Los Angeles have been so different from one another in their intensity, duration, and lethal consequences. The main empirical findings are that race riots have thus far been more short-lived and less lethal in New York than in Chicago and Los Angeles, and that each city has developed its own culture of rioting and police/political response that develops over time and demonstrates certain continuities. But that was only the beginning. The real problematic was to explain why. The answer required a historically informed configurational analysis that stressed the interaction among variables that are often disaggregated, parceled out to different disciplines, and illuminated by different theories.

Although it is impossible to summarize all of the arguments in a long book, I can single out a few that are central, notably space and politics. My theoretically informed explanations are drawn from demographic diversity, the organization of space, how minorities have been inserted in the economic base, and the political structures and cultures of each city. But I view these dimensions not as independent variables but as interacting spheres or configurations. The very different configurations in the three cities offer complex explanations, based on the theoretical assumption that cities are interactional systems of local actors whose behavior, in turn, is shaped by the past, by opportunity structures afforded within larger national and even global conditions and constrained by legal and economic forces. In this book, I contend that race riots represent temporary breakdowns or crises in which these systems are revealed more transparently, much in the way that Kai Erikson approached *Everything in Its Path.*[12]

The major actors include:

1. *City residents:* their composition and diversity by race, ethnicity, immigrant origin, class; their distribution in space, the degree of their segregation from one another; their awareness of and learned attitudes toward one another; and their relative levels of political savvy and organization within and between different communities.

2. *Political structures and culture:* the degree of diffuseness or concentration of local government structures and political parties, the flexibility and openness of these structures to wider representation and empowerment without recourse to violence, which in turn depend not only on spatial and social organization, but on local political opportunity structures and outcomes anticipated on the basis of past conflict resolutions. Here, too, space, in terms of political boundaries, plays a role, even if it is the unintended historical result of successful or unsuccessful annexations.

3. *Forces of law and order:* the size and ethnic composition of the police force; the organization and degree of discipline exercised over their behavior and culture; the better or worse mechanisms they have developed for crowd control; and their relative ability to restore order without depending upon external military forces such as the National Guard.[13] Here, too, space, segregation and density play their parts, allowing or limiting the strategies that police departments can use to counteract civil disturbances or inadvertently heighten tensions and reactions.

I shall try to highlight briefly the specific contrasting characteristics of the three cities, working in concert, that account for (explain?) why their race riots have been so different.[14]

The City Residents: Population in Space

Not unexpectedly, all three cities were multicultural and multiracial in their foundings and have been the recipients of subsequent waves of settlers from Europe, Africa, and Asia, but the original mix was different in each city. Tiny New Amsterdam drew its early settlers from seventeen different language groups and was hospitable to escaped slaves. In the Revolutionary War, local blacks who volunteered to fight the British were freed in recognition of their service, and in 1827 state law abolished slavery. From the start, the city attracted immigrants from various Caribbean islands.

Chicago's first settler was of mixed black/French descent and married to an Indian. However, the state of Illinois tolerated slavery well into the nineteenth century, eventually replacing it by the infamous "black laws" of indenture that were little better. Free blacks came from nearby states. The original founders of Los Angeles hailed from Mexico and were multiracial (a few "white" Spaniards, but mostly mulattoes, blacks, and Indians). After the mid-nineteenth century, once California was conquered from Mexico, Americans established a legalized hierarchy of rights that placed American whites on top, Mexicans next, then blacks, and, at the bottom and ineligible for citizenship, Native Americans and Chinese whose status as Asians was elided to Indians. White numerical majority was not achieved until an influx of primarily midwesterners was facilitated by the completion of railroad links, massive publicity, and heavily subsidized tickets.

By the turn of the twentieth century, the racial and ethnic compositions of the three cities had diverged radically. In Los Angeles, Anglos were in the majority, followed by persons of Mexican origin, a very small black community, and a minority of Chinese who were the object of racial exclusion and occasional violence. Chicago had absorbed a large influx of immigrants from Eastern Europe, who joined the Irish and German workers in its large-scale slaughterhouses, metal manufacturing plants, and eventually, steel mills. Its small African-American population was scattered throughout the city, although there were small concentrations on the south and west sides. New York had become host to Italians, Jews from Russia, and a highly diversified set of other nationalities. Immigrants, by then, accounted for some 40 percent of the city's population, a proportion not again matched until the floodgates opened after 1965.

And yet, at the start of the twentieth century, less than 2 percent of each city's population was African American, because the great migration from the South had not yet taken off in earnest, and indeed would be delayed for decades in Los Angeles. But their conditions differed markedly in New York and Chicago. In the former city, whose economic base was still concentrated in small firms,[15] entry into the labor force was more open, as was better access to the housing market[16]—an unintended consequence of the metropolitan confederation that in 1898 unified the borough of Manhattan with its four outlying boroughs (including Brooklyn, once the second largest city in the United States, where ten thousand African Americans, largely still employed as farmers, were added to the city's population base).

The consolidation added vast, sparsely settled territories for future urban expansion that would amply accommodate much of the white flight in the post–Second World War period, keeping many initial movers within the city limits and thus the electorate. In addition, concessions granted to entice confederation established parallel hierarchies of political representation, which multiplied the number of elected offices, lowered the bar for entry into politics, and led to more balanced tickets.

In contrast to this over-bounding of New York City, annexation of Chicago's adjacent suburban towns was vigorously resisted by their build-ers,[17] which created under-bounding of the city's jurisdiction and led to the virtual exclusion, until very recently and then in only isolated locations, of African Americans from the white ring of Chicago's collar counties. Exclusion from most of the city's housing market was also more extreme in Chicago than in New York and was intensified by the white-on-black race riot of 1919 that resulted in defensive withdrawal to the South Side black belt of African Americans, who were previously more scattered. Segregation was then solidified by race-restrictive covenants (not deemed unenforceable until 1948) and by more violent attacks on blacks defined as invaders into white forbidden turf.

Housing open to black residents was not only more constricted in Chicago but was in far worse condition than that in New York, where consolidation, coupled with overbuilding at a time of market collapse in 1908, opened the fine new residential neighborhood of Harlem to blacks and facilitated a relatively conflict-free transition there, from Jewish to black occupancy. This pattern would be repeated in Brooklyn's Bedford-Stuyvesant district decades later and for a similar reason: a temporary collapse of a new real estate market. The cultural efflorescence associated with the Harlem Renaissance in the 1920s had little parallel in Chicago. To some extent, this contrast was due to the diversity of Harlem's black population, since the area served as a magnet for talented blacks from the Caribbean and other northern cities.

These differences persisted. In the heightened demand for labor, at first during the First World War, and then even more in the Second World War, New York's recruiters sought black migrants from American cities in the

South and then workers from Puerto Rico. This was in sharp contrast to Chicago's labor recruiters for the large-scale Fordist industries, who drew primarily from the Deep South, for example Mississippi's less-educated displaced farmers escaping both poverty and Jim Crow.

It would not be until the expansion of port developments in Los Angeles beginning after the construction of the Panama Canal (in 1913) and the development of heavy industry there during the Second World War that the city's African-American population grew dramatically, paralleling those changes that had taken place in New York and Chicago's racial composition during the First World War. These newcomers, however, competed with established blue-collar Mexican Americans and faced a common housing shortage and white hostility. They joined Latinos, primarily in Watts and South Central.[18]

But the spatial pattern of Los Angeles differed radically from both highly dense Manhattan and modestly dense Chicago. Whereas Manhattan, constrained by its island site, had come to sprout high-rise rental and office structures from the 1920s on and Chicago's skyscrapers were still largely contained within its Loop, Los Angeles sprawled over a vast area filled with single-family houses, its low density decentralization facilitated by builder-sponsored streetcar lines and later by heavier dependence on the automobile. Consolidation of this expanding urbanized territory within a single municipal administration, however, proved even more elusive than in Chicago. Resistance to annexation grew and settlements could even opt to de-annex. Many did so to avoid sharing their wealth via city taxation (such as those where oil was discovered) or to preserve their exclusive cachet and autonomy (such as Beverly Hills). The fragmented Swiss-cheese boundaries of the city had important implications for its political system, forcing some functions upward to the county level and distorting its distribution of power.

A final contrast between the spatial patterns established over time in the three cities was their relative dependence on mass transit, which in turn yields a distinctive characteristic of New Yorkers: their greater exposure to, if not universal enthusiasm for, social diversity. To a limited extent, this may be attributable to the city's fragmented and fine-grained spatial pattern, knitted together by, and dependent on, a mass transit system that throws together a wide range of people of varied appearances and behavior patterns, who are inadvertently exposed, at least visually, to one another and have thus developed unique forms of, if not tolerance, studied social nonobservance of one another.[19] (This accommodation is not without its occasional frictions and even dangers.) These daily reminders of diversity are also replicated, at variable scales, in the juxtaposing or overlapping divisions in both public and private space and along shared major pedestrian pathways—true not only in Manhattan but also in denser parts of the Outer Boroughs. The mass transit system also makes it possible for minority workers to reach jobs distant from their residences, thus importing diversity into the workplace, even when residences may be segregated.

The other side of fragmentation is that it applies to all neighborhoods, regardless of whether they are predominantly occupied by native-born whites of various extractions,[20] by blacks, and/or by immigrants from different continents. Certainly, there is segregation by race, ethnicity, and class, but the fine-grained spatial patterns of the city's racial, ethnic, and class mosaic are complex, often broken up into multiple same-race/same ethnic-origin zones that are not necessarily contiguous.[21] On the other hand, the scattered patterns of black and Hispanic segregation throughout at least four of the five boroughs also reduce the probability of a concerted, simultaneous rebellion.

At the opposite extreme is Los Angeles, knitted together by freeways that separate drivers from one another and that form impassable barriers between neighborhoods. Paralleling these developments was actually the disassembly of the streetcar system initially used to open peripheral areas for mass community builders; this led to the isolation of black areas and encouraged, although it did not cause, the decentralization of large-scale industry and the associated disappearance of nearby industrial jobs.[22]

Chicago represents a mixed case, combining mass transit with freeways designed to both intensify its radial divisions into north, west, and south, and to reclaim land for post-slum development and/or to barricade racial groups from one another. Since these, along with racially based decisions about the locations of public housing, were products of considered policies on land use, they are more logically treated in the next section on political structures.

Political Structures and Political Cultures

Although the social and economic grievances of minorities that are the deep causes of periodic protests may be similar in all three cities—lack of decent job opportunities, denials of equal justice, barriers to open housing, neglected social services, and inferior schools, health, and recreational facilities attributable in part to spatial segregation—the institutional structures of local government contrast markedly with one another. These differences affect the potential for minority community mobilization and influence government actors' differential responsiveness to them. Up to now, the African-American community in New York has been better organized for actions short of riots to pressure for reforms and has met with greater governmental responsiveness than comparable communities in Chicago and Los Angeles.

While James Weldon Johnson attributed this to New Yorkers' more liberal political beliefs,[23] Martha Biondi rightly gives more credit to the sophistication and commitment of New York's black leadership.[24] Articulation of grievances and governmental response came together in the aborted Harlem uprisings of 1935 and 1943, when Mayor Fiorello La Guardia succeeded not only in defusing anger but also in responding to grievances with positive concern and reforms, setting a precedent or at least a model for how to bring the parties together. Although the areas of protest were cordoned off (a tactic facilitated by dependence on subways), the police were cautioned against provocative attacks, the state and National Guards were not deployed, the Mayor resisted condemnation in his appeals for peace, and immediate relief was provided. In contrast to the police-dominated post-riot committees of investigation that followed the 1965 riots in Los Angeles and the 1968 riots in Chicago, the blue ribbon biracial committee appointed by Mayor La Guardia in 1935 diagnosed the major problems in Harlem and made serious recommendations for reform.[25] Although not fully implemented to this day, they gave voice to legitimate complaints, at least some of which were addressed, albeit within the limitations of Depression-reduced financial straits (i.e., public housing, school construction, hospital reforms, and enhanced recreational facilities). Again, in 1943, the city, at La Guardia's initiative (albeit responding to well-organized

African-American pressures), passed Fair Employment regulations that were later incorporated into national laws, and averted rent gouging in a dual housing market through its now much maligned rent control/regulation laws that, for all their flaws, slowed down although they did not prevent white flight to the suburbs in the postwar era.

When this pattern of sympathetic response was violated in 1964, the result was a more prolonged and destructive riot. Mayor Robert Wagner attempted, albeit belatedly and with less success, to follow La Guardia's example to tamp down the flames of rebellion and to avoid punitive measures. But his initial absence, his failure to discipline his police commissioner's insensitivity and incompetence, and his unwillingness to confront police resistance to the greater civilian control demanded by minority leaders were disappointing and shortsighted.[26] Those policies were not reversed until two years later by John Lindsay, the same mayor who, in 1968, allegedly averted the spread to New York of riots from Chicago and other cities that were responding to the assassination of Martin Luther King Jr. Indeed, Lindsay vigorously castigated Mayor Daley for his demand that arsonists be shot and looters maimed.

I posit a political culture in the city that has evolved from social learning and from the unique history of the city as a port of entry for diverse immigrant groups. One might describe this political culture as a constant jockeying for position in a negotiated order of competitive coexistence, necessitated by the inability of any one group to establish stable dominance. This pattern of negotiated order occurs in spite of, or possibly because of, the fact that no political party or ethnic group has had a permanent lock on local power. Even though New Yorkers tend to vote overwhelmingly Democratic at the national level, mayors have been drawn from diverse sources: patricians, Whigs, Tammany Boss Tweed types, Republicans,[27] Fusion tickets, Democratic-machine bosses, and even some, like Michael Bloomberg, the present mayor, Democrats posing as Republicans. Mayors have been Protestant, Catholic, and Jewish. Each has come to power through changing coalitions in an electorate whose fragmentation mirrors, but not exactly, the city's racial and ethnic diversity and its diffused spatial distribution. One downside of this fluidity is that few reforms introduced by one set of incumbents are guaranteed to last, but must constantly be renegotiated. This has been especially the case with imposing permanent constraints on provocative police behavior. Enforcement tightens and loosens at the discretion of the mayor and his police chief.[28]

Chicago's governmental structure and political culture are in marked contrast to New York's. As we have argued, racial/ethnic animosities were inscribed, early on, in Chicago's class system and its spatial organization—long before African Americans came to constitute a noticeable fraction of its population. Racial apartheid has persisted to the present, albeit on shifting and contested terrains. It seems no accident that two of the most serious race riots of the twentieth century have taken place in that city.[29]

The nascent Fordism of its powerful industrial base toward the end of the nineteenth century pitted nouveaux riches capitalists not against African Americans but against their white immigrant workers, drawn sequentially from Germany and Ireland and later from eastern and southern Europe. The barons of the Lake Shore facade did not need to become politicians; they only needed to control them. In the ward system of the large city council, zones occupied by the immigrant workers and their families held the numerical plurality and the leaders of Chicago's thriving vice industries were aligned with them.[30] Reforms to clean up the system failed, but by the opening decades of the twentieth century, the two contenders had granted each other a fair amount of autonomy, especially after the capitalist moguls of the Chicago Club got their lakefront plan (by Burnham in the early twentieth century), which served to insulate them from the masses.

A turning point in ethnic power came around the First World War when, in a campaign that played on anti-Catholic (anti-Irish) feelings, "Big Bill" Thompson was elected mayor on the Republican ticket in 1915, receiving support from Chicago's black (Protestant) voters, who retained their traditional loyalty to the party of Lincoln.[31] This may have taunted Irish Democrats, including Ragen's Colts who, in 1919, initiated the invasion across the dead line into the expanding black ghetto east of Wentworth. Indeed, Thompson deployed his local police to defend the black community. He remained in office, with one interruption, until 1931, when the Democrats retook city government—and never let it go.[32]

The Democratic Party machine, under Irish hegemony, has governed Chicago, with rare exceptions, into the present.[33] As the African-American community grew in numbers and geographic extent of segregation, African-American politicians eventually surfaced (viz. in the west side's "plantation" wards[34] as well as Dawson's more autonomous south side wards), but they had little bargaining power in city government. There was no counter power or viable opposition political party to which they could appeal or work through. By the 1930s and even more in the 1940s, the Democratic Party, with greater black support, consolidated its lock on city government that it never really relinquished.

The Party's control extended to the wards that elected representatives to the potentially strong but disciplined and complicit city council and, given the mayor's power to appoint important managers in the city's bureaucracy, to the agencies that actually ran the city's day-to-day operations. An example of how these three forces worked together to strengthen racial segregation in Chicago is provided by the Chicago Housing Authority, which built and managed public housing, and later, under urban redevelopment/renewal legislation, the offices of land clearance and redevelopment that were empowered to buy, clear, and resell slumland to developers for "higher uses."

It is illuminating to contrast Chicago's experience with New York's, where public housing not only succeeded in eventually producing far more units of subsidized housing than any other city, but was freer to locate its projects throughout Manhattan and three out of four Outer Boroughs to accommodate its growing minority populations. The difference lay in the multiple competing power centers in a government that had learned to strike deals as its chief mode of operating. Whereas in Chicago, the power of site selection for public housing was given to the city council, each suggested site was proposed individually for the council's approval. In the end, the only sites approved (with a sole exception intended to punish a recalcitrant member) were either in the existing black ghettos or in areas immediately adjacent to them, thus hardening the lines of racial segregation.[35] In contrast, "czar" Robert Moses insisted on proposing "balanced ticket sites" that could be voted up or down as a unit by the Board of

Aldermen. Vetoes were therefore rare, not only because the city saw public housing as a positive development in itself, but because low-income minorities demanded help. (I ignore Los Angeles in this discussion since opposition from the real estate lobby, lack of enthusiasm for "socialism," and fear of racial integration combined to defeat referenda on public housing, which meant that almost none was built. Indeed, voter rejection of both open housing and public housing initiatives helped precipitate black revolts in that city.)

It was within Chicago's monolithic political system that Richard J. Daley asserted his control over the Democratic Party and the city in the mayoral race of 1955, which he won with strong support from black politicians from the south side. For over twenty years, he ruled with such a strong hand that he became known as The Boss. The overwhelming vote he received in his reelection in 1967, albeit with declining black support,[36] may have emboldened him during his subsequent struggles with Martin Luther King Jr. and encouraged his draconian response to the riot of April 1968,[37] for which he suffered no adverse political consequences. After the riot, Mayor Daley appointed a committee[38] to inquire into the causes of the riot and, more particularly and in greater detail, to make recommendations to avert—and more efficiently control—any further outbursts of racial unrest. Not only did the committee's report place the most blame on the black community itself and its leaders, but it devoted most of its recommendations to improving police equipment and streamlining court procedures for handling massive arrests.

Daley died in 1976. After a dozen years of inconclusive interregnums,[39] his regime was reestablished when his son, Richard M. Daley, was elected mayor in 1989 in the most racially polarized vote in the city's history.[40] He has subsequently been reelected (five terms and counting), although with declining turnouts that are symptomatic of the degree to which potential opponents have capitulated and/or resigned themselves to cooperating with his powerful machine.

He has tried to undo the "dis-reputation" his father earned during the 1968 race riot/rebellion, largely through co-opting some black leaders who place peace, personal power, and potential profits above deep transformation. He had little choice of strategy, given the under-bounded borders of his city in relation to the metropolitan region and the pluralities of racial/ethnic minorities within these constrained city limits. Doing business with Daley promises to preserve Chicago from the fate of economic blowout suffered by Gary, Indiana, and Detroit, among others. (Interestingly enough, Daley's success in getting wealthy Chicagoans to fund the new and impressive Millennium Park at the lakefront recapitulates and expands the Burnham Plan that was used almost a century ago to separate the classes.)[41] Reforms of the police and greater local controls over the failing school system have also made Daley Jr. the least bad alternative.

Even though their numbers are declining slightly, African Americans remain the largest potential voting bloc in the city and therefore could have a powerful voice in Chicago's politics, despite increases in the proportion of other minorities (Puerto Ricans, Mexicans, and Asians). Short of taking over control of the Democratic Party, however, they are unlikely to radically alter Chicago's political culture.[42] In the meantime, the destruction of the "projects"[43] offers a selective depopulation of the ghettos, and HOPE holds out some chance for real estate profits to be made by black entrepreneurs, at least on the near south side. To this must be added the increased incarceration of young black and Latino males, a strategy that not only removes them from the scene but, when they return, removes them from the voter rolls as well. We return to this discussion below, which has implications for potential riot prevention in all three cities.

In contrast to the political continuities noted in New York and Chicago, and despite the similarities between the Los Angeles riots of 1965 and 1992, it is difficult to infer that a consistent long-term political culture accounts for them. In Los Angeles there have been at least three major phases of racial and ethnic relations, conditioned by changes in its governance, economic base, and demographic composition. A fourth stage is apparently now beginning, what some are calling the *reconquista*. Los Angeles's narrow-based structure of local government, set during the Progressive Era, has made it sluggish in responding to these changes.

By the opening decades of the twentieth century, Los Angeles had solidified characteristics that distinguished it from Chicago and New York. First, its population had become overwhelmingly Anglo. Only 10 percent were

Mexicans in 1930, when the U.S. Census counted them separately instead of including them in the white category,[44] and an even smaller percentage were black. Second, the vast fortunes of its leading citizens had been created chiefly through expanding the transportation lines and developing the ports (both with help from Washington), which yielded related and commensurate gains in booming real estate values. Their social values, expressed in Chandler's powerful newspaper, were far from progressive: they favored unfettered capitalism, albeit with state subsidies, suppressed progressive movements (deemed communist in the Red Scare of 1911), and fought unionization, which threatened to undermine their treasured "open shop" for labor.[45] Their racism, if not their conservative economic philosophy, was shared by most Anglos, as evidenced by their general satisfaction when, at the beginning of the Depression, eighty thousand Mexicans were deported.[46] Nor did they protest the removal and internment of the Japanese in 1943. In both cases, no distinctions were made between native-born citizens and foreigners.

The entrepreneurial, self-styled patriciate controlled a pliant political system that did not interfere with either its corporate interests or its links to federal authorities.[47] The structure of local government for both Los Angeles city and county was lean indeed, based on the philosophy of the Progressive Era that favored an apolitical managerial system of government based on civil service, limited size, and even less power vested in the city council, and dependence on citizen referenda for major policy changes. This structure explains why, in the third phase of Los Angeles's history during which the two race riots occurred, the clearly provocative behavior of the police department was insulated from civilian control and why (criminal) negligence of duty in 1965 and 1992 by its chiefs of police went unpunished. (Chief Daryl Gates, for example, resisted the call for his resignation because he was protected by law from politically motivated dismissal.) In addition, the small size of the ward-based city council and the even smaller number of county commissioners were increasingly unable to represent the growing minority population.

The third phase that began with World War II saw the growth of heavy industries and the economic, but not political, integration of the metropolis's sprawling region.[48] The rapidly increasing demands for labor attracted significant numbers of African American migrants, especially since immigration of Mexicans was restricted solely to meeting the shortage of farm laborers, under the federal bracero program. It was the expanded demand for labor in the nearby industrial district along the tracks and in the port area where the tracks ended that led to an influx of African Americans during and after the war. The city's black population increased from under 39,000 in 1940 to more than 113,000 by 1945–46 and 171,300 in 1950. By 1965, the county's black population had risen to 650,000, most piling up in the already degraded Watts and the older and only slightly better (south) Central Avenue district to its west. The shortage of housing and the tight noose of segregation were among the grievances that had accumulated[49] even before the riot that erupted in Los Angeles on the evening of August 11, 1965. This riot, which raged relatively unchecked until it was finally extinguished with the aid of the California National Guard six plus days later, was if not the most lethal (34 dead) to date, certainly one of the best documented ghetto uprisings of the 1960s.

The insensitive governmental response left much to be desired. The official, and therefore authoritative, version is laid out in the report of the *Governor's Commission on the Los Angeles Riots,* the so-called McCone Report submitted to Governor Pat Brown on December 2, 1965. Although it is only 109 pages long, in large print and with wide margins, it claims to be based on records and testimonies that filled eighteen volumes of transcripts! Like the equally brief report of Mayor Daley's appointed commission to investigate the 1968 (chiefly) West Side riot in Chicago, it seems naively straightforward, if too accepting of a law and order perspective that basically exonerates the police and the National Guard and instead blames the riot on the irrational and lawless behavior of ghetto residents.[50] Not surprisingly, the local government remained unresponsive to grievances and failed miserably to rebuild the area destroyed in the riot.

But one thing did eventually change. In 1973, with coalition support from the black-dominated wards and that of the white, so-called liberal west side,[51] the city elected a black mayor, Tom Bradley, who had first entered politics in 1963 as one of the first three black representatives on the city council. Some attributed his attractiveness to backlash from the 1965 riots, when it was hoped that his pigment would placate racial dissent. However, only his skill as a cooperative coalition player with the big business leaders, who always operated behind the scenes of elected government, and the managerial bureaucracy, could have guaranteed his twenty-year survival. But it was at the end of his watch that the city would experience a replay of its bloody riot—in roughly the same depressed zone now shared equally by the poorest blacks and an even poorer population of Latino recent immigrants.[52] The precipitating event was similar to the trigger of 1965, police brutality, but Bradley's actions only succeeded in gaining a year's reprieve.

Within a few days of the savage beating of Rodney King on March 3, 1991, by four apparently out-of-control L.A. uniformed police officers while some seventeen other officers stood by, the FBI, the L.A. District Attorney's Office, and the L.A. Police Department's Internal Affairs Division began their investigations. The Police Commission, a civilian panel charged with overseeing the operation of the police department, also began an inquiry. On May 1, 1991, Mayor Bradley created an independent commission to investigate the case, appointing Warren Christopher, former deputy secretary of state, as chair. Christopher had been vice chair of the McCone Commission and principal drafter of the much-maligned report, but this time he was in a stronger political position.[53] Unlike the after-the-riot McCone Report that depended on and defended official LAPD records, Christopher was charged with investigating police behavior that could potentially touch off a riot. After a thorough investigation,[54] the commission issued its report on July 9, 1991.[55] It came down hard on the L.A. Police. According to Raphael J. Sonenshein,

> it was a shocker. Unexpectedly, the commission issued a stinging report, which highlighted the failure of the LAPD and other city officials to rein in police brutality. Most dramatically, the commission released transcripts of police conversations on car computers. The transcripts contained numerous examples of racist and sexist phrases, including the infamous reference to "gorillas in the mist."[56]

The report concluded that "the department suffered from a . . . siege mentality," called upon Gates to retire, and recommended "greater civilian control of the police department."[57] In September 1991, the L.A. City Council approved a ballot referendum incorporating many of the recommendations of the Christopher Commission, including greater civilian control over the police department. By early June 1992, Los Angeles voters overwhelmingly approved Proposition F to reform the police department and to restore civilian control over it, but it was too little and much too late. The city had already exploded at the end of April in response to the trial verdict that had found the four policemen, charged with using excessive brutality, not guilty. In this explosion, fatalities were even higher and destruction more extensive than in 1965. When consultants were called in from the Police Foundation to evaluate police planning before and their behavior during the ten days of violence when federalized California and National Guardsmen were called in to restore order, their report was highly critical and called for massive reforms.[58]

This brings us to our third and most proximate difference between riots in the three cities, namely, the roles played by the local police in triggering and exacerbating riots and the degree to which their behavior is subject to political control.

Comparing Police Behavior in the Three Cities: Space Matters

As I insist in my book, legal boundaries are important. Given the significance of police actions in triggering and intensifying riots and that police administrations are under the control of city governments, the decisions local governments make are crucial. They determine the size and budget for their police departments. They set limits on the relative degree of police autonomy, i.e., the extent to which they are free to set the rules of engagement in situations of civil unrest or are constrained by and/or subject to civilian controls. On this dimension, the three cities have had very different histories. In general, where local police forces are trained to respond with restraint, where there is greater familiarity and less underlying animosity between protesters and the police, and where careful planning and disciplined responses by the police are able to avert or defuse lethal confrontations, the chances for minimizing the duration and costs of the riot are enhanced. In contrast, the wider the social and ethnic gap between the police and the protesters, the more haphazard the planning, the more panicky and unrestrained the police, and the greater the dependence on imported and untrained armed members of the national guard to handle the emergency, the more prolonged the riot and the greater its destructive results.

Paul Chevigny's *Edge of the Knife* contends that the

> governments of New York City and Los Angeles . . . have taken almost opposite approaches to policing. The Los Angeles police . . . have had a reputation as the quintessential anticrime force, with a semimilitary attitude both to the job and the public. There have been no major corruption scandals for decades, and morale has been good . . . at least until the Rodney King scandal. In contrast, the . . . NYPD . . . has been concerned with controlling the discretion of its officers and maintaining good relations with the public and political forces . . . While each of the cities has had endemic problems with the abuse of non-deadly force—police brutality . . . Los Angeles made no serious attempt to control such violence before 1991 [whereas] . . . New York long ago took the lead in the nation in trying to make officers accountable and reduce the use of deadly forces.[59]

Regardless of police styles, minorities in all three cities complain about police brutality and about being specifically targeted in a general system of unequal justice.[60]

In response, a number of reforms have been instituted in all three cities to control police brutality. In New York, the black community organized early to protest discriminatory treatment and eventually achieved civilian review and a complaints procedure,[61] although this has resulted largely in multiplying unresolved complaints. Los Angeles, in the wake of the 1992 riots, has imposed term limitations for police chiefs and greater civilian supervision. All three cities now have programs in community policing, a policy strongly promoted by the National Center for the Study of Police and Civil Disorder.

Community policing, however, depends heavily on street foot patrols and the development of sympathetic relations between the officers and the communities to which they are assigned.[62] Its feasibility, therefore, depends not only on procedures and self-discipline but also on spatial factors. The spatial density of New York facilitates street monitoring by foot patrols, as does the size and composition of the force—three times larger than Los Angeles's as well as more ethnically diverse.[63] Locality-based decentralization is still feasible in Chicago's moderately dense setting, where it was introduced experimentally in 1993 in five districts and has subsequently been expanded citywide. Its results are being monitored annually.[64] However, at least some Chicago studies suggest that whereas community policing may make residents less fearful and more satisfied with police services, it alone does not necessarily reduce crime.[65] And without some assurance that this more personalized contact will not simply permit the freer exercise of racism and discriminatory targeting, the attitudes of police officers must be changed, a policy also advocated by the Police Foundation.

Conclusions

This discussion has shown how people, place, and politics are differently configured in our three cities and that, to some extent, has resulted in different histories of racial violence. But it would be foolish to ignore the convergent effects of recent supralocal social and legal changes that are now impinging more and more on the probabilities of future race riots. Among these are the increased incarceration rates of black males in the criminal [in]justice system over the past generation, due to federal and state laws in the war on drugs, mandatory sentencing, and "three strikes and you're out." In the short run, this may reduce the probability of racial uprisings by selectively removing potential participants from the streets, but it can only intensify their alienation and grievances. Paradoxically, the civil rights movement enhanced both social mobility and escape from center-city ghettos by educated blacks at the same time it intensified the isolation of the poor and excluded. National changes in workfare policy, without provisions for child care, can increase the number of neglected children, and the growing competition between blacks and Latinos for jobs and political voice may increase tensions between them. To this must be added the potential effects of current wars, since there has always been a cyclical association between wars and riots. These are all factors that may overcome the relative abilities of local areas to forestall future riots by judicious and enlightened political and police cultures.

Notes

1. I find theories drawn from political economy particularly powerful for macro-analysis but have found sociopsychological and cross-cultural theories fertile for understanding variations in behavior in cities.

2. I am indebted to Dr. Steven Hutchinson for providing me with this translation from Jorge Luis Borges, *El Hacedor,* 143–44. That work—which purports to be a seventeenth-century account attributed to Suarez Miranda, *Viajes de varones prudentes,* book 4, chapter 45 (Lerida, Spain, 1658)—is, of course, a wise satire on science's attempts to reflect the world accurately.

3. Roderick McKenzie and Louis Wirth are often added to the pair.

4. The much-maligned association of the Chicago School with "human ecology" as God's little acre, devoid of sociocultural forces, betrays a deep misunderstanding of Park's theoretical contribution. In his mature statement of 1936, Park presented a Parsonian synthesis that offers a set of potential interactional/process/effects between what he termed the "subconsensual" or biotic level (geographic/sociospatial environment) and what he called the moral or cultural level (economic, social, and legal institutions). See his "Human Ecology," *American Journal of Sociology* 42 (July 1936): 1–15.

5. Burgess's contribution has also been simplified to focus on a particular outcome, namely, the shape of Chicago in the 1920s, rather than the socioeconomic process of land values that created that pattern. Actually, Burgess's (mindlessly misapplied) diagram of concentric circles did employ a theory of process, based on a model from "Adam Smith" urban land economics, which was more powerful in 1923 and more time/space constrained than it acknowledged. Just as Park borrowed some new theories from University of Chicago geographers (Barrows), so Burgess borrowed from the new field of land values being developed by economists at the University of Wisconsin.

6. Manhattan is a walking city, which forces one to pay attention to detail; the Outer Boroughs demand greater mobility and often present themselves discontinuously, subway stop to subway stop. Robert Park exhausted his students by making them accompany him on his rapid reconnaissance walks. Los Angeles is so spread out that its ecology cannot be grasped except by car and is distorted by freeways. Cameras mounted on vehicles have been used to trace changes along the major surface avenues.

7. I can pinpoint the exact moment this happened to me. Accompanying my husband to Egypt, my first experience outside the United States, I took a job teaching urban sociology at the American University in Cairo—and discovered with a jolt that nothing I had learned in

Chicago applied to that city! The layers of the city could only be unpeeled historically, which is how I became a historian.

8. I take pride in escaping classification by school, just as I take pride in the fact that I have been identified over the years as a planner (which I was), a sociologist (which I still am), and even a historian, an economist, an anthropologist, and a geographer (which I strive to be). Urbanists may be the last of the universalists!

9. Kurt H. Wolff, *Surrender and Catch: Exploration and Inquiry Today*, ed. Robert S. Cohen and Marx W. Wartofsky (Reidel Publishing Co., 1976).

10. Perhaps the most explicit, concise formulation may be found in Robert E. Park and W. I. Thomas, "Participation and Social Assimilation," in Kimball Young, ed., *Source Book for Social Psychology* (New York: Knopf, 1927), 47–53, although a fuller treatment can be found in Thomas's methodological note to the first volume of the *Polish Peasant* series with his collaborator, Florian Znaniecki (Chicago: University of Chicago Press, 1918). I suspect that Park's contribution in this instance was largely as a cover for Thomas who, in 1918, the same year the *Polish Peasant* was published, had been dismissed from the University of Chicago because of a personal scandal.

11. Janet Abu-Lughod, *Race, Space, and Riots in Chicago, New York, and Los Angeles* (New York: Oxford University Press, 2007). This book, in turn, drew on the context of their detailed histories presented in my *New York, Chicago, Los Angeles: America's Global Cities* (Minneapolis: University of Minnesota Press, 1999).

12. Kai Erikson, *Everything in Its Path: Destruction of Community in the Buffalo Creek Flood* (New York: Simon and Schuster, 1978).

13. Careful histories of these and other urban riots reveal the important role played by police behavior in triggering (although not causing) outbursts of racial violence, and the deleterious effect of importing trigger-happy troops unfamiliar with the site and the people in exacerbating riot behavior. The overwhelming proportion of fatalities in most riots, with the possible exception of lynchings and Chicago in 1919, come from police/imported troops, not from alleged snipers.

14. In the following section, I draw heavily on the first half of chapter 8 in my book, *Race, Space, and Riots*, although obviously the supporting evidence appears in chapters 2–7. A defense of my use of the ambiguous and ultimately unsatisfactory terms "race" and "riots" appears in chapter 1.

15. See Edward Ewing Pratt, *Industrial Causes of Congestion of Population in New York City* 45, no. 1, Columbia University Studies in History, Economics, and Public Law (New York, 1911).

16. Mary White Ovington identified five areas scattered across Manhattan in 1900. See her *Half a Man: The Status of the Negro in New York* (New York: Longmans, Green, 1911).

17. See Ann Durkin Keating, *Building Chicago: Suburban Developers and the Creation of a Divided Metropolis* (Columbus: Ohio State University Press, 1988).

18. The Mexican settlement of "Mudtown," later renamed Watts, originally housed workers imported to build the railroad connecting Los Angeles with the port of Long Beach via what is still referred to as "the shoestring addition," the most anomalous example of the city's irrational boundaries, pockmarked by independent towns.

19. Massive and diverse immigration has helped to sustain the city's population growth in recent decades, and the proportion of foreign-born now rivals the situation that obtained at the turn of the last century. For information on the numbers and diverse origins of immigrants, see, inter alia, New York City Department of City Planning, *The Newest New Yorkers 1990–1994: An Analysis of Immigration to NYC in the Early 1990s* (New York: New York City Department of City Planning, 1997), which updated their 2-vol. ed., *The Newest New Yorkers: An Analysis of Immigration into New York City during the 1980s* (New York: New York City Department of City Planning, 1992).

20. This is not to deny that there have been numerous ethnic-specific territorial conflicts as well as individual attacks on blacks viewed as invaders, such as in the Howard Beach case, or more collectively, in portions of Brooklyn, viz. Jonathan Rieder, *Canarsie: The Jews and Italians of Brooklyn against Liberalism* (Cambridge, Mass.: Harvard University Press, 1985). Such tensions provided the theme for Spike Lee's film, *Do the Right Thing.*

21. I was unable to locate a single map of the city depicting the complex distribution of racial/ethnic groups in overlapping and multiple spaces. See *Atlas of New York City for 2000,* produced by William Bowen (http://130.166.124.2/atlas.nyc/ny6_20.gif). Separate maps in this atlas show the percentage distribution of blacks in the five boroughs and the size distributions of blacks of various ancestries (overlapping in Venn diagram form with "Black Hispanics"), but these maps cannot be combined except by inspection and verbal descriptions.

22. The isolation of Watts and South Central, despite its proximity to downtown (a dubious label) was intensified by the death of street railroads and the construction of the Santa Monica freeway to its north and the Harbor thruway to its east, which split Watts from South Central but lacked exit ramps into these areas.

23. James Weldon Johnson, *Black Manhattan* (New York: Knopf, 1930).

24. Martha Biondi, *To Stand and Fight: The Struggle for Civil Rights in Postwar New York City* (Cambridge, Mass.: Harvard University Press, 2003), but see early history in her chapter 1.

25. Mayor La Guardia's Commission, *The Complete Report of Mayor La Guardia's Commission on the Harlem Riot of March 19, 1935* (preliminary publication in the *Amsterdam News,* July 1935). Transcript of this newspaper clipping reprinted in the Mass Violence in America series (New York: Arno Press, 1969).

26. Michael W. Flamm, "New York's Night of Birmingham Horror: The NYPD, the Harlem Riot of 1964, and the Politics of 'Law and Order,'" in Richard Bessel and Clive Emsley, eds., *Patterns of Provocation: Police and Public Disorder* (New York: Berghahn Books, 2000): 81–98.

27. Both La Guardia (Fusion) and Lindsay (Republican) were liberals. In New York, given its historical association between the Democratic Party and corruption, reform candidates have often been not so much Republican as antimachine.

28. Giuliani favored the police over citizen rights and established the notorious street crime control units, whose commando tactics resulted in several unprovoked shootings of innocent men, whereas Bloomberg has opposed the modus operandi of police out of uniform.

29. There are structural similarities between the economies and spatial patterns of Chicago and Detroit that make these cities stand out in their degrees of racial animosity.

30. For fuller details, see Abu-Lughod, "Chicago Becomes Fordist," *New York, Chicago, Los Angeles,* chapter 5, 100–132.

31. Black voters did not begin to shift party affiliations to the Democrats until the Depression.

32. In 1931, Democrat Anton Cermak (of Bohemian descent) won the mayor's race with strong Irish backing. When he was killed in an early assassination attempt on Roosevelt's life, the Irish politicos stepped out from behind to take over the party.

33. The most relevant theory is still Robert Michel's *Political Parties* (published in German in 1911; first English trans. by Glencoe, Ill: The Free Press of Glencoe, 1949).

34. See William J. Grimshaw, *Bitter Fruit: Black Politics and the Chicago Machine, 1931–1991* (Chicago: University of Chicago Press, 1992).

35. The sordid tale of how city council members vetoed sites for public housing in their own wards is recounted in Martin Meyerson and Edward Banfield, *Politics, Planning and the Public Interest* (Glencoe, Ill.: The Free Press of Glencoe, 1955). A more apologetic analysis of the role of the University of Chicago in renewing its neighborhood is Peter Rossi and Robert Dentler, *The Politics of Urban Renewal: The Chicago Findings* (New York: The Free Press of Glencoe, 1961).

36. See ward-specific votes reproduced in Len O'Connor, *Clout: Mayor Daley and his City* (Chicago: Regnery, 1975), 192–93.

37. His notorious complaint that his chief of police had failed to follow his orders to "shoot to kill any arsonist or anyone with a Molotov cocktail in his hand … and to maim or cripple anyone looting any stores" was delivered at a press conference within two weeks of the riot's start. *Chicago Daily News,* April 17, 1968.

38. See *Report of the Chicago Riot Study Committee to the Hon. Richard J. Daley* (Chicago: Chicago Riot Study Committee, 1969).

39. Achieved through Democratic primary elections, including the three-way Democratic contest (that included Daley Jr.) won by Harold Washington, making him Chicago's first and only black mayor. Reelected to a second term, Washington died of a heart attack in the first year of the new term. This proved only a brief interlude between the Irish mayors.

40. Significantly, Wesley G. Skogan and Susan M. Harnett, in *Community Policing Chicago Style* (New York: Oxford University Press, 1997) suggest that the younger Daley's initial interest in the community policing experiment was motivated by his search for a reform issue that could unite all races and especially the overly victimized and underprotected black community: namely, crime reduction. It seems to me, however, that extending the responsibilities of beat patrolmen to encompass broader activities such as calling for improved city services, in response to expressed complaints from neighborhood residents, begins to approximate the old role played by precinct captains in the Chicago machine.

41. See Timothy Gilfoyle, *Millennium Park* (Chicago: University of Chicago Press, 2006).

42. Barack Obama would have been a likely prospect for a black mayor, had he not aspired to a higher office.

43. According to Chicago Housing Authority reports, before their destruction, over 90 percent of their non-senior project units were occupied by African Americans.

44. See Table 6.1 in Abu-Lughod, *New York, Chicago, Los Angeles,* 141.

45. This period is well covered by Mike Davis in *City of Quartz: Excavating the Future in Los Angeles* (New York: Verso, 1990).

46. Figures from Armando Morales, *Ando Sangrando! (I Am Bleeding!): A Study of Mexican American-Police Conflict* (La Puente, Calif.: Perspectiva, 1972). For a broader treatment of this nationally, see Abraham Hoffman, *Unwanted Mexican Americans in the Great Depression: Repatriation Pressures, 1929–1939* (Tucson: University of Arizona Press, 1974). Mexicans had already found their way to the Chicago region to work on the railroads and as migrant farm workers. Their settlements were also emptied out, at least temporarily.

47. For a fine-tuned analysis of the evolution of Los Angeles's political culture between 1880 and 1932, see Steven Erie, "The Local State and Economic Growth in Los Angeles, 1880–1932," *Urban Affairs Quarterly* 27, no. 4 (1992): 519–54.

48. See Abu-Lughod, *New York, Chicago, Los Angeles*, "Los Angeles Becomes Industrial," chapter 9, 237–68.

49. Indeed, one of the grievances acknowledged by the California Governor's Commission on the Los Angeles Riots in *Violence in the City—An End or a Beginning? A Report by the Governor's Commission on the Los Angeles Riots* (Dec. 2, 1965), commonly referred to as the McCone Report, was the passage of Proposition 14 by two-thirds of the voters in November 1964, a referendum that repealed the Rumford Fair Housing Act and thus foreclosed the possibility of reducing housing segregation. Reprinted in Robert M. Fogelson, comp., in Mass Violence in America series (New York: Arno Press, 1969).

50. But unlike the 1968 Chicago case, which was never independently investigated, a quite different story, in great detail that is more credible and explanatory, is told by historian Robert Conot, in his best-selling and widely acclaimed *Rivers of Blood, Years of Darkness* (New York: Bantam, 1967).

51. The best explication of this system I have found is Raphael J. Sonenshein, *Politics in Black and White: Race and Power in Los Angeles* (Princeton, N.J.: Princeton University Press, 1993): see especially the map series of City Council Districts, 15–17. For details on the 1963 city council elections, see 36–48. Note the parallel to the Chicago coalition between blacks and "lakefront liberals" that would elect Harold Washington fifteen years later.

52. Changes in U.S. immigration laws in 1965 liberalized the entry of special classes of immigrants, including those from Latin America and selected Asian countries, and provided a cover for entrants of similar appearance to join them without proper documentation. Many of the latter settled in Watts and South Central.

53. Lou Cannon, *Official Negligence: How Rodney King and the Riots Changed Los Angeles and the LAPD* (New York: Times Books/Random House, 1997), 122–123. This almost seven-hundred-page source is the most detailed and balanced account I have found of the events surrounding the riot and the politics of policing in L.A.

54. His large staff interviewed some 450 police officers (current and past) and experts on policing and law enforcement, reviewed some 1,240 personnel complaints filed against the police, examined 100,000 pages of transcripts of MDT (Mobile Digital Terminal) communications, 700 police personnel files, and held five public hearings. See Cannon, *Official Negligence*, 129.

55. See Independent Commission on the Los Angeles Police Department, also called the *Christopher Commission Report* (Los Angeles: July 1991).

56. Sonenshein, *Politics in Black and White*, 218–19, citing the *Christopher Commission Report*, 1991, 71–74. Cannon provides details on how this quote was obtained in *Official Negligence*, 79. The insulting remark about "gorillas in the mist" was traced to Officer Lawrence Powell, one of the two officers found guilty in the second (federal) trial for violating King's civil rights (i.e., being racist). Immediately after the beating, Powell sent a computer message to a fellow officer on MDT, which included the phrases "I haven't beaten anyone this bad for some time" and "It was right out of gorillas in the mist." Transcripts of these MDTs were released on March 18 and quoted on TV. A random sample of sixteen months of MDTs had been reviewed in preparation for the *Christopher Commission Report*. Although most were routine, hundreds contained derogatory comments about racial and ethnic minorities, women, and gays—some "patently offensive." See Cannon, *Official Negligence*, 137.

57. Hiroshi Fukurai, Richard Krooth, and Edgar W. Butler, "The Rodney King Beating Verdicts," chapter 4 in Mark Baldassare, ed., *The Los Angeles Riots: Lessons for the Urban Future* (Boulder, Colo: Westview Press, 1994), 79. The fullest account of the trials can be found in this chapter.

58. William H. Webster and Hubert Williams, *The City in Crisis: A Report by the Special Advisor to the Board of Police Commissioners on the Civil Disorder in Los Angeles*, submitted October 21, 1992 (2 vols., privately printed and copyrighted by the authors).

59. Paul Chevigny, *The Edge of the Knife: Police Violence in the Americas* (New York: The New Press, 1995), introd. The costs of each approach are obvious: militarism can lead to higher shooting deaths; good relations may lead to collusion and corruption.

60. The most succinct case for this is made by David Cole in *No Equal Justice: Race and Class in the American Criminal Justice System* (New York: New Press, 1999).

61. See Marilynn Johnson, *Street Justice: A History of Police Violence in New York City* (Boston: Beacon Press, 2003) for a detailed account of these reforms.

62. One unintended consequence in New York has been the facilitation of corruption (deals and payoffs to officers walking the same beat over time), which has sometimes required regular reassignments. In 1999, an LAPD scandal erupted in the Rampart district where some seventy locally assigned policemen were found to have been robbing, murdering, and framing gang members for many years.

63. Size matters. Up to now, Los Angeles has depended on vehicular mobility and helicopter surveillance. See, inter alia, Sewell Chan, "Counting Heads Along the Thin Blue Line," *New York Times*, March 26, 2006, on plans to increase New York's police force by 1,200, even though the city already has 4.5 officers for every thousand residents (or 118 per square mile), as contrasted with Los Angeles's 2.4 officers per 1,000 residents (only twenty per square mile). The new mayor of Los Angeles and Bratton, his police chief, are seeking to increase the LAPD force by 1,000 officers but "so far there has been little action." See also Jennifer Steinhauer, "A Tough East Coast Cop in Laid-Back Los Angeles: Bratton Poised for Second Term as Chief," *New York Times*, September 3, 2006, where the Ramparts scandal is mentioned. Bratton later resigned.

64. Wesley Skogan has been evaluating this innovation and has written several accounts of its progress. See, for example, Skogan and Harnett, *Community Policing Chicago Style*; Wesley G. Skogan, *On the Beat: Police and Community Problem Solving* (Boulder, Colo.:

Westview Press, 1999); Wesley G. Skogan, *Police and Community in Chicago: A Tale of Three Cities* (New York: Oxford University Press, 2006).

65. In Skogan's *Community Policing Chicago Style,* he suggests that the experimental program was least successful in Hispanic areas, and in his ten-year review, he admits that although the policy has now been extended citywide, it has not had an impact on Chicago's high murder rate.

3

The Chicago of Jane Addams and Ernest Burgess

Same City, Different Visions

▪ Daphne Spain

Chicago at the turn of the twentieth century was an amazing place. Incorporated in 1837, burned to the ground in 1871, host to the glorious World's Columbian Exposition in 1893, and magnet for thousands of European immigrants, this was a city that was constantly reinventing itself. One of Chicago's prominent citizens at the time was Jane Addams. Acknowledged leader of the American settlement house movement, Addams was the most famous American woman of the Progressive Era. With her friend Ellen Gates Starr, she opened the Hull House settlement on Halsted Street in 1889. It was the base from which she conducted vigorous campaigns to improve living and working conditions for immigrants. In 1902 Addams published *Democracy and Social Ethics,* a treatise on her belief that democratic principles were best learned by practicing them.[1] John Dewey credited Addams with the shift to thinking of democracy as a way of life rather than just a political system.[2]

Soon after Addams and Starr opened the doors of Hull House, the American Baptist Educational Society, with the help of John D. Rockefeller, established the University of Chicago. The first department of sociology in the United States was created there in 1892. When Robert Park joined its faculty in 1914, he had already been a teacher, a newspaper reporter, and an aide for seven years to Booker T. Washington. Ernest Burgess, who earned his sociology degree at the University of Chicago and returned there to teach, collaborated with Park on urban research throughout the 1920s.[3]

Their 1925 edited volume, *The City*, became the bible of the Chicago school of urban sociology.

This chapter explores the different visions of the city held by participants in the settlement house movement, epitomized by Jane Addams, and members of the Chicago school of urban sociology, as represented by Ernest Burgess. In a volume on different schools of urban theory, the chapter provides a counterbalance to the hagiography surrounding the Chicago School. Park and Burgess knew of Addams's work, yet chose to dismiss it.[4] That decision would have significant consequences for the divergence of sociological theory and practice. Park and Burgess's Chicago consisted of natural areas of "social junk" characterized by disorder and vice. In contrast, Addams saw the promise of democracy. Both Addams and Burgess based their work on Chicago, and both drew conclusions that influenced American scholarship for decades. But where Burgess and his colleagues perceived urban anomie from a distance, Addams and other settlement house residents experienced communities up close. The Chicago School emphasized theory, settlement workers demanded action. The juxtaposition of Addams and Burgess reveals a gender disparity in approaches to the city informed less by essentialist gender qualities than by actual experiences.

Contrasting Visions

In *Seeing with Their Hearts* (2002), historian Maureen Flanagan proposed that activist women in Chicago between the 1870s and 1930s had a vision of "the good city," a democratic city that promoted the welfare of all its citizens, not just the interests of the business elite. That meant suffrage for women, homes in which all residents could raise healthy children, and protection from polluted air and water. In contrast, argues Flanagan, men of the business community placed profits above the public welfare.

Men's and women's responses to the Great Fire of 1871 were an example of their different priorities. The fire killed 300 people, destroyed 2,000 acres, and inflicted $200 million worth of damage to property. The city was in ruins. Almost one-third of all residents lost their homes, and one-third of the downtown buildings were lost.[5] Mayor Roswell Mason turned over

$5 million in relief donations to the Chicago Relief and Aid Society, a private organization run by the city's most prominent businessmen. The society imposed strict rules about eligibility, where relief would be distributed, and who would provide supplies for rebuilding. Women, who were excluded from the society, objected to its overly bureaucratic rules. They formed their own Ladies' Relief and Aid Society to provide survivors with food, clothing, and money. Contemporary sketches depicting the differences in relief efforts portrayed men meeting around a large table in a comfortable room, deciding how to dispense aid, while women were shown mingling in the slums with the homeless, handing out food.[6] The dichotomy between masculine theory and feminine practice took shape early in Chicago's history.

Jane Addams

Jane Addams was a standard bearer for the women's vision of the city. Her writings are permeated with castigations of men's values. In 1899, she thought Chicago was a city where "well-to-do men of the community . . . are almost wholly occupied in the correction of political machinery and with concern for the better method of administration, rather than with the ultimate purpose of securing the welfare of the people."[7] On corporate evasion of property taxes in 1900: The entire community would have to exert pressure "until it shall be a great disgrace that any great corporation does not pay its adequate taxes; until any shareholder shall be ashamed to receive a dividend if out of that dividend has not first been paid that which is legitimately owed to the city."[8]

Addams's *Democracy and Social Ethics* was a collection of essays codifying her theory that a new *social* morality must take the place of *personal* morality if true democracy were to flourish. For Addams, democracy was more than a political system; it was a way of life that informed daily activities. Faith in the equality of humans carried with it the responsibility to support others in reaching their potential. Addams and her settlement house colleagues were especially committed to helping immigrants become American citizens.[9] In fact, Hull House was the first social settlement in the United States to offer citizenship preparation classes.[10] More important than the classroom, however, was first-hand experience in the political process. The Hull House Men's Club ran a candidate in the 1893 alderman's race, and the Women's Club campaigned vigorously for garbage removal.[11] The corrupt ward boss system, vote-buying, and retreat from municipal service delivery were all targets of progressive reform. Addams believed that good governance was possible only to the extent that all citizens engaged in the democratic process.

Living in the midst of impoverished immigrant neighborhoods reinforced Addams's commitment to a socially just city. She saw, every day, the effects of intense industrialization on ethnic communities. Addams's 1910 memoir, *Twenty Years at Hull-House,* was a philosophical reflection on her daily encounters with neighbors.

Over and over in *Twenty Years,* she recited stories of infant abandonment, worker injuries, starvation, and derelict housing. Yet she also told of strong ethnic communities. Italian families visited Hull House on Saturday nights and on national holidays. On their nights, German families sang folk songs and read German history and literature in the drawing room. Addams attempted to preserve the best of the old traditions while bringing immigrants into contact with American customs. She was most proud of the Labor Museum, which featured the handwork of immigrant women. Addams also invited Italian, Syrian, Greek, and Russian women to bring their spindles to Hull House for an exhibition of old-world spinning and weaving skills. She hoped to illustrate the evolution of the industry to children who worked in the local textile factories, producing what her friend John Dewey called a "continuing reconstruction of experience." Addams attributed her inspiration for the museum to her "exciting walk on Polk Street," where she had first seen an old woman spinning.[12] The city was an adventure for Addams and her colleagues, despite the grimy surroundings.

Addams applied her democratic ideals to the fight for woman suffrage. In a 1913 *Ladies Home Journal* article ironically titled "If Men Were Seeking the Franchise," she set forth a hypothetical world in which women, but not men, could vote. She imagined the following responses from enfranchised women when men pleaded for the vote: "You [men] have always been so eager to make money; what assurance have we that in your desire to get the greatest amount of coal out of the ground in the shortest possible time you would not permit the mine supports to decay and mine damp to accumulate, until the percentage of accidents among miners would be simply heartbreaking?" Women would also point out to men demanding the vote that men's preoccupation with profits would block legislation to ensure factory workers' safety, and that men might expect very young children to work fourteen-hour days in those factories.[13] Both conditions were true at that time.

Ernest Burgess

Compare Addams's vision with that of the Chicago urban sociologists. In "The Growth of the City," Burgess identifies the city as the crucible of social problems such as divorce, delinquency, and social unrest that "alarm and bewilder us."[14] In Burgess's Concentric zone theory, Hull House would have been located in the "Zone in Transition" surrounding the Central Business District. According to Burgess, it was a "zone of deterioration" that included "slums and bad lands, with their submerged regions of poverty, degradation, and disease, and their underworlds of crime and vice." Its rooming house districts were a "purgatory of lost souls," and immigrant colonies were full to overflowing. Burgess saw a dangerous urban world, but Addams and Starr were fearless. In the excitement of their first night at Hull House, they forgot to close a side door opening onto Polk Street. They awoke to find all their possessions intact and were "much pleased in the morning to find that we possessed a fine illustration of the honesty and kindliness of our new neighbors."[15]

Burgess acknowledged that there might be some hope for residents of this zone: "The area of deterioration, while essentially one of decay . . . is also one of regeneration, as witness the mission, *the settlement,* the artists' colony, radical centers—*all obsessed with the vision of a new and better world.*"[16] Burgess seems to have had little patience for the utopian visions of progressive reform. Nor did he see a role for the university in solving the social problems that plagued the slums. For purely academic reasons, students and faculty in the sociology department conducted dozens of case studies of Chicago's neighborhoods. These included reports on boys' gangs, the Central Business District, the natural history of vice areas, the slum, and the Lower North Side.[17]

Points of Intersection

Burgess and Addams knew of each other's work, for Addams and her colleagues published frequently in the leading professional journal. Residents of settlement houses had been writing about social problems since the 1890s. Between 1896 and 1911, the *American Journal of Sociology (AJS)* published nearly twenty articles by Chicago authors, most of whom were affiliated with one of the thirty-four settlement houses in the city. Addams and her colleagues at Hull House were regular contributors to *AJS*. Addams's "Trade Unions and Public Duty" and Florence Kelley's "The Working Boy" both appeared in 1896. Addams's first book, *Democracy and Social Ethics*, was reviewed in *AJS* in 1902, the same year it was published. Sophonisba Breckinridge and Edith Abbott's articles on Chicago's housing problems appeared in a 1909 issue.[18]

Two settlement houses had direct ties to the University of Chicago. The most closely connected was the University of Chicago Settlement, established in 1894 by the Philanthropic Committee of the university's Christian Union. Head resident Mary McDowell belonged to the Chicago Free Bath and Sanitary League and succeeded in having the city's third municipal bath opened in her district. McDowell earned a reputation as "The Garbage Lady" for her tireless crusade to clean up her Packingtown neighborhood.[19] She saw it as an industrial community, not a slum, where the dreary quality of life resulted from the vile work and low wages in the nearby stockyards. McDowell's article about these deplorable conditions appeared in *AJS* in 1901.[20]

Graham Taylor's Chicago Commons also opened in 1894. In 1903, Taylor created the first class in social work at the University of Chicago, and his students visited frequently to gain firsthand knowledge of poverty in the Seventeenth Ward. In addition to the many programs sponsored by the Chicago Commons, Taylor secured a new public school that offered kindergarten classes in the mornings and adult classes at night. His article about the scientific value of social settlements appeared in *AJS* in 1902. Taylor also founded the Chicago School of Civics and Philanthropy in 1903, which for four years was operated in cooperation with the University of Chicago's extension program. Taylor appointed Jane Addams, Julia Lathrop, Sophonisba Breckinridge, and Edith Abbott to the board when the school became independent. Nearly one thousand students enrolled in its programs over the next seven years.[21]

Unlike Burgess, settlement house workers did more than write about urban conditions. Like McDowell, they lobbied for public baths and sanitary reforms. Like Taylor, they offered educational programs to children and adults. And Addams was famous for garnering city resources for her neighborhood. When months of complaints about trash removal were ignored, Addams applied for, and was appointed to, garbage inspector of the Ninth Ward.[22]

Nearly every piece of significant housing reform legislation during the Progressive Era was based on research conducted by settlement house residents. *Hull House Maps and Papers*[23] contained thorough documentation of the squalid living conditions in the Hull House neighborhood. The district contained "filthy and rotten tenements, dingy courts and tumble-down sheds, foul stables and dilapidated outhouses, broken sewer pipes, and piles of garbage fairly alive with diseased odors."[24] Rooms served multiple purposes; residents might cook, sleep, eat, and work in a single room. Florence Kelley's chapter on the "sweating system," in which women and children sewed clothing in poorly lit and ventilated rooms, contributed to the regulation of tenement sweatshops and to labor reforms.[25]

Members of the Chicago School had an uneasy alliance with settlement house residents. Burgess thought settlement work represented a devoted, idealistic, and intelligent phase of social work. The settlement exhibited a "love of truth" and "the spirit of science" because, according to Burgess, it had originated as an extension of the university. But residents' contact with immigrants represented only the first stage in the "trend of neighborhood work toward a scientific basis." Settlement workers completed the second stage when they collected statistics about living and working conditions, as *Hull House Maps and Papers* had done. But this type of work, one step removed from personal experience, only documented *factors,* whereas real science, for Burgess, was concerned with *forces,* not with factors. A factor was a concrete cause of an individual event; a force was an abstract cause for general events. For Burgess, neighborhood work had to study social forces to become scientific. The department of sociology was sponsoring a series of research projects to do just that, using the city as a laboratory. Burgess assumed that results from these studies could be generalized to other neighborhoods in other cities.[26]

Jane Addams had been living at Hull House for nearly thirty years by the time Burgess and his colleagues developed their urban theories. What did she think of their work? Although *Twenty Years at Hull-House* (1910) was written long before *The City* (1925), it provides clues to her attitude toward the relationship between the university and the settlement house. Addams had experience with the University of Chicago before Park and Burgess joined its faculty. She became a member of the university's extension staff soon after it was founded, she was in close contact with Taylor and McDowell, and she frequently invited professors from the university to speak at Hull House. Although Addams perceived the need for an affiliation, *Twenty Years* reveals some of her reservations.

First, she disliked the idea that the settlement was merely an experimental site for the work of scholars: "I have always objected to the phrase 'sociological laboratory' applied to us, because Settlements should be much more human and spontaneous than such a phrase connotes."[27] Second, she would have asserted that the settlement was a precursor to the university, not the other way around, as Burgess claimed. Hull House preceded the University of Chicago by one year. Moreover, the Hull House "Working People's Social Science Club," formed in 1890, predated the sociology department by two years.

The Social Science Club met in the Hull House drawing room from 8:00 to 10:00 p.m. every Wednesday for seven years. On any given night, forty to one hundred men would assemble to discuss political, social, and economic issues that directly affected them. Although arguments could become heated, the club prided itself on rules of decorum. After all, according to Addams, "radicals are accustomed to hot discussion and sharp differences of opinion" and took the exchanges in stride. Not so some of the guests. During the seven-year history of the club, only twice had a speaker lost his temper. In each case, it had been a college professor who "wasn't accustomed to being talked back to."[28]

Hull House was an extension center for the University of Chicago. One of the most direct collaborations was in the Sunday evening lecture series, when nearly seven hundred men would assemble in Bowen Hall to hear illustrated lectures delivered by faculty from the university. Addams despaired of the shortcomings of academic lecturers, however. She archly observed that their "habit of research and the desire to say the latest word upon any subject" often overcame their ability to connect with the audience, whereupon they would "insensibly drop into the dull terminology of the classroom." There were exceptions: "We had twelve gloriously popular talks on organic evolution, but the lecturer was not yet a professor—merely a university instructor—and his mind was still eager over the marvel of it all."[29]

Finally, Addams would have disagreed with Burgess on the failure of settlement houses to grasp social forces, rather than merely record social factors. Addams identified the settlement house movement as "an experimental effort to aid in the solution of the social and industrial problems which are engendered by the modern conditions of life in a great city. It insists that these problems are not confined to any one portion of a city. It is an attempt to relieve, at the same time, the over-accumulation at one end of society and the destitution at the other."[30] As a member of the middle class dependent on industrialists for financial support, Addams was acquainted with both ends of the spectrum. Her talent was the ability to distill abstract principles of capitalism from concrete examples of hunger, disease, and intolerable housing.

Addams saw the gulf between the haves and the have-nots as a threat to democracy. According to Addams, it was the duty of every settlement worker to "arouse and interpret the public opinion of their neighborhood toward the redistribution of social and educational resources."[31] The settlement house movement focused on teaching immigrants how to participate in democratic processes that would facilitate that redistribution. This was a controversial idea in a xenophobic nation. Settlement house residents were branded as socialists, with some basis in fact. Vida Scudder, who founded College Settlement in New York City the same year as Hull House, readily described herself as a "Christian Socialist."[32] Addams traveled to Russia to meet with Tolstoy, and Hull House resident Florence Kelley translated into English Friedrich Engels's *The Condition of the Working Classes in England in 1844*.[33] In retrospect, Addams thought the Social Science Club might have been the reason Hull House achieved its early reputation for radicalism.[34] With settlements sheltering self-proclaimed socialists and those who consorted with them, it is little wonder that the movement's ideas failed to gain currency with conservative academics.[35]

Conclusion

Addams and her colleagues, and Burgess and his colleagues, lived in Chicago at the same time. Yet they had significantly different visions of the city. Settlement house workers were surrounded by filthy conditions, but were convinced that democracy could thrive in the worst of circumstances. They used the data in *Hull House Maps and Papers* to lobby for reform legislation, offered classes in citizenship, and mobilized their neighbors to demand municipal services. Sociologists, however, were intent on creating theories that would explain social forces in cities other than Chicago. They studied some of the same neighborhoods in which settlement workers lived, but they saw places with the detached eye of the analyst who could go back to the university and ponder his findings.

Settlement house workers and sociologists documented social problems associated with rapid industrialization, yet they had different priorities. The urban sociologists saw themselves as academic theorists; settlement house residents considered themselves activists. Where Burgess saw social breakdown, Addams saw community strengths. Because they had minimal interaction, their respective visions of the city barely touched.

The potential for collaboration between sociological theorists and practitioners clearly existed in Chicago during the 1920s. They lived in the same city and addressed similar issues, but Park and Burgess worked in the ivory tower while Addams, McDowell, and Taylor toiled in the trenches.

Chicago School sociologists *wrote about* the city while settlement workers *lived in and tried to reform* the city by coercing officials to provide public baths, schools, and clean streets. Although sociological theory and practice could have converged in Chicago during the 1920s, the historical moment was lost. The two became estranged and social work became a mostly separate and less academically prestigious profession. Yet many conditions that characterized cities one hundred years ago are being reproduced today. Millions of immigrants, many of whom are poor, are arriving in cities just as government-funded social services are declining. Asian and Hispanic newcomers face many of the same barriers, and contribute as much to cultural change, as did their predecessors from Europe during the late nineteenth century. Perhaps now is the time to consider whether the continued separation of the fields is good for the disciplines, or for immigrants.

Notes

1. Jane Addams, *Democracy and Social Ethics* (Cambridge, Mass.: Belknap Press of Harvard University Press, 1964).

2. Charlene H. Seigfried, "Introduction to the Illinois Edition," *Democracy and Social Ethics* (Urbana: University of Illinois Press, 2002), xi.

3. James F. Short, *The Social Fabric of the Metropolis: Contributions of the Chicago School of Urban Sociology* (Chicago: University of Chicago Press, 1971), xi–xlvi.

4. Elsewhere, I have argued that the Los Angeles School, despite its efforts to distance itself from the Chicago School, was equally guilty of ignoring women's contributions to urban theory. See Daphne Spain, *How Women Saved the City* (Minneapolis: University of Minnesota Press, 2001); Daphne Spain, "What Happened to Gender Relations on the Way from Chicago to Los Angeles?" *City and Community* 1 (June 2002): 155–67.

5. Carl Smith, *Urban Disorder and the Shape of Belief: The Great Chicago Fire, the Haymarket Bomb, and the Model Town of Pullman* (Chicago: University of Chicago Press, 1995).

6. Maureen Flanagan, *Seeing with Their Hearts: Chicago Women and the Vision of the Good City, 1871–1933* (Princeton, N.J.: Princeton University Press, 2002).

7. Ibid., 7.

8. Ibid., 69.

9. Seigfried, *Democracy and Social Ethics.*

10. Jean Bethke Elshtain, *Jane Addams and the Dream of American Democracy: A Life* (New York: Basic Books, 2002), xix.

11. Jane Addams, *Twenty Years at Hull-House, with Autobiographical Notes* (New York: New American Library, 1960), 202–22.

12. Ibid., 169–73.

13. Jane Addams, *Twenty Years at Hull-House with Autobiographical Notes,* ed. Victoria Bissel Brown (Boston: St. Martin's, 1999), 232–38.

14. Robert E. Park, Ernest Burgess, and Roderick D. McKenzie, *The City : Suggestions for Investigation of Human Behavior in the Urban Environment* (Chicago: University of Chicago Press, 1925; reprint, 1967), 47.

15. Addams, *Twenty Years at Hull-House* (1960), 79.

16. Park, Burgess, and McKenzie, *The City,* 56; emphasis added.

17. Ibid., 62; Short, *The Social Fabric of the Metropolis.*

18. See Mary Jo Deegan, *Jane Addams and the Men of the Chicago School, 1892–1918* (New Brunswick, N.J.: Transaction Books, 1988); David Sibley, "Gender, Science, Politics, and Geographies of the City," *Gender, Place, and Culture* 2 (1995): 37–49.

19. Caroline M. Hill, *Mary McDowell and Municipal Housekeeping* (Chicago: Chicago Council of Social Agencies, 1938).

20. Deegan, *Jane Addams and the Men of the Chicago School;* Sibley, "Gender, Science, Politics."

21. Deegan, *Jane Addams and the Men of the Chicago School.*

22. Addams, *Twenty Years at Hull-House* (1960), 200–4.

23. Hull-House Residents, *Hull-House Maps and Papers* (1895; New York: Arno Press, 1970).

24. Agnes Sinclair Holbrook, "Map Notes and Comments," *Hull-House Maps and Papers,* 3–23.

25. Kathryn Kish Sklar, *Florence Kelley and the Nation's Work: The Rise of Women's Political Culture, 1830–1900* (New Haven, Conn.: Yale University Press, 1995).

26. Park, Burgess, and McKenzie, *The City,* 142–43.

27. Addams, *Twenty Years at Hull-House* (1960), 217.

28. Ibid., 134–40.

29. Ibid., 296–97.

30. Ibid., 98.

31. Ibid.

32. Ruth Crocker, *Social Work and Social Order: The Settlement Movement in Two Industrial Cities, 1889–1930* (Urbana: University of Illinois Press, 1992), 114.

33. Sklar, *Florence Kelley and the Nation's Work.*

34. Addams, *Twenty Years at Hull-House* (1960), 137.

35. Deegan, *Jane Addams and the Men of the Chicago School.*

Part II

The View from Los Angeles

Urban Politics and the Los Angeles School of Urbanism

■ Michael Dear and Nicholas Dahmann

The Los Angeles School of urban studies refers to a loosely affiliated group of scholars who since the 1980s have made Los Angeles their research focus. Initial work highlighted the emergence and consequences of economic restructuring in Southern California but quickly broadened to consolidate the knowledge base for what had hitherto been a relatively neglected city-region. Almost concurrently, a subset of researchers recognized in L.A. a particular form of contemporary urban transition that was characteristic of what they labeled as "postmodern urbanism." Finally, by the late eighties, came the realization that many lessons from L.A. were relevant to scholars beyond Southern California, and the aggregate of these findings became codified as the L.A. School of urbanism.

Over the past two decades, critical engagements with the L.A. School have become increasingly common in geography, sociology and urban studies, but also in American studies, anthropology, architecture, history, and international relations.[1] Yet with a few notable exceptions, the discipline of urban politics remains relatively untouched. This is not to suggest that L.A.'s politics has been left unexamined; on the contrary, there are strong analytical traditions deriving from both mainstream political science and urban political economy. But neither approach has systematically embraced the challenges of the L.A. School; nor, incidentally, have they entered into a critical dialogue with each other about their complementary interpretations of urbanism and governance.

The purpose of this essay is to bring urban politics, urban political economy, and the L.A. school of urbanism into the same discursive space. Its origins lie in a spring 2007 conference held at the University of Chicago, organized by Dennis Judd and Dick Simpson. Researchers from Chicago, Los Angeles/San Diego, and New York City were joined by international scholars from Europe and Latin America and charged with uncovering the common ground among their varying perspectives. Naturally, no clear resolutions emerged over the few short days of the meeting, and these first published pieces are best understood as an invitation to extend the debate begun during those snowy days of a typical Chicago spring. Our contribution is a perspective from the L.A. School. It is unabashedly polemical, politely confrontational, and constructively critical. It is lightly referenced and does not presume to offer any critique of urban politics as an academic field of inquiry.

From Modern to Postmodern Urbanism

Consensus has it that we have entered a global urban age, in that the majority of the world's population now lives in cities. Yet there is precious little understanding about what this trend entails, beyond the customary Malthusian-inspired cries of apocalypse. The proliferation of neologisms describing emergent urban forms is more indicative of confusion rather than intellectual grasp. Is this a "postmodern urbanism," a "splintered urbanism," or "post-suburbanism"? Are we confronted by "city-regions," "micropolitan regions," an "exopolis," or what? Attempts at clarification by contextualizing the urban process within a wider social dynamic are only confounded by a facile retreat to fashionable reductionisms such as "globalization" or "neoliberalism" that fail to capture the complexity of global and local transformation. In our efforts to rebuild urban theory, we (like others) have turned to Los Angeles.

The principal dimensions of urban change in Los Angeles are by now well documented. For instance, the detailed empirical analyses contained in *From Chicago to L.A.*[2] reveal multiple shifts in the practices of urban place production: demographic, economic, political, social, cultural, and virtual. These include, inter alia, that population diversity is becoming the norm in contemporary cities and the conventional divide between black and white in many American cities is being submerged by a minoritizing polity; that waves of immigration are altering practices of community and citizenship; that the principal tropes of contemporary urbanism include edge cities, privatopias, and other mutant urban forms; that the rise of post-Fordism and the network society are transforming urban economic geographies everywhere; that religious affiliations are atomizing, as diverse, multicultural populations with transnational ties recreate spiritual traditions beyond conventional religions; and that the crisis of sustainability has repositioned nature and environment as key components of the urban question. The book's contributors also convey that altered ways of reading and representing the city are needed if we are to recognize and accumulate evidence measuring urban change. No one claims that these adjustments, both material and mental, are unique to Los Angeles, nor that they lack a history; but taken together, they represent a major transformation in the processes of urban place—production that is affecting many cities across the world beyond L.A. (although not in equal proportion). To put it succinctly, L.A. is simply one of the best currently available counterfactuals to conventional urban theory and practice, and as such it is a valuable foundation for excavating the future of cities everywhere.

In our view, the L.A. School's account of postmodern urbanism offers an especially productive template for generating alternative urban theories, no matter what one feels about postmodernism. In this section, we briefly recapitulate this template, contrasting the imperatives of modernist conceptions of the urban (in the style of Chicago) with that of a postmodern perspective (based on Los Angeles).

During recent decades, the term postmodern has accumulated so many meanings as to have reached the limits of language. However, this should not detract from its enduring interpretive propositions, which devolve into three broad categories:

- *Postmodernism as style,* that is, a series of distinctive cultural and stylistic practices that in and of themselves are intrinsically interesting and consequential;
- *Postmodernism as epoch,* or the totality of emergent practices viewed as a cultural ensemble characteristic of contemporary capitalism (often referred to as postmodernity); and

- *Postmodernism as philosophy/method,* representing a set of philosophical and methodological discourses that are antagonistic to foundational constructs of whatever persuasion and (most particularly) the hegemony of any single intellectual persuasion.

All these approaches are germane to the contemporary urban question: in, for instance, the burgeoning styles or texts of urban morphology (such as edge cities); indicators of epochal change (e.g., the rise of cybercities); and the putative demise of previous urban rationalities (including the end of master planning). Implicit in each approach is the notion of radical break, that is, a fundamental discontinuity between past and present practices. There is ample evidence to support the notion of major adjustments in each category, and we regard with suspicion any effort to corset emerging urbanisms into existing (but obsolete) analytical containers.

From such presuppositions, it is but a simple step to the central conceit of postmodern urbanism[3]: just as the core beliefs of modernist thought have been displaced by multiple ways of knowing, so has the notion of a universal urban process been dissolved by the multiplying logics that transform city-building. In modernist urbanism, the impetus for growth and change proceeds outward from the city's central core to its hinterlands. In postmodern urbanism, this logic is precisely reversed: the evacuated city core no longer dominates its region; instead the hinterlands organize what is left of the center. By this, we mean that urban space, time, and causality have been altered:

- the heterogeneous *spatial logics* that characterize contemporary urban development derive from the outside-in, not inside-out as in modernist urbanism;
- in the sequence of urban development , a center—if one ever emerges—appears *chronologically later* than the peripheries;
- the direction of *causality* is from periphery to center, even if (as often happens) this finds expression as an absence of pressure or direction; and
- as a consequence, an urban center (if it exists) has *altered structural and functional relationships* with the surrounding city-region that are radically different from relationships in the modernist city.

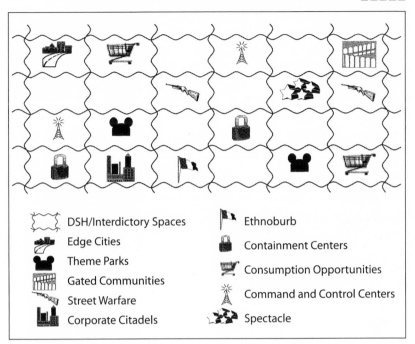

Figure 4.1 "Postmodern Urbanism."

The remainder of this essay is an exploration of some consequences of this fundamental realignment. For us, industrial Chicago of the late-nineteenth and twentieth centuries remains the foundational example of the modernist city. The core-to-hinterland causality of a universal urban process was best captured in E. W. Burgess's account of the evolution of differential urban social areas within the city. Burgess observed that outward from the urban core, the city would take the form of a series of concentric rings of diminishing density and diverse composition.[4] Now imagine a city where fragmentation and decenteredness are the primary urban drivers: there are many urban cores, not one; independent edge-cities spring up with allegiance to no city center; conventional town centers are no longer part of contemporary urban process; conventional suburbs, understood as peripheral accretions to existing urban cores, no longer exist; and the agglomeration dynamics that historically produced cities has been so altered as to bring into question the whole concept of a city. This is the world of postmodern urbanism; this is what Dear and Flusty call "keno capitalism" (Figure 4.1).

Keno capitalism assumes a world of ubiquitous connectivity, courtesy of the Information Age. Urbanization occurs on an undifferentiated grid of opportunities where each land parcel is (in principle) equally available for development as a consequence of its access to the information superhighway (the wavy lines in Figure 4.1). Capital settles on a land parcel while ignoring opportunities on adjacent lots, thus sparking urban development. The relationship between development in one lot and another is a disjointed, unrelated affair, because conventions of urban agglomeration have been replaced by a quasi-random collage of noncontiguous, functionally independent land parcels. Only after considerable time will these isolated parcels collide with other developed lots, and *take on the appearance* of what we normally regard as a city. However, there is no necessity for such an agglomeration to occur, because the keno capitalism grid is (again, in principle) infinitely expandable in any direction, allowing a fragmented urbanism to occur piecemeal as long as potential development parcels remain wired.

This straightforward rereading of urban form provides many clues about the changing nature of cities, but how does the spatial structure of postmodern urbanism relate to concurrent social process? At the risk of oversimplification, there seem to be five principal social dynamics underlying the altered urbanisms of today's world:

- *Globalization,* including the emergence of a relatively few world cities as centers of command and control in a globalizing capitalist world economy;
- *Network society,* including the rise of the cybercities of the Information Age;
- *Polarization,* the increasing gap between rich and poor, nations, different ethnic, racial and religious groups, genders, and between those on either side of the digital divide;
- *Hybridization,* the fragmentation and reconstruction of identity and cultural life (including the political) brought about by international and domestic migrations; and
- *Sustainability,* including a widening consciousness of human-induced environmental change.

Needless to say, these categories do not provide an exhaustive account of the dynamics of contemporary capitalism. But together with the geography of postmodern urban form, they define a preliminary analytical frame for the problematic of contemporary urban governance.

What's at Stake in the Theory Wars?

At the Chicago meetings, Robert Beauregard asked a very good question: what's at stake in the confrontation among urban theorists? Our response is that *everything* in urban theory and urban politics warrants a thorough reconsideration. Of course, it's not simply postmodern urbanism or Los Angeles that is causing this upheaval. But these foci, buttressed by the five dynamics and their manifest consequences, surely give credence to the notion of a radical break. And while these tendencies may find formal equivalence in previous eras (e.g., the claim that there have been earlier manifestations of globalization), the present *is* different because they have never before appeared in concert, never before penetrated so deeply, never before been so geographically extensive, and never before overtaken everyday life with such speed. In short, there has never been anything as globally universal as the rise of the Information Age. It is likely to prove as profoundly altering as the advent of the Agricultural and Industrial Revolutions. This is not a claim that modernist urbanism and politics are dead, although they may everywhere be tending toward obsolescence. Just as some places in the American West and Southwest are already predominantly postmodern in their urban process, many older cities in the Northeast and Midwest retain their modernist ways. However, even places of persistent modernism (including Chicago) are now being overwritten by the texts of postmodern urban process. It is as if a postmodern scrim were being laid over the archeology of the modern city, providing compelling evidence of urban and social change—if we care to see it.

In this essay, our central proposition is that geography has trumped government; that the *altered geographies of postmodern urbanism are redefining the meaning and practice of urban politics*. This is because the extension of cities beyond conventional political jurisdictions negates the notion of representative democracy, compromises the ability of the local state to serve the collective interests of its constituents, and may even intensify the subordination of the local state to plutocratic privatism. The tendency for geography to outgrow government may appear to be a restatement of a familiar problem, namely, the question of regional government in a fragmented metropolis. Arguments in favor of supracity government have long been advanced, provoking many rebuttals championing the proliferation of small urban jurisdictions on the grounds that interjurisdictional competition and differentiation maximizes residential choice and promotes efficient public service delivery. Today, however, we hold that jurisdictional fragmentation in megacity regions has become a pathological, iatrogenic condition. That is to say, the clash between urban hypertrophy and obsolete government itself causes new problems and prevents government from meeting its obligations. The sheer scale of urban Los Angeles, for example, is mind-boggling: the five-county region (Los Angeles, Orange, Riverside, San Bernardino, and Ventura counties) contains about 17 million people in 177 cities spread over 14,000 square miles and overlain by more than 1,000 special districts. In Los Angeles County, there are only five supervisors representing more than 8 million inhabitants. Daily life in L.A. testifies to the notion that local government in L.A. is fundamentally undemocratic and dysfunctional, its practitioners lacking both the capacity and will for collective political action.

As a corollary, the central normative question in contemporary urban political geography pertains to the appropriate scales of (re)territorialization of local governance. What is the optimal scale of regionalization to ensure effective representative democracy and efficient public service provision in the hyperextended metropolis? Existing theories have failed to come up with effective answers to this question, and indeed, today the question merely slumbers in too many academic minds. In the meantime, millions of people are effectively disenfranchised, un- or underserved, and even actively harmed by these *failed local states*. So, this is what is at stake in the theory wars: a proper reconceptualization of the process and form of local politics. Existing theories will not achieve this; something different is required. In the remainder of this essay we outline a new direction involving the intersection of territoriality/scale, postmodern urbanism, and politics.

Redefining the Urban

Urban geographers in the latter half of the twentieth century uncovered many systematic ways to describe urban form and process, based largely on the Chicago School. In particular, the quantitative turn in urban geography after the 1960s catalogued a wide range of statistical regularities that found expression in "laws" of urban structure both at the intraurban (within-city) and interurban (between-city) scales. These empirical regularities included the rank-size rule (relating to the primacy of a single major city in the urban hierarchy of each nation), as well as central place theory, referring to consistencies in the size and spacing of cities, and based in the earlier works of Christaller, Losch, and von Thunen).[5] At the same time, there was an explosion of interest in methodology, including especially the use of multivariate statistical techniques (such as factor analysis to reduce the complexity of large data sets).

Most if not all the statistical regularities that characterized our twentieth-century understanding are now challenged by the revised geographies of intra- and interurban structure. At the macroscale of interurban change, for instance, rapid urban growth in the United States has shifted decisively to the Sun Belt cities of the West and Southwest; and across the nation, the fastest-growing urban areas are those "micropolitan districts" outside established cities, representing a radical flattening in the hierarchy of American urban places. At the intraurban scale, we have already described manifestations of change under the rubric of postmodern urbanism/keno capitalism. It is worth emphasizing that early traces of a fragmented urbanism have long been evident, though not universally recognized or theorized. For example, Eugene Moehring described the phenomenon of leapfrog growth in mid-twentieth-century Las Vegas, referring to the tendency for development to occur in disjointed, noncontiguous parcels. This produced what Charles Paige called a "checkerboard effect," i.e., "large residential subdivisions connected by commercial strips along major streets and separated by equally large squares of undeveloped land."[6]

Adjustments in the size, spacing, and internal structure of cities are clues to fundamental changes in urban process, including the agglomeration economies that brought the modernist city into existence. Yet if we are to understand the material evidence, adjustments in our mental processes are also necessary, in the way we see cities. Chief among the consequent epistemological and ontological challenges is the need for a new urban lexicon that redefines the categories used in urban analysis. For instance, a single, dominant downtown urban core is now best regarded as an historical artifact; in no way can it be construed as *the* nerve center of its region. By extension, there is no longer such a thing as suburbanization, understood as a peripheral accretion in a center-dominated urban process: edge cities may look like conventional suburbs, but they most certainly are not. Perhaps the most pressing categorical revision in our dictionary relates to the term *sprawl*. For some, this much-maligned appellation invokes all that is bad about uncontrolled urban growth, but for others it is the benign realization of millions of American suburban dreams, and what could possibly be wrong about that? In our new dictionary, the definition of sprawl as uncontrolled suburbanization is a secondary, even antiquarian term; instead, its primary usage should describe the principal formal expression of the postmodern urban process. Sprawl thus becomes an urban theoretical primitive, one of the most fundamental categories in our revised lexicon. An important consequence of framing sprawl in this way is to reposition sustainability at the core of the urban question. Until very recently, conventional urban theory considered environmental issues as peripheral. But as cities expand, habitats are destroyed, species eliminated, and biodiversity patented, the viability of life on earth is truly under threat.

All this is not to suggest that many established concepts, categories, and preoccupations in urban analysis should be summarily scrapped. Such traditional concerns as residential segregation, housing affordability, and so forth retain their purchase. Nevertheless, L.A. and its postmodern urbanism have put us on notice that the urban question is radically changing.

Reconsidering the Political

Sprawl affects urban governance overwhelmingly. This much is obvious from myriad urban political studies of minoritization, dissolving notions of community, identity, and citizenship, and the seemingly ubiquitous elevation of individual rights over collective obligations. In some fundamental way, the future of electoral politics, representative government, and even the *possibility* of local democracy have been brought into question. We are only now coming to grips with a politics of urban pathology. The pioneering work of Evan McKenzie on the rise of privatopias is indicative of what we regard as a pathological urban form—a perverse doctrine of antidemocratic residential apartheid that now comprises 18 percent of America's housing stock and houses one-sixth of the nation's population. Underwritten by the politics of privatization, common interest development (CIDs) are described by McKenzie as maturing into an orchestrated attempt to replace public municipal government with unaccountable private agencies.[7] Another form of secession in Los Angeles has been the incorporation of new cities—about thirty since the late 1970s—whereby political boundaries become the jurisdictional walls separating Us from Them. These various political geographies of privatization, secession, and balkanization are profound threats to the urban polity and should be recognized as such. Even in neighborhoods without political or material fortifications, a rabid NIMBYism (Not in My Back Yard) is eroding any lingering sense of community. Years ago, when Ed Koch stepped down as mayor of New York, he warned that NIMBY sentiments were the greatest threat to that city's future. Yet strong and weak mayors alike confront intensifying neighborhood exclusionism; NIMBYism is being rapidly transformed into a BANANA (Build Absolutely Nothing Anywhere Near Anybody) world.

Paradoxically, sprawling cities also provide enclaves where intense local autonomies are possible, enabling tightly knit communities to realize their goals below the radar of formal politics. Such movements include the activities of the much-vaunted "creative classes," or advocates of "green urbanism." In addition, the potential of revitalized local social movements, globalization from below, and recovered human agency all point optimistically to a grassroots political renaissance.[8] Local governments themselves also find incentives and opportunities to experiment. For instance, in Southern California, Riverside County has been attempting to manage rapid urban growth by invoking federal endangered species legislation; in Ventura County similar land-use management objectives were sought through a broad-based coalition of grassroots movements. Same goal, different political means.

Urban politics is also about public policy. If, as we have argued, urban process is changing and urban theory requires revision, then surely our policy prescriptions and practices too will require adjustment? So if, for example, postmodern urbanism suggests that conventional downtowns are becoming obsolete, does it really make sense to promote megaprojects for downtown renewal when the principal urban dynamic has shifted to the periphery? Not only that, but traditional corporate and philanthropic leadership has also quit the center. Of course, it is still possible to defend downtown revitalization on the basis of efficient reuse of physical and social infrastructural investments already in place. However, such policy must be recognized for what it is: a hugely risky investment strategy, perhaps fatally undermined by a compromised political leadership, that current theory suggests is doomed to failure. For some time now in Southern California, peripheral urban developments occur without conventional downtowns, which are sometimes added later for aesthetic and identification/branding purposes, or simply to promote consumption opportunities. In such cases, downtowns or town centers become, in effect, externalities of the postmodern urban process. If we take seriously the theory-practice link (and we do), then an altered urban theory necessarily involves an altered public policy. This includes puncturing the expectation that center-city/suburb alliances are the panacea for urban ills.

Invitation to a Debate

It was impossible to sit in Hull House, the site of most of our Chicago meetings, without feeling its palpable history and inspiration. Urban experts joined for an open-minded exchange on comparative urbanism that well realized the intentions of the conference organizers. Now it is time for others to join the debate. Yet for several reasons we may not be as well-positioned for debate as we would like. An obsessive focus on the empirical characterizes much urban political analysis, as it does urban sociology. This may be blinding practitioners to the need for an overhaul of urban political theory and limiting our prescriptive capacities as engaged academics. A preference for the empirical in the Chicago deliberations also emerged as an antitheory bias voiced by some who denigrated theory as mere "words about words." This was echoed by an unseemly rush to distance oneself from the Burgess model, disparagingly described by one participant as those "silly concentric ring circles," thus dismissing a foundational theoretical framework that is still good to think with and still maintains its stranglehold on textbooks and anthologies as well as a great many current conceptualizations of the city. We reject these rejections. What is needed, for now at least, is more theory not less.

So, Chicagonistas may do well to forget about the mayors Daley for awhile, and New Yorkers would be better off checking their rhetoric and romanticism at the door. Yes, New York is demonstrably a leading world city, but comparative urbanism is not about status and rankings; it is much more about identifying the generic and specific in urban process and outcome, plus their consequences. Thankfully, none of the New York–based conference contingent reached for the rhetorical heights so effortlessly achieved by a recent book, which was, without trace of irony, "dedicated to New York, the greatest city in the world." Neither a celebratory ethos born out of surviving New York's mean streets, nor an abiding nostalgia for the city's glorious past are adequate bases for a revitalized urban theory, yet they persist like some narcotic miasma over theme park Manhattan.

Eighty years ago, power brokers altered local political boundaries in Chicago to more adequately reflect the community boundaries identified by Burgess and his Chicago School cohort. Before our research can attain such levels of everyday political relevance, we urgently need to revise our obsolete theoretical and analytical apparatuses. A good start was made in Chicago but the work has only just begun. We hope others will now join this debate.

Notes

This essay was written while Dear was resident at the Mesa Refuge in Point Reyes Station, California. Thanks to Common Counsel for making this stay possible; to Peter and Cornelia for hosting; and to fellow residents Augustina Fields and Michael Stoll for helpful conversations.

1. Michael J. Dear et al., "Critical Responses to the Los Angeles School of Urbanism," *Urban Geography* 29, no. 2 (2008): 101–112.

2. Michael J. Dear, ed., *From Chicago to L.A.: Making Sense of Urban Theory* (Thousand Oaks, Calif.: SAGE Publications, 2002).

3. Michael J. Dear, *The Postmodern Urban Condition* (Malden, Mass.: Blackwell Publishing, 2000), ix.

4. Ernest Burgess, "The Growth of the City: An Introduction to a Research Project," in Robert E. Park, Ernest Burgess, and Roderick D. McKenzie, *The City: Suggestions for Investigation of Human Behavior in the Urban Environment* (Chicago: University of Chicago Press, 1925; reprint 1967).

5. Walter Christaller, *Central Places in Southern Germany* (Englewood Cliffs, N.J.: Prentice Hall, 1966); August Lösch, *The Economics of Location* (New Haven, Conn.: Yale University Press, 1954); Johann Heinrich von Thünen, *Der Isolierte Staat in Beziehung auf Landwirtschaft und Nationalekonomie* (1826; Stuttgart: Gustav Fischer, 1966).

6. Eugene P. Moehring, *Resort City in the Sunbelt: Las Vegas, 1930–1970* (Reno: University of Nevada Press, 1995), 238.

7. Evan McKenzie, "Constructing the Pomerium in Las Vegas," *Housing Studies* 20, no. 2: 187–203.

8. See, respectively, Roger Keil, *Los Angeles: Globalization, Urbanization and Social Struggles* (New York: Wiley, 1998); Steven Flusty, *De-Coca-Colonization: Making the Globe from the Inside Out* (New York: Routledge, 2004); and Michael P. Smith, *Transnational Urbanism: Locating Globalization* (Malden, Mass.: Blackwell Publishing, 2001)—all notably working at least in part from an L.A. perspective.

5

The Sun Also Rises in the West

■ Amy Bridges

There is a certain irony to the fact that something as public and palpable as the energy a social movement unleashes has flown under our analytic radar screen.

—Karen Brodkin, *Making Democracy Matter: Identity and Activism in Los Angeles*

Portraits of Southern California and Los Angeles are prominent in noir novels, and "*noir* has . . . remained the popular . . . anti-myth of Los Angeles."[1] James Cain, Raymond Chandler, and, more recently, Walter Mosely have written stories with ironic and grim outcomes. In these stories no one is really good. At best, people are all too fallible, more likely they are selfish, criminal, or downright evil; the déclassé among them "invariably choose murder over toil."[2] Contemporary academics similarly portray L.A. In Michael Dear's accounts we see that "as the modern public expanded, it shattered into a multitude of fragments speaking incommensurable private languages. Thus fragmented, modernity loses much of its capacity to organize and give meaning to people's lives."[3] Here community is elusive. There are "genuine neighborhoods to be found in Los Angeles," Edward Soja writes, but they are few and far between. "Indeed, finding them . . . has become a popular local pastime, especially for those so isolated from propinquitous community in the repetitive sprawl of truly ordinary-looking landscapes that make up the region."[4] For Mike Davis, the sorrow of Los Angeles lies in the self-dealing of elites, the selfishness and racism of the affluent, and "fortress L.A.," the carceral city that is their creation.

In this essay, rather than echo these presentations, I tell a more cheerful story about L.A. by providing an account of the Justice for Janitors (JfJ) campaign, which began there in 1988. I offer parallels to events in other cities, both contemporary and earlier in the twentieth century. Having shown that in this instance L.A. is not altogether peculiar but an example of processes both current and historical, I turn to the L.A. School and the Chicago School to see how either provides insight into the successes of janitors' mobilization for justice.

Justice for Janitors in Los Angeles

Service workers suffer low pay and a long list of other occupational burdens: long hours, intermittent and unpredictable employment, absence of benefits (health insurance, vacation, holidays, pension), unpaid weeks of "training" or "internship," failure to receive overtime pay, and lack of equipment for worker safety. Organizing service workers presents particular challenges. In every city and occupation the Service Employees Industrial Union has embraced, many of the workers are immigrants, often unaware of their rights as workers and some especially vulnerable because they are illegal. Although in some occupations service workers toil at large workplaces (hospitals, airports), in others workers are scattered over many sites, individually or in small groups (janitors, home health care workers) and, in the case of janitors, work at night.

SEIU is the fastest-growing workers' organization in the United States. In 2007 the proportion of workers in the United States who were union members rose for the first time since 1979, led by the new unions built by the SEIU.[5] In California, SEIU has several victories to its credit. Most impressive was the organization of home health care workers. In 1999, 74,000 home health care providers joined a single negotiating unit, the largest successful organizing effort in U.S. history next to the UAW in 1937.[6] The Justice for Janitors campaign began in Pittsburgh in 1985 and the next year began organizing in Denver. Subsequently, JfJ has successfully organized citywide bargaining for janitors in two dozen U.S. cities.

JfJ came to Los Angeles in 1988. Janitors in L.A. had a long history of union membership. First organized by the Building Service Industrial Union in 1921, by the early 1980s janitors were earning hourly wages as high as $12.50.[7] In the late 1970s, however, building owners began releasing janitors from their payrolls and instead contracting the work out to cleaning companies, only some of which were unionized. A large pool of immigrants provided workers willing to mop floors for the minimum wage of $4.25, and sometimes less.[8] In this way, the well-paid, unionized, mostly African-American men who worked as janitors in Los Angeles were replaced by nonunionized, poorly paid, mostly immigrant women workers, Latinas.

The major newspapers in Los Angeles, the *L.A. Times* and *La Opinión*, were more than sympathetic to the Justice for Janitors campaign (so much so that their reporting and their editorializing are hard to tell apart), and in their pages we can follow the public face of the janitors' movement. The papers were dogged in presenting the poor working conditions and straitened circumstances of janitors. Early in the L.A. campaign, janitors joined a nationwide vigil in support of union organizing efforts. The *L.A. Times* reported, "the janitors protesting here Wednesday typically make between $3.60 and $4 an hour and receive no overtime, health insurance, or paid vacations." One organizer commented, as janitors were working to clean offices of lawyers, doctors, and corporate executives, "It is wrong to have such poverty among such riches."[9] Over the next twenty-seven months, the press repeatedly reported evidence of poor working conditions, low wages, and employer indifference to janitors. In December 1988 the story of Edwin Osorio was featured. Osorio worked for Bradford Building Services for five weeks in an alleged training program, for which he received no pay at all. In response to a complaint by Local 399, the company paid Osorio $1,173.[10] In August 1989 UCLA released a report showing "America's working poor are getting poorer, and evidence of that sad fact is apparent after dark in many of the nation's most lavish office buildings. That's when crews made up primarily of *Latinos,* immigrants and blacks—most of them women— clean the steadily increasing supply of those expensive, handsomely furnished buildings."

In Los Angeles, janitors' wages were down 36 percent from six years before; fully 17.5 percent of janitors were earning wages at or below the poverty line. The story was headlined, "While Building Owners' Profits Soar, Janitors Get Poorer."[11] The result was that although working as a janitor in the United States looked good from Central America, in Los Angeles it quickly became clear that the life it provided was not so good. When Aura Canted was twenty, she

> watched the family hock its refrigerator to get her one-way bus fare out of Guatemala's grinding poverty. Her first janitor job paid $3.35 an hour. She lived with 16 others in a one-room apartment; they took turns sleeping by day and night . . . A decade after arriving there is little improvement. Her two young children help her scrub houses on her days off; Canted sells tamales she cooks and sells Avon products . . . She recently pawned a ring for food. When her daughter suffered convulsions . . . the hospital bill totaled $700. It took two years to pay it off.

Canted welcomes the presence of the SEIU: "I know with a union we will get more."[12]

Readers were also often reminded of the benefits unions brought to janitors. Three months after the vigil, Eric Mann, an SEIU organizer, wrote an op-ed essay in support of janitors and the union, noting that unionized workers earned $5.50 an hour and benefits, while janitors without unions earned $4.25 an hour (or less) without benefits. Mann also scolded L.A. Mayor Tom Bradley and city councilman Zev Yaroslavsky for not joining the union's effort to pressure employers.[13]

Alternating with stories of the janitors' burdens was reporting of their boisterous demonstrations, meant to bring public attention to their struggle and embarrassment or shame to their employers. In September 1988, papers reported that SEIU was suing Western Cleaners. Although Western Cleaners itself had a union contract, the protest claimed that it also operated Century Cleaning Contractors, which employed janitors without union representation.[14] In November, fifty janitors from Local 399 protested the firing of four custodians who had participated in a union organizing drive in the

Banco Popular Building. Providing an early victory for the union, on the same day L.A.'s Community Redevelopment Agency (CRA)—a tenant in the building—announced it would hire its own janitors, rather than contracting with a cleaning company.[15] This was quite a coup for the janitors; nothing can be built in Los Angeles without CRA approval. Afterward, a spokesman for the CRA explained the agency's position. "We have a moral obligation," he said, "to care for the invisible people who maintain our facilities. It's unconscionable for many downtown employers to pay their janitors subsistence wages and none of the standard benefits most of us are accustomed to receiving."[16]

In February, 230 janitors "snaked [their] way along financial district sidewalks and through office tower lobbies . . . waving signs and broom handles while chanting union slogans in Spanish" to call attention to their campaign for a living wage. The demonstration ended in the lobby of an office tower, where "the whistle-blowing demonstrators refused to leave until a building management representative agreed to address them."[17] Not all demonstrations were so unruly. In March, a demonstration outside International Tower took place one week in advance of the Tower's choice of a new cleaning contractor. Were the contractor to be nonunion, fifteen janitors would lose their jobs. In this instance, publicity focused on janitors' families, bringing attention to the fact that many janitors were women. A photograph of a four-year-old boy, walking with his mother, was given an Old Testament caption, "A Child Shall Lead."[18]

The boisterous assertion of workers' presence and grievances might have alienated more than building and cleaning company owners. The same loud demonstrators who intimidated the owners and invaded office buildings may well not have seemed at all like the upright, hard-working, family-supporting janitors the public was reading about in the press. "It is not surprising that . . . tenants often complained to building managers about JfJ activities."[19] To soften opposition on the part of workers where JfJ campaigned, other tactics were developed. A union member explained to Waldinger, "Secretaries' Day . . . we brought huge boxes of carnations, thousands of them, and we passed them out as a sort of token of appreciation from janitors to secretaries. We said, 'There's been five demonstrations, it's probably very difficult for you, but we ask for your support as we fight for our rights.' And it turned out to have a positive impact." [20]

In addition to demonstrations, guerilla theater was a key element in the Justice for Janitors campaign. As Christmas approached in 1989, Jono Shaffer, a Local 399 organizer, dressed as Santa Claus and walked into Century Towers. Santa declared Century Towers a naughty company, because janitors there were not provided with protective gloves. The building owners admitted to no responsibility, arguing that the cleaning contractor, International Service Systems, was the guilty party. Security helped Santa leave the building.[21]

That winter, SEIU organizers were looking for an appropriate site to organize janitors and then be in a position both to pressure a landlord with sizable holdings and to bargain with a large contract cleaning company. Century City provided the perfect opportunity. Century City is a complex of 21 high-rise office buildings built in 1965 to create a small second down-town for Los Angeles.[22] In 1989, a single firm owned a majority of the office space. And a single firm, International Service Systems (ISS) cleaned more than half of the buildings. Together, the buildings required many janitors each night, an exceptionally large gathering of workers in one place. As its name implies, ISS is a multinational firm (a subsidiary of a Danish company). ISS employed a total of 43,000 people in 1990, 14,000 in the United States.

In April, janitors demonstrated, claiming that a majority had signed union cards, and calling for union recognition from ISS.[23] With no response from ISS, most ISS employees went on strike May 31. On June 2, 400 janitors marched at Century City office buildings to bring attention to their demand for union recognition. The *L.A. Times* described the event:

> To the beat of Conga and snare drums, the chanting marchers barged into office lobbies and blocked traffic as they paraded across Century City Park East . . . The group tossed bags of garbage into the revolving doors of one office building and pasted tiny orange stickers reading 'Who will clean your offices?' on the walls, doors and windows along the way . . . At one point, 15 Los Angeles police officers equipped with riot helmets and batons ordered the group to disperse. But the marchers ignored their commands, leaving the officers standing in formation, outnumbered and unable to stop the two-hour demonstration.[24]

Over the next two weeks, a series of demonstrations maintained pressure on Century City building owners and ISS. On June 15, a demonstration of janitors was joined by James Wood (assistant executive secretary of the Los Angeles Labor Federation and president of L.A.'s Community Redevelopment Agency) and other prominent officials and labor leaders. Police blocked their march; when marchers protested, police broke up the demonstration with considerable violence. These events were witnessed, reported, broadcast, and bemoaned by the media. Mike Davis reported on the police: "A small, blonde female officer who had wielded her club with . . . sadism was practically lifted on the shoulders of her male comrades. She had made it through the rite of passage to macho solidarity . . . A hulking motorcycle cop was boasting to admiring comrades how he had taken down one of the marchers. He mimicked a janitor crying in pain or fear."[25]

On the op-ed page of the *L.A. Times,* under the headline "Corporate America's Security-Guards-In-Blue," Antonio Rodriguez and Gloria Romero wrote,

> The brutal assault by Los Angeles police officers on striking janitors and their supporters last week . . . will be remembered in labor history as a classic example of the use of police force to defend corporate interests against workers' movements . . . Dozens were bloodied and suffered injuries . . . The action of the LAPD violated the strikers' rights to organize, assemble, have freedom of movement and be free of police violence—all guaranteed by the Constitution . . . Had the crackdown occurred in the Soviet Union, China, or in . . . Nicaragua, everyone from . . . [the President to the police chief] . . . would have condemned it.[26]

Police behavior brought tremendous public attention (this was before Rodney King), loud denunciations of Police Commissioner Gates and the LAPD, and insistent support for the janitors from Mayor Bradley and Councilman Zev Yaroslavsky.[27] A year later, the *Times* reminded readers that the confrontation was "the ugliest local labor confrontation in recent memory."[28]

Events in L.A. were not quite enough to push ISS to recognize the union. Negotiations took place in Chicago, where the CEO of ISS-USA and SEIU representatives attempted to reach a settlement. Meanwhile, police violence in Los Angeles mobilized JfJ allies in New York City. Gus Bevona, head of the Building Service Division of SEIU as well as SEIU Local 32B-32J in New York, went to ISS headquarters there and said that if ISS failed to recognize the union and negotiate in Los Angeles, New York's five thousand janitors would go on strike. That was the last straw for the cleaning company. Soon thereafter, ISS in Los Angeles acceded to the demands of SEIU Local 399. Janitors secured raises, health insurance, vacations, sick pay, and of course, union recognition.[29]

SEIU aimed to organize janitors from as broad a swath of greater Los Angeles as possible. In May 1992, JfJ targeted West L.A.; in October 1992, JfJ demonstrated at Toyota in Torrance and El Segundo (six and twelve miles northwest of downtown, respectively). For Local 399 there were many other downtown and nearby targets, among them, the University of Southern California, Los Angeles International Airport, Pacific Bell, Rebuild Los Angeles and its chair, Peter Ueberroth. Unionizing efforts did not stop there; JfJ ventured farther afield. In February 2000, JfJ was organizing in Long Beach, about twenty miles south of downtown; in April, Janitors were organizing in Irvine, thirty-five miles south of downtown (in Orange County). With greater goals still, SEIU began planning for contract negotiations just over the horizon, to be simultaneous from sea to shining sea.

Explaining the Success of the Justice for Janitors Campaign in L.A.

Even with supportive press, talented and committed organizers, and the unintentionally cooperative L.A. police force, the organization of Local 399, a union of poor immigrant workers, and the agreement by nationwide and multinational employers to negotiate with them, were tremendous accomplishments. To what can we attribute the success of JfJ in L.A.? The campaign to organize janitors and gain union recognition in the Century City complex contained all the elements of future Justice for Janitors campaigns in Southern California. Its style seemed to observers altogether innovative. As opposed to business unionism, the mobilization of janitors was an example of "social movement unionism," in which a coalition of unions and other activists sought social justice for the working poor.[30]

Roger Waldinger and colleagues point to three key elements of the JfJ campaign: centralized union leadership, "industry-specific strategy and tactics," and "the presence of a critical mass of class conscious immigrant workers."[31] I add here SEIU's brilliant public relations campaign. Preston Rudy calls attention to the changing configuration of Los Angeles politics, and how globalization shaped that change. In addition, Rudy points to a conjunctural element: the dramatic rise in real estate values in the city. It also helped that the JfJ campaign happened at a propitious time, as a multiplicity of activists and groups were campaigning for greater equity in metropolitan Los Angeles. Finally, the ever-increasing *political* importance of Latinos in Los Angeles and California raised the stakes of the janitors' campaign, as its outcome promised (or threatened) to affect the fortunes of politicians who supported or failed to support their efforts.

By centralized union leadership, Waldinger calls attention to the top-down initiative to organize janitors. This was not a campaign begun at the grass roots, and locals did not always welcome missionaries from the International union (the local stopped contributing material support to the campaign early in 1989). SEIU's commitment to organizing service sector workers is its central mission; in 1984 the union began taxing each member $8 monthly toward that goal, and soon after fully 25 percent of SEIU's national budget was devoted to organizing.[32]

Without the commitment of the International to the organization of janitors, it is not likely the campaign would have succeeded, and not only because of lack of leadership in the local. The commitment of the International brought resources of several sorts. Most prominent was the leadership of Stephen Lerner, director of Business Service Organizing at SEIU, the prime mover and strategist of the national effort to organize janitors. Lerner recognized that janitors were the fourth most rapidly growing occupation in the service sector, and so should be an SEIU priority. As the national effort proceeded, it became clear to Lerner that to be effective, organization had to embrace a majority of janitors citywide (rather than proceeding firm by firm), securing a single contract for all of them. In Los Angeles, that single contract required a sizable area. Since outlying employers and down-town businesses constituted a single labor market, union organizers made joining them in a single contract their strategic goal.

SEIU sent experienced organizers, with the ability to train new orga-nizers on-site. SEIU provided intelligence for the effort, information about the structure of the local market, about the conditions of work for employ-ees, and about the cost of janitors' services to contractors and business owners. One official explained, "When you meet with workers ... you have your whole market analysis of the relationship between the janitors and the building owners and how we think it works. We try to educate them about how their industry works."[33] Organizers also educated workers about their rights on the job. An important element of JfJ campaigns was bringing suit against employers for violating laws protective of labor.[34] In addition, SEIU sent staff to Los Angeles who researched the working conditions of L.A. janitors. The great majority of janitors worked too many hours, using antiquated equipment; janitors worked in closed buildings with insufficient air-conditioning, and of necessity used dangerous chemicals in their work. SEIU planned to create health and workplace safety committees to inform workers of their rights and provide training for using their equipment.[35]

There are precedents for union organizing supported from the center, and we can see in those events collective labor experience from which the Justice for Janitors campaign benefited. Most important of prior leaders was John L. Lewis who, as president of the United Mine Workers, promoted and subsidized the organization of industrial unions in the auto, steel, and rubber industries in the 1930s.[36] Another example came at midcentury. In the 1960s, New York City pharmacists were organized in Retail Drug Employees Union Local 1199. The union could not extend its reach geo-graphically without encroaching on the jurisdiction of other pharmacists' unions. Two leaders, Leon Davis, president of the local, and Elliott Godoff, devised a plan for 1199 to grow. Godoff was trained as a pharmacist, but his heart was in organizing. Godoff saw a future for 1199 in organizing hospital workers—although many pharmacists worked in drugstores, others worked in hospital pharmacies; all were members of 1199. In 1957, Godoff spoke to a meeting of 1199 leaders, offering a history of hospital employees and his hopes for their future. If the pharmacists committed themselves to organizing hospital workers and delivered improvement in working conditions and earnings for hospital employees, 1199 membership would grow. Without much discussion, the meeting approved that goal.

Hospital employees (laundresses, cafeteria workers, engineering staff, orderlies) lived in poverty, yet they were not the receptive workers who joined SEIU in the 1980s and 1990s. Nor did they think of themselves as a community; black and Puerto Rican, they did not always see one another as colleagues in a shared struggle. Their organization into 1199, then, was a project of persuasion, education, and persistence with the workers, as well as sustained pressure on their employers. As for JfJ later, "a sense of theater pervaded . . . 1199 activities." In November 1961, Brooklyn Jewish Hospital offered employees a raise of two cents an hour. Elliott Godoff called for a "burial" of the raise. "Workers at Brooklyn Jewish formed a funeral procession, complete with a coffin covered with wax flowers and carried by pallbearers, [accompanied by mourning workers], and marched up the hospital's front steps." Management blocked their entrance, but the next month awarded the workers an additional 6.25 cents an hour, which totaled $2.50 per week.[37] As the *L.A. Times* did forty years later, the *New York Times* published stories about the poverty of hospital workers.[38] Like JfJ later, 1199 was successful at gathering support from other unions (AFSCME District 65, Harry Van Arsdale) and political and civic leaders (Emmanuel Celler, Jacob Javits, Eleanor Roosevelt, Thurgood Marshall, Martin Luther King).[39]

The extended first strike, which lasted from May 8 until June 19, 1959, bore little result. Employees won neither collective bargaining nor recognition of the union, gaining only the minimal wage improvements offered before the strike and a formal grievance procedure. Henry Nicholas, an 1199 organizer for years to come, offered this judgment of the strike: "It was a defeat, but the greatest defeat the union ever encountered." For Nicholas, the most important result of the strike was that "the struggle . . . had convinced the hospital workers that they 'were part of a movement.'"[40] SEIU's "movement organizing" is also part of labor's legacy to the janitors.

JfJ brought, and refined, its developing strategy and tactics to the organization of Century City and subsequent Los Angeles campaigns. The strategy and tactics of the JfJ campaign were aimed at the problem that the companies employing the janitors were not located in the buildings the janitors cleaned. Janitors' demonstrations where they worked directly pressured building owners; it was the building owners who contracted with cleaning companies. It was in this indirect way that the demonstrations served to bring pressure on their employers, since landlords were susceptible to the disruption and confrontation janitors brought to their doors. So newspapers reported many large, disruptive, and noisy demonstrations. These were public confrontations that shamed and embarrassed both building owners and cleaning contractors. The demonstrations were very effective, and owners were bitter. "They pick a target and beat them into submission by whatever methods are necessary," explained a lawyer for a cleaning company. "They are extortive [sic]," complained George Vallen of American Building Management. The costs were substantial. ABM "paid $60,000 in legal fees to fend off union attacks and . . . lost two cleaning contracts, worth $50,000 in combined monthly billings." Managers and building owners offered weak defenses. A manager at Mattel, for example, claimed, "These janitors don't work under deplorable conditions, but in beautiful, modern buildings. We have not found the injustices the janitors speak of . . . This is a free-market system. People can change jobs for better pay and benefits."[41]

If sometimes strategies and tactics were tailored to janitors' specific situation, in some ways JfJ's strategies and tactics were responses to more general developments in labor-management relations. The SEIU endeavored to avoid strikes. Reporting the "fresh tactics" of hotel employees, the *L.A. Times* explained that "workers generally avoid strikes" because the likely result is that they will be fired.[42] Demonstrations could be so persuasive that strikes were unnecessary. Even more than avoiding strikes, the goal of the demonstrations was to sidestep the need for an NLRB (National Labor Relations Board) election. Although the election was an advance when first devised, in more recent years employers developed a range of tactics to delay elections and discourage workers from participating. By contrast, either the union card strategy (getting a majority of employees to sign union membership cards), or demonstration and disruption, were more effective in securing union recognition and negotiation for the janitors.[43]

In addition, the JfJ campaign's success in Los Angeles is unimaginable absent SEIU's well-wrought publicity campaign and the cooperation of the media in support of that campaign. The demonstrations, the presentation of worthy workers, often mothers, at those demonstrations, the newspaper coverage of their difficult work and meager compensation—all contributed to public support. Leaving nothing implicit, SEIU and the newspapers contrasted the thin economic resources of janitors and their families with the salaries of professionals working in the same buildings. The *L.A. Times* headlined, "Union Strategy Targets High-Rise 'Sweatshops' to Organize Custodians."[44] And in an article describing SEIU's efforts to educate workers about their rights, as well as the union's organizing tactics and guerilla theater actions, a description of janitors' exploitation contrasted their earning "$30 a night cleaning offices where, by day, lawyers make $300 an hour."[45] The very name of the campaign called the public's attention not to a desire for shorter hours or more money, but to simple justice for those who labored to clean the places where middle-class and affluent administrators, support staff, and professionals worked. The Los Angeles Police Department added the final flourish to building public support. Public support pressured and prompted politicians to act.

Waldinger also credits the large Latino community of Los Angeles. An SEIU organizer observed about immigrants from El Salvador that "there, if you were in a union, they killed you ... Here ... you lost a job at $4.25."[46] As a consequence, in Los Angeles, although there were tensions among Latinos from different countries, Latinos were very receptive to union organizing.

The SEIU did not anticipate any of this, not the geographic size of the Latino community, nor its sheer numbers, nor its dominance of service occupations; and they did not have a plan for educating immigrant workers about their rights. Moreover, SEIU organizers were not hopeful about the capacity of Latinos to build effective unions. A measure of how ill-prepared the organizers were is that when they arrived in Los Angeles, none spoke Spanish. Five years later, Jono Shaffer explained to *La Opinión,* "Our union was not prepared to organize Latinos who filled in where once African

Americans and Anglos worked. *We had no bilingual personnel,* nor did we understand how to educate them about U.S. [labor] laws."[47]

SEIU organizers were not the only group surprised by the Latino community. Social scientists, possibly thinking of the small, close-knit immigrant communities that supported the organization of needlewomen, meatpackers, and others earlier in the century, thought the geographic extent of the Latino community, reaching well across the city, would be a hindrance to solidarity. On the contrary, the community is well-networked. During the drywallers' strike (in 1992), one employer lamented, "Unfortunately, the community, the Hispanic community is pretty tight, most of these people know where everybody lives."[48] As an SEIU organizer remarked, "Even though L.A. is famous for no community, we found a community of janitors."[49] Two contemporary processes facilitated JfJ's success. The first was the intensely competitive real estate market in L.A. at the moment JfJ arrived. These were "the halcyon days of the 1980s when investors were falling over themselves to build . . . in downtown L.A." as its role as a world city of finance and corporate headquarters intensified.[50] In 1986, still early days in this transformation, "Beverly Hills, Century City, and Westwood" housed more than sixty corporate headquarters, a veritable "citadel of corporate power."[51] For JfJ, of course, this was important, since the demand for building maintenance and cleaning escalated with the rapidly increasing square footage of office space and the price of real estate.

Second, the arrival of JfJ in Los Angeles coincided with the beginnings of a broad stream of activism in workplaces, communities, and among nonprofit organizations, often joining nationally and racially diverse supporters. Karen Brodkin has argued that in the same years Justice for Janitors was organizing, Los Angeles was home to an array of workers', immigrants,' and progressive activist groups who were forming "a network of people and groups . . . [that was] strategically innovative and engaged in building complex coalitions in their organizing."[52] Unions were central to this network; like the janitors' union, several are unions of immigrants. Although their names may be new, they are descendants of the labor movement writ large. The Union of Needlework, Industrial and Textile Employees is a good example. UNITE is a product of the merger of the International Ladies'

Garment Workers' Union (ILGWU) and the United Food and Commercial Workers. Each union was challenged first by the movement of clothing manufacture overseas, and second, by the reorganization of what remains of the domestic clothing industry along lines parallel to the changes in building maintenance: into manufacturers (Guess, Jones New York, and the like) on one hand, and on the other, into contractors who employ garment workers to assemble the clothing. Reorganization has meant the reappearance of the sweatshop in Los Angeles. Indeed, the similarities between Maria Soldatenko's description of women who were sewing at home in Los Angeles in 1992[53] and Mary Van Kleeck's description of *Artificial Flower Makers*[54] four generations earlier in New York—their age, gender, and immigrant status, the struggle with piece rates and low wages, the unhealthy environment of their work, the intense competition of small contractors—is chilling. Efforts to unionize today's garment workers have met little success; that the ILGWU found its beginnings in the New York of the flower makers is encouraging. The Hotel Employees and Restaurant Employees have been successful at rescuing their union from decline by energetic efforts to recruit immigrants.[55] By the mid-1990s, then, Los Angeles was home to "intense and broadly framed social justice activism."[56] The achievements of social justice activism—a living wage ordinance in L.A., for example—came after 2000, but the beginnings were contemporaneous with the Justice for Janitors campaign.[57]

The success of the JfJ campaign rested on, and was part of, the steadily increasing presence of Latinos in the political life of Los Angeles and California. The state assembly has been a site of increasing Latino representation since 1962, when Phil Soto and John Moreno were the first two Latinos elected to that body. In 1990, the assembly's four Latinos held 5 percent of the seats; by 1996, sixteen Latinos formed 20 percent of the assembly.[58] In the same years, the growth of the Latino population considerably outdistanced their presence in the electorate. Latino turnout has increased significantly since. Organizations supporting Latino turnout have existed since California LULAC (League of United Latin American Citizens) was founded in 1945; they received a boost from an unlikely source in 1994. In a spectacular instance of unexpected consequences, votes and citizenship became considerably more valuable in that year, when Governor Pete Wilson supported passage of Proposition 187, which denied public services to undocumented immigrants and their children. The measure passed but was found unconstitutional by the California Supreme Court. Between 1996 and 2003, half of the Latinos who now make up 18.5 percent of the California electorate had registered.

In Los Angeles, organized labor was an important part of Mayor Tom Bradley's (1973–1993) coalition and afterwards was among the supporters of Mayor James Hahn (1971–1975). One consequence of the transformation of the L.A. labor force was that Latinos replaced not only Anglo and African-American workers but also Anglo and African-American labor leaders. Labor organizations continued to be important actors in L.A. politics as their membership and leadership changed in step with the reorganization of work and the migration of Mexican-Americans to the city. The L.A. County Federation of Labor ("the Fed") has a long history as part of Democratic governing coalitions in Los Angeles. In addition, the executive secretary of the Fed is appointed president of the L.A. County Redevelopment Agency. Miguel Contreras held both positions in 1996. Under Contreras and subsequently, the Fed has become an active political force in Los Angeles—getting out the vote and endorsing candidates for L.A. mayor and city council and the California Legislature.[59]

There was yet another way that the Mexican-American presence in the labor movement resulted in increased political muscle. Politicians' personal histories as union activists powered their name recognition and honed their political skills, key assets when they sought political office. Antonio Villaraigosa is the outstanding example of this trajectory, having volunteered in support of the United Farm Workers of America's (UFW) first grape boycott when he was fifteen; subsequently he worked for the United Teachers of Los Angeles.[60]

JfJ in Los Angeles and the L.A. and Chicago Schools

What insights do the Los Angeles or Chicago Schools lend to this account of Justice for Janitors? Edward Soja and Michael Dear present what Charles Tilly called Big Structures and Large Processes. The reality of the L.A.

School's portrait—L.A.'s multi-centered and enormous geographic footprint, the increased importance of the center, and the role of globalization in the economic and geographic organization of L.A.—structured the course of the JfJ efforts in the city. Although Soja and Dear study Los Angeles, they do not study Angelenos. They offer economic and geographic contexts but no community and little politics or agency. Steve Erie's research contravenes that description. Erie has long argued that L.A.'s government worked toward state-driven growth and development (and without the morose undertones of L.A. noir).[61] Mike Davis has presented portraits of L.A. politics grounded in political economy and, more recently, an account of the effects of growing Latino populations on the city.[62] The story of the Justice for Janitors campaign is very much a story of community, politics, and agency. For community, politics, and agency, L.A. scholars might well consult the Chicago School.

The Los Angeles School emphasizes globalization processes structuring L.A. politics and economy. Simultaneous with the continuing growth of L.A.'s already extensive map, there was another dynamic: the emergence and assertion of the center as more important in the economy and politics of Los Angeles than it ever was earlier in its modern history. Although the Los Angeles School long emphasized the multinucleated metropolis, the same scholars have been attentive to how globalization has increased the importance of the center.[63] Globalization appears in several guises, both in the geographic spread of Los Angeles and in the reassertion of the center. The disparities in the labor markets of the United States and Mexico power the sustained wave of immigration from south to north. Globalization creates the territory of the multinational firms employing L.A. janitors. And, Preston Rudy has argued, globalization aggravated the destabilization of L.A.'s governing coalition, just as Mayor Bradley stepped down from office.

The geographic spread of Los Angeles created a single labor market over the city's broad reach. Employers' size, and the unified labor market serving them (as well as smaller employers), required and enabled the ever-broader range of JfJ organizing. The ever-increasing radius of JfJ organizing was a response to the reach of the labor market shared by janitors across the metropolitan region.

Globalization made possible the giant corporations that contract to service office buildings in the United States and elsewhere. The reach of their employers, and the strategic advantage of negotiating from equal ground, conditioned SEIU's strategy to work toward a metropolitan, statewide, and, finally, a nationwide presence and nationwide bargaining. Immigration provided a large, receptive, and militant workforce. Despite its extensive territory in L.A. County, the immigrant community was a networked and close-knit one. Although janitors' wages were sufficient to attract immigrant workers, it quickly became clear that those wages were insufficient to support families. The steady increase in the number of Latinos holding political office, as well as support for the janitors among politicians and L.A. city and county governments, played an important part in the janitors' success. Political support followed not only from public sympathy, but also, and more directly, from the effective increase in Latino mobilization (citizenship, registration, voting) and their consequent rising political importance.

The initial sites of JfJ organizing—Century City and downtown Los Angeles—represent developments in economy and society that mark the new importance of the center. Century City was built forty years ago. A harbinger of things to come, it has been joined by many more high-rise offices and homes. The office towers are evidence of the growing economic importance of downtown. The sixty headquarters of global corporations, the growth of financial services, and FIRE industries (finance, insurance and real estate) create both the necessity for and the tenants of this new construction. In Davis's description of the Los Angeles renaissance,

> neighborhoods were Manhattanized beyond recognition. Seemingly overnight, Ventura Boulevard in Encino metamorphosed from a low rise landscape of delis and used car lots into a concrete jungle dominated by high rise Japanese banks. Startled hillside homeowners . . . found themselves looking directly into the windows of North Hollywood's and Universal City's new Skyscrapers . . . Affluent residents . . . watched in horror as the quaint, Spanish Colonial style intersection of Westwood and Wilshire boulevards became a windy canyon.[64]

There are other dynamics at play here. Downtowns across the country have gained economic and social centrality as the baby boom generation—the first generation to grow up in the suburbs—has aged to become empty nesters, poised to migrate from their suburban homes to condominiums in the center. For empty nesters, downtown is attractive because it promises simplified living arrangements (no more staircases or lawns) as well as proximity to work and many amenities. The same people are attractive to developers and politicians. Still healthy, affluent, in the labor force (some with rising incomes), and now childless, the middle aged are the perfect low-demand, high-spending, and taxpaying residents. Changes in population dynamics make another contribution to the importance of downtown. People marrying later, putting in more years in the labor force as singles or with partners but without children, has resulted in hundreds of thousands of downtown residents among white-collar workers in their twenties and thirties. They share critical characteristics with older domestic migrants—rising incomes and tax contributions, good health, and few demands for public services. For younger and older residents alike, downtown has become their neighborhood in L.A., New York, Chicago, Washington, D.C., and a host of other cities.

L.A.'s government has moved along the same trajectory as the city's economy and population. Since Robert Fogelson's *Fragmented Metropolis* was published in 1967,[65] Los Angeles city government has represented frailty, fracture, and division. The ultimate manifestation of this division was the threatened secession of the San Fernando Valley in 1995, a threat not deterred until a referendum in 2002. The importance of the center was affirmed in the process of writing and approving—by popular vote—a new city charter. Even before that, Michael Dear observed that although L.A.'s population and the economy were spread out, "the government is all in one place." This mattered for the janitors' campaign. For SEIU organizers, as one explained to Preston Rudy, Los Angeles was "an easy place to organize, because everything was concentrated downtown, including City Hall and the Board of Supervisors."[66] The central and directing offices of the region's largest corporations, where janitors worked, were also there.

The Los Angeles School theorizes Los Angeles in its broad economic and geographic outlines, but does not study Angelenos. Possibly for this reason, and in recognition of the size and influence of the city's immigrant communities, two contributors to *From Chicago to L.A.* comment, "A revival of the ethnographic tradition as pioneered by the Chicago School would be a welcome addition to contemporary scholarship."[67] A brief review of the contributions of the Chicago School explains why.

Like the theorists of the Los Angeles School, the theorists of the Chicago School were taken with the power of geography. This is the role of the famous Burgess map. The map is not simply an extension of the ecological approach, but the representation of a theory of urban growth. In Burgess's thinking, in a city and its region all economic growth begins in the central business district downtown. This argument became both the consensus at universities and the common-sense premise of government policy. The theory of urban growth captured by the Burgess map was also the theory of urban renewal. In the 1940s, when leaders were worried about the postwar economies of the cities, what could they do? Their answer was urban renewal, which we may think of as Keynesian stimulus for the central city. Who has not drawn the Burgess map, in half-circles to accommodate Lake Michigan, as urban renewal is introduced in lecture? The Burgess map has not represented every city, but it did represent the growth of the great majority of U.S. cities for generations, especially in the Northeast and Midwest.

The geographic pattern is clear in the implementation of urban renewal legislation in the 1950s and 60s. As New Haven, Philadelphia, Chicago, and New York scrambled for federal funds, Albuquerque, Phoenix, San Antonio, Dallas, and Houston were laggards. The reason for the reluctance of southwestern cities was that (as has been observed of Los Angeles) their growth was directed from the edges, not the center. Their governments were developers' regimes, and developers' fortunes were made in the communities that ringed the downtown. Not coincidentally, outlying communities were also home to the core constituents of the cities' leading politicians. In these cities it was only in the 1970s and 1980s that the center became the focus of economic and political leaders.[68]

Chicago School scholars were concerned not only with geography in its large-scale configurations, but also its small-scale reality, the neighborhood. Morris Janowitz offered the ecological definition of community: "community is when I and the guy sitting across the room take our shirts to the

same laundry." Community was about proximity, about paths crossing. In
their studies of community, Chicago sociologists listened to residents. The
result was an array of community portraits that remain classic accounts of
city life—*The Gold Coast and the Slum* (1929),[69] *Black Metropolis* (1945),[70]
The Politics of Urban Renewal (1961, about Hyde Park),[71] and many others.
The community studies introduce the reader to Chicago's people: the young
woman from midwest farm country who comes to the city hoping to earn
her living and keep her honor; black workers who have joined the new CIO
unions; self-righteous liberal professionals and the self-serving interests
with which they were allied.

Just as the University of Chicago was an important place in the
early development of sociology, so too early in the twentieth century the
University of Chicago was home to the new field of political science and to
the study of city politics. Charles Merriam studied city politics and was an
early student of voting behavior. He was a politician, too, long a member of
the Chicago City Council. Harold Gosnell charted the organization of the
city's politics in two volumes, *Negro Politicians: The Rise of Negro Politics
in Chicago* (1935)[72] and *Machine Politics, Chicago Model* (1937).[73] Gosnell's
books have provided a guide to the institutions of machine politics for every
study of machine politics that has followed.

Gosnell documented the machine as a hierarchical and disciplined
organization, from the precinct captain, to the ward committeeman, to city
and county bosses. Like his colleagues in sociology, Gosnell was energetic
in his efforts to listen to the dramatis personae of his work. For *Machine
Politics,* Gosnell charted the work and motivations, and assembled the
records, of 900 precinct captains and 197 ward leaders. For *Negro Politicians,*
Gosnell and his students interviewed dozens of African-American voters,
revealing their values, their views of the two major political parties, their
memories of disfranchisement in the South, and the tremendous importance they placed on the ballot. Gosnell saw his observations of the Black
Belt as a political battleground in the context of the subordinate status of
blacks in American society, and he showed how the style and agenda of
black politicians followed from that subordinate status.

The social scientists of the Chicago School studied geography and
economy; they studied Chicago's residents and communities, its citizens

and their politics. Were they on the West Coast in the last few decades, Chicago School sociologists would have written portraits of the janitors, their goals and motivations, their children and their communities. If Harold Gosnell had studied government in Los Angeles, he would have presented the institutions of L.A. politics, the relations of Anglos, Latinos, Asians, and blacks to one another, and also the relations between the many and the few. Had he done so, we might better understand Latinos' path to a place in both governing and electoral coalitions. We might understand too how the far-flung and multinational Latino residents of L.A. function as a community, a prospect not imagined in the Chicago of Park, Burgess, Merriam, and Gosnell, by Rossi and Dentler a generation later, or by SEIU's organizers. The story of the successful campaign of Justice for Janitors is inseparable from the environment of big structure, large processes, and huge comparisons in which it is played out. The plot of the story, however, is about politics, purposive action, organizations, and the press. It is a story about the janitors, their labor and their resolve, their community and the communities that supported them. The story reveals that the janitors have lost neither the capacity to organize nor the dignity and strength of meaningful lives.

Notes

I am indebted to Alexander Gomez, who assembled an extensive database of newspaper articles for me. I also relied heavily on the brilliant dissertation of Preston Rudy, cited throughout, which provides a sophisticated and nuanced analysis of the SEIU in California. Dennis Judd and Dick Simpson have been patient and encouraging beyond measure.

1. Mike Davis, *City of Quartz: Excavating the Future in Los Angeles* (New York: Vintage, 1992), 21.

2. Ibid., 40.

3. Michael Dear, "In the City, Time Becomes Visible: Intentionality and Urbanism in Los Angeles, 1781–1991," in Allen J. Scott and Edward Soja, *The City: Los Angeles and Urban Theory at the End of the Twentieth Century* (Los Angeles: University of California Press, 1996), 76–105, especially 81–82.

4. Edward W. Soja, *Postmodern Geographies: The Reassertion of Space in Critical Social Theory* (New York: Verso, 1989), 246.

5. "As SEIU Leads Growth of Union Membership, SEIU 721 Launches Twenty-first Century Member Resource This Labor Day Week," *Los Angeles Times*, Sept. 1, 2008.

6. Ruth Milkman, *L.A. Story: Immigrant Workers and the Future of the U.S. Labor Movement* (New York: Russell Sage, 2006), 130; Ruth Milkman, ed., *Organizing Immigrants:*

The Challenge for Unions in Contemporary California (Ithaca, N.Y.: Cornell University Press, 2000).

7. Preston O. Rudy, "Labor, Globalization, and Urban Political Fields: A Comparison of Justice for Janitors in Three California Cities" (PhD diss., University of California, Davis, 2003), 80.

8. Ibid.

9. Harry Weinstein, "Janitors Stage Vigil as Part of National Protest," *Los Angeles Times*, March 31, 1988.

10. *La Opinión*, Dec. 30, 1988.

11. Harry Bernstein, "While Building Owners' Profits Soar, Janitors Get Poorer," *Los Angeles Times*, Aug. 15, 1989.

12. Sonia Nazario, "Column One," *Los Angeles Times*, Aug. 19, 1993. "For This Union, It's War. Protesters scream and bang drums. Recruiters sneak into buildings. Decried by critics, the militant Justice for Janitors campaign has been wildly successful in uniting those who clean L.A. high-rises."

13. Eric Mann, "Janitors Toil in Limbo Behind Downtown's Glitter," *Los Angeles Times*, June 26, 1988.

14. "Local News in Brief: 'Justice for Janitors' Suit Filed by Union," *Los Angeles Times*, Sept. 1, 1988.

15. "Firing of Janitors in Union Is Protested," *Los Angeles Times*, Nov. 23, 1988.

16. Rudy, "Labor, Globalization," 85.

17. Paul Feldman, "Janitors Get Attention with Rally," *Los Angeles Times*, Feb. 11, 1989.

18. J. Albert Diaz, *Los Angeles Times*, Mar. 24, 1989 (photo caption). Cf. Isaiah, chapter 11, vol. 6, "The wolf also shall dwell with the lamb, and the leopard shall lie down with the kid; and the calf and the young lion and the fatling together; and a little child shall lead them."

19. Roger Waldinger et al., "Helots No More: A Case Study of the Justice for Janitors Campaign in Los Angeles"(Working Paper 15, Lewis Center for Regional Policy Studies, School of Public Policy and Social Research, University of California, Los Angeles, 1996), 14.

20. Ibid., 15.

21. Bob Baker, "Santa Offers Presents to Aid Cause of Janitors' Labor," *Los Angeles Times*, Dec. 21, 1989.

22. Martha Groves, "Century City May Be Looking Up," *Los Angeles Times*, July 30, 2005.

23. "Janitors Threaten Century City Strike," *Los Angeles Times*, Apr. 27, 1990.

24. Vicki Torres, "Talking Trash: Strike Supporters Sweep through Century City," *Los Angeles Times*, June 2, 1990.

25. Mike Davis, "Police Riot in Century City," *LA Weekly*, June 6, 1990.

26. Antonio M. Rodriguez and Gloria J. Romero, "Corporate America's Security Guards in Blue," *Los Angeles Times*, June 22, 1990.

27. Rudy, "Labor, Globalization," 91–94; Bob Baker, "Inquiry into Strike Violence Ordered," *Los Angeles Times*, June 16, 1990.

28. Bob Baker, "Column One: Unions Try Bilingual Recruiting," *Los Angeles Times*, March 25, 1991.

29. Rudy, "Labor, Globalization," 94–95; Bob Baker, "Multinational Cleaning Contractor ISS fires Janitors," *Los Angeles Times,* June 26, 1990.

30. Rudy, "Labor, Globalization," 41.

31. Waldinger et al., "Helots No More," 16.

32. Rudy, "Labor, Globalization," 26.

33. Waldinger et al., "Helots No More," 19.

34. Ibid., 20. See, e.g., *La Opinión,* June 30, 2003.

35. Jose Ubaldo, "Estudio revelta falta de securidad para empleados de la limpieza de LA," *La Opinión,* Oct. 8, 1993.

36. Melvyn Dubofsky and Warren Van Tine, *John L. Lewis: A Biography* (New York: Quadrangle Books, 1997), 232ff.

37. Leon Fink and Brian Greenberg, *Upheaval in the Quiet Zone: A History of Hospital Workers' Union, Local 1199* (Chicago: University of Illinois Press, 1989), 100.

38. "Benito Nieves . . . lives with his wife and seven children in a three room basement apartment," *New York Times,* July 13, 1959.

39. Fink and Greenberg, *Upheaval in the Quiet Zone,* 102.

40. Ibid., chapter 4.

41. Nazario, *Los Angeles Times,* August 19, 1993.

42. Stuart Silverstein, "Unions Trying Out Fresh Tactics," *Los Angeles Times,* Sept. 6, 1993.

43. *Ibid.;* see also Baker, "Column One: Unions Try Bilingual Recruiting."

44. Ken Ellingwood, "Union Strategy Targets High-Rise 'Sweatshops' to Organize Custodians' Labor," *Los Angeles Times,* May 31, 1992.

45. Nazario, *Los Angeles Times.*

46. Waldinger et al., "Helots No More," 117, cited in Milkman, *Organizing Immigrants,* 9.

47. *La Opinión,* Feb. 10, 1994, emphasis added.

48. Milkman, *Organizing Immigrants,* 183.

49. Milkman, *L.A. Story,* 135.

50. Waldinger et al., "Helots No More," 21.

51. Edward Soja, cited in Rudy, "Labor, Globalization," 62.

52. Karen Brodkin, *Making Democracy Matter: Identity and Activism in Los Angeles* (Piscataway, N.J.: Rutgers University Press, 2007), 42.

53. Maria Angelina Soldatenko, "The Everyday Lives of Latina Garment Workers in Los Angeles: the Convergence of Gender, Race, Class, and Immigration" (PhD diss., University of California, Los Angeles, 1992).

54. Mary Van Kleeck, *Artificial Flower Makers* (New York: Russell Sage Foundation, 1913).

55. Miriam J. Wells, "Immigration and Unionization in San Francisco Hotel Industry," in Milkman, *Organizing Immigrants,* 109–129 passim.

56. Brodkin, *Making Democracy Matter,* 3.

57. Ibid., 31–40.

58. I am indebted to Thad Kousser for these numbers. Sixteen remains the minimum across subsequent assemblies; the maximum number of Latino assemblymen, 26 (32.5 percent), were elected in 2006.

59. Larry Frank and Kent Wong, "Dynamic Political Mobilization: The Los Angeles County Federation of Labor," *Working USA* 8, No. 2 (2004), 155–181.

60. Jack Gould, "The Movement's Mayor," *Los Angeles Weekly*, Feb. 22, 2001.

61. Steven P. Erie, "How the Urban West Was Won: The Local State and Economic Growth in Los Angeles, 1880–1932," *Urban Affairs Quarterly* 27, no. 4 (June, 1992): 519–54; Steven P. Erie, *Globalizing L.A.: Trade, Infrastructure, and Regional Development* (Palo Alto, Calif.: Stanford University Press, 2004); Steven P. Erie, *Beyond Chinatown: The Metropolitan Water District, Growth, and the Environment in Southern California* (Palo Alto, Calif.: Stanford University Press 2006).

62. Davis, *City of Quartz*; Mike Davis, *Magical Urbanism: Latinos Reinvent the U.S. Big City* (London: Verso, 2000).

63. Edward Soja, "Economic Restructuring and the Internationalization of the L.A. Region," in Michael Peter Smith and Joel Feagin, *The Capitalist City* (Oxford and New York: Basil Blackwell, 1991), 178–98.

64. Davis, *City of Quartz*, 190.

65. Robert W. Fogelson, *The Fragmented Metropolis: Los Angeles, 1850–1930* (Cambridge, Mass.: Harvard University Press, 1967).

66. Rudy, "Labor, Globalization," 68.

67. Jerome Straughan and Pierrette Hondagneu-Sotelo, "From Immigrants in the City to Immigrant City," in Michael J. Dear, ed., *From Chicago to L.A.: Making Sense of Urban Theory* (Thousand Oaks, Calif: SAGE Publications, 2002), 199.

68. Amy Bridges, *Morning Glories, Municipal Reform in the Southwest* (Princeton, N.J.: Princeton University Press), chapter 7, esp. 151–59.

69. Harvey Warren Zorbaugh, *The Gold Coast and the Slum: A Sociological Study of Chicago's Near North Side* (Chicago: University of Chicago Press, 1929).

70. St. Clair Drake and Horace R. Cayton, *Black Metropolis: A Study of Negro Life in a Northern City* (New York: Harcourt, Brace, 1945).

71. Peter H. Rossi and Robert A. Dentler, *The Politics of Urban Renewal* (New York: Free Press, 1961).

72. Harold Gosnell, *Negro Politicians: The Rise of Negro Politics in Chicago* (Chicago: University of Chicago Press, 1935).

73. Harold Gosnell, *Machine Politics, Chicago Model* (Chicago: University of Chicago Press, 1938).

6

From the Chicago to the L.A. School
Whither the Local State?
■ Steven P. Erie and Scott A. MacKenzie

Over the past two decades, Los Angeles has gone from an understudied metropolis to a critically acclaimed new paradigm for urban development around the world. One important factor accounting for L.A.'s recent prominence is the emergence of the L.A. School of Urbanism, composed of a core group of "Marxist geographers" and postmodernist scholars, and a larger interdisciplinary community of academics working in research centers across Southern California.[1] The L.A. School is known for its focus on the urban periphery; eclectic theories about the "social construction of urban space"; and lingering pessimism about the future of urban life. But the L.A. School is perhaps best known for offering Los Angeles as a new paradigm of urban growth challenging the iconic concentric circles model developed in the 1920s by the Chicago School of Sociology.

This essay critically reexamines the L.A. School growth paradigm. We argue that the L.A. School, like the Chicago School before it, offers an inadequate account of political institutions and the local state as forces shaping urban and metropolitan growth. Many of the L.A. School's adherents perpetuate a Chinatown myth of the local state. As depicted in the famed 1974 noir movie about an L.A. developer-led water grab from unsuspecting farmers, political actors are seen as having neither the will nor the capacity to pursue policies independent of the desires of powerful private actors. The Chinatown myth implies that urban democracy has failed, a belief that partly explains the L.A. School's pessimism. It also understates the importance of local politics and public entrepreneurship to understanding Los Angeles's precocious rise as a regional imperium and global city.

Our argument is organized in five parts. First, we consider Los Angeles historiography and offer explanations for early scholarly neglect versus current prominence. Second, we revisit the research program of the Chicago School of Sociology, contrasting it with work being done contemporaneously by political scientists in Chicago. Third, we critically reevaluate the L.A. School's growth paradigm and its adequacy as an account of L.A.'s rise as a regional imperium and global city. Fourth, we offer an alternative account of L.A.'s improbable yet rapid twentieth-century growth, focusing on public entrepreneurship and local state capacity and relative autonomy. Finally, based on the L.A. case, we suggest that any new urban growth paradigm needs to bring the local state back in.

From Backwater to Bellwether

Compared to the steady stream of books and articles produced on Chicago and New York, scholarship on Los Angeles lagged for much of the twentieth century. Only in the 1990s did interest in L.A. and the broader Southern California region approach the level of attention devoted to older industrial cities and regions. There are many reasons for this scholarly disparity. L.A. developed later than most major American cities, with its early population heavily native-born rather than immigrant. Until the 1980s and 1990s, there were few research centers dedicated to studying Los Angeles. Moreover, L.A. was considered an anomaly with respect to leading analytic frameworks, such as the machine-reform dialectic, driving much of the discourse in urban politics. Only recently have scholars come to see Los Angeles as a place where "everything comes together."[2]

Los Angeles's emergence as a global city has been comparatively recent. In 1900, New York's population approached 3.5 million residents, twice the size of Chicago (1.7 million). L.A., meanwhile, had barely cracked the 100,000 mark. Until 1920, San Francisco, not Los Angeles, was the largest city on the West Coast. In the early twentieth century, L.A. grew prodigiously. Its 1930 population of 1.2 million outstripped Boston and St. Louis. By this time, however, New York had 6.9 million residents and Chicago 3.3 million. Until the 1980s, the population of L.A. remained stubbornly homogenous; less than 15 percent were foreign-born, and less than 20 percent were nonwhite. H. L. Mencken once derisively called Los Angeles "double Dubuque" because of its large midwestern population. New York was the nation's prime international gateway, with close to 30 percent of its residents foreign-born prior to World War II. For scholars studying ethnicity, race and assimilation, New York and Chicago, rather than Los Angeles, occupied the front lines of research. L.A.'s population did diversify substantially starting in the 1970s. Today, more than 40 percent of Angelenos are foreign-born, with diverse Hispanic and Asian communities in the urban core and periphery.[3]

Inattention to L.A. also was due to a perception that the city was an anomaly with respect to the machine-reform dialectic that dominated urban politics research at midcentury.[4] Unlike the well-studied cities of the Northeast and Midwest, L.A. was never governed by classic party machines using patronage to cement support among ethnic voting blocks. Instead, early L.A. was controlled by the Southern Pacific Railroad, which fashioned a potent bipartisan political organization. This interest-group machine was top-down (i.e., buying off political elites) rather than bottom-up (i.e., distributing jobs and services to key voting constituencies).

In addition to its anomalous status vis-à-vis cities in the Northeast and Midwest, Los Angeles resisted the reform impulses that swept through the Southwest prior to World War I. While cities like Dallas, San Antonio, and Phoenix adopted commission and council-manager governance arrangements, L.A. retained and even strengthened its mayor-council form of government. And unlike other southwestern cities, L.A. in the mid-1920s adopted a district system of city council representation. Festering separatism in the recently incorporated San Fernando Valley and elsewhere in the far-flung city made district elections attractive.

L.A.'s failure to follow the typical reform playbook is curious since it exhibited all of the features—e.g., absence of partisan machines, cohesive leadership by local business elites—that Bridges argues led to this initial round of reform.[5] Los Angeles, however, was the vanguard reform city in California, pioneering civil service reform and direct democracy, the initiative, referendum, and recall measures that would be adopted statewide.

Significantly, L.A. also was a bureaucratic pioneer. If as Lowi argues, the legacy of reform was powerful and autonomous municipal bureaucracies replacing party machines,[6] then reform succeeded earlier in L.A. than nearly anyplace else in the country. The 1925 L.A. city charter empowered semiautonomous proprietary departments to oversee water, power, ports and, later, airports, and partially insulated them from mayoral and councilmanic oversight.

In the postwar era, Los Angeles would begin to command scholarly attention. With the 1965 Watts riots, L.A. was ground zero for the racial unrest sweeping the country. In 1973, the election of African-American Mayor Tom Bradley, featuring a biracial coalition of blacks and Jews, represented a new, more diverse form of minority incorporation.[7] Meanwhile, scholars began noticing that Southern California's distinctive decentralized development pattern was being copied in cities and regions around the world. No longer a West Coast backwater, L.A. was being hailed as a twenty-first-century urban prototype. In the early 1990s, L.A. experienced another severe racial riot. If, as one critic noted, "every single American city that is growing, is growing in the fashion of Los Angeles,"[8] then the problems facing Southern California might reappear elsewhere. Suddenly, there were new reasons to study L.A. and added urgency to understanding the causes of its racial tensions and unrest.

The L.A. School justifies its focus on Southern California by proclaiming it to be a prototype for urbanization patterns in the United States and around the world. In Los Angeles, its leading adherents argue, all of the essential features of the new urban growth model are apparent. The L.A. School's unique blend of geospatial analysis, Marxism and postmodern thought has brought a new perspective to understanding traditional urban phenomena. The question for students of L.A.'s politics is whether studying the city as a prototype or from a postmodern perspective sheds any light on its unconventional rise as a global city. Does the urban growth model proposed by the L.A. School contribute new insights into L.A.'s political organization? To answer this question, it is necessary to delve more deeply into the L.A. School model and the concentric circles model it seeks to replace. We begin with a discussion of the substantive and methodological contributions of the Chicago School before turning to a more detailed analysis of the L.A. School research agenda, in particular its proposed alternative to the concentric circles model, and its explanation of L.A.'s rise as a global city.

The Chicago Schools

The Chicago School label conjures up very different associations for scholars of different disciplines. Geographers and sociologists use the Chicago School label or "Chicago Sociology" to denote the research program developed by William I. Thomas and Robert Park at the University of Chicago during the interwar years.[9] Economists associate the Chicago School with the work of Milton Friedman, George Stigler, and other Chicago economists on free markets and regulatory policy.[10] For students of politics, the early empirical analyses of voting behavior, machine politics, and race relations by Harold Lasswell, Charles Merriam, and Harold Gosnell, together with the detailed studies of public administration by Leonard White, form a Chicago School of Political Science. Sociologists also recognize a second Chicago School of Sociology that flourished in the 1950s. The proliferation of Chicago schools owes much to the fertile intellectual and institutional environment of the University of Chicago, which for much of the twentieth century exercised extraordinary influence over the social sciences.[11]

This section focuses on the original Chicago School of Sociology, particularly its broad conception of urbanism and surprising inattention to politics. Scholars continue to debate the legacy of this Chicago School. Indeed, current understanding about Chicago Sociology owes much to attempts by individual researchers to claim its authority, or displace its basic theories and methodological approaches.[12] Understanding how a research agenda relates to the substantive and methodological concerns of the Chicago School reveals much about its predispositions. Leaders of the L.A. School, for example, have defined their research agenda in opposition to the concentric circles model that appears in chapter 2 of *The City*.[13] This narrow reading of the Chicago School legacy, ignoring both its core substantive and methodological concerns, underscores the preoccupation of geographers with the spatiality of the urban environment.

While scholars continue to debate the legacy of Chicago Sociology, several basic features of the research produced by its core members are worth highlighting. These include: (1) *Strong empirical emphasis.* Thomas, Park and others stressed the importance of empirical observation, especially firsthand experience with the urban environment being studied. (2) *Eclectic subject matter.* The Chicago School incorporated a broad range of subject matter, including an expansive definition of urbanism. (3) *Focus on the individual.* Most studies posited relationships between the individual, i.e., his observable behavior and unobserved mental state, and the environment. (4) *Induction.* The investigative approach was primarily inductive with the expressed purpose of verifying broadly generalizable claims and theories.

These features are readily apparent in the classic works produced by the Chicago School. Thomas's *The Polish Peasant in Europe and America* addressed the social problems associated with the assimilation of recent immigrants.[14] Thomas used reams of transcribed letters sent back and forth between immigrants and their families in Poland to construct comparable life histories and document the challenges faced by new Americans. Zorbaugh's *The Gold Coast and the Slum* utilized personal interviews, maps, and statistical tables to construct a detailed portrait of residential segregation on Chicago's north side.[15] Wirth's *The Ghetto* looked at the condensed Jewish communities in Chicago and Frankfurt in search of generalizations about the effects of neighborhood and culture on individual personality.[16]

Urban scholars recognize *The City,* a collection of eight papers by Park, Ernest W. Burgess, and Roderick McKenzie, as the first systematic attempt to understand the causes and consequences of urbanization. In the introductory essay, Park defines the city in broad terms—"a state of mind"— and proposes a scheme for studying the physical organization, occupational structure, and culture of cities.[17] The essay views urban life, including the physical and social order of the city, as a reflection of human nature. Each subject area is divided into subtopics. For the latter, Park proposes research questions that are readily amenable to social scientific (usually quantitative) analysis. In the introduction and third chapter, Park and McKenzie introduce the ecological approach to social inquiry, which purported to understand the natural evolution of urban development.[18] *The City* is full of ecological metaphors, e.g., succession, invasion, metabolism, and so forth, drawn from the study of plants and animals.

Representing the city as a state of mind, as opposed to a political entity with legally defined physical boundaries, vastly expands the range of acceptable inquiry. In *The City*, for example, the authors consider the nature and consequences of physical expansion, explain the emergence of local newspapers, explore the effects of neighborhood organization on crime and individual personality, trace the causes of juvenile delinquency, offer a vivid characterization of the homeless population, and prescribe a set of best practices for social workers. This expansive view of how cities ought to be studied is also reflected in the comprehensive bibliography compiled by Wirth. The academic scope he defines for urban sociology incorporates boilerplate topics like zoning, trade, growth, and administration as well as less traditional issues like communication, fertility, religion, public morale, and social mobility.

The second chapter of *The City* has received the most scrutiny from the L.A. School. In it, Burgess presents a model that relates the physical expansion of cities to social organization. The model represents the city as a series of concentric circles radiating from a central business district.[19] Urban expansion occurs as inner zones extend their areas by invading the spaces of adjacent outer zones. Expansion also involves the concentration of transportation networks, business activity, and political and cultural life on the central business district. It is this representation of the city that the L.A. School strenuously objects to, as it appears to poorly characterize the decentralized development pattern of modern Los Angeles. L.A. is not divided into neatly circumscribed residential and industrial zones, nor is the region organized by a central business district.

The concentric circles model initiated an empirical research agenda by sociologists attempting to verify the descriptive accuracy of Burgess's "zonal hypothesis" for cities around the world.[20] As a scientific model of urbanization, however, the concentric circles model is underdeveloped. Burgess never explains why inner zones "invade" outer zones, or what prompts a spurt of succession. Indeed, the concentric circles model of the urban environment is essentially a sideshow to the central question of the essay: "How far is the growth of the city, in its physical and technical aspects, matched by a natural but adequate readjustment in the social organization?" Burgess was most interested in the effects of expansion on the social organization of cities, especially with respect to the assimilation of newcomers into urban life. He worried about the potential dangers of rapid expansion, e.g., the impact on urban life of a large influx of African-Americans and European immigrants into northern cities. The latter portion of the essay introduces a broad conception of mobility ("change, new experience, stimulation") and laments its tendency to confuse and demoralize the individual.

Rather than view the concentric circles model as an analytical device, urban scholars might better think of it as a visual representation of residential segregation, itself the result of individual responses to increasing size, density, heterogeneity, and other outgrowths of industrialization. More precisely, the model is one answer to the question of what the city would look like if the posited relationship between industrialization on the one hand, and individual behavior on the other, were allowed to develop unchecked. Hise has suggested that the model was in part a reaction to the perceived chaos of growth around the turn of the century, i.e., a *prescriptive*, as well as *descriptive* model; for generations, planners across the country accepted it as such.[21] The model does not perfectly explain urban expansion in Chicago; nor was it ever meant to. Implied in the concentric circles model is a Euclidean zoning scheme, with a hierarchy of land uses. Park and Burgess favored locating "higher" uses away from the urban core. Whatever its original intent, the model has been influential with academics and policy makers alike, with largely negative consequences for urban residents.

The preoccupation of the Chicago School with the relationship between individual behavior and the size, density and heterogeneity of cities comes across more clearly in a later Wirth article.[22] Where Park offers an expansive definition of the city, Wirth's is purposely minimal. In contrast to the inductive approach that characterizes most studies produced by Chicago Sociology, Wirth engages in a deductive exercise, deriving testable hypotheses that posit size, density, and individual heterogeneity as independent variables for a variety of social, economic, and psychological phenomena. With the exception of Zorbaugh, who assumed a concentric

circles development pattern,[23] Chicago School sociologists paid little attention to Burgess's thought experiment. From this perspective, the concentric
circles model is secondary to the more important task of relating the characteristics of cities to their social organization. It never was a major component of the Chicago research agenda.

Urban scholars can learn more from Wirth's article than the concentric
circles model in *The City*. In it, he warns against confusing urbanism with
industrialism and modern capitalism. The rise of cities in the modern world
is not independent of modern technology, mass production, and capitalistic
enterprise, but many cities predate these forces. Similarly, Wirth suggests
that the purpose of a theory of urbanism is to assist our understanding
of the differences between cities and to inform empirical research on the
relationships between the characteristics of cities and their consequences.
Positing a single model of urbanization, as Burgess does in *The City*, does
little to explain variation in outcomes across urban settings.

While subsequent generations of sociologists have found much to
admire and emulate in the Chicago School, neither *The City* nor its other
seminal works dramatically improve our understanding of urban politics.
Politics was seldom among the list of factors that concerned Chicago Sociology. This is not surprising, given its focus on individual behavior. Politics
involves collective action and the use of public authority. More surprising is
the inattention to local politics as one characteristic of cities affecting individual behavior. Political organizations, including federal, state, and local
agencies, political machines, and other organizations are conspicuously
absent from many of the foundational works of the Chicago School.

The inattention to politics, either as an independent variable affecting social organization, assimilation, and individual behavior, or a dependent variable influenced by community norms and behavior, is particularly
baffling, given the work being conducted by political scientists sharing
office and classroom space with Chicago sociologists during the 1920s and
1930s. Leading members of the Chicago School were aware of the theoretical insights and empirical relationships uncovered by members of the
Chicago School of Political Science. Park suggested the title for and wrote

the introduction to Gosnell's *Negro Politicians* (1935). Chicago sociologist William Ogburn wrote the introduction to *Machine Politics* (1937).

These and other works by the Chicago School of Political Science show the substantial influence of Chicago Sociology. In *Non-Voting,* Merriam and Gosnell bring the modern data collection and analytical techniques emphasized by Park, Ogburn, and others to bear on the question of why citizens frequently fail to show up at the polls.[24] Their discovery that 25 percent of those interviewed cited "general indifference" as a reason for not voting ought to have drawn greater interest from a group of scholars interested in questions of assimilation and the demoralizing effects of urban life. In both *Machine Politics* and *Negro Politicians,* Gosnell explores the social and economic roots of voting behavior, and the effects of machine rule on individual behavior. In doing so, he tapped primary source materials, conducted personal interviews, and served as an active party worker—the kind of first-hand experience emphasized by Chicago sociologists. Gosnell found that the penetration of machine propaganda and exchange relationships was extensive. The consequences, he argues, were largely negative. White's work on city managers similarly shows the potential of political leadership and administration for shaping life in big cities.[25] Claims about the importance of public administration are supported by extensive field work conducted in thirty-one cities across the country.

These efforts argue for the importance of political organization to the character of urban life. Merriam, Gosnell, and White found much to emulate in the research agenda of the Chicago School. Influence, however, only flowed one way. The findings of political scientists were not incorporated into the later work of Chicago sociologists in any meaningful way. In many respects, serious consideration of the implications of political organization began not with the Chicago School of Sociology, but with these early studies of machine politics and administration and the comprehensive textbook published by Banfield and Wilson (1966). Those authors utilize the insights of sociologists on the emergence of neighborhood values and ethnic culture to inform explanations of machine politics and reform movements and the formation of labor unions, civic associations, and other interest groups in big cities.

The L.A. School and Urban Growth

The L.A. School of Urbanism emerged as a collective enterprise in urban geospatial analysis and social critique following a fateful 1987 meeting of geographers and planners in the San Bernardino Mountains.[26] By then, Michael Dear, Edward Soja, and others who would become leaders of the L.A. School had already produced important essays on the form and function of urbanism in Southern California.[27] Nevertheless, the 1987 meeting signaled the beginning of a fruitful, collaborative, interdisciplinary effort that has resulted in a series of research conferences, policy monographs, and edited volumes on Los Angeles.[28]

The body of work produced by the L.A. School is large and eclectic. Like the Chicago School, the L.A. School embraces an expansive definition of urbanism. Its scholarly activities range from efforts to catalogue the city's architecture; understand the economic foundations of regional prosperity; alleviate problems of poverty and homelessness; study the rise of L.A. as a global city; assess the impact of federal, state, and local public policies; and chronicle the emergence of ethnic and religious communities. Much of this work cannot be reviewed here. In the following sections, we critically reexamine two major components of the L.A. School research agenda: (a) its proposed alternative to the concentric circles model developed by sociologists at the University of Chicago in the 1920s and (b) its explanation of L.A.'s rise as a global city.

Just as the legacy of the Chicago School is a continuing subject of debate, urban scholars are attempting to come to grips with the ideas and influence of the L.A. School. Halle claims that three characteristics distinguish the L.A. School's research program. The first is its focus on the urban periphery.[29] Dear has stated that in Los Angeles, "the central core no longer organizes the hinterland."[30] Second, the L.A. School places great emphasis on Southern California's excessive political fragmentation, including weak mayoral powers and limited legislative oversight within the city, and a multitude of autonomous local governments. Third, there is a belief that Los Angeles represents the new urban paradigm. The L.A. School seeks to change the perception of L.A. from urban exception to developmental prototype of the twenty-first century.

None of these factors, however, is new or unique to the L.A. School's research program. Decentralization and political fragmentation are the major themes of *The Fragmented Metropolis,* the classic study of early L.A. development.[31] Indeed, the foreword to the 1993 edition of Fogelson's work hints that the L.A. School is merely "repeating in the language of French post-structuralism the crucial insight that Fogelson presents in his book."[32] This charge is too critical of the L.A. School and, we hasten to add, overly generous to Fogelson. The L.A. School has devoted far greater attention to the causes and consequences of decentralization and fragmentation, with much of this work focusing on postwar Los Angeles.

Those who live and work in L.A. and those who write about it have been billing Los Angeles as a future city since the beginning of the twentieth century. In adopting the principles of the garden city movement, planners in L.A. self-consciously identified their task as building a city of the future. Through comprehensive planning, future cities like Los Angeles could avoid the problems plaguing the congested cities of the East and Midwest. Nearly a decade before Fogelson published *The Fragmented Metropolis,* researchers already were recognizing L.A.'s decentralized development pattern and fractionalized politics, and advertising it as a prototype for the automobile-centered cities of the late-twentieth century. In an insightful, but obscure, article, Arthur L. Grey identifies decentralization and fragmentation as key features of L.A.'s distinctive development pattern.[33] Entitled "Los Angeles: Urban Prototype," Grey's article argued that other U.S. cities would soon exhibit the characteristics of Los Angeles. These included a transportation system dominated by the automobile, residential and commercial decentralization, political fractionalization, and racial polarization. Published six years before the 1965 Watts riot, Grey's warnings about the housing problems of black residents were especially prophetic.

If neither the twin themes of decentralization and fragmentation distinguish the L.A. School, what does? We believe a combination of six characteristics best describes the L.A. School research agenda: (1) *Focus on Los Angeles.* The L.A. School is admittedly fractured and incoherent. What unites members is their focus on Los Angeles. (2) *The search for a new theory of urban growth.* The L.A. School has become well known for its attempts to elaborate an alternative to the concentric circles model. (3) *Emphasis on the link between physical development and global capital.* The L.A. School cites the shift from assembly line to flexible modes of production as a decisive factor in L.A.'s industrial and residential dispersion. (4) *The* Chinatown *theory of the local state.* Much research by the L.A. School's leading scholars either ignores local politics and political institutions or views the local state as a wholly owned subsidiary of the business community. (5) *Bearish take on urban fortunes.* The scholarship of the L.A. School has a distinct noir flavor, imagining both the loss of individual autonomy and a nightmarish collective future. (6) *Methodological agnosticism and interdisciplinary flavor.* Many L.A. School projects combine the perspectives of planners, sociologists, political scientists, historians, and theorists.[34] However, the L.A. School's general aversion to modern statistical techniques and research design is in stark contrast to the Chicago School.

Urban Growth and the Postmodern Project

From the beginning. the L.A. School focused on creating a model of urban growth capable of explaining the development pattern of postwar Los Angeles. Efforts to replace the concentric circles model began in the early 1980s. In *Urbanization and Urban Planning in Capitalist Society,* Dear and Scott gathered an interdisciplinary group of scholars to explore the relationship between capitalist modes of production and the physical development of urban space.[35] Subsequent work by Scott investigates this relationship more fully. In *Metropolis,* Scott argues that the division of labor in capitalist economies shapes the urban landscape.[36] The shift from an economy of large composite firms performing many tasks to one characterized by small firms performing specialized tasks contributed to industrial and residential dispersion. Tradeoffs among land, labor, and location costs underlie a "transactional" logic. This logic is a variation of transaction cost economics, or the study of vertical integration. In the latter, the concern is with explaining the boundaries of the firm, i.e., which contracts are organized within firms and which contracts are transacted between firms or via markets.[37]

Scott's innovation is to consider the consequences of changes in the boundaries of the modern industrial firm for urban space.

Scott's recent work offers empirical support for the connection between modes of production and urban space. In *Technopolis,* Scott collected information about production processes used in firms, the internal labor force, production and sales figures, and relationships with suppliers, subcontractors, and purchasers.[38] Scott finds that industrial activity has migrated from the core to the periphery, where agglomerations of high-technology firms have arisen. A large proportion of contracting activity is intraregional, with firms placing a premium on proximity to business partners. Scott concludes that Southern California was well poised to take advantage of postwar changes in industrial organization by virtue of its deep labor pool and large number of small firms providing specialized products and services. Scott finds similar patterns in the San Fernando Valley and Ventura County areas.[39] Maps of population density and firm location at three points in time (the mid-1950s, 1973, and 1990) show that residential dispersion, including racial minorities, followed industry to these remote locations.

Scott's attention to changes in industrial organization highlights an important dynamic contributing to industrial and residential dispersion. However, this dynamic by itself hardly seems sufficient in explaining both the scale and timing of these trends in Southern California. Nor can it explain other salient aspects of the region's physical development. Subsequent efforts attempt to provide a more complete model of urbanization. These essays traffic in the abstractions of Marxist analysis and postmodern theory, and, in contrast to Scott's work, eschew both formal deduction and empirical verification. In *The Postmodern Urban Condition,* Dear proposes a model of urbanization that organizes urban space as a checkerboard landscape characterized by an undifferentiated and decentralized development pattern ("keno capitalism").[40] Dear and Flusty[41] argue that this pattern better describes L.A. and other cities in the "post-Fordist" phase of urbanization.[42] Other factors driving this pattern include deindustrialization, globalization, nationalism, and the rise of the Pacific Rim.[43]

Like the concentric circles model, the checkerboard model is theoretically underdeveloped. None of the explanatory factors constitute variables;

they are historical events. How one gets from events to outcomes is not entirely clear, as the model lacks identifiable change agents. Dear and Flusty finesse issues of agency (obscuring responsibility for the dystopia they imagine) in writing that postmodern urbanism is "the result of the interaction among ecologically-situated human agents in relations of production, consumption, and coercion."[44] Unnamed developers and corporations appear as deus ex machina. Consumers enter as an undifferentiated mass, buying up products offered by the capitalist economy, seemingly unaware of their own long-term interests. The state arrives intermittently to lend a hand to the undemocratic self-interested schemes of big business. Neither a theory proper nor a scientific model, keno capitalism is a hodgepodge of urbanisms, incorporating elements of the edge city,[45] privatopia,[46] theme parks,[47] and the fortified city.[48]

Like the concentric rings model, the checkerboard model has problems as a descriptive representation, let alone analytical model, of the physical development of cities. One major shortcoming is its relative inattention to the local state, either as an independent variable affecting urban space or a dependent variable affected by geospatial relationships. Local politics, like all politics, is territorially based. Presumably, any theory that adequately accounts for the distribution of people and resources into geographically defined spaces will address the contributory roles of political interest groups and institutions. None of the urbanisms acknowledged by Dear[49] and Dear and Flusty[50] adequately represents state-society relations.

Another shortcoming, related to the first, is the model's built-in economic determinism. Like the concentric rings model, it is driven almost entirely by economic factors (industrialization in the case of the former, postindustrial economic organization in the latter). In Scott's economic essentialism and Dear and Flusty's patchwork urban theory, the implication is that urban space develops to fulfill the needs of capitalist economic organization, with the impersonal forces of global finance leading the way. Ultimately, the reliance on a single model or variable to explain the physical growth of cities has theoretical and empirical shortcomings. To repeat Wirth's admonition,[51] the purpose of a theory of urbanism is to assist our understanding of the differences between cities, and inform empirical research on the relationships between the characteristics of cities and their consequences. Neither the concentric circles diagram nor the checkerboard model help one understand the causes of differences between cities. To our knowledge, such models have not generated much empirical research on the consequences of urban space.

L.A. History through Sunshine and Noir

The characteristics cited above are also evident in a second component of the L.A. School research program: explaining the rise of Los Angeles as a global city. Devoted less to the abstract pattern of physical development than to explaining particular events, trends, and outcomes, the L.A. School's efforts along these lines make for unconventional histories. Here, the focus is not the people of Los Angeles, the political activities of its leaders, the regional economy, nor other subjects that form traditional subjects of historical analysis. The goal is not to posit L.A. as a prototype of physical development elsewhere, but to describe how the city and region itself have been shaped by a confluence of urban processes over time.

In this vein, Mike Davis's *City of Quartz*[52] is a landmark effort to explain the evolution of urban space in Los Angeles. It is also a natural starting point for understanding the L.A. School's approach to historical inquiry. Unlike Dear and Flusty's model,[53] change agents abound in *City of Quartz*. The main players are vaguely defined social classes: an underclass composed of new immigrants and the working poor, and the city's social and economic elite. Davis cites a succession of growth coalitions, beginning with the one headed by the virulently antiunion *Los Angeles Times*, and culminating in the contemporary regime of land bankers, homebuilders, commercial developers, and land-intensive industries. Davis describes a world of looming class conflict, with urban space as a battleground and channeler of conflict. These conflicts are played out at the microlevel, with homeowner associations, gangs, and the Los Angeles Police Department struggling to control pieces of L.A.'s geography.

One of Davis's original contributions is his attention to L.A.'s image-makers. Parallel to the battle for urban space is the struggle to define the image of Los Angeles. On one side is an alliance of developers and boosters; on the other side is a coterie of architects, writers, movie producers, and like connoisseurs of high culture. The former helped manufacture a sunshine image of Los Angeles designed to appeal to tourists and newcomers. The other side consists of intellectuals dedicated to debunking L.A.'s booster myths while producing a rich genre of noir literature and film that depicts the dark underbelly of L.A. life. The contrast between sunshine and noir forms a powerful dialectic affecting those who write about Los Angeles and those who make its policies.[54] Davis and much of the L.A. School lean heavily toward the noir. *City of Quartz* has been enormously influential in shaping both the L.A. School's and global intellectuals' views of Los Angeles.

If the L.A. School's theory of growth is a hodgepodge of urbanisms, the historical narratives of L.A.'s rise as a global city have been written as a collection of geographies, i.e., urban processes. This is how Soja organizes his historical account of Los Angeles between Watts and the multiethnic riots of 1992.[55] The geographies that emerge in this period are captured (appropriately) in neologisms. The term *exopolis,* for example, denotes peripheral urbanization, i.e., the rapid growth in pockets of Orange County, the San Fernando Valley, along the Pacific coast, and the Inland Empire. Flexcities similarly signify the deindustrialization of the local manufacturing base and rise of specialized districts housing craft-based production networks that are highly responsive to international markets. Several additional geographies are consequences of metropolitan transformation. The more important include repolarization—the increasing gap between rich and poor—and the carceral city, the erection of fortress-like structures and surveillance systems for monitoring public spaces.[56]

These geographies constitute important departures from pre–World War II development patterns. Soja makes a compelling argument that they were triggered, in part, by the Watts riots in 1965. Watts marked an important change in the relationship between the people and urban space of Los Angeles, a phenomenon he calls urban restructuring. In urban restructuring, the dominant urban processes are transformed, giving rise to new processes that shape both urban space and how individuals interact with and understand them.[57] These geographies have solved some problems but created others. Soja believes the combination of repolarization and the carceral city contributed to the 1992 multiethnic riots. He suggests that L.A. has gone from a crisis-generated restructuring to a restructuring-generated crisis. The new crisis includes the collapse of L.A.'s historically strong civic will.[58]

Scott picks up the economic theme from Soja in an essay on Southern California's industrial urbanism.[59] Whereas East Coast and midwestern cities like Pittsburgh, Chicago, and Detroit experienced rapid growth in the Fordist era, Los Angeles emerged in the post-Fordist phase. The post-Fordist city departs from the Fordist industrial metropolis in its low level of unionization among workers; polarization of occupational structures (i.e., a highly paid cadre of professionals and a large stratum of low-paid, low-skilled manual workers); reduced opportunities for upward mobility; diverse, but unassimilated workforce; and tight links between local economic activity and international market forces. Concerned about the consequences of these trends, Scott, like Soja, suggests that they contributed to the 1992 riots. Left unchecked, they threaten to transform Southern California into a *Bladerunner*-like dystopia.

Like the L.A. School's theory of urban growth, these histories of L.A.'s development as a global city generally are inattentive to political development and institutions. In *City of Quartz*, public officials, when they appear, are portrayed as junior partners or handmaidens to the private sector newspaper publishers, developers, and homebuilders that run Los Angeles. Despite such shortcomings, these histories of L.A.'s development hold greater promise than the attempt to elaborate a single theory of urban growth. They highlight several enduring patterns of order (i.e., urbanisms or geographies) and seek to identify the forces that gave rise to them. The L.A. School has offered searching critiques of their consequences (i.e., the erosion of public authority, and Babel-like disintegration of L.A.'s civic culture). Davis, Dear, Soja, and others have drawn attention to the manner in which the urban landscape is socially constructed as well as physically manufactured by developers, industry, and consumers. The key challenge facing L.A. scholars is to understand the political manifestations of these trends and their implications for urban democracy in Los Angeles and beyond.

We suggest two ways of moving forward. The first is to specify whether the geographies uncovered by the L.A. School are unique to Southern California. To date, work by the L.A. School straddles both sides of the exception-prototype dichotomy. To the extent that these geographies are generated by crisis events, e.g., the Watts riots of 1965, they are likely to be exceptional. However, peripheral urbanization, rising inequality, and international interdependence appear to be widespread. For these broader trends, it is important to identify how local governments are responding to shape and even mitigate their effects. Janet Abu-Lughod provides this kind of analysis in her comparative study of urban responses to changes in the international political economy.[60]

The second way forward involves focusing on the political implications of the geographies identified by the L.A. School. Whether or not repolarization constitutes a geography, it has pregnant implications for politics. At the national level, for example, there has been a resurgence of partisan polarization in recent years, exacerbated by the unprecedented electoral parity between the major political parties. Political scientists have argued about whether polarization is elite-driven or a reflection of polarization in the electorate.[61] The work of the L.A. School offers reason to expect that polarization is driven primarily by the spatial distribution of jobs and residents. Interestingly, polarization is less evident in both the electoral and institutional arenas of urban politics. In contrast to national legislatures, voting in city councils tends to be consensus-based, not conflict-driven. In recent years, a large proportion of the votes in the New York, Los Angeles, and Chicago legislatures has been unanimous or near-unanimous. Local consensus in the face of widening social disparities is a puzzle that deserves greater attention.

Why has the dystopian future imagined by the L.A. School and others failed to materialize? The answer perhaps lies in the ability of the local state to manage conflict and shelter itself from some of the more divisive issues that animate state and national politics. Explaining how this is accomplished puts the focus squarely back on political institutions such as nonpartisanship, the artificial construction of municipal boundaries and legislative districts within municipalities, and the interference of state and national entities, which has removed many contentious issues from the local sphere. In any case, understanding how local governments have frustrated the more dire predictions of the L.A. School requires bringing the local state and its policies back into the study of places like Los Angeles.

Bringing the Local State Back In

One of the major implications of work by the L.A. School is that politics and political institutions play a minor role, if any, in shaping the urban landscape. To characterize the entire output of the L.A. School as "stateless," however, would be unfair. Dear, Scott, and Wolch have experimented with state-centered analyses.[62] Others have cited municipal institutions like the initiative process and commission system in arguing that the city and region are ungovernable.[63] In a recent essay, Dear suggests that L.A.'s history reflects the interplay between private and public authority, with the balance having shifted over L.A.'s 150-plus years of history.[64] Nevertheless, these efforts are more the exception than the rule. The L.A. School's efforts to develop an alternative to the concentric circles model and explain the rise of modern Los Angeles generally demonstrate an inattention to politics that needs correction.

This inattention undoubtedly reflects the dearth of political scholarship on Los Angeles before the late 1980s. L.A. did not fit easily into the dominant frameworks in urban politics, e.g., the machine-reform dialectic, regime theory,[65] and Sun Belt model of urban governance.[66] There were few book-length studies of L.A.'s political system and power structure comparable to heavily studied cities such as Atlanta, New Haven, New York, and Chicago.[67] Those that did appear seldom reached more than a regional audience.[68]

In the past twenty years, however, political scholarship on Los Angeles has proliferated. Sonenshein's work on charter reform and local government structures, for example, provides a much-needed examination of local institutions.[69] Political scientists have tackled difficult subjects like minority political incorporation,[70] race and ethnic coalition building,[71] and the 1992 multiethnic riots.[72] Others have written on the rise of labor, environmental, and neighborhood groups.[73] In addition, L.A. has become a popular subject of comparative analysis.[74] Interestingly, much of this research pairs Los Angeles with New York but not Chicago. Whether it is demographics,[75] voting patterns,[76] or mayoral politics,[77] New York is generally considered a more relevant comparison.

Bringing the local state back in involves arguing for the importance of the political organization of cities. The state is not merely an arena of conflict, but a set of institutions with the potential, realized or not, to shape private sector activity, determine the distribution of rights, responsibilities, and benefits of collective action, and rearrange policy to suit its own narrow interests as well as those of various publics.[78] For this potential to be realized, it is necessary for public actors to marshal state capacity and achieve a level of autonomy from social interests. State capacity and autonomy cannot be assumed by the analyst, but must be described and demonstrated through empirical research. Similarly, the alignment of interests between government and governed—the objective of institutional design and expectation of democratic theory—is a subject for both theoretical and empirical analysis.

L.A. School efforts to analyze the local state have one major shortcoming. The state is treated as monolithic and subservient to the economic system. As a result, local state autonomy is neglected and its component parts are rarely differentiated. In Clark and Dear (1984), both the form and functions of the state are derived from the capitalist economic system. The goals of the state—e.g., to secure spaces for production and accumulation— and the nature of its activity do not differ according to state structures (e.g., regional, county, or municipal level; executive, legislative, bureaucratic, or judicial function) or policy area (e.g., public safety, social policy, or economic development). As a result, the L.A. School generally equates the interests of the state with the preferences of the ruling class. Scott, for example, views local planning apparatuses in Los Angeles as tools of the economic elite.[79] This reductionist view is inconsistent with the approach advocated here.

Bringing the local state back in requires differentiating the components of local government and exploring how state activity varies by policy area and over time. For example, Erie offers a state-centered analysis focusing on the contributions of municipal bureaucracies and public infrastructure to Los Angeles's early development.[80] For the period 1870 to 1930, he distinguishes two growth regimes: an entrepreneurial regime (1880–1906) characterized by a business-run, low-tax, caretaker government pursuing private strategies of economic development, and a more state-centered regime (1906–1932) featuring a high-tax, high-debt, activist local government pursuing public economic development strategies in the face of growing business opposition. The latter relied heavily on the municipal bond market to finance large-scale infrastructure projects, aided by the legal and financial latitude granted home-rule cities like L.A. by the California Constitution. Los Angeles acquired nearly all of its territory after 1906, using its water monopoly to annex neighboring communities.[81]

More generally, Erie describes Los Angeles as a developmental city-state where public entrepreneurs and municipal agencies such as L.A.'s Department of Water and Power used electoral strategies (e.g., bond and charter amendment elections) to publicly finance and independently manage the public infrastructure needed for urban and regional development. Crucial to L.A.'s rise from frontier town to regional imperium was a permissive state constitutional framework. California's Constitution allowed home-rule cities like L.A. substantial flexibility (i.e., a high debt ceiling) to finance needed infrastructure investments. By 1920 Los Angeles was using more of its extensive borrowing capacity on infrastructure projects than any other city in the country. L.A.'s semiautonomous proprietary departments (Water and Power, Harbor, and, later, Airports) successfully campaigned for voter-approved city charter amendments that insulated these agencies from elected officials and even the powerful business community.

This statist approach diverges sharply from traditional urban development theories that emphasize local growth constraints,[82] and the catalytic role of business elites.[83] This approach also helps explain L.A.'s curious reform experience. L.A. differed from liberal growth regimes such as New York's that sought to balance redistribution demands and economic imperatives.[84] Similarly, L.A.'s state-centered growth regime deviated from the laissez-faire growth regimes of southwestern cities.[85] L.A.'s experience, however, was typical of West Coast cities such as San Francisco and Seattle, where the local state was actively used for economic development. In the late nineteenth century, the West was an economically backward region. In a classic study, Gerschenkron explains how economically backward states can achieve industrialization in the absence of well-developed capital markets.[86] In these countries, the state uses its public fiscal capacity to substitute for the private capital provided by private banks in more advanced societies. The local state played precisely this role in L.A., which lacked both a manufacturing sector and well-developed private capital markets. The exigencies of economic and industrial development under conditions of backwardness help explain the early state-centered strategies adopted by West Coast cities and their meteoric rise in the twentieth century.

Recent work by L.A. scholars on city planning and regional water provision further illustrates that the local state is both pervasive and, frequently, relatively autonomous from local economic and social interests.[87] In both arenas, the L.A. School has characterized local state involvement as a function of private interests. Hise, however, taps an impressive array of archival sources to restore the role of public planning in building modern Los Angeles.[88] He finds that suburban development in Southern California was the joint product of public and private planning, not the disorganized, unplanned sprawl it is typically portrayed as. Similarly, Hoffman, Libecap, and others have culled the historical record to refute the conspiracy alleged in the movie Chinatown about how the city acquired vast water supplies from the Owens Valley.[89] Erie shows how the Metropolitan Water District of Southern California, initially opposed by conservatives in the L.A. business community, halted L.A.'s territorial expansion by putting an end to its water monopoly.[90] Since the 1950s, MWD has charted an independent course, making decisions on capital improvements, environmental protection, and cost-sharing measures that powerfully shaped the Southern California landscape.

Conclusion

The scholarship reviewed above reveals both the promise and shortcomings of the L.A. School's research agenda. The L.A. School's model of urban growth can be distinguished from the concentric rings model by its emphasis on changes in economic organization and its observation that the center no longer drives development at the periphery. Like Los Angeles, many fast-growing cities in the West and Southwest lack traditional downtown cores. In studying this new pattern of urbanization, however, the L.A. School has ignored the contribution of the local state. In this regard, work by the L.A. School shares an affinity with the Chicago School, which also failed to incorporate local politics and political organization as a key independent variable shaping the urban landscape. The L.A. School's greatest departure from the Chicago School consists of its reliance on abstract theory and historical generalizations rather than rigorous empirical research. Postmodern theory, however, is not a sufficient strategy for demonstrating the veracity of an urban growth model. More detailed empirical work, currently being conducted by L.A. School scholars and others, will undoubtedly bring greater nuance and clarity to the L.A. School model.

The local state has played a critical role in shaping the physical and economic development of Los Angeles and Southern California. Particularly crucial have been L.A.'s bureaucratic machines such as the Los Angeles Department of Water and Power. Equally important was the role of local voters in supporting efforts to bring the railroad to Los Angeles, introducing direct democracy, and significantly adding to the municipal tax burden to finance massive public infrastructure projects. Efforts to characterize Los Angeles as a politically fragmented and incoherent metropolis largely incapable of local collective action miss the forest for the trees. Similarly, depicting the region's development as merely a response to the needs of powerful, private economic interests effectively reduces urbanization to a functionalist logic.

In fairness, many of the seminal works of the L.A. School were written during a tumultuous period in the history of the city and region. The late 1980s and 1990s were characterized by depression-like conditions caused by defense downsizing and the collapse of the aerospace industry in Southern California. The early 1990s witnessed the disintegration of the Bradley coalition and eruption of multiethnic race riots that caused more damage than nearly any other episode of urban unrest in U.S. history. Secession movements in the San Fernando Valley and the harbor district threatened to break up the city. In the face of these challenges, the local state appeared adrift and powerless. It was in this context that Davis published his nightmarish predictions of overweening developer greed, environmental catastrophe, and racial strife.[91]

Since the late 1990s, L.A.'s economic and political fortunes have markedly changed. Southern California recovered from its severe post–Cold War economic slump, largely on the strength of new jobs created by L.A.'s rapid rise as a major international trade hub. Local voters rejected secession in 2000 and instead approved a new charter designed to both centralize local government and give neighborhoods greater local control. Los Angeles, once a bastion for antilabor sentiment, has become a labor stronghold. In 2005, voters elected former labor organizer Villaraigosa as mayor. L.A. now sits on the cutting edge of progressive politics, having passed a living-wage ordinance requiring firms that do business with the city to pay their workers enough to afford housing and healthcare. Efforts to revitalize the aging downtown area have borne fruit. Finally, the Villaraigosa administration has reinvigorated the old Bradley liberal coalition, but with a new combination of Latino incorporation and environmentally-friendly policies. The business community, once the dominant force in local politics, has been reduced to the status of coequal, if not junior, partner.

Perhaps reflecting this new climate, L.A. School scholars are beginning to incorporate the local state and public policy as important factors in their analyses. For example, Wolch, Pastor, and Dreier's anthology *Up against the Sprawl* considers "how government policy has shaped the development of greater Los Angeles."[92] The view that metropolitan areas develop primarily as a result of market and consumer forces is characterized as the naive legacy of public choice theories. Admitting the importance of public policy as an independent force shaping urban and regional development is a promising step. It suggests that the relationship between those who study L.A. politics and those interested in its urban spaces flows both ways.

Urban scholarship on Los Angeles has been immeasurably enhanced by the L.A. School's collaborative undertakings, such as its efforts to connect economic organization and urban space. A major challenge for L.A. scholars going forward is to better explain how political institutions and public policy are shaping the development of Southern California and, by implication, other metropolitan areas across the country and globe. By bringing the local state back in, L.A. scholars can offer a more robust urban growth paradigm.

Notes

1. The term "Marxist geographers" is from Mike Davis, *City of Quartz: Excavating the Future of Los Angeles* (New York: Verso, 1990). In this essay, the L.A. School refers to the work of its leading members, e.g., Michael J. Dear, Edward W. Soja, Allen J. Scott, and Jennifer Wolch. Where appropriate, we separately cite additional scholars who have collaborated with members of the L.A. School or contributed to bound volumes edited by Dear, Soja, and others.

2. Edward W. Soja, *Postmodern Geographies: The Reassertion of Space in Critical Social Theory* (New York: Verso, 1989).

3. A. A. Beveridge and S. Weber, "Race and Class in the Developing New York and Los Angeles Metropolises, 1940–2000," in David Halle, ed., *New York and Los Angeles: Politics, Society, and Culture —A Comparative View* (Chicago: University of Chicago Press, 2003), 49–78.

4. See J. Q. Wilson, *The Amateur Democrat: Club Politics in Three Cities* (Chicago: University of Chicago Press, 1962); E. C. Banfield and J. Q. Wilson, City Politics (New York: Vintage, 1963).

5. Amy Bridges, *Morning Glories: Municipal Reform in the Southwest* (Princeton, N.J.: Princeton University Press, 1997).

6. T. J. Lowi, "Machine politics—old and new," *Public Interest* 9 (1967): 83–92.

7. Raphael J. Sonenshein, *Politics in Black and White: Race and Power in Los Angeles* (Princeton, N.J.: Princeton University Press, 1993).

8. Joel Garreau, *Edge City: Life on the New Frontier* (New York: Anchor Books, 1991).

9. The Chicago School of Sociology is the subject of countless articles and several books. Among the more useful are Martin Bulmer's *The Chicago School of Sociology: Institutionalization, Diversity, and the Rise of Sociological Research* (Chicago: University of Chicago Press, 1984) and Andrew Abbott's *Department and Discipline: Chicago Sociology at One Hundred* (Chicago: University of Chicago Press, 1999).

10. See G. J. Stigler, "The Theory of Economic Regulation," *The Bell Journal of Economics and Management Science* 2, no. 1 (1971): 3–21; S. Peltzman, "Toward a More General Theory of Regulation," *Journal of Law and Economics* 19, no. 2 (1976): 211–40; R. A. Posner, "Theories of Economic Regulation," *The Bell Journal of Economics and Management Science* 5, no. 2 (1974): 335–58; G. S. Becker, "A Theory of Competition Among Pressure Groups for Political Influence," *The Quarterly Journal of Economics* 98, no. 3 (1983): 371–400.

11. Bulmer, *The Chicago School of Sociology,* 6–8.

12. Abbott, *Department and Discipline,* 10–18.

13. See Michael J. Dear and Steven Flusty, "Los Angeles as Postmodern Urbanism," in Michael J. Dear, ed., *From Chicago to L.A.: Making Sense of Urban Theory* (Thousand Oaks,

Calif.: SAGE Publications, 2002), 61–84; Michael J. Dear and Steven Flusty, "The Resistible Rise of the L.A. School," in Dear, *From Chicago to L.A.*, 3–17.

14. W. I. Thomas and F. Znaniecki, *The Polish Peasant in Europe and America: Monograph of an Immigrant Group* (Boston: Richard G. Bader, 1918–1920).

15. H. W. Zorbaugh, *The Gold Coast and the Slum: A Sociological Study of Chicago's Near North Side* (c. 1929; Chicago: University of Chicago Press, 1969).

16. L. Wirth, *The Ghetto* (Chicago: University of Chicago Press, 1928).

17. Robert E. Park, Ernest Burgess, and Roderick D. McKenzie, *The City: Suggestions for Investigation of Human Behavior in the Urban Environment* (Chicago: University of Chicago Press, 1925), 1–46.

18. Ibid., 1–46, 63–79.

19. Ibid., 47–62.

20. See J. A. Quinn, "The Burgess Zonal Hypothesis and Its Critics," *American Sociological Review* 5, no. 2 (1940): 210–18, for an early review of efforts to see whether and how cities exhibit concentric zones. See also A. M. Guest, "Retesting the Burgess Zonal Hypothesis: The Location of White-Collar Workers," *American Journal of Sociology* 76, no. 6 (1971): 1094–1108, which finds that the decentralization of white-collar workers predicted by the theory reflects the location of larger, newer housing on the periphery.

21. G. Hise, "Industry and the Landscapes of Social Reform," in Dear, *From Chicago to L.A.*, 97–130.

22. L. Wirth, "Urbanism as a Way of Life," *American Journal of Sociology* 42, no. 4 (1938): 493–509.

23. Zorbaugh, *The Gold Coast and the Slum.*

24. C. E. Merriam and H. F. Gosnell, *Non-Voting: Causes and Methods of Control* (Chicago: University of Chicago Press, 1924).

25. L. D. White, *The City Manager* (Chicago: University of Chicago Press, 1927).

26. Dear and Flusty, "The Resistible Rise of the L.A. School."

27. See Michael J. Dear and Allen J. Scott, eds., *Urbanization and Urban Planning in Capitalist Society* (New York: Methuen, 1981); Michael J. Dear, "Postmodernism and Planning," *Society and Space* 4, no. 3 (1986): 367–84; Michael J. Dear and Jennifer R. Wolch, *Landscapes of Despair: From Deinstitutionalization to Homelessness* (Princeton, N.J.: Princeton University Press, 1987).

28. See, for example, Michael J. Dear, "Los Angeles and Chicago Schools: An Invitation to Debate," *City and Community* 1, no. 1 (2002): 5–32.

29. David Halle, "The New York and Los Angeles Schools," in David Halle, ed., *New York and Los Angeles: Politics, Society, and Culture—A Comparative View* (Chicago: University of Chicago Press, 2003), 1–46.

30. D. W. Miller, "The New Urban Studies," *The Chronicle of Higher Education* 46, no. 50 (2000): A15–A16.

31. Robert M. Fogelson, *The Fragmented Metropolis: Los Angeles, 1850–1930* (Berkeley: University of California Press, 1967).

32. R. Fishman, "Foreword," in Fogelson, *The Fragmented Metropolis: Los Angeles, 1850–1930* (Berkeley: University of California Press, 1993); xv–xxviii; see xxi.

33. A. L. Grey, "Los Angeles: Urban Prototype," *Land Economics* 35, no. 3 (1959): 232–42.

34. See Dear, "The Resistible Rise of the L. A. School"; Allen J. Scott and Edward W. Soja, eds., *The City: Los Angeles and Urban Theory at the End of the Twentieth Century* (Berkeley: University of California Press, 1996); Michael J. Dear, H. Eric Schockman, and Greg Hise, eds., *Rethinking Los Angeles* (Thousand Oaks, Calif.: Sage Publications, 1996).

35. See Dear and Scott, *Urbanization and Urban Planning.*

36. Allen J. Scott, *Metropolis: From the Division of Labor to Urban Form* (Berkeley: University of California Press, 1988).

37. See R. H. Coase, "The Nature of the Firm," *Economica* 4 (1937): 386–405; A. A. Alchian and H. Demsetz, "Production, Information Costs, and Economic Organization," *American Economic Review* 62, no. 5 (1972): 777–95; O. E. Williamson, "The Logic of Economic Organization," *Journal of Law, Economics, and Organization* 4, no. 1 (1988): 65–93.

38. Allen J. Scott, *Technopolis: High Technology and Regional Development in Southern California* (Berkeley: University of California Press, 1993).

39. Allen J. Scott, "High Technology Industrial Development in the San Fernando Valley and Ventura County," in Scott and Soja, *The City: Los Angeles and Urban Theory at the End of the Twentieth Century,* 276–310.

40. Michael J. Dear, *The Postmodern Urban Condition* (Malden, Mass.: Blackwell Publishers, 2000).

41. See Dear and Flusty, "Los Angeles as Postmodern Urbanism."

42. Allen J. Scott, *New Industrial Spaces: Flexible Production Organization and Regional Development in North America and Western Europe* (London: Pion, 1988).

43. See Dear, *The Postmodern Urban Condition.*

44. Dear and Flusty, "Los Angeles as Postmodern Urbanism."

45. Garreau, *Edge City.*

46. E. McKenzie, *Privatopia: Homeowner Associations and the Rise of Residential Private Government* (New Haven: Yale University Press, 1994).

47. See Soja, *Postmodern Geographies;* M. Sorkin, "Introduction: Variations on a Theme Park," in M. Sorkin, ed., *Variations on a Theme Park: The New American City and the End of Public Space* (New York: Hill and Wang, 1992), xi–xv.

48. Mike Davis, "Fortress Los Angeles," in Sorkin, *Variations on a Theme Park,* 154–180.

49. Dear, *The Postmodern Urban Condition.*

50. Dear and Flusty, "The Resistible Rise of the L.A. School."

51. Wirth, *The Ghetto.*

52. Davis, *City of Quartz.*

53. Dear and Flusty, "Los Angeles as Postmodern Urbanism."

54. Davis, *City of Quartz,* 15–98.

55. Edward W. Soja, "Los Angeles, 1965–1992," in Scott and Soja, *The City: Los Angeles and Urban Theory,* 426–62.

56. Davis, "Fortress Los Angeles."

57. Soja, *Postmodern Geographies.*

58. Scott and Soja, *The City: Los Angeles and Urban Theory.*

59. Allen J. Scott, "Industrial Urbanism in Late-Twentieth-Century Southern California," in Michael J. Dear, ed., *From Chicago to L.A.: Making Sense of Urban Theory* (Thousand Oaks, Calif.: SAGE Publications, 2002), 3–17.

60. Janet Abu-Lughod, *New York, Chicago, Los Angeles: America's Global Cities* (Minneapolis: University of Minnesota Press, 1999).

61. M. P. Fiorina, *Culture War? The Myth of a Polarized America* (New York: Pearson Longman, 2005); G. C. Jacobson, "Polarized Politics and the 2004 Congressional and Presidential Elections," *Political Science Quarterly* 120, no. 2 (2005): 199–218; N. McCarty, K. T. Poole, and H. Rosenthal, *Polarized America: The Dance of Ideology and Unequal Riches* (Cambridge, Mass.: MIT Press, 2006).

62. Jennifer Wolch, *The Shadow State: Government and Voluntary Sector in Transition* (New York: The Foundation Center, 1990); Allen J. Scott, *The Urban Land Nexus and the State* (London: Pion, 1980); Gordon L. Clark and Michael J. Dear, *State Apparatus: Structures and Languages of Legitimacy* (Boston: Allen & Unwin, 1984).

63. H. Eric Schockman, "Is Los Angeles Governable? Revisiting the City Charter," in Dear, Schockman, and Hise, *Rethinking Los Angeles,* 57–75.

64. Michael J. Dear, "In the City, Time Becomes Visible: Intentionality and Urbanism in Los Angeles, 1781–1991," in Scott and Soja, *The City: Los Angeles and Urban Theory,* 76–105.

65. C. Stone, *Regime Politics: Governing Atlanta, 1946–1988* (Lawrence: University of Kansas Press, 1989).

66. C. Abbott, *The New Urban America: Growth and Politics in Sunbelt Cities* (Chapel Hill: University of North Carolina Press, 1981); R. M. Bernard and B. R. Rice, eds., *Sunbelt Cities: Politics and Growth Since World War II* (Austin: University of Texas Press, 1981).

67. See Stone, *Regime Politics;* R. Dahl, *Who Governs? Democracy and Power in an American City* (New Haven, Conn.: Yale University Press, 1961); W. Sayre and H. Kaufman, *Governing New York City: Politics in the Metropolis* (New York: W. W. Norton, 1960); E. C. Banfield, *Political Influence: A New Theory of Urban Politics* (New York: Free Press, 1961).

68. W. W. Crouch and B. Dinerman, *Southern California Metropolis: A Study in Development of Government for a Metropolitan Area* (Berkeley: University of California Press, 1963); F. M. Carney, "The Decentralized Politics of Los Angeles," *The Annals of the American Academy of Political and Social Science* 353 (1964): 107–21; E. C. Banfield, *Big City Politics* (New York: Random House, 1965).

69. Raphael J. Sonenshein, *The City at Stake: Succession, Reform, and the Battle for Los Angeles* (Princeton, N.J.: Princeton University Press, 2004); Raphael J. Sonenshein, *Los Angeles: Structure of a City Government* (Los Angeles: League of Women Voters of Los Angeles, 2006).

70. Sonenshein, *Politics in Black and White;* F. J. Gilliam Jr., "Exploring Minority Empowerment: Symbolic Politics, Governing Coalitions and Traces of Political Style in Los Angeles," *American Journal of Political Science* 40, no. 1 (1996), 56–81.

71. M. Jones-Correa, ed., *Governing American Cities: Inter-Ethnic Coalitions, Competitions, and Conflict* (New York: Russell Sage Foundation, 2001); Raphael J. Sonenshein, "The Dynamics of Latino Incorporation: The 2001 Los Angeles Mayoral Election as Seen in *Los Angeles Times* Exit Polls," *PS: Political Science and Politics* 35, no. 1 (2002): 67–74.

72. M. Baldassare, *The Los Angeles Riots: Lessons for the Urban Future* (Boulder, Colo.: Westview Press, 1994).

73. J. A. Regalado, "Organized Labor and Los Angeles City Politics: An Assessment in the Bradley Years, 1973–1989," *Urban Affairs Quarterly* 27, no. 1 (1991): 87–108; S. P. Erie, *Globalizing L.A.: Trade, Infrastructure, and Regional Development* (Palo Alto, Calif.: Stanford University Press, 2004);. M. Pastor, J. Sadd, and R. Morello-Frosch, "The Air Is Always Cleaner on the Other Side: Race, Space, and Air Toxics Exposures in California," *Journal of Urban Affairs* 27, no. 2 (2005): 127–148.

74. Abu-Lughod, *New York, Chicago, Los Angeles;* Halle, "The New York and Los Angeles Schools."

75. Beveridge and Weber, "Race and Class in the Developing New York and Los Angeles Metropolises."

76. J. H. Mollenkopf and T. Ross, "Immigrant Political Participation in New York and Los Angeles," in Jones-Correa, *Governing American Cities,* 17–70.

77. J. H. Mollenkopf, et al., "Race, Ethnicity, and Immigration in the 2005 Mayoral Elections in Los Angeles and New York" (working paper, Institute of Urban and Regional Development, University of California, Berkeley, 2006).

78. P. D. Evans, D. Rueschemeyer, and T. Skocpol, eds., *Bringing the State Back In* (New York: Cambridge University Press, 1985).

79. See Scott, *The Urban Land Nexus and the State.*

80. Stephen P. Erie, "How the Urban West Was Won," *Urban Affairs Quarterly* 27, no. 4 (1992): 519–54; S. P. Erie, "Los Angeles as a Developmental City-State," in Dear, *From Chicago to L.A.,* 131–59.

81. Erie, "How the Urban West Was Won."

82. P. E. Peterson, *City Limits* (Chicago: University of Chicago Press, 1981); J. H. Mollenkopf, *The Contested City* (Princeton, N.J. : Princeton University Press, 1983); P. Kantor, *The Dependent City Revisited: The Political Economy of Urban Development and Social Policy* (Boulder, Colo.: Westview Press, 1995).

83. S. Elkin, *City and Regime in the American Republic* (Chicago: University of Chicago Press, 1987); T. Swanstrom, *The Crisis of Growth Politics: Cleveland, Kucinich, and the Challenge of Urban Populism* (Philadelphia, Pa.: Temple University Press, 1985); W. B. Friedricks, *Henry E. Huntington and the Creation of Southern California* (Columbus: Ohio State University Press, 1992).

84. M. Shefter, *Political Crisis, Fiscal Crisis: The Collapse and Revival of New York City* (New York: Basic Books, 1985); Swanstrom, *The Crisis of Growth Politics.*

85. Bernard and Rice, *Sunbelt Cities.*

86. A. Gerschenkron, *Economic Backwardness in Historical Perspective* (Cambridge, Mass.: Belknap Press, 1962).

87. See Steven P. Erie and Scott A. MacKenzie, "The L.A. School and Politics Noir: Bringing the Local State Back In," *Journal of Urban Affairs* 31, no. 5 (2009): 537–57, for a discussion of how research in these areas relates to the urban growth model and historical narratives of the L.A. School.

88. G. Hise, *Magnetic Los Angeles: Planning the Twentieth-Century Metropolis* (Baltimore, Md.: Johns Hopkins University Press, 1997).

89. A. Hoffman, *Vision or Villainy: Origins of the Owens Valley–Los Angeles Water Controversy* (College Station: Texas A&M University Press, 1981); G. D. Libecap, *Owens Valley Revisited: A Reassessment of the West's First Great Water Transfer* (Palo Alto, Calif.: Stanford University Press, 2007).

90. Steven P. Erie, *Beyond Chinatown: The Metropolitan Water District, Growth, and the Environment in Southern California* (Palo Alto, Calif: Stanford University Press, 2006).

91. See Davis, "Fortress Los Angeles"; Mike Davis, *Ecology of Fear: Los Angeles and the Imagination of Disaster* (New York: Metropolitan Books, 1998).

92. Jennifer Wolch, Manuel Pastor Jr., and Peter Dreier, "Making Southern California: Public Policy, Markets, and the Dynamics of Growth," in Jennifer Wolch, Manuel Pastor Jr., and P. Dreier, eds., *Up against the Sprawl: Public Policy and the Making of Southern California* (Minneapolis: University of Minnesota Press, 2004), 1–44.

Part III

The View from New York

7

The Rise and Decline of the L.A. and New York Schools

■ David Halle and Andrew A. Beveridge

From the 1960s to the end of the twentieth century, the nation's two largest cities each helped to nurture a distinct approach to urban analysis. In his introduction to this book, Dennis Judd discusses the Los Angeles School and a New York School. The former tended to emphasize the decentralization and fragmentation of urban areas; the latter the potential of the urban core. Each school offered valuable insights applicable to the study of all major urban regions, not just New York and Los Angeles. In this chapter we argue that it is time to move beyond the framework of these schools. Partly this is because their contributions have been widely acknowledged. More importantly, it is because both schools were reacting, in different ways, to a common view that American cities were in decline while the periphery was expanding. These processes were captured by the terms "white flight" and "ghetto," which described the mass movement of the middle and working classes from the central cities to the suburbs and the concentration of the poor and minorities within cities. This account of urban decline dominated scholarly analysis for much of the second half of the twentieth century, mainly because it had a basis in the real situation of American cites. That this perspective is no longer widely held reflects the fact that it is no longer a compelling account of the actual situation of urban development. No dominant alternative discourse has yet emerged. Any new discourse must recognize that American cities are in a state of change.

The data we present in this chapter suggest some of the basic elements of a new discourse. These involve: (1) key demographic changes, including especially changing birth rates for racial and ethnic groups; (2) the rise and collapse of the housing bubble; (3) demographic changes that transform our understanding of ghettos, an issue that we approach via a case study of changes in Harlem, once the country's most famous urban ghetto; (4) the environmental movement, which we consider via a case study of Manhattan's High Line, the long-disused, above-ground railroad that environmentalists are turning into a park and whose June 2009 opening has drawn enormous attention. The High Line is an early example of some of the issues faced in New York and Los Angeles by environmentalism, which has raced to a central place in the mayoral agenda of both cities. For example, the High Line case shows that even when we understand large-scale social and economic trends, public policies can change the patterns of urban development in profound and unpredictable ways. Although our two case studies—Harlem and The High Line—focus on New York, we believe that their implications and lessons can be generalized to other cities. Overall, our analysis is inevitably exploratory and tentative. No account can be truly comprehensive; it is too soon for that.

The New York and the L.A. Schools and Their Fading Usefulness

David Halle's *New York and Los Angeles*, which appeared in 2003, began with a statement about the limitations of the L.A. School, which had focused almost exclusively on the decentralization and fragmentation of urban regions.[1] Halle proposed that beginning in the 1950s, New York had produced a school of its own that focused on the potential and importance of the urban center. The contrast between these two schools was useful both for describing different patterns of urban development and also for referring to divergent theoretical tendencies. We use the term *school* here to refer to any group having at least the first two of the following four features: (1) some shared perspectives and ideas; (2) a common agenda of research; (3) an overt sense of membership in a distinct school; (4) residence in the same area/region. If the latter two characteristics exist as well, then it is likely that the school gains an additional measure of coherence.

The New York School

As Halle described it, the New York School that flourished in the latter decades of the twentieth century was characterized by several distinguishing features: first, a strong interest in the central city, especially Manhattan; second, a determination to improve city life; third, a utopian belief that the central city could and should be a place where the wealthy, the middle class, the working class, and the poor can coexist; and fourth, a belief that city life is superior to suburban life.

Some key figures of the New York School were Jane Jacobs, arguably its intellectual and organizational founder, whose 1961 *The Death and Life of Great American Cities* remains widely regarded as the best analysis of how to make cities work;[2] historian Kenneth Jackson, whose 1985 *Crabgrass Frontier* contains a biting critique of how government policies (federal, state, and local) undermined the health of American cities especially from the 1920s to the 1970s;[3] architect Robert Stern, who provided some of the key ideas associated with the rejuvenation of Times Square;[4] and sociologists Richard Sennett,[5] William Whyte,[6] and Sharon Zukin.[7] The latter's 1982 *Loft Living* arguably pioneered the study of gentrification, with an analysis of the famous conversion of Soho industrial lofts to residence-workspaces.

The overview of the New York School presented in *New York and Los Angeles* included several caveats. The first was that there are "many important urban researchers in New York City and the region whose work scarcely, or only partly, fits this New York School model." The point was just that the New York School perspective is a distinct and important approach to cities exemplified by a cluster of distinguished analysts in the nation's largest city. The second caveat was that the basics of the New York School perspective are clearly not confined to discussion of New York City. For example, Manhattan-centrism is, with different names, transferable to many other cities. The third was that most of the New York School did not, and do not, think of themselves as a school. This was not, we argued, a reason to avoid using the term. It just depends what is meant by a school, an issue on which there is no clear consensus. But according to the criteria introduced earlier, the New York School has features 1 and 2, and for the most part 4, but not 3.

The Los Angeles School

The Los Angeles School writers stressed, when analyzing Los Angeles and many (but not all) major urban areas, their "sprawling, polycentric character," which contained "multiple urban cores" or "edge cities" or "techno-cities" spread around the periphery of the traditional city center. The central point was that "edge cities" were not just "bedroom suburbs" from which people commuted to the central city. Instead, they were complex urban centers in their own rights. Formally, edge cities could be defined, following Garreau,[8] as "places that have substantial leasable office and retail space, have more 'jobs than bedrooms,' are perceived by their populations as a unitary place, and have appeared in the past thirty years." Key figures in the Los Angeles School were Robert Fogelson (arguably the founding thinker), Joel Garreau, Robert Fishman, Michael Dear, Jennifer Wolch,[9] Allen Scott, Edward Soja,[10] and Michael Davis.

The thinkers classified as the Los Angeles School, on the whole, met criteria 1 for being a school: a shared idea—an emphasis on the polycentric character of urban areas, though there were disagreements on other ideas—and 2, a research agenda that focused on urban dispersal. A majority of these scholars also met criterion 4 since most of them resided in the Los Angles region, though some lived and worked elsewhere: Robert Fogelson in Boston, Joel Garreau in the Washington, D.C., area, and Robert Fishman in the New York–New Jersey region.[11]

Regarding criterion 3, several members of the L.A. School regarded themselves as a distinct school at some point in the 1980s and 1990s. The embryo of the school was a series of meetings and publications in the late 1980s, which included, for instance, Michael Dear, Allan Scott, Ed Soja, and Jennifer Wolch. Over time, however, the sense of membership began to disappear as various intellectual disagreements surfaced. For example, Dear grafted a strong version of the Frankfurt school of sociology's approach to culture onto the Los Angeles School's central idea, arguing that individuals who purchased tract homes in the suburbs were part of a giant latifundia dominated by real estate interests, patrolled by a kind of Praetorian Guard, and requiring a complex new vocabulary to be understood.[12] This was too elaborate and explicit for most of the other members of the school. By 2008, when several key figures from the school's early days gathered for a retirement party for Soja held at UCLA, only Dear was willing to advocate for the continued existence of the Los Angeles School. The rest denied the current usefulness of the category, mostly on the grounds that its key idea had been acknowledged, and also that there were numerous intellectual disagreements between its former members.

New York and Los Angeles argued that the ideas of the Los Angeles and the New York schools could fruitfully be applied to most urban regions in the United States and elsewhere. Several of the analyses in that book drew, in an eclectic and open-minded way, on the best insights of the two schools. For example, the chapter on riots tried to correct a common perception that Los Angeles was more riot-prone than New York in the period after World War II, and did so by looking at riots in a broader, regional perspective, not just one confined to the respective cites. From this point of view, the City of Los Angeles had two mega riots (Watts in 1965 and Rodney King in 1992), but there were no major or mega riots elsewhere in the Los Angeles region. By contrast, New York not only had New York City's ("blackout") mega riot of 1977 and major riots of 1964 (Harlem–Bedford Stuyvesant), 1991 (Crown Heights), and 1992 (Washington Heights), but also several riots in the region, including Newark's 1967 mega riot, and major riots in Plainfield (1967), Jersey City (1967 and 1970), and Englewood (1967). From a broad regional perspective, New York was at least as riot-prone as Los Angeles. Looking back from the vantage point of the economic and real estate boom that Los Angeles and New York experienced from 2002 to 2007, it is clear that despite their differences, a similar dynamic provided the foundation for both schools. Each was reacting, though in quite different ways, to the perceived decline of central cities and to the growth of the urban periphery. The reaction of the scholars of the L.A. School was to focus on studying the expanding periphery (edge cities and the like), while the New York School's reaction was to focus on the revival of the urban core.

Today's context—an increasingly perceived and to some extent actual resurgence of urban life—creates a far more complex and balanced situation. When cities and suburbs are more equally valued, there is far less opportunity or need for scholars to take distinct sides, for example to either vigorously defend underappreciated cities, as in the New York School, or to shift attention to a burgeoning suburban and peripheral context, as in the

Los Angeles School. (We wish to stress, however, that many urban scholars never did take sides.)

The two opposing perspectives have been overtaken by recent developments that we describe in this chapter. In New York the demand for housing in Manhattan and the resurgence of the city's outer boroughs, especially Brooklyn and Queens, and more modestly the Bronx (Staten Island never really flagged), means that one key component of the New York School's perspective, namely its advocacy of the superiority of urban over suburban life, is less and less needed; the case now has many adherents. Likewise, the Los Angeles School's nearly exclusive focus on the periphery looks unbalanced, given the somewhat successful efforts to renew downtown Los Angeles, attract a more affluent and diverse population, and in the process eliminate downtown's main perceived blemish, Skid Row. The developments in both cities mean that our understanding of the processes influencing urban spatial development must be reevaluated.

Comparing the Los Angeles and New York Metropolises

Though New York City and Los Angeles are both major cities, they are also the major urban agglomerations in their two regions, which include numerous counties and municipalities and, in the case of New York City, a population spread over several states. We divided each region into three roughly comparable zones, which are presented in Figure 7.1. The New York metropolitan area is relatively easy to divide in this fashion. There is Manhattan, the Outer Boroughs (Bronx, Brooklyn, Queens, and Staten Island), and the rest of the metropolitan area, which includes all the counties outside New York City and which we call the "Suburbs." For Los Angeles, we made a comparable tripartite division. We specified an area in the city as "West of Downtown," a term often used locally to define a highly affluent area that includes West L.A., Century City and the like, and also some areas outside the City of Los Angeles (e.g., Beverly Hills and Malibu). Our two other zones are the rest of the City of Los Angeles and the remainder of the Los Angeles metropolitan area.[13] By specifying these three zones, we are able to compare equivalent areas of the two metropolitan areas. For example, Manhattan and West of Downtown have a variety of similarities.

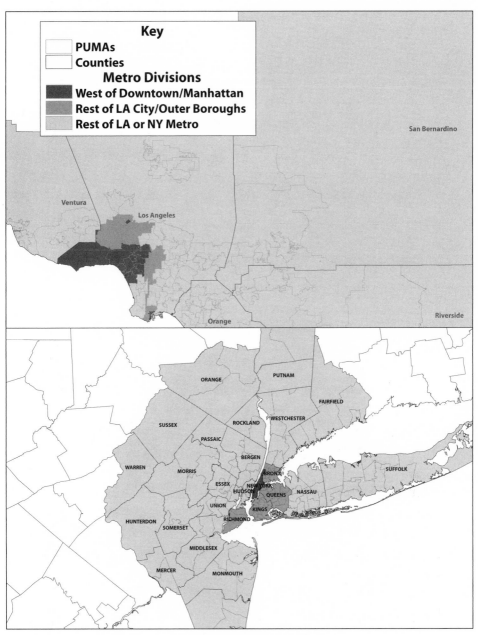

Figure 7.1 Metropolitan divisions, New York and Los Angeles.

White Flight and Families with Young Children

Although suburbanization began long before 1945, after World War II it gained enormous traction as large proportions of the better-paid working class and middle and upper middle class moved away from the city into suburbs.[14] The flight out of major American cities, including Los Angeles and New York City, had become so obvious that when journalists and others

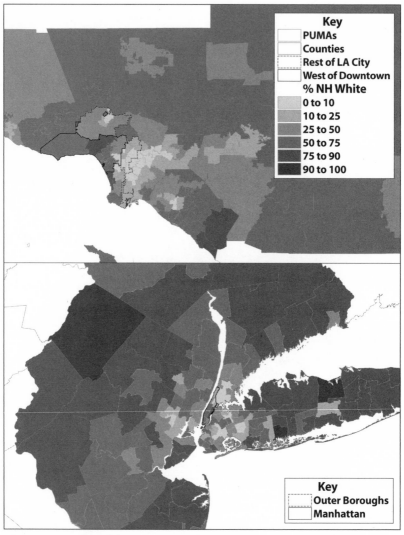

Figure 7.2 Percentage of the non-Hispanic white population by PUMA in the New York (bottom) and Los Angeles (top) metropolitan areas, 2006.

noticed it had reversed, it was newsworthy.[15] This reversal is fueled by the changing composition of family and labor force in the major cities, most particularly the changing role of women in the workforce, as well as changing economic opportunities. Still, although the overall trend seems to have reversed, the way it is playing out in different parts of the Los Angeles and New York metropolitan areas varies in significant ways.

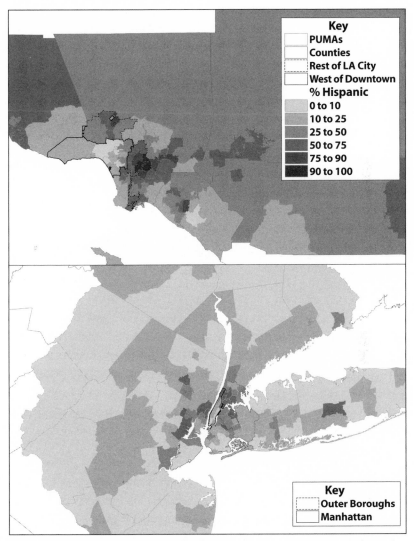

Key
PUMAs
Counties
Rest of LA City
West of Downtown
% Hispanic
0 to 10
10 to 25
25 to 50
50 to 75
75 to 90
90 to 100

Key
Outer Boroughs
Manhattan

Figure 7.3 Percentage of the Hispanic population by PUMA for the New York (bottom) and Los Angeles (top) metropolitan areas, 2006.

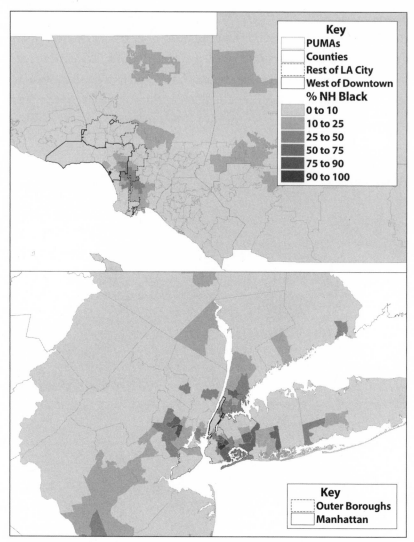

Figure 7.4 Percentage of the non-Hispanic black population by PUMA for the New York (bottom) and Los Angeles (top) metropolitan areas, 2006.

Figures 7.2–7.5 show, in map form, the spatial distribution of racial and ethnic groups in New York and Los Angeles in 2006. These patterns are not frozen in time. The overall demographic changes in the demographic profiles of the two regions from 2000 to 2006 are displayed in Tables 7.1 and 7.2. In the Los Angeles region, the following general trends for the

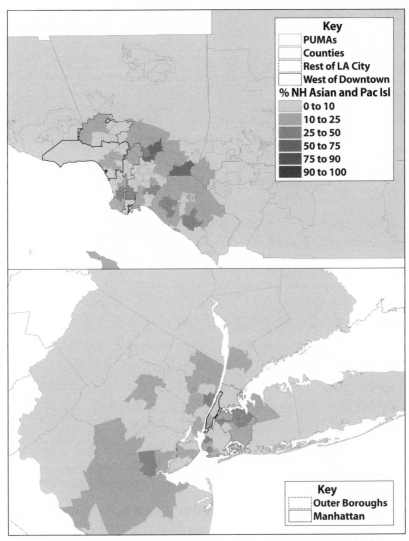

Figure 7.5 Percentage of the non-Hispanic Asian and Pacific Islander population by PUMA for the New York (bottom) and Los Angeles (top) metropolitan areas, 2006.

Los Angeles metropolitan region (the agglomeration that includes all our three zones) occurred from 2000 to 2006: an increase in the Hispanic population, from 39.0 percent to 42.9 pecent; a decline in the non-Hispanic white population, from 40.6 percent to 36.4 percent; a continuing, albeit slight, fall in the non-Hispanic black population, from 6.7 percent to

6.54 percent; and a slight increase in the Asian population, from 10.9 percent to 11.8 percent.

These trends vary a great deal within the three zones, however. Table 7.1 shows changes in the racial and ethnic composition of the Los Angeles metro area for 1990, 2000, and 2006. Notably, in West of Downtown the non-Hispanic white population is barely changed (53.4 percent to 52.9 percent between 2000 and 2006); the Hispanic population increased only slightly (22.5 percent to 23.6 percent), the Asian population held steady (10.2 percent to 10.4 percent), and the non-Hispanic black population has continued to decline (13.2 percent to 12.1 percent).

However, as Table 7.2 shows, a striking development becomes clear if we examine only demographic changes involving those people aged 0 to 4 years old. West of Downtown, the proportion of non-Hispanic whites aged 0 to 4 increased markedly from 2000 to 2006, from 39.7 percent of all children to 47.6 percent.

Table 7.3 shows that the general patterns from 2000 to 2006 for the New York metropolitan region (the agglomeration that includes all our three zones) are similar to the Los Angeles statistical pattern: an increase in Hispanics, from 18.6 percent to 20.4 percent; a decrease in non-Hispanic whites (from 56.5 percent to 53.6 percent) and non-Hispanic blacks (from 17.1 percent to 16.6 percent), and an increase in the Asian population (from 7.2 percent to 8.8 percent). In Manhattan, by contrast, the number and proportion of non-Hispanic whites has increased from 46.6 percent to 48.7 percent.

Furthermore, as shown in Table 7.4, in Manhattan there is a very striking increase in the number and percent of children aged 0 to 4 who are non-Hispanic whites, from 34.8 percent to 44.4 percent. Thus, in the most desirable (or at least expensive) urban sections of both major metropolitan regions, there has been a marked increase in non-Hispanic white young children. In Manhattan there has also been a substantial increase in the number of children overall, from 76,300 in 2000 to 99,841 in 2006.

One trend that seems to be fueling the increases in the number of non-Hispanic white children in Manhattan and the West of Downtown area is the income gap with respect to sex for full-time workers aged 20 to 29. In

	Hispanic	White Non-Hispanic	Black Non-Hispanic	Asian and/or Pacific Islander Non-Hispanic	Other Race Non-Hispanic	American Indian/ Alaska Native Non-Hispanic	Total
West of Downtown							
1990	310,211	741,359	188,368	144,536	4,053	4,235	1,392,762
	22.3%	53.2%	13.5%	10.4%	0.3%	0.3%	
2000	304,148	721,032	178,794	137,530	4,237	4,520	1,350,261
	22.5%	53.4%	13.2%	10.2%	0.3%	0.3%	
2006	318,698	714,648	164,196	140,177	9,342	4,710	1,351,771
	23.6%	52.9%	12.1%	10.4%	0.7%	0.3%	
Rest of LA City							
1990	1,082,154	773,700	296,480	201,143	5,949	7,408	2,366,834
	45.7%	32.7%	12.5%	8.5%	0.3%	0.3%	
2000	1,453,865	669,601	267,812	267,715	4,098	7,476	2,670,567
	54.4%	25.1%	10.0%	10.0%	0.2%	0.3%	
2006	1,577,033	627,268	248,599	280,640	14,115	6,079	2,753,734
	57.3%	22.8%	9.0%	10.2%	0.5%	0.2%	
Rest of LA Metro							
1990	3,301,517	5,733,836	678,570	949,308	21,169	51,431	10,735,831
	30.8%	53.4%	6.3%	8.8%	0.2%	0.5%	
2000	4,819,633	5,261,530	824,619	1,377,531	19,422	52,286	12,355,021
	39.0%	42.6%	6.7%	11.1%	0.2%	0.4%	
2006	5,870,963	5,130,796	889,301	1,668,468	67,456	43,815	13,670,799
	42.9%	37.5%	6.5%	12.2%	0.5%	0.3%	
LA Metro Total							
1990	4,693,882	7,248,895	1,163,418	1,294,987	31,171	63,074	14,495,427
	32.4%	50.0%	8.0%	8.9%	0.2%	0.4%	
2000	6,577,646	6,652,163	1,271,225	1,782,776	27,757	64,282	16,375,849
	40.2%	40.6%	7.8%	10.9%	0.2%	0.4%	
2006	7,766,694	6,472,712	1,302,096	2,089,285	90,913	54,604	17,776,304
	43.7%	36.4%	7.3%	11.8%	0.5%	0.3%	

Sources: Analysis of PUMS data 1990, 2000, and 2006 from IPUMS files available from Minnesota Population Center. County Boundary files from the National Historical Geographic Information System and PUMA boundaries from US Bureau of the Census.

Table 7.1 Changing racial and Hispanic composition of the Los Angeles metropolitan area and various regions, 1990, 2000, and 2006.

	Hispanic	White Non-Hispanic	Black Non-Hispanic	Asian and/or Pacific Islander Non-Hispanic	Other Race Non-Hispanic	American Indian/ Alaska Native Non-Hispanic	Total
West of Downtown							
1990	29,456	29,673	13,104	139	7,447	604	80,423
	36.6%	36.9%	16.3%	0.2%	9.3%	0.8%	
2000	27,696	28,944	10,439	106	5,206	439	72,830
	38.0%	39.7%	14.3%	0.1%	7.1%	0.6%	
2006	23,515	35,865	8,674	218	5,999	1,009	75,280
	31.2%	47.6%	11.5%	0.3%	8.0%	1.3%	
Rest of LA City							
1990	124,550	42,447	26,561	553	12,644	1,282	208,037
	59.9%	20.4%	12.8%	0.3%	6.1%	0.6%	
2000	156,817	31,396	18,934	474	13,354	414	221,389
	70.8%	14.2%	8.6%	0.2%	6.0%	0.2%	
2006	165,435	27,708	15,453	742	14,208	1,583	225,129
	73.5%	12.3%	6.9%	0.3%	6.3%	0.7%	
Rest of LA Metro							
1990	384,356	384,828	66,040	3,054	70,900	3,508	912,686
	42.1%	42.2%	7.2%	0.3%	7.8%	0.4%	
2000	528,592	283,944	69,993	2,762	76,416	1,850	963,557
	54.9%	29.5%	7.3%	0.3%	7.9%	0.2%	
2006	605,330	251,016	72,881	779	88,592	6,439	1,025,037
	59.1%	24.5%	7.1%	0.1%	8.6%	0.6%	
LA Metro Total							
1990	538,362	456,948	105,705	3,746	90,991	5,394	1,201,146
	44.8%	38.0%	8.8%	0.3%	7.6%	0.4%	
2000	713,105	344,284	99,366	3,342	94,976	2,703	1,257,776
	56.7%	27.4%	7.9%	0.3%	7.6%	0.2%	
2006	794,280	314,589	97,008	1,739	108,799	9,031	1,325,446
	59.9%	23.7%	7.3%	0.1%	8.2%	0.7%	

Sources: Analysis of PUMS data 1990, 2000, and 2006 from IPUMS files available from Minnesota Population Center. County Boundary files from the National Historical Geographic Information System and PUMA boundaries from US Bureau of the Census.

Table 7.2 Changing racial and Hispanic composition, population aged 0 to 4, of the Los Angeles metropolitan area and various regions, 1990, 2000, and 2006.

	Hispanic	White Non-Hispanic	Black Non-Hispanic	Asian and/or Pacific Islander Non-Hispanic	Other Race Non-Hispanic	American Indian/ Alaska Native Non-Hispanic	Total
Manhattan							
1990	375,850	723,673	263,668	106,752	3,134	2,223	1,475,300
	25.5%	49.1%	17.9%	7.2%	0.2%	0.2%	
2000	427,171	720,145	246,656	146,621	6,359	3,030	1,549,982
	27.6%	46.6%	15.9%	9.5%	0.4%	0.2%	
2006	409,036	783,850	237,809	173,689	4,701	1,666	1,610,751
	25.4%	48.7%	14.8%	10.8%	0.3%	0.1%	
Outer Boroughs							
1990	1,348,962	2,441,499	1,599,712	387,850	14,576	12,207	5,804,806
	23.2%	42.1%	27.6%	6.7%	0.3%	0.2%	
2000	1,723,794	2,186,564	1,794,072	678,676	51,889	19,782	6,454,777
	26.7%	33.9%	27.8%	10.5%	0.8%	0.3%	
2006	1,867,604	2,099,438	1,752,744	791,233	76,308	15,500	6,602,827
	28.3%	31.8%	26.5%	12.0%	1.2%	0.2%	
Suburbs							
1990	990,062	8,686,800	1,194,912	364,654	13,663	15,390	11,265,481
	8.8%	77.1%	10.6%	3.2%	0.1%	0.1%	
2000	1,601,542	8,511,008	1,418,380	639,948	30,917	18,774	12,220,569
	13.1%	69.6%	11.6%	5.2%	0.3%	0.2%	
2006	1,965,486	8,244,249	1,452,716	864,376	54,943	14,418	12,596,188
	15.6%	65.5%	11.5%	6.9%	0.4%	0.1%	
NY Metro							
1990	2,714,874	11,851,972	3,058,292	859,256	31,373	29,820	18,545,587
	14.6%	63.9%	16.5%	4.6%	0.2%	0.2%	
2000	3,752,507	11,417,717	3,459,108	1,465,245	89,165	41,586	20,225,328
	18.6%	56.5%	17.1%	7.2%	0.4%	0.2%	
2006	4,242,126	11,127,537	3,443,269	1,829,298	135,952	31,584	20,809,766
	20.4%	53.6%	16.6%	8.8%	0.7%	0.2%	

Sources: Analysis of PUMS data 1990, 2000, and 2006 from IPUMS files available from Minnesota Population Center. County Boundary files from the National Historical Geographic Information System and PUMA boundaries from US Bureau of the Census.

Table 7.3 Changing racial and Hispanic composition of the New York metropolitan area and various regions, 1990, 2000, and 2006.

	Hispanic	White Non-Hispanic	Black Non-Hispanic	Asian and/or Pacific Islander Non-Hispanic	Other Race Non-Hispanic	American Indian/ Alaska Native Non-Hispanic	Total
Manhattan							
1990	28,338	24,443	19,609	52	5,113	486	78,041
	36.3%	31.3%	25.1%	0.1%	6.6%	0.6%	
2000	29,413	26,556	13,780	127	6,019	405	76,300
	38.5%	34.8%	18.1%	0.2%	7.9%	0.5%	
2006	28,428	44,339	16,665	182	9,846	381	99,841
	28.5%	44.4%	16.7%	0.2%	9.9%	0.4%	
Outer Boroughs							
1990	128,521	128,056	131,638	1,015	27,474	4,683	421,387
	30.5%	30.4%	31.2%	0.2%	6.5%	1.1%	
2000	151,582	116,952	136,941	1,925	44,160	5,174	456,734
	33.2%	25.6%	30.0%	0.4%	9.7%	1.1%	
2006	156,940	123,581	134,606	697	54,860	2,844	473,528
	33.1%	26.1%	28.4%	0.1%	11.6%	0.6%	
Suburbs							
1990	87,834	543,396	95,699	822	29,602	2,345	759,698
	11.6%	71.5%	12.6%	0.1%	3.9%	0.3%	
2000	141,464	530,822	111,928	1,258	47,079	3,142	835,693
	16.9%	63.5%	13.4%	0.2%	5.6%	0.4%	
2006	178,883	460,157	103,654	1,241	54,204	4,931	803,070
	22.3%	57.3%	12.9%	0.2%	6.7%	0.6%	
NY Metro							
1990	244,693	695,895	246,946	1,889	62,189	7,514	1,259,126
	19.4%	55.3%	19.6%	0.2%	4.9%	0.6%	
2000	322,459	674,330	262,649	3,310	97,258	8,721	1,368,727
	23.6%	49.3%	19.2%	0.2%	7.1%	0.6%	
2006	364,251	628,077	254,925	2,120	118,910	8,156	1,376,439
	26.5%	45.6%	18.5%	0.2%	8.6%	0.6%	

Sources: Analysis of PUMS data 1990, 2000, and 2006 from IPUMS files available from Minnesota Population Center. County Boundary files from the National Historical Geographic Information System and PUMA boundaries from US Bureau of the Census.

Table 7.4 Changing racial and Hispanic composition, population aged 0 to 4, of the New York metropolitan area and various regions, 1990, 2000, and 2006.

both metropolitan areas, younger women workers earned higher salaries and wages than did younger male workers.[16] This seems to be largely due to the increasing gap with respect to education between men and women. When one examines the household income of young children, it is clear that regardless of race and ethnic backgrounds, there was a rapid growth of income for these families from 2000 through 2006, from $54,450 to $81,502.

These trends represent a major reversal of a long-standing pattern and require a rethinking of the basic storylines about cities and suburbs. Women are now in the labor force in large numbers. In the 1948 classic *Mr. Blanding Builds His Dream House,* Cary Grant plays Mr. Blanding, an advertising man, and Myrna Loy his wife Muriel, who decide to move with their two children to a house in Connecticut. It isn't quite the dream move they expected: Muriel wrestles with the two children and housing renovations, Mr. Blanding with the travails of a long commute. Today Muriel would more likely be working in her own professional-level job and would eschew the commute, if she could. The city would be a realistic option.

Income, Rent, and Housing Bubbles

Examining income trends in more detail in both metro areas, only in the preferred areas were there real income gains. (See Table 7.5.) From 2000 to 2006, median household income rose by 3.5 percent West of Downtown and by 8.4 percent in Manhattan. There are two key points here. First, there was a major housing bubble in both regions from 2000 to 2006, but the overall bubble was far greater in the overall Los Angeles region than in New York. In New York for all three of our areas, house values rose from between 42 percent and 48 percent, while in Los Angeles for all three of our areas house values rose from between 106 percent and 123 percent. Only in Manhattan did house values rise substantially in the decade before 2000, rising 29 percent. In that sense, Manhattan has had its own housing bubble.

In all three sections of each region, rents rose sharply during the period 2000 to 2006, with rises ranging from 12 to 22 percent. Table 7.5 shows the more or less stagnant median household income in all sectors of the region except the preferred sections, the economic pressure on renters is apparent.

	1990	2000	2006	% change 1990 to 2000	% change 2000 to 2006
Median Household Income (2006 Dollars)					
LA Metro	$58,756	$54,934	$55,341	-6.5%	0.7%
West of Downtown	$55,277	$54,450	$56,347	-1.5%	3.5%
Rest of LA County	$48,774	$41,140	$40,248	-15.7%	-2.2%
Rest of LA Metro	$61,780	$58,201	$58,359	-5.8%	0.3%
NY Metro	$61,780	$60,500	$60,170	-2.1%	-0.5%
Manhattan	$52,026	$55,297	$59,969	6.3%	8.4%
Outer Boroughs	$45,661	$42,592	$42,763	-6.7%	0.4%
Suburbs	$72,933	$72,600	$70,433	-0.5%	-3.0%
Median House Value (2006 Dollars)					
LA Metro	$270,815	$215,514	$480,155	-20.4%	122.8%
West of Downtown	$465,297	$358,456	$799,455	-23.0%	123.0%
Rest of LA County	$307,932	$231,046	$478,009	-25.0%	106.9%
Rest of LA Metro	$277,953	$218,391	$486,168	-21.4%	122.6%
NY Metro	$279,341	$295,787	$422,543	5.9%	42.9%
Manhattan	$395,923	$510,862	$756,431	29.0%	48.1%
Outer Boroughs	$279,909	$285,131	$406,222	1.9%	42.5%
Suburbs	$280,364	$304,315	$433,570	8.5%	42.5%
Median Gross Rent (2006 Dollars)					
LA Metro	$995	$855	$1,036	-14.1%	21.2%
West of Downtown	$996	$927	$1,097	-7.0%	18.3%
Rest of LA County	$882	$731	$885	-17.2%	21.1%
Rest of LA Metro	$1,026	$882	$1,077	-14.1%	22.2%
NY Metro	$841	$866	$996	3.1%	15.0%
Manhattan	$791	$931	$1,097	17.6%	17.9%
Outer Boroughs	$753	$805	$926	7.0%	15.0%
Suburbs	$970	$927	$1,046	-4.4%	12.8%

Sources: Analysis of PUMS data 1990, 2000, and 2006 from IPUMS files available from Minnesota Population Center. County Boundary files from the National Historical Geographic Information System and PUMA boundaries from US Bureau of the Census.

Table 7.5 Median household income, median house value, and median gross rent for the Los Angeles and New York metropolitan areas and various regions, 1990, 2000, and 2006.

This review of income, house value, and rental trends suggests a key basis of the now collapsed housing bubble. Overall in the region, house values rose rapidly from 2000 to 2006, as did the cost of renting, while income for most people did not substantially increase. The likelihood that those who wished to enter the housing market would be enticed by a loan that would allow them to borrow above their means is apparent.

Does "the Ghetto" Remain an Appropriate Term? Is Harlem a "Ghetto"?

One of the most distinctive features associated with American cities after World War II was the ghetto, an inner-city section inhabited primarily by blacks living in areas of concentrated poverty. A current debate about the term *ghetto* reveals how American cities are changing. The long-standing movement of Latinos into ghetto areas long inhabited by blacks in poverty, especially into Central Los Angeles, and the well-publicized movement of some (non-Latino) whites into Harlem, reveals the magnitude and speed of the changes. What Latinos call "barrios," which translates roughly as "neighborhoods," are not equivalent to the category of ghetto, with its various negative connotations. Also, in Harlem the rapid increase in the number of properties that sell for well over $1 million raises obvious issues and questions about the suitability of the concept ghetto.

Harlem: Demographic Changes, 1910–1980

Major changes in Central Harlem and New York City from 1910 to 2006 are shown in Table 7.6. "Central Harlem" is defined as set out by Gilbert Osofsky in his 1966 book *Harlem: The Making of a Ghetto.*[17] Central Harlem is basically north of Central Park and east of Morningside and St. Nicholas Avenues. The southern edge starts at 96th Street on the East Side; at Fifth Avenue and Central Park it goes up to 110th, and then cuts over to 106th Street on the West Side. The northern boundary in most places is 155th Street, though it extends a bit further up on the East Side.

In 1910, Central Harlem was about 10 percent black, Greater Harlem was a little more than 4 percent black, while the rest of New York City was

	Central Harlem	Greater Harlem	Rest of NYC			Central Harlem	Greater Harlem	Rest of NYC
1910					**1970**			
Black	9.89%	4.28%	1.73%		Black	95.42%	63.53%	18.48%
White	90.01%	95.64%	98.12%		White	4.28%	34.44%	79.82%
Other	0.10%	0.08%	0.15%		Other	0.29%	2.02%	1.70%
Total	181,949	593,598	3,191,962		Total	157,178	430,567	7,083,455
1920					**1980**			
Black	32.43%	12.28%	1.46%		Black -NH	94.17%	58.76%	22.20%
White	67.47%	87.60%	98.39%		Hispanic	4.32%	28.46%	19.45%
Other	0.15%	0.14%	0.15%		White-NH	0.62%	10.29%	53.98%
Total	216,026	652,529	4,767,727		Other-NH	0.89%	2.49%	4.37%
					Total	108,236	339,490	6,732,149
1930					**1990**			
Black	70.18%	34.82%	1.99%		Black -NH	87.55%	52.37%	23.93%
White	29.43%	64.78%	97.80%		Hispanic	10.14%	33.94%	23.90%
Other	0.39%	0.40%	0.21%		White-NH	1.50%	10.85%	44.74%
Total	209,663	580,277	6,168,984		Other-NH	0.80%	2.85%	7.43%
					Total	101,026	334,076	6,988,199
1940					**2000**			
Black	89.31%	48.32%	2.65%		Black -NH	77.49%	46.03%	23.67%
White	10.48%	51.38%	97.10%		Hispanic	16.82%	38.02%	26.47%
Other	0.21%	0.31%	0.25%		White-NH	2.07%	10.45%	36.11%
Total	221,974	576,846	6,677,187		Other-NH	3.62%	5.50%	13.75%
					Total	109,091	354,057	7,654,221
1950					**2006**			
Black	98.07%	57.52%	5.64%		Black -NH	69.27%	40.54%	23.40%
White	1.76%	41.89%	94.03%		Hispanic	18.58%	38.24%	27.22%
Other	0.17%	0.60%	0.33%		White-NH	6.55%	14.80%	36.06%
Total	237,468	593,246	7,078,650		Other-NH	5.60%	6.42%	13.33%
					Total	118,111	374,854	7,838,724
1960								
Black	96.71%	58.53%	10.71%					
White	2.94%	40.55%	88.62%					
Other	0.35%	0.92%	0.67%					
Total	163,632	467,634	6,829,199					

Sources: 1910 to 1940, Census Tract Data from National Historical Geogrpahical Information System, Compiled by Andrew A. Beveridge and Co-workers; 1950, Ellen M. Bogue File, as edited by Andrew A. Beveridge and coworkers; 1960 through 2000, Tabulated Census Data from National Historical Geographic Information System; 2006 Data from American Community Survey, U.S. Bureau of the Census. Boundary Files from National Historical Geographic Infomration System 1910 to 2000, U.S. Bureau of the Census, 2006. All data and boundary files available from Minnesota Population Center. Since results are tabulated from the sources indicated, they may not necessarily match Census published figures for population and race.

Table 7.6 Population and racial composition of Harlem and New York City, 1910 to 2006.

less than 2 percent black. By 1930, during the Harlem Renaissance, Central Harlem had become a definably black area in a largely white city. Central Harlem was over 70 percent black and Greater Harlem was about 35 percent black, but the rest of New York City was still less than 2 percent black. By 1950, Central Harlem was about 98 percent black, while Greater Harlem was 57.5 percent black. Central Harlem remained almost entirely black through 1980, with the black population never dropping below 94 percent. In the early years, Harlem was quite diverse economically, but as the great migration of blacks from the American South continued, and the size of the black population expanded, an area of sharply bounded concentrated poverty developed.

The period from 1950 to 1980 was the "classic" period of the American urban ghetto. Over these three decades, Harlem went into a steep population decline. Central Harlem lost more than half of its population, dropping from roughly 237,000 to 101,000, and Greater Harlem also saw its population drop, from roughly 593,000 to 339,000. This also marked the era of urban renewal, and many older housing units were razed, either for public housing projects or for other apartment developments, though the new developments did not come close to housing the same number of people that were displaced. At the same time, areas farther out, such as southeast Queens, attracted affluent black families. The extreme concentration of black families in poverty or relative poverty in the postwar era made the term *ghetto* into a mainstay of American political discourse.

A review of recent demographic changes in Harlem also makes clear why it is less often referred to as a ghetto than in the past. The map displayed in Figure 7.6 shows the relationship between Central and Greater Harlem.

Since 1980, Central Harlem has become less black. By 2006, the black population had dropped to 69 percent, just below its 1930 level of 70 percent. At the same time, white and Hispanic populations have increased. Hispanics accounted for 4.3 percent of Harlem residents in 1980, the first year they were classified separately in the U.S. Census. In 2006, that number reached 18.6 percent. In 1980, there were just 672 non-Hispanic whites in Central Harlem, constituting about 0.6 percent of the population. By 2006, there were 7,741, or about 6.6 percent. Further, the non-Hispanic white

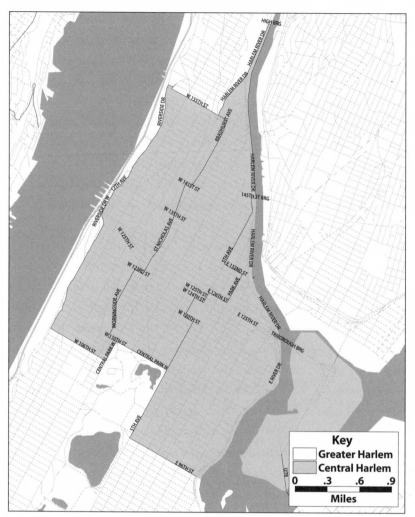

Figure 7.6 Central and Greater Harlem area, delineated.

population that had moved to Harlem by 2000 was distributed in many different places throughout Harlem.

It appears that areas of Harlem are sought after once again. By 2000 and 2006, there were areas of some highly affluent black and white residents. Median household income in Central Harlem rose from about $13,765 in 1950 to over $26,161 in 2006, in 2006 dollars. (This figure is, however, still well below the median of $46,285 for the rest of New York City.) The traditional townhouse areas around Strivers Row, Sugar Hill, and Marcus Garvey Park have undergone a rebirth. At the height of the housing boom, in 2006, some sold for $1 million to $3 million. Stores and restaurants catering to the affluent have opened in West Harlem, and Magic Johnson opened a Starbucks and a Multiplex on 125th Street, near where former President Bill Clinton has his office suite. A planned expansion of Columbia University will bring more change to West Harlem.

Figure 7.7 compares the concentration with respect to the black population in 1980 and 2000 at the tract level. As the map reveals, the deconcentration of the black population in Harlem is happening in many different areas. It is not that the non-African American population, which is largely non-Hispanic, is moving into enclaves, but rather that many parts of Harlem are becoming less black. Of course, the large stock of public housing and the relatively low income of many residents ensure that high levels of poverty will continue to be a feature of Harlem. Harlem is not likely to lose its black majority or its high concentrations of poverty anytime soon. Even so, it no longer displays the features associated with the postwar American ghetto.

The "Greening" of Los Angeles and New York

Policy initiatives may be leading in the direction of convergence between the center and the periphery, and between metropolitan areas. What social and economic change does not accomplish, public policy often does. The current mayors of New York and Los Angeles have both placed development at the top of their agendas, and in both cases development has often proceeded under the mantle of environmentalism. Antonio Villaraigosa, inaugurated as mayor in July 2005, proclaimed as one of his key goals that "Los Angeles become the greenest big city in America." On a parallel track, two years later, in April 2007, Mayor Bloomberg's administration published its ambitious plan for managing New York City's population growth, which is projected to grow from its current 8.2 million to 9.0 million by 2030. Almost every page of the "Plan NYC: A Greener, Greater New York" makes a bow in the direction of greening the city and making it more environmentally

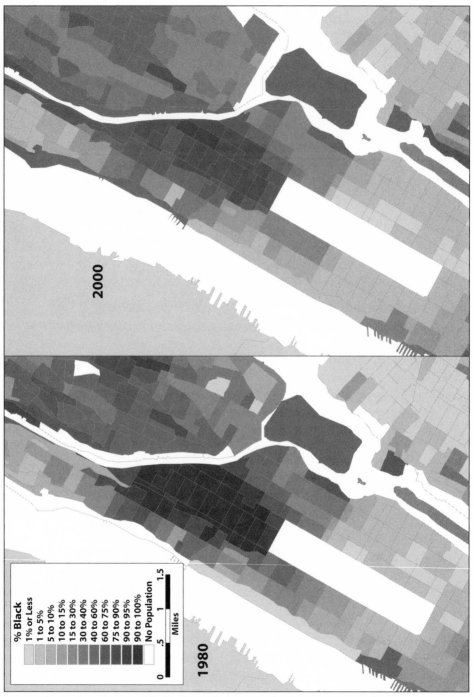

Figure 7.7 Percentage of the black population in Harlem by trace, 1980 and 2000.

sustainable. Announcing itself as "the most sweeping plan to enhance New York's urban environment in the city's modern history," the plan proposed projects to enhance the quality of the city's land, air, water, energy, and transportation, and asserted (not to be outdone by Los Angeles) that New York "can become a model for cities in the twenty-first century."[18] Nonetheless, many of the details of Plan NYC focused on increasing transportation, power and other infrastructural resources, while clearing the way for massive development in many parts of the city through zoning changes.

Environmentalism raises acute political questions—basically what to aim for and how to achieve it. These political issues are apparent in both cities. In Los Angeles, Villaraigosa appointed a slate of new environmental activists and policy people to powerful commissions such as the city's Department of Water and Power and the Harbor Department, which guides the nation's largest port complex. He also rolled out a plan for renewable energy and a climate plan to reduce Los Angeles's overall carbon footprint 30 percent below 1990 levels by the year 2030. The Port of Los Angeles and the Port of Long Beach collaborated for the first time on a shared air policy, passing its first Harbor-wide Clean Air Action Plan (CAAP), with the city adopting a Clean Truck Plan, a key objective in the CAAP that transforms the current trucking system into a system requiring licensed motor carriers to hire employees instead of relying on independent contractors.

As these initiatives were rolled out, the mayor began to confront the political realities of governing in a city and a region with some of the most protracted environmental problems in the country. At the same time, the movement activists began to confront the realities of how to continue their own activism and push their own agendas while positioning themselves in relation to a mayor who had emerged from the same movements and embraced a progressive (including a strong environmental) agenda when he took office.

The Case of the High Line

In New York, environmentalism has also become a key element in development politics. However, environmentalist values, when successfully implemented, also risk becoming a wedge for raising land values to levels affordable only by the most affluent residents. The High Line project provides a fascinating case study showing the spatial development of urban areas is affected as much by organized policy as by economic and social trends. It also shows the difficulty such organized, policy-oriented activity can have in producing the intended, and not unintended, results.

The High Line is an elevated freight rail line that was originally built between 1930 and 1934 on the Far West Side of Manhattan in order to remove dangerous trains from Tenth Avenue by raising them up. High Line trains served the key function of bringing freight, food, and other merchandise, after it had been offloaded from the waterfront, to factories and warehouses along New York City's busy industrial West Side. It ran from 34th Street (now the Hudson Rail Yards) down to Spring Street, just south of Canal Street.

By the 1960s, the growth of trucking made the High Line obsolete. Its last freight run was in 1980, when it took a carload of frozen turkeys to the Gansevoort Meat Market. The High Line's southern part, below 16th Street, was demolished in the 1980s. From then until 1999, when two young environmentalists proposed turning it into an elevated park, it languished. No longer necessary for its original purpose, yet valuable as an unobstructed right-of-way through Manhattan, it lingered on, its tracks overrun with wild vegetation. At the time of the movement to turn it into a park, it was owned by Conrail and managed by Conrail shareholder CSX Corporation.

In 1999, a group of neighborhood residents, businesses, design professionals, and civic organizations joined forces to form Friends of the High Line, a not-for-profit (501c3) organization, hoping to save the remaining 1.5 miles of track. The key figures were two Chelsea residents, Joshua David and Robert Hammond, who first met at a Community Board meeting where the High Line was discussed and its owner, CSX Corporation, which was opposed to tearing down the railroad, proposed as one of several alternatives the park conversion idea. David and Hammond discovered that they both liked this idea, and then came across the precedent of Paris's Promenade Plantée. The Promenade Plantée is an unused rail viaduct whose conversion to a park was in process in 1999 (the first section had only just opened). It has since become one of Paris's most popular parks. Hammond believed that the High Line could improve on the Promenade Plantée design.

Still, in 1999, the High Line's prospects were dim. Many residents saw it as a blight. As far back as 1992, the railroad had been put under an order, won by the Chelsea Property Owners, to demolish the structure. The Chelsea Property Owners consisted of those who owned property next to and under the High Line and were eager to develop their property. They had been formed by a parking-lot and storage-facility operator in the area, around 1990, to force CSX Transportation to tear down the structure. The actual demolition, however, had been held up because of disagreement among the Chelsea Property Owners about how the demolition costs would be shared.

Hammond had helpful connections. His Princeton roommate had been Gifford Miller, the president of the city council, so Miller favored the High Line early on. The Friends of the High Line created a powerful board, which included, for example, Phil Aarons, a principal in Millennium Partners, a real estate development firm. Amanda Burden, later chair of the Department of City Planning, who lived in the Village nearby, was also an early supporter. The Friends of the High Line commissioned landscape photographer Joel Sternfeld to take photos for a book they produced celebrating the High Line and especially the wild vegetation that grew along its tracks. In 2001 the High Line got a big boost when all six mayoral candidates declared support for the project.

In December 2001, in the final week of his administration, aware that incoming mayor Bloomberg had promised to save the High Line, Mayor Giuliani signed a demolition agreement with the Chelsea Property Owners seeking to compel CSX to demolish the High Line. He was doubtless moved to act by the Chelsea Property Owners, who were more eager than ever to kill the movement to preserve the High Line. In response, the Friends, joined by the city council and by Manhattan Borough President C. Virginia Fields, filed a lawsuit to require the High Line demolition to go through the city's review process, the Uniform Land-Use Review Procedure. This gave the Friends several months of breathing space and ultimately a victory when the courts ruled in their favor in March 2002.

Newly elected Mayor Bloomberg had been a big High Line supporter during his campaign, but then in early 2002 he said that the serious economic problems triggered by 9/11 meant that all bets were off. The city requested an economic feasibility study and Deputy Mayor for Economic Development Dan Doctoroff said city support would depend entirely on the economic case. "Does it make sense for the city to support the High Line financially?" In response, Hammond and the Friends showed that, over a twenty-year period, the revenue to the city would add up to an estimated $140 million, over twice the cost of the $65 million price tag for development. The Bloomberg administration subsequently reaffirmed its support for developing the High Line.

On December 17, 2002, a year after Bloomberg's election as mayor, the city filed an application to the Federal Surface Transportation Board (STB) to begin negotiations to transform the High Line into an elevated public walkway. To accomplish this, it formally requested a Certificate of Interim Trail Use, or CITU. The biggest obstacle remained the Chelsea Property Owners, which insisted that the structure was a dangerous eyesore and derided the Friends of the High Line as "romantics." The Chelsea Property Owners had considerable influence with STB, and by 2003, word had come from Washington that the STB would not grant the Certificate of Interim Trail Use to allow the High Line to convert to a park unless the Chelsea Property Owners were compensated.

The eventual key to winning over the Chelsea Property Owners was the West Chelsea Rezoning, which Amanda Burden first proposed as an idea in September 2003. The rezoning gave the Chelsea Property Owners an alternative method of making an equivalent profit to what they would have made if they had been allowed to develop their properties adjacent to and under the High Line. The rezoning would allow them to sell their air rights to special "receiving sites"—basically potential condo sites—that did not adjoin the High Line though they were in the area. Actually, new development could still also occur adjacent to the High Line, but subject to a series of building bulk and use controls to encourage connections to the High Line and the preservation of light, air, and views. Very tall buildings could be put up only in the special "receiving zones" some distance from the High Line. As a result, the Chelsea Property Owners dropped their opposition to the High Line, and the Certificate of Interim Trail Use was granted on June 13, 2005, nineteen days after, and clearly as a result of, the Department of City Planning's adoption of the West Chelsea Rezoning on May 25, 2005.

The High Line created enormous excitement and buzz for several years before an inch of it had opened. Advocating for the project in a *New York Times* op-ed piece in 2003 while the struggle for approval was still under-way, Kenneth Jackson said: " Just as everyone loves Central Park because its meadows and glades allow us to forget that we are in the midst of a huge city, a High Line Park could become a public open space of an altogether different sort, a place that celebrates density and diversity, that shows us how nature can persevere in even the grittiest circumstances, that enables us to understand history not through a book or through a movie but through our own eyes." After the last major approval hurdle — obtaining the Certificate of Interim Trail Use — was crossed, the High Line was also widely hailed as proof that New York could still pull off visionary projects despite the complex approval processes always entailed.

So successful was the High Line idea that the chair of the city planning department, Amanda Burden, received a planning prize in April 2006 from the American Planning Association for the new West Chelsea zoning district. Still, by early 2008, the High Line, which had not yet opened, had already triggered a frenzy of condominium development, driven basically by the belief that rich people would pay huge sums for residences with views of the new park.

In an April 2007 article for *New York Magazine,* journalist Adam Stern-bergh brilliantly captured the unease with which many people now viewed the flood of condominium developments associated with the High Line.

What you'll get, in other words, is a thoughtfully conceived, beautifully designed *simulation* of the former High Line—and what more, really, do we ask for in our city right now? Isn't that what we want: that each new bistro that opens should give us the *feeling* of a cozy neighborhood joint, right down to the expertly battered wooden tables and exquisitely selected faucet knobs? And that each new clothing boutique that opens in the space where the dry cleaner's used to be—you know, the one driven out by rising rents—should retain that charming dry cleaner's signage, so you can be *reconnected* to the city's hardscrabble past even as you shop for a $300 blouse? And that each dazzling, glass-skinned condo tower, with the up-to-date amenities and Hudson views and *en suite freaking parking*, should be nestled in a charming, grit-chic neighborhood, full of old warehouses and reclaimed gallery spaces and retroactively trendy chunks of rusted urban blight? Isn't that exactly what we ask New York to be right now?

The High Line . . . will one day look to us like a monument to the time we live in now. A time of great optimism for the city's future. A time of essentially unfettered growth. A time when a rusted rail bed could beget a park and a park could beget a millionaire's wonderland. And a time when the city was, for many, never safer, never more prosperous, and never more likely to evoke an unshakable suspicion: that more and more, New York has become like a gorgeous antique that someone bought, refurbished, and restored, then offered back to you at a price you couldn't possibly afford.[19]

The first section of the High Line opened in June 2009 and was an instant success, drawing enormous crowds and becoming a major tourist attraction. By chance, it opened at a time when New York City's real estate market had entered a severe down-turn (part of the national financial and economic crisis) and there were several temporarily abandoned construction sites nearby. This timing probably blunted the critique of the relation between the High Line and property development.

The High Line case also illustrates the power of public policies to dramatically alter land-use patterns. The lesson is that in New York, and elsewhere, it is essential to understand that the spatial patterning of urban regions is not determined solely by large-scale social and economic trends; if it were, it would be easier to devise general theories of the city.

Conclusion

We have argued that the New York and Los Angeles schools of urban analysis were each rooted in a context of urban decline that is no longer valid. Instead, the fate of cities such as New York and Los Angeles is fluid and constantly changing, subject to multiple and simultaneous forces that cannot be easily anticipated.

We have, therefore, taken the opportunity to sketch out some new trends and issues. Whether these will eventually coalesce into a major direction or school is just unclear. There is some slowdown or reversal of white flight, at least for those able to afford the most desirable sections of each city, with the effects clearest when one looks at the rising numbers of non-Hispanic white children in the most desirable sections of each city. There was the massive rise in housing prices in each region from 2000 to 2006 (overall much faster in the Los Angeles region than in the New York region, though Manhattan's prices have been rising far longer than elsewhere in either region). This, together with the failure of most people's income to keep pace with these housing price increases, provided an important underpinning of the now collapsed housing bubble. There are the changing demographics of areas such as Harlem, which raise the question of whether the term *ghetto* remains an appropriate description. Finally, there is the case of the High Line in New York, which poses key issues for the burgeoning environmental movement, including the dilemma of using public funds for a project that then makes a section of the city so desirable that those with the greatest economic resources (the wealthy) move there and are most able to enjoy it.

These observations have serious implications for the project of theorizing the city. If cities no longer present several of the major features that produced a classic discourse about them, it makes sense to think that urban scholarship will regroup and reassess. Finally, the demographic changes and policy initiatives we have presented reveal that any new paradigm must account for the interaction between social and economic processes and the policies that attempt to give them direction.

Notes

The authors would like to acknowledge National Science Foundation support for aspects of the paper presented here (awards 0919993 DUE and 0940804 SBE).

1. David Halle, ed., *New York and Los Angeles: Politics, Society, and Culture — A Comparative View* (Chicago: University of Chicago Press, 2003).

2. Jane Jacobs, *The Death and Life of Great American Cities* (New York: Random House, 1961).

3. Kenneth Jackson, *Crabgrass Frontier: The Suburbanization of the United States* (New York: Oxford University Press, 1985).

4. Robert Stern, Thomas Mellins, and David Fishman, *Architecture and Urbanism between the Second World War and the Bicentennial* (1960; New York: Monacelli Press, 1997).

5. Richard Sennett, *The Conscience of the Eye* (New York: Alfred Knopf, 1990).

6. William H. Whyte, *Rediscovering the Center* (New York: Doubleday, 1988).

7. Sharon Zukin, *Loft Living: Culture and Capital in Urban Change* (New Brunswick, N.J.: Rutgers University Press, 1989).

8. Joel Garreau, *Edge City: Life on the New Frontier* (New York: Doubleday, 1988).

9. Jennifer Wolch, *The Shadow State* (New York: Foundation Center, 1990).

10. Allen J. Scott and Edward W. Soja, eds., *The City: Los Angeles and Urban Theory at the End of the Twentieth Century* (Berkeley: University of California Press, 1996).

11. Robert Fishman, *Bourgeois Utopias: The Rise and Fall of Suburbia* (New York: Basic Books, 1987).

12. Michael Dear, *The Postmodern Urban Condition* (Oxford: Blackwell, 2000).

13. The three areas of each metropolitan area were defined in terms of PUMAs. PUMAs are Public Use Microdata Areas and contain a population of at least one hundred thousand. Because of their size, they give a general idea of the distribution of race and Hispanic population. PUMAS are the only geographic unit from the American Community Survey (the large, yearly survey that is the replacement for the Census long form) that allows for an accurate analysis of the metro areas.

14. Robert Beauregard, *When America Became Suburban* (Minneapolis: University of Minnesota Press, 2006).

15. Conor Dougherty, "The End of White Flight," *Wall Street Journal,* July 19, 2008; Sam Roberts, "'White Flight' Has Reversed, Census Finds," *New York Times,* September 23, 2008.

16. Andrew Beveridge, "No Quick Riches for New York's 'Twentysomethings,'" *Gotham Gazette,* June 2007.

17. Gilbert Osofsky, *Harlem: The Making of a Ghetto: Negro New York 1890–1930* (New York: Harper and Row, 1963).

18. New York City Department of City Planning, *Plan NYC: A Greener, Greater New York* (2006), http://www.nyc.gov/html/planyc2030/html/downloads/the-plan.shtml.

19. Adam Sternbergh, "The High Line: It Brings Good Things to Life," *New York Magazine,* April 29, 2007.

8

School Is Out
The Case of New York City
■ John Hull Mollenkopf

> New York is nothing like Paris; it is nothing like London; and it is not
> Spokane multiplied by sixty, or Detroit multiplied by four. It is the loftiest
> of cities . . . Manhattan has been compelled to expand skyward because of
> the absence of any other direction in which to grow.
> —E. B. White, *Here Is New York*, 1949

Is There a New York School of Urbanism?

Los Angeles, for Michael Dear, is all about the central importance of the
deconcentration and fragmentation of social and political activities within
a highly dispersed city-region, sometimes in "mutant" forms like gated
communities. Viewing the L.A. region as the archetype of the postmodern epoch, he arrives at the distinctive proposition that urban periphery is
now organizing the center. In his words, "the direction of *causality* is from
periphery to center, even if (as often happens) this finds expression as an
absence of pressure or direction."[1] Old urban power relations, he thinks,
have melted away in a postmodern welter of new possibilities. From such
seeds, he and Jennifer Wolch, Ed Soja, Mike Davis, and Allen Scott are said
to have grown a Los Angeles School of urban studies.

Many people, including me, think that New York City, by contrast, is all
about how the dense concentration of information exchange and analysis,
decision making, and deal making makes New York a central node not only
in the life of the region and the nation, but the globe. This concentration is

housed within an institutional environment characterized by a strong local government and is surrounded by dense residential neighborhoods where personal interactions between unlike people are more or less compulsory, as distinguished from the autocentric, detached, politically fragmented, and gated living in Los Angeles. The immensity of New York City's economy and its elaborate division of labor foster a vast array of small worlds, each attaining a scale not often found elsewhere. But do these distinctive characteristics provide the intellectual kernel for a New York School?

David Halle argues that a focus on the vitality of neighborhood life and the superiority of urban over suburban living,[2] as exemplified by the work of Jane Jacobs or Richard Sennett, constitutes a distinctive New York School of analysis. The trajectories of New York neighborhoods, including both the downward spiral of residential abandonment and concentrated poverty of the 1970s and the subsequent processes of gentrification, immigrant neighborhood formation, and urban revitalization, have certainly yielded a huge and rich literature. But to say that this topic alone has generated a New York School ignores a huge range of work on other aspects of the city and region. Terry Clark, who has also weighed in on this subject, dismisses New York–based scholarship as a hopeless relic of class analysis.[3] While one cannot come to grips with New York—or for that matter Chicago—without understanding the power of economic elites and the processes that generate economic inequality, Clark fails to understand that New York is just as Catholic as Chicago, has many more old and new immigrant ethnic groups and subcultures than that city, and has also produced a rich literature on these characteristics.[4] So his view of what constitutes a New York School also seems skewed and incomplete.

New York certainly does loom large in the discussion of global cities.[5] That literature also does not constitute a New York School, however, because it focuses on the global system of cities and the internal dynamics thought to be more or less common to its key nodes. Indeed, historians, political scientists, sociologists, economists, and planners have generated a vast number of individual studies on the city and region, not least in the four volumes that the Social Science Research Council Committee on New York

City commissioned in the late 1980s to rekindle scholarly interest in the city as a peer to Chicago as a model for urban studies.[6] But no one basic orientation or theoretical thrust dominates or unifies this scholarship.

The major works on the city's political development offer a case in point. Wallace Sayre and Herbert Kaufman's pluralist classic, *The Government and Politics of New York City*,[7] focused on the central tension between revenue-providing and spending-dependent interests, while Theodore Lowi's *At the Pleasure of the Mayor*[8] enlightens readers about the social bases and political strategies of urban reformers, stressing the dynamics of ethnic and ideological coalition-formation. Raymond Horton and Charles Brecher's *Power Failure*[9] echoes Sayre and Kaufman's concern that hungry interest groups would overwhelm city officials in their study of the fiscal crisis and economic collapse of the mid-1970s and its political aftermath. Ester Fuchs's *Mayors and Money* locates the source of New York City government's inability to withstand spending demands—compared to Chicago— in the decay of its political parties.[10] Meanwhile, others emphasize how race and class are interwoven in the city's political economy.[11] The variety of theoretical orientations across these works makes it hard to categorize them as a school. (Moreover, New York lacked an institution, like the University of Chicago, that devoted itself to creating one.)

Even though a coherent New York School does not exist, we can say that certain common themes or assumptions run through works on New York City and its region: that the city center remains an interesting place, that suburban growth is not inconsistent with continued, even increased vibrancy in the center, that government and politics shape the city's trajectory, that public services help to organize urban life, that the struggle over getting and spending is thus an important matter, and that density and scale foster heterogeneity. New York City is certainly not a place where scholars feel compelled to construct a Web site touting a New York School. Nor do its public intellectuals worry much about being outpaced by Los Angeles. (The few who do feel this need occasionally import Joel Kotkin.) If they worry about competition from other cities, they are more likely to think about London or Shanghai than Chicago or Phoenix.[12] Finally, New Yorkers do not take second place to those who work in Los Angeles on matters of diversity, cultural innovation, ethnic hybridity, or any other aspect of postmodern life.

The L.A. School through Chicago's Eyes

Geographically as well as theoretically, Chicago lies somewhere between the two poles of decentralized Los Angeles and concentrated New York, probably closer to the latter. Scholars who used Chicago as their laboratory have certainly had a profound impact on urban theory. Brilliant faculty working at the University of Chicago included not only the founders of the Chicago school of sociology, Robert Park, Ernest Burgess,[13] and Louis Wirth, but political scientists Charles Merriam and Harold Gosnell, whose studies of Chicago launched the scientific analysis of American politics and whose students, like V. O. Key, also had a profound impact on political science.[14] The Chicago School continues to influence contemporary theories of urbanism through those educated at UC, such as Herbert Gans, William Kornblum, and Mitchell Duneier, or members or former members of its faculty, such as William J. Wilson, Robert Sampson, Michael Dawson, and Cathy Cohen.

Although you might not know it from scholars who criticize or dismiss the Chicago School, often without having read or reread its founding texts, its members were highly attuned to the global, transnational, and regional nature of urban change. Modern capitalism, they thought, had loosened transborder flows of people to congregate in the major metropolitan areas that were the driving force behind the emerging global economy. Shaped partly by natural features, partly by the shifting geography of economic activities, and partly by political institutions, but mostly by their own actions and strategies, succeeding groups would compete against each other within these metropolitan realms for space or place, material gain, and favored positions in the cultural mainstream. They would assimilate into the larger economic, cultural, and political systems, but the stages and trajectories of their assimilation would be framed by opportunity structures that themselves reflected the successes and failures of prior groups seeking to establish themselves within the urban realm.

Given that corporate headquarters were concentrated in downtown Chicago and manufacturing activities near it, members of the Chicago School observed that more powerful economic activities had clustered in the center and that less powerful ones spread out in roughly concentric zones reflecting their relative influence in the larger society. Patterns established by earlier groups would constrain the paths taken by later groups, blocking them from some areas while attracting them into others by creating a vacuum as the earlier ones departed. But the land-use maps constructed by the Chicago School reveal that the concentric circle diagram was not a fetish or iron law, only a metaphor.[15] Nothing about the basic ideas or research methodologies of the Chicago School was inconsistent with a spatial layout where conditions might instead motivate economic activities and ethnic groups to locate on the periphery, such as happened in metropolitan Los Angeles.[16] Their primary goal was to understand how the power relations among various groups were related to their spatial locations, not how close they were to the city center.

Dear and other members of the L.A. School use similar conceptual tools to paint their portraits of metropolitan Los Angeles and, by extension, contemporary urbanism. Indeed, in stressing that many interests want to escape the influence of the central city, members of the Chicago School foreshadowed the conclusions of the L.A. School. Metropolitan decentralization was already apparent in the 1930s and was well captured in *Our Cities—Their Role in the National Economy,* the 1937 report by the urbanism committee of the National Resources Planning Board, authored by Louis Wirth.[17] In the years after World War II, Jean Gottman's *Megalopolis: The Urbanized North-Eastern Seaboard of the United States* outlined trends that Dear describes as being uniquely characteristic of contemporary Los Angeles.[18] The Regional Plan Association's New York Metropolitan Region Study of the late 1950s[19] lacks the L.A. School's emphasis on cultural innovation, but its thesis was that powerful forces were undermining the region's core relative to its periphery and the region as a whole relative to the rest of the country.[20] So it seems a stretch to say that the Los Angeles experience represents a sharp break from past trends or that L.A. provides the different template for the urban future. The L.A. School seems more an interesting extension of prior thinking than a major departure from it.

Toward a School of Comparative Urbanism

We may conclude, therefore, that the case of New York has not produced a coherent school of urban studies, that the L.A. School may not be much more than new California wine in old Chicago bottles, and that the old Chicago School still has intellectual legs. These are not the most interesting questions, however. More important is whether a comparison of New York, Chicago, and Los Angeles can help us identify the crucial dynamics of metropolitan areas and unpack their implications for urban theory. Put another way, we need to ask what critical dimensions of urban and metropolitan life are present in all three cities, how they vary, and what we should learn from these variations.

The nation's three largest cities (and metropolitan areas) do share important commonalities. Compared to other metropolitan areas or the country as a whole, they are physically big and sprawling, economically dynamic and rich, and demographically and culturally complex. From the air or ground, you see them from a long way off. Upon entering them, you know that you are not in Kansas anymore. All three are basing points for economic clusters of corporate headquarters, the corporate service activities that are at the heart of global capitalism (investment banks, law firms, consulting firms, print and digital media) and high-level social services, including higher education, cultural production, health services, and so on.

Of course, each has distinctive specializations. New York is the biggest capital market, Chicago is the center of commodities exchanges, and Los Angeles has the entertainment industry. Yet all three are members of a certain class of cities, global cities, which contain concentrations of higher-level service functions associated with the global economy.[21] As such, their labor pools contain large and growing shares of highly educated professionals, their economic bases have had to adapt to the revolution in corporate organization and location that has taken place over the past fifty years, and they have large and heterogeneous service sector working class populations.

At the same time, we can observe important variations across the three cities, some of which are summarized in Table 8.1. Perhaps the most obvious is that they experienced their most rapid phases of economic and demographic growth at different historical points under different economic and technological conditions. This gave each a distinctive physical form reflecting that period, which in turn shaped subsequent physical development patterns. New York City is the oldest, biggest, densest, and arguably most centralized of the three. Having the best harbor on the eastern seaboard, building the Erie Canal (in 1825) to link that harbor to a hinterland reaching through the Great Lakes, constructing the Croton water system (1837–1842) to provide an ample supply of what may be the best municipal water in the country, and tying it all together with an intricate rail mass transit system (in the late nineteenth to early twentieth century) enabled New York to become the first urban colossus in the nation. Including Brooklyn, then a separate city, New York's population first hit one million in 1860. New York could be called a city of sail, steam, and barge.

Chicago followed, in a somewhat symbiotic way. Its population first hit one million in 1890. Its growth was propelled by being at the trading center for agricultural products, including grain and beef, facilitated both by water-borne transport connections between the Mississippi Valley and the Great Lakes and becoming the central node in the emerging transcontinental railroad system. Chicago also facilitated the construction of the national rail system by becoming a great center of steel manufacturing. It could be called a city of rail and commodities trading and shipping. Like New York, it reached its fairly full geographic extent well before the arrival of the automobile, and mass transit was central to its geographic expansion.

Los Angeles, by contrast, is a city of the twentieth century. Its population did not reach one million until 1930. For most of the nineteenth and early–twentieth century, San Francisco was a more important metropolitan area. Transcontinental rail came to Los Angeles in 1881 (Southern Pacific) and 1885 (the Santa Fe), William Mulholland began constructing the Owens Valley water system in 1905–1913, and the opening of the Panama Canal in 1913 heightened the importance of the port. Movie production and the oil industry were also established in the early decades of the twentieth century. The

	New York	Chicago	LA[a]
City Population (2005 ACS – excludes group quarters)	7,962,148	2,694,642	3,729,655
Metro Area Population (2005 ACS – excludes group quarters)	19,371,905	8,567,103	17,355,098
City Area (miles^2)	309	227	469
City Density in 2005 (persons/ miles^2)	25,770	11,871	7,952
City Share of Metro Population in 2005	41.1%	31.5%	21.5%
City NH white (2005 ACS)	34.5%	30.2%	28.5%
City NH black (2005 ACS)	23.8%	34.3%	9.6%
City NH Asian (2005 ACS)	11.5%	4.7%	11.2%
City Hispanic (2005 ACS)	27.8%	29.3%	48.6%
City NH White Share of Voting Age Citizens (2005 ACS)	42.7%	38.3%	43.7%
City Foreign Born (2005 ACS)	36.5%	22.6%	40.4%
City Naturalized among Foreign Born (2005 ACS)	50.7%	37.6%	37.5%
Naturalized FB Share of Voting Age Citizens (2005 ACS)	29.9%	13.4%	29.3%
Votes in Last Mayoral General Election	(05) 1,315,360	(07) 456,765	(05) 498,729
Votes as Share of 2005 Voting Age Citizens (2005 ACS)	27.8%	27.5%	26.6%
Democratic Share of 2004 Presidential Election Vote	71.9%	81.3%	71.4%
Global Advanced Services Connectivity Ranking[b]	2	7	9
GDP (2005 in 2001 dollars)[c]	$974 billion	$419 billion	$697 billion
GDP Per Capita	$50,280	$48,909	$40,161
City Median HH Income Per Capita (2005 ACS)	$15,667	$13,333	$13,000
Remainder of Metro Area Median HH Income Per Capita	$24,167	$22,033	$16,320
City Median HH Income as Share of Remainder of Metro Area	64.8%	60.5%	79.7%
City Tax Burden Per $100 Gross Taxable Resources[d]	($4.51) $5.62	$3.57	$2.87
State Tax Burden Per $100 Gross Taxable Resources	$3.40	$2.33	$4.01
Total Central City Taxes Per $100 in Taxable Resources 2003-04[b]	$9.02	$5.89	$6.88
City Budget (FY 2006)	$54 billion	$5.2 billion	$6.7 billion
County Budget (pro-rated to city)	NA	$1.6 billion	$4.3 billion
School Board/Water Board	NA	NA	$7.3/$3.2 billion
Total City-County Budget/Person	$6,782	$2,305	$5,766
Miles of Rail Mass Transit	722	222	73
Mass Transit Riders (millions/weekday)	7.0	1.5	1.6

a Metro LA includes LA-Long Beach-Santa Ana CBSA, Thousand Oaks-Oxnard-Ventura CBSA, and San Bernardino CBSA.
b Bureau of Economic Analysis, U.S. Department of Commerce (2007), "BEA Introduced New Measures of the Metropolitan Economy," Table 1.
c P.J. Taylor, G. Catalano, and D.R.F. Walker, "Measurement of the World City Network," Urban Studies 39, no. 13 (2002): 2367–76
d Independent Budget Office, City of New York, "Comparing State and Local Taxes in Large U.S. Cities," IBO Fiscal Brief (February, 2007).

Table 8.1 A comparison of New York, Chicago, and Los Angeles, 2005.

first Academy Award was given in 1929, the year UCLA built its campus in Westwood. While the city once had a wonderful mass transit system, the Pacific Electric Railway, it grew up under the dominion of the automobile. The construction of the regional freeway system in the 1950s sealed this pattern. The result was a much greater extent and lower density. As is obvious to anyone who spends time there, L.A. is the city of the car, the freeway, and the movie theater.

This timing sequence has had many consequences. New York was always and remains by far the densest of these cities, with a highly centralized transport system and a big public sector to support it, while Los Angeles has a density less than a third that of New York and less than half that of Chicago. Both Chicago and New York annexed substantial adjacent municipalities and a great deal of land area at the end of the nineteenth century. It also has a large and strongly centralized public sector, with county government becoming vestigial. While New York City's share of the metropolitan population has been dropping steadily, it remains extremely dense by national urban standards. Its overall population has remained high and, contrary to many other large, old industrial cities of the Northeast and Midwest, it rebounded considerably after dropping over ten percent in the 1970s. While the city has postwar suburban neighborhoods on its periphery, such as Canarsie, they are noticeably denser than similar areas of Chicago or most residential neighborhoods in L.A. When one ponders the shocks New York has faced, from racial transition to near-bankruptcy to a volatile business cycle to the impact of immigration to the September 11 attack, its neighborhoods seem amazingly resilient and adaptive. The scholarly interest in neighborhood life noted by David Halle is a logical consequence.

Chicago, also a nineteenth-century city, was built on a fairly flat plain around the place where the Chicago River empties into Lake Michigan. It served as the gateway, or linchpin, between the previously developed East and the rapidly developing West.[22] While it had, and still has, a heritage of late-nineteenth-century buildings and land uses and a rail mass transit system, its outward expansion occurred largely in the era of the automobile. When the Chicago School sociologists began to study the city intensively in the 1920 and 1930s, it had just come through an explosive period of growth similar in many ways to that which had taken place in New York.

(Its population grew from 1.7 million in 1900 to 3.4 million in 1930; New York grew from 3.4 million to 6.9 million people in the same period.) While Chicago's municipal government has a complicated institutional structure that involves Cook County as well as the city, the Cook County Democratic Party dominance over both jurisdictions gave a strongly partisan cast to a formally nonpartisan system. The original Chicago School (and before them the researchers associated with Hull House) also came by its interest in the outward movement of social groups, ethnic succession, intergroup relations, and urban politics naturally. Terry Clark's interest in ethnicity, religion (specifically Catholicism), and culture stems from the same source.

As the late developer of the trio, Los Angeles is the least dense and most fragmented. Its housing stock has a much higher share of detached, single family dwellings, and many more people commute to work alone in their automobiles than in the other two cities. As Table 8.1 shows, its density is far below that of either Chicago or New York. Many have called it a collection of suburbs. Recently, the city went through a major discussion of whether the area north of the mountains, the San Fernando Valley, would secede.[23] Despite the importance of the Los Angeles Department of Water and Power in the region's development,[24] the City of Los Angeles is but one of the eighty-eight municipalities in Los Angeles County. It has a far narrower range of powers than New York City; the DWP and the L.A. Unified School District are both vast bureaucratic operations with considerable autonomy. L.A. County government has jurisdiction over most social services. The City of Los Angeles thus offers a virtually polar case to New York City in terms of how central city politics are to the life of the region, prompting quite interesting work comparing the two.[25]

Four Dimensions of Difference

The political, economic, social, institutional, and spatial consequences of this urban development sequence mostly place New York City and Los Angeles on opposite ends of several continua, with Chicago in between. These are: (1) the importance of city government and urban politics in shaping the quality of everyday life, (2) the impact of density on the vitality of neighborhood life and local public spaces, (3) the impact of immigration (in this respect, Los Angeles and New York both differ from Chicago), and (4) the political dynamic of regionalism.

First of all, Table 8.1 clearly shows that New York has much higher levels of public spending, tax burden, and mass transit usage than the other cities. As a result, the politics of how these resources are secured and allocated is a high-profile matter in New York—as it surely is in the other two cities, but possibly to a lesser extent, especially in Los Angeles, where the county takes on a much greater role. Interestingly, underscoring the "party control hypothesis" separately advanced by Ester Fuchs and Terry Clark, Chicago, not Los Angeles, has the most parsimonious local public spending viewed as a total, per capita, or in relationship to local income. Los Angeles is often thought to have a small government, which is certainly true when one looks only at the city budget. But other layers of local government in Los Angeles also exercise significant budgetary powers. The Los Angeles school system, for example, is not counted in the Los Angeles city budget, while that of New York City is. Though Los Angeles's public sector is vastly more fragmented than New York's, the differences between the two narrow when one adds up all the layers, levels, and functions in Los Angeles.

The importance of the local political economy in New York has generated a vast literature. Many scholars have focused on the tension between revenue providers and public service consumers, beginning with Sayre and Kaufman (1960) and continuing through the work of Fuchs (1991), Shefter (1992), Brecher, Horton, Cropf, and Mead (1993), and Mollenkopf (1992). J. Phillip Thompson has focused on how these forces placed excruciating crosscutting imperatives on Mayor David Dinkins.[26] A second major focus in the political economy perspective are those works concerned with the interaction of the public and private sectors around the promotion of growth and the distribution of gains produced by growth. In addition to the previously cited work by the Fainsteins and Mollenkopf, one could mention work by Robert Caro, Peter Marcuse, and many others.

While Fuchs contrasts New York and Chicago and many scholars have traced the political wars leading up to the Washington victory in Chicago and the subsequent rise of the second Daley regime, Chicago does not appear to have generated the same level of policy concern for the structure and functioning of local government or its role in the political economy of the region. (Clearly, Simpson and Kelly provide an exception to this over-generalization.)[27] Similarly, while Sonenshein has written brilliantly about political development in Los Angeles,[28] no analysis takes on Los Angeles County as a whole, and members of the L.A. School have not paid much attention to fiscal and policy issues or the work of political scientists. Erie and MacKenzie make the point that the absence of a strong, central local government in Los Angeles is itself an important topic of study.[29] This dimension of a New York–L.A.–Chicago school of urbanism needs fuller development across all three cities. The L.A. School's relative silence on local politics and government may be taken, if not as a deficit, then as an area for improvement.

Second, New York City has produced a raft of wonderful neighborhood studies and ethnographies; a full set of citations would run into the hundreds. While Terry Clark thinks the community of scholars studying New York City focuses too much on class and not enough on ethnicity and culture, that does not seem to be a fair assessment of work dating back to Glazer and Moynihan's *Beyond the Melting Pot* and going forward to Jonathan Reider's study of Jews and Italians in Canarsie, Ida Susser's study of the Polish neighborhood of Greenpoint, Janet Abu-Lughod's study of the East Village, Wendell Pritchett's study of Brownsville, or Steven Gregory's study of the African American neighborhood of Corona—all of which address racial and ethnic tensions in the context of group succession. Mitchell Duneier has studied the role of street vendors in public space on Sixth Avenue, while Terry Williams, William Kornblum, Philippe Bourgeois, and Martin Sanchez-Jankowski have studied gangs, and the list could go on and on.

Scholars studying contemporary Chicago have certainly built on the Chicago School's original lead on studying neighborhood processes (one thinks, for example, of Eric Klinenberg's *Heat Wave,* Sudhir Venkatesh's studies of Chicago projects, and the magisterial study of neighborhood effects reported in recent papers by Felton Earls, Jeanne Brooks-Gunn, Stephen Roudenbush, Robert J. Sampson, Jeffery Morenoff, and other colleagues).

Perhaps because everyone is stuck on the freeway, however, L. A. scholars do not seem to have produced much work on neighborhood life. Given how important residential neighborhoods are in organizing daily life in all three cities, and the interesting and varied internal dynamics of these neighborhoods, this topic ought to be central to a new New York–L.A.–Chicago school of comparative urbanism.

Third, the arrival, establishment, and political development of various immigrant groups have been and will be crucial for the development of all three cities. New York has produced an immense amount of work on this topic. The work includes recent comprehensive studies by Kasinitz, Mollenkopf, and Waters, and Kasinitz, Mollenkopf, Waters, and Holdaway;[30] studies on specific ethnic communities including incisive work on Asian immigrant communities by Peter Kwong, Pyong Gap Min, Claire Kim, Min Zhou, and Margaret Chin; analysis of Afro-Caribbean communities by Philip Kasinitz, Mary Waters, Reuel Rogers, Milton Vickerman, and Francois Pierre Louis; study of older and newer Latino groups by Angelo Falcon, Patricia Pessar, Michael Jones Correa, Robert Smith, and Nicole Marwell; and work by Roger Sanjek that describes how ethnic groups interact in Queens neighborhoods influenced by an aging but still vital regular Democratic county political organization.

While Los Angeles has also produced rich studies of the immigrant experience, particularly of Mexican-Americans, and Waldinger and Bozorg-mehr provide a fine overview,[31] this literature neither seems to match that on New York in terms of breadth and depth nor to have been integrated very well into, or have had much impact on, the L.A. School. Similarly, though immigration has had an increasingly significant impact on Chicago, scholars have mainly seen politics in that city through the lens of "Politics in Black and White," to borrow Sonenshein's title for Los Angeles politics. Clearly, this profound demographic transition has pervasive political, social, cultural, and economic implications for all three metropolitan areas and also deserves to be a pivotal point of comparison.

Finally, scholars based in New York take the comparative study of regions seriously. Well-known theorists on regional comparison based in

New York or heavily influenced by its experience include, in no particular order, David Harvey, Peter Marcuse, Saskia Sassen (returning from her sojourn in Chicago), Richard Sennett, Susan Fainstein, Bob Beauregard, and Neil Brenner, not to mention the original Regional Plan study of 1927, the New York Metropolitan Region study in the late 1960s, and classic work by Robert Wood, Jameson Doig, and Michael Danielson. As outlined above, regionalism and metropolitan development were already well advanced and long-studied phenomena in metropolitan New York before the founding of the L.A. School. The point here is not to deny that the L.A. School has reached important and sometimes counterintuitive findings based on the Los Angeles experience as a decentered metropolis, but to understand why intrametropolitan dynamics vary across regions in the way they do. The L.A. School's implicit claim that all other regions may be converging on the Los Angeles model may or may not be correct. Certainly, the New York metropolitan area remains a vital and successful region in a far more centered mode than in Los Angeles. Since almost all the emerging large metropolitan areas will be in China and India, not North America, it seems unlikely that any of the three cities will provide the ideal type for new metropolitan growth at a global scale.

To conclude by stating the obvious, we don't really need a Chicago, Los Angeles, or New York School that privileges the distinctive characteristics of one city as in our understanding of comparative urban theory. We do need a nuanced comparative analysis across metropolitan areas that draws on characteristics that are more or less prominent across them, or even absent in some. The Los Angeles School certainly draws our attention to the ways in which the various parts of the metropolis relate to one another far differently in Los Angeles today than in Chicago eighty years ago. For that we are grateful. But New York, Chicago, and many other big, important, nodal cities also have distinctive features that provide equally valid bases for generating theory. The New York example suggests four such features—a large urban political economy, a vital neighborhood life, group succession driven by immigration, and close ties to other key nodes in the global urban system. The time has come to shift our attention from whose model is better to how and why these important dimensions vary across places.

Notes

1. Michael J. Dear and Nicholas Dahmann, "Urban Politics and the Los Angeles School of Urbanism"(2007; this volume, chapter 4).

2. David Halle, ed., *New York and Los Angeles: Politics, Society, and Culture—a Comparative View* (Chicago: University of Chicago Press, 2003), 15–230.

3. Terry Nichols Clark, "The New Chicago School: Notes Toward a Theory"(2007; this volume, chapter 11).

4. According to the 2000 Religious Congregations and Membership Study, 2.15 million of Cook County's 5.38 million residents were Catholic adherents (40 percent), as were 2.97 million of New York's 8.0 million residents (37 percent).

5. Saskia Sassen, *The Global City: New York, London, Tokyo,* second ed. (Princeton, N.J.: Princeton University Press, 2001); Janet Abu-Lughod, *New York, Chicago, Los Angeles: America's Global Cities* (Minneapolis: University of Minnesota Press, 1999); Susan S. Fainstein, *The City Builders: Property Development in New York and London, 1980–2000,* second ed., rev. (Lawrence: University Press of Kansas, 2001); Neil Brenner and Roger Keil, eds., *The Global City Reader* (New York: Routledge, 2006).

6. John Mollenkopf, ed., *Power, Culture, and Place: Essays on New York City* (New York: Russell Sage Foundation, 1988); John Mollenkopf and Manuel Castells, eds., *Dual City: Restructuring New York* (New York: Russell Sage Foundation, 1991); David Ward and Olivier Zunz, eds., *The Landscape of Modernity* (New York: Russell Sage Foundation, 1992); Martin Shefter, ed., *Capital of the American Century: The National and International Influence of New York City* (New York: Russell Sage Foundation, 1993).

7. Wallace S. Sayre and Herbert Kaufman, *Governing New York City: Politics in the Metropolis* (New York: Russell Sage Foundation, 1960).

8. T. J. Lowi, *At The Pleasure of the Mayor: Patronage and Power in New York City 1898–1958* (New York: Free Press, 1961).

9. Charles Brecher and Raymond D. Horton, with Robert A. Cropf and Dean Michael Mead, *Power Failure: Government and Politics in New York City Since 1960* (New York: Oxford University Press, 1993).

10. Ester Fuchs, *Mayors and Money: Fiscal Policy in New York and Chicago* (Chicago: University of Chicago Press, 1991).

11. See Ira Katznelson, *City Trenches: Urban Politics and the Patterning of Class in the United States* (Chicago: University of Chicago Press, 1982); Norman I. Fainstein and Susan S. Fainstein, "Governing Regimes and the Political Economy of Development in New York City, 1946–1984," in Mollenkopf, *Power, Culture, and Place;* Martin Shefter, *Political Crisis/Fiscal Crisis: The Collapse and Revival of New York City* (New York: Columbia University Press, 1992); John Mollenkopf, *A Phoenix in the Ashes: The Rise and Fall of the Koch Coalition in New York City Politics* (Princeton: Princeton University Press, 1992).

12. PricewaterhouseCoopers, *Cities of Opportunity: Business-readiness Indicators for the 21st Century* (New York: Report to the New York City Partnership, 2007).

13. Robert E. Park, Ernest Burgess, and Roderick D. McKenzie, *The City: Suggestions for*

Investigation of Human Behavior in the Urban Environment (Chicago: University of Chicago Press, 1925; reprint, 1981).

14. Michael T. Haney and John Mark Hansen, "Building the Chicago School," *American Journal of Political Science* 100, no. 4 (November 2006): 589–96.

15. See http://www.lib.uchicago.edu/e/su/maps/ssrc/; Louis Wirth, "Urbanism as a Way of Life," *American Journal of Sociology* (July 1938): 1–24; Louis Wirth, "The Limitations of Regionalism," in Merrill Jensen, ed., *Regionalism in America* (Madison: University of Wisconsin Press, 1951), 381–93. As Wirth said in "Urbanism as a Way of Life," 3, "As long as we identify urbanism with the physical entity of the city, viewing it merely as rigidly delimited in space, and proceed as if urban attributes abruptly ceased to be manifested beyond an arbitrary boundary line, we are not likely to arrive at any adequate conception of urbanism as a mode of life." Later, in "The Limitations of Regionalism," 386, he wrote that "regions based on the principle of interdependence and the dominance of a focal center are not only vaguely defined but are subject to infinite flux."

16. See James Paul Allen and Eugene Turner, *Changing Faces, Changing Places: Mapping Southern Californians* (Center for Geographical Studies, California State University Northridge, 2002). Indeed, Park and Burgess in *The City*, 185, concluded that Chicago was experiencing "centralized decentralization" through the "development of satellite cites" which "may exert a determining influence upon the direction of the city's growth."

17. Urbanism Committee, National Resources Planning Board, *Our Cities: Their Role in the National Economy* (Washington, D.C.: National Resources Planning Board, 1937).

18. Jean Gottmann, *Megalopolis: The Urbanized Northeastern Seaboard of the United States* (New York: The Twentieth Century Fund, 1961).

19. This document is summarized in Raymond Vernon, *Metropolis 1985: An Interpretation of the Results of the New York Metropolitan Region Study* (Cambridge: Harvard University Press, 1960).

20. It is worth noting, too, that New York's population gain during the 1990s was half again larger than that of Los Angeles and that Chicago, Boston, and San Francisco also gained population after previous declines.

21. The Global and World Cities Study Group and Network has done excellent work on their positions in the global urban system. http://www.lboro.ac.uk/gawc/group.html; for an overview of related issues, see Brenner and Keil, *The Global City Reader*.

22. William Cronon, *Nature's Metropolis: Chicago and the Great West* (New York: W.W. Norton, 1991).

23. Raphael J. Sonenshein, *The City at Stake: Secession, Reform, and the Battle for Los Angeles* (Princeton, N.J.: Princeton University Press, 2004).

24. Steven P. Erie and Scott A. MacKenzie, "From the Chicago to the L.A School: Whither the Local State?" (2007; this volume, chapter 6).

25. See Halle, *New York and Los Angeles;* Karen M. Kaufmann, *The Urban Voter: Group Conflict and Mayoral Voting Behavior in American Cities* (Ann Arbor: University of Michigan Press, 2004); Janelle S. Wong, *Democracy's Promise: Immigrants and American Civic Institutions* (Ann Arbor: University of Michigan Press, 2006); John Logan and John Mollenkopf, *People*

and Politics in America's Big Cities (New York City: Drum Major Institute, 2003); John Mollenkopf et al., "Race, Ethnicity, and Immigration in the 2005 Mayoral Elections in Los Angeles and New York" (paper presented at the annual meeting of the American Political Science Association, Philadelphia, Pa., 2006).

26. J. Phillip Thompson, *Double Trouble: Black Mayors, Black Communities, and the Call for a Deep Democracy* (New York: Oxford University Press, 2005).

27. Dick Simpson and Tom Kelly, "The New Chicago School of Urbanism and the New Daley Machine" (chapter 10, this volume).

28. Raphael J. Sonenshein, *Politics in Black and White: Race and Power in Los Angeles* (Princeton, N.J.: Princeton University Press, 1994); Sonenshein, The City at Stake.

29. Erie and MacKenzie, "From the Chicago to the L.A. School."

30. Philip Kasinitz, John H. Mollenkopf, and Mary C. Waters, eds., *Becoming New Yorkers: Ethnographies of the Second Generation* (New York: Russell Sage Foundation, 2004); Philip Kasinitz, John Mollenkopf, Mary Waters, and Jennifer Holdaway, *Inheriting the City: The Children of Immigrants Come of Age* (Cambridge and New York: Harvard University Press and the Russell Sage Foundation, 2008).

31. Roger Waldinger and Mehdi Bozorgmehr, eds., *Ethnic Los Angeles* (New York: Russell Sage Foundation, 1996).

9

Radical Uniqueness and the Flight from Urban Theory

■ Robert A. Beauregard

Imagine, for the moment, a world in which each and every city is incontestably unique. I do not mean simply different but so dissimilar that if you were to enter a city for the first time, having no prior knowledge, you would be wholly disoriented. Nothing that you know about, say, La Paz or Kiev would be applicable to Mumbai. Cities would be profoundly incomparable.

In such a world, a world of radical uniqueness, urban studies—based as it is on a comparative perspective—would come to a halt. Although one might study Mumbai while in La Paz, there would be little point in doing so. La Paz offers no lessons for, or insights into, anyplace else. Mumbai is where one should study Mumbai. There, one's experiences will reinforce one's research. Mumbai, moreover, is where Mumbai scholars would likely congregate. A Mumbai scholar in La Paz would merely be a curiosity hoping through sheer persistence to turn the irrelevant into the exotic.

With all knowledge irresistibly local, thinking about cities would be transformed. Urban theory would be of little value. If theory's intent is to generalize from one city to the next or to set places in context—for example, in a national system of cities or global commodity chains—theory would be impossible. If the purpose of theory is to discover the logic that makes cities into cities, this too would be a hopeless task since doing so requires that a category of cities exist to which such logic applies.

A unique city is an autarkic city; self-sufficient, it has nothing in common with any other. With comparison impossible, thinking beyond the single case would be useless; one might as well compare octopi with ski lifts. Consequently, only city-specific theory would remain; that is, theory focused solely on the conditions and dynamics within particular places.

Barcelona would have an urban theory, Lagos a different one, Kyoto a third, Vancouver a fourth, Helsinki a fifth, and on and on wherever a single urban scholar resides. A metatheory of the city would be confined to one insight: all knowledge is local.

Radical uniqueness, of course, is a theoretical conceit. Nonetheless, it serves a rhetorical purpose as regards the claims of the Los Angeles school of urbanism and other city-based urban theories. It also signals my intent to convince you that city-based theories, regardless of the city in which they originate, are antithetical to the larger urban project. Suffering ontological flaws, they obstruct rather than facilitate critical thinking about cities. Larry Bourne has written that such labeling is "inherently selective, frequently distorting, and potentially exclusionary."[1]

I agree.

Unique Cities

Few scholars—in fact, I know of none—embrace radical uniqueness. Even Terry Clark, who begins his chapter in this volume on the new Chicago School with the sentence "Every city is unique," later and judiciously qualifies his original position. He turns to general processes—the deep structures—that characterize all cities and that are "combined in unique ways in each location," a comment that points to mediated commonalities rather than radical uniqueness. Later, Clark repeats his bold claim: "Like cities, every individual is unique," a surprising observation from a social scientist but one intended to suggest that schools of thought cannot truly exist since individuals hold different ideas, itself a problematic statement. To be fair, Clark is arguing the distinctiveness of Chicago as a city and the benefits of an internal point of view, not Chicago's radical uniqueness.

Consider the statement that Los Angeles is the precursor of the twenty-first century city; that is, "the first consequential American city to separate itself decisively from European models" of urbanism.[2] Such a claim implies that Los Angeles is—or was—unique for only an historical moment and that other American cities will eventually catch up. Los Angeles is presented as a prototype. Subsequently and inevitably, its uniqueness will disappear.

Take another example—New York City. The architectural historian Robert A. M. Stern's wonderfully rich histories of architecture, planning, and urbanism offer the proposition that New York City travels through history alone. Stern does not state this explicitly. Rather, he proposes that adversity often impinges on the city from the outside, yet he treats that "outside" as less a force for change than an occasion for response. The city's particular strengths enable it to prevail and prosper; what New York City has accomplished is due wholly to its genetic makeup. Its people, institutions, buildings, and political leaders make it great.[3]

Prior to World War II, as Stern and his coauthors note, New York City was "both a miniature and distillation of America."[4] And, writing a few years earlier about the interwar years, they comment that "even if New York did not embody the nation in all its complexities, it surely gave life to its fantasies."[5] In short, Stern pulls the world into the city's orbit. To understand New York, you need know next to nothing about any other place; developmentally, the city is self-sufficient.

Radical uniqueness, of course, is most pronounced when other cities are similar to each other. The contrast is what makes the claim dazzle. Within the category of not–New York City, distinguishing Seattle from Boston or Boston from San Francisco is of little intellectual interest. Their differences can thus be ignored. Having much in common with each other, these other cities are simply ordinary.

In a world of radical uniqueness, urban categories such as "not–New York City" are themselves suspect; the antithesis is meaningless without its thesis, thereby making radical uniqueness less plausible. Without a category to which a city can be incomparable, radical uniqueness is deflated. Or, to say it differently, the conceit of radical uniqueness depends on the contradictory—dialectic—existence of a prior category of cities.

Unnatural Categories

A nonhypothetical world, one without radical uniqueness, is a world of nested categories.[6] Such categories—cities, governance, infrastructure, ethnicity, morphological patterns—enable us to explore and then interpret our perceptions. As data come to us, we sort through them, create bundles of facts and opinions, and attach labels; we make sense of the world. As individual categories fill up, they suggest lines of inquiry and novel points of view. Learning more about the category "informal economies," we discover what we do not know and form attitudes, hypotheses, and arguments. And, we think about the relationship between and among categories, for example, when we recognize the difference between resurgent cities undergoing growth after a period of stagnation and declining cities faced with continued depletion of jobs, residents, and tax revenues.

Categories are the foundation of theory. They enable us to group together and then juxtapose matters of fact, move beyond single cases, and communicate easily with others. Being able to put data and sense impressions into categories, moreover, engenders a sense of security in the face of information overload. Categories are the antithesis of radical uniqueness.

Within the social sciences, the dominant categories are those of the academic disciplines: economics, sociology, politics, anthropology, and history.[7] Social science, of course, is itself a category; it shares knowledge with the humanities, the natural sciences, and religion—more categories. Such foundational distinctions have a major impact on how we think about and what we think about the city. Many urban theorists, however, argue that the city is so complex, so multidimensional, that exploring its qualities from within one or another of these categories does the city a disservice. Savage and Warde[8] comment that life in cities is "a subject whose boundaries [can] not be delimited," while Hubbard[9] writes of the multiplicity of meanings that adhere to the city—"a spatial location, a political entity, an administrative unit, a place of work and play, a collection of dreams and nightmares, a mesh of social relations, an agglomeration of economic activity"—and defeat a simple or singular disciplinary perspective. Consequently, the city calls for an interdisciplinarity that draws from the various social sciences, the natural sciences, and the humanities, together offering an elusive ontological logic that embraces the spaces of multiplicity.[10]

The assertion that the city's complexity requires interdisciplinarity assumes that the city's qualities are naturally arrayed in disciplinary categories. This is not the case. The relevant qualities of a city are always theory-dependent; they follow from the point of view that we bring to the case at hand. Qualities are socially constructed. Moreover, the notion that a category anticipates a case is problematic; categories come into existence only through multiple cases. Cases often exist before the category is formed, as when the study of Durban or Johannesburg leads to the category of apartheid city. In addition, the belief that sense perceptions compel certain, and not other, categories is an untenable position, one related to the notion of naturalism, a point to which I will return. Two regrettable consequences of a fixed view of qualities and categories ensue: a rejection of the malleability of language and suppression of reality's social and discursive construction.[11]

All of this points to the obvious; intellectual schools are social constructs.[12] They are created by individuals and groups as a way to address a specific task or project, whether it be painting (the Ashcan School), philosophy (the Vienna Circle), city planning (New Urbanism), or architecture (the Bauhaus). And because they are socially created, this means that their motivations are not simply or purely intellectual or utilitarian. Motives having to do with publicity, status, personal advancement, and institutional advantage also operate.[13] These are neither lesser motives nor independent of the concern to think more clearly or act more effectively. Nevertheless, they cannot be ignored when thinking about the Los Angeles school of urbanism, its "new" Chicago counterpart, the evanescent New York School, or even the original Chicago School. What sense are we to make of such "exceptionalist narratives."[14]

City-Based Schools

To a great extent, the Los Angeles School owes its prominence to Michael Dear, professor of geography at the University of Southern California in Los Angeles. Although acknowledging a late-1980s meeting of scholars from and of Los Angeles, Dear was the one who wrote the school into existence. The first signs of its emergence occurred in 1993 when Charles Jencks (an architectural critic) and Marco Cenzatti (an urban planning professor) made public mention of a group of planners and geographers writing on Los Angeles from a shared perspective.[15] Not until Dear's "Postmodern

Urbanism" was published in the *Annals of the Association of American Geographers* in 1998, though, was the school given a full-blown debut and, most importantly, contrasted with the original Chicago School of urban studies. In that article, Dear and Flusty claimed Los Angeles as a "special place" and a clear break from prior patterns of urbanization and urbanism, particularly that based on a monocentric model of urban form.[16] This morphological break with the past, they argued, compelled a new theory of the city. Moreover, Los Angeles attracted a host of scholars, including Edward Soja, Mike Davis, and Allen J. Scott. To greater and lesser degrees, these scholars distanced themselves from modernist social theory and turned instead to an emerging postmodernism that reflected the multiplicity, indeterminateness, and elusiveness of the contemporary city.[17] Yet, they did not wholly abandon the Chicago School. They retained the critical significance of space, ignored gender,[18] and marginalized culture.[19] Nevertheless, Los Angeles was offered as a paradigmatic place where the "dynamics of capitalist spatialization" all come together.[20]

The L.A. School is presented, particularly by Michael Dear, as a classic Kuhnian revolution[21]—a paradigm shift.[22] (For a critique, see Beauregard[23] and for a defense see Dear et al.)[24] This strong rhetorical move is most apparent in *From Chicago to L.A.: Making Sense of Urban Theory*, edited by Dear in 2002. The book is organized as an alternative to the Chicago School, with each topical grouping of chapters prefaced with an excerpt from Robert Park's *The City*, a text that Dear asserts is that school's "basic primer."[25] The excerpts are meant to provide a "point of departure"[26] for subsequent chapters and the intent is to challenge the "hegemony"[27] of the Chicago School and offer "*alternative* analytical frameworks."[28]

Dear's goal is clear—a displacement of the "ruling" paradigm that had "remained coherent for most of the twentieth century"[29] despite his declared misgivings regarding the advisability of another hegemonic metanarrative for the "myriad global and local trends that surround us."[30] And, in a comment meant to seal the fate of the Chicago School for evermore, Dear suggests that Louis Wirth in his chapter in *The City* had anticipated the shift from modern to postmodern cities and thus "foreshadow[ed] the *necessity* of the transition from the Chicago to the L.A. School."[31] The Chicago School was thus fated for self-destruction; it did not need the L.A. School to effect its demise.

Except for an attempt by Jan Nijman[32] to declare Miami as the city that best deserves to anchor urban theory in the twenty-first century, few scholars have taken up the challenge posed by Dear to tie urban theory to a specific place. One who did was David Halle, professor of sociology at the University of California Los Angeles and a resident of New York City. Whereas Dear was and has been forceful in his advocacy, Halle has been muted. Buried in the introduction to his edited book *New York and Los Angeles: Politics, Society, and Culture—a Comparative View* was the first mention of the New York School.[33] Halle described it as being primarily concerned with the central city of the metropolitan area and, more narrowly, with Manhattan. (As Dear might remark, the New York School is stuck in the "centered" perspective of the modernist paradigm.) Halle noted that the putative members of the New York School—Jane Jacobs, Sharon Zukin, Richard Sennett, Kenneth Jackson, William H. Whyte—focus on street life, ignore the suburbs, worry about class-based disparities, and attend closely to the oppositional politics that infuse gentrification, redevelopment, and ethnic succession.[34]

Halle, however, has not further elaborated his claim. Moreover, he acknowledges that some urban scholars, such as Herbert Gans, who live and work in New York City do not fit this profile. Neither does he claim that the New York School is the replacement paradigm for the Chicago School nor offer it as an alternative to the L.A. School. Most telling, Halle never suggests that any of the scholars to which he refers identify themselves as part of a defined, intellectual community. And, unlike Dear, he leaves himself out of the school.[35] For Halle it seems, the existence of such a school is merely an interesting phenomenon that supports the comparison posed by his book.

Not until the spring of 2007 did Halle publicly repeat his New York School argument. He did so at a conference held at the University of Illinois Chicago Circle, which was sponsored in part by the Department of Political Science and the Great Cities Institute there.[36] The conference began with the political scientist Dennis Judd acknowledging the L.A. School and the Chicago School while noting the emergence of a second Chicago School.

Judd related how a group of urban scholars in Chicago had begun to meet informally in the fall of 2001 to discuss urban issues. After a number of meetings, they came to the realization that existing urban theories were irremediably deficient. Moreover, these urban scholars concluded that understanding change within Chicago, or any city, meant attending to that city's distinctive political culture. Or, to cast this claim more broadly, Chicago can be understood only by investigating what happens within Chicago.

The declaration of a second Chicago School is most apparent in Terry Clark's "The New Chicago School: Notes Toward a Theory," chapter 11 in this volume. Unlike Halle, Clark engages the first Chicago School. He begins his chapter by writing that "older Chicago paradigms are inadequate" and that Chicago is too unlike Los Angeles for the L.A. School to be applicable. Both schools ignore politics and culture, particularly as the latter is manifested in innovation and consumption.[37] These other schools are also inattentive to globalization, a factor that distinguishes Chicago from other cities. Clark's main argument, though, is that Chicago requires its own theory because it is "distinct," though I think he means "unique," since a city can be distinct (as Edmonton is from Calgary) without requiring a tailored, theoretical treatment. He claims that Chicago is the country's largest major city with a strong tradition of Catholicism, it was a frontier town and is thus less freighted with tradition, is strongly individualistic, has clearly delineated neighborhoods, and its local government is relatively autonomous from the state and federal governments. Unique, it deserves its own point of view.

Interestingly, other Chicago Schools have been sighted—a second Chicago School of sociology after the 1920s and, possibly, a third in the 1960s,[38] not to mention a first Chicago School of architecture that emerged in the 1880s around Louis Sullivan and William Holabird. When compared to Dear's historiography, though, Clark is indifferent to the antecedents of contemporary Chicago urbanism and this diminishes his theoretical project. Accusations of scholarly opportunism would be deflected by situating the new Chicago School more centrally in current debates and historical developments. Of course, once one decides to believe that Los Angeles is the prototype of the twenty-first century city or that New York or Chicago is unique, then all other cities and the theories associated with them fade away. We should object. The turn to city-based theories is unhelpful for understanding cities and crafting urban theory.

Critique

Claims regarding the uniqueness of individual cities evoke more than the complexity of cities or the fertile minds of urban theorists. Much more is at stake here, particularly if one accepts Dear's argument regarding the profound transformation of cities and the corresponding need to reformulate how we think about them. At minimum, the debate suggests a dissatisfaction with urban theories built on the original Chicago model. Less obvious is a deep disregard for Marxist-based political economy. In fact, the erasure of Marxist-based urban political economy by all of the advocates of the putative schools is quite surprising, particularly given that it was Marxist urban political economists who initially launched the assault against and displaced the ecological paradigm of the first Chicago School.[39] The Marxist critics cast cities as epiphenomena; what needed to be explained was not urbanization but the historical geography of capitalism. Individual cities were thus precluded from being independent sites for theory-building. That and the postmodern disdain for metanarratives, I suspect, is more than sufficient reason to suppress mention of Marxist political economy.

Clearing the ground for urbanization, though, does not necessarily privilege a city-based approach. Dissolving cities in the spatiality of capitalism or constructing urban theory around a single city are only two of many possibilities. Numerous theorists[40] have used categories such as mega-, global, and Southeast Asian cities as the source and object of their theoretical and empirical work. The choice of a single city with which to anchor urban theory and from which to derive empirical understandings is neither obvious nor necessary.

A critical assessment of city-based urban theories might begin by questioning their empirical validity; for example, asking about the degree to which Los Angeles earns its prominent status because of its historical position or Chicago's political culture actually sets it apart from other cities. The debate, though, is not solely about empirical correspondence. It is also, and mostly about representation, that is, how we think about cities. Thus, an empirical assessment is beside the point—though, see Wasserstrom.[41] Nor is the issue one of specifying the distinctiveness of these cities so as to validate their atypical status. Rather, a critique should focus on how we think about cities and how we think theory should be written.

To this end, let me reveal but not defend my criteria for assessing an urban theory. First, urban theory should connect generalities with particularities, identifying the path between larger trends, deeper logics, or spatially extensive forces and the way they are manifest and mediated by specific places and times. Thus, and second, an urban theory has to attend to the historical geography of cities. This means that spatial and temporal comparisons are essential.[42] Third, it has to capture the "reality" of cities by descending from the heights of abstraction, targeting what is concrete and particular about such places, while avoiding the seduction of empiricism. Fourth, and related, theory must do more than recognize and explain what is; it also has to capture what lies hidden or behind "reality." To this extent, urban theory has to grasp not just the actuality of cities and life within them but their potential as well. Theory has to confer meaning by attending to what could have happened. This cannot be done if the reality of cities is conflated with what actually occurred. Finally, urban theory must be simultaneously inclusive and discriminating. That is, it must reject radical uniqueness along with its close imitations and accept both the general category of cities and the necessity of differentiating among them. Individual cities have to be conceived as simultaneously similar and distinct and ripe with theoretical possibilities.[43]

Drawing on these criteria, I will touch on four theoretical sins being committed by those who call for a city-based urban theory. The transgressions are: a tendency to radical uniqueness, the embrace of naturalism, a flattening of space and place, and intellectual permissiveness.

To begin, individual cities are unique only in a specific sense; they are not radically unique. Their uniqueness stems from our perception—that is, we choose to perceive and emphasize certain qualities (and thus differences) and not others—and from the way in which cities are overdetermined and mediated sites. Overdetermined, cities offer innumerable choices as regards how to think about them. In this sense, the city is chaotic.[44] Because of this, theorists systematically and purposively unpack the city. A city-based theory privileges the characteristics that best suit the broader claims being made for it. So, Terry Clark attaches significance to Chicago's Catholicism and Michael Dear emphasizes Los Angeles's polynucleated urban form. Chicago, though, also has edge cities (that is, is polynucleated) and many of the residents of Los Angeles are Catholic (for example, most Mexicans). These latter qualities, however, are less useful to their respective counterparts and so are ignored. And though Los Angeles and Chicago have major industrial districts, industrial districts are resonant of the past. As a result, they go unmentioned; to do so would dilute the claim that the city represents the future.

Mediated, any city's uniqueness emerges from its specific embeddedness in time and space. Uniqueness is a contingent and not a necessary quality of cities.[45] Cities are unique only conjuncturally. And, then, they are unique only under theoretical strictures that give primacy to certain qualities and not others. In short, uniqueness is socially constituted and thus always problematic. Thus, a city-based urban theory is a truncated, partial, and compromised view of the nature of cities and even of the named city itself. By denying the ordinariness of cities, cities themselves are denied.

Second, city-based urban theories suffer from the presumption that the named city is meaningful because its dynamics and conditions are deeply "real." The city, it is being claimed, is neither fictional nor, even more importantly, symbolic. If it were either, the city's radical uniqueness would be trivialized. The city's unmediated qualities are what compel our attention.

This is naturalism, and it is a doubtful claim. It deproblematizes representation and assumes that reality presents itself to us as itself, that is, is unmediated. We are asked to believe in the necessity of what exists and to ignore its social constructedness and potential otherness. To this extent, naturalism precludes rhetoric, a loss that would cramp the style of many proponents of the Los Angeles School who believe that new realities require new language. And, to the extent that naturalism has an affinity for determinism, it takes all of the fun out of making bold theoretical claims and doing urban theory.

In fact, to be simultaneously committed to an unmediated uniqueness of the city and the importance of postmodern representational strategies is contradictory. Postmodernists, almost by definition, embrace the malleability and instability of language and its tenuous connection to something called reality. If this is so, then claims of uniqueness are seriously weakened. Radical uniqueness is untenable. What is defensible, though, are mediated distinctions. For example, few cities can quite match in sheer, sudden, technological violence the fates of Hiroshima and Nagasaki at the end of World War II. Many cities, though, have experienced large-scale wartime destruction.

Third, city-based urban theories distort the role of space and place and thereby undermine the necessity of historical geography. Space must be part of any urban theory, but this does not mean that urban theories should be spatially confined and labeled. To propose that urban theory should be crafted around the spatiality of a single city such as Los Angeles is to embrace space as absolute space, that is, as self-contained. Radical uniqueness, in fact, rests on the notion that a place can exist independently of all other places; once independent, the chosen city can be unique. Yet, this is a caricature of the spatial qualities of cities. Space is partitioned so as to achieve a sharp disjuncture between the space of one city and that of all others. Space, though, is not functionally discontinuous in this way. Differentiated, it is relational.[46] To deny these two qualities by isolating a single city is antithetical to urban theory.

City-based urban theories, then, contain a narrow conception of how to think about place. Cities are conceived as geographically coherent, clearly defined, and stable.[47] In actuality, places like Los Angeles, Chicago, or Mumbai are geographically fragmented. That is, they are not singularities. And while these urban scholars recognize that cities are multiscalar, that is not my point. Rather, consider New York. It is geographically located along the eastern seaboard of the United States and at the mouth of the Hudson River. It also exists north of its municipal boundaries, where it owns and controls land for water provision; in Ohio, where it transports its trash (leaving behind pieces of Queens and Brooklyn); in Washington, D.C., and Albany, N.Y., where it has a political lobbying presence; in London, where its financial service and legal firms facilitate the worldwide flow of capital; and in other countries, where it has stationed police to intervene in drug trafficking. One can hardly conceive of New York and other cities as stable, fixed, and coherent entities able to anchor a more extensive urban theory. Cities do not occupy a single, privileged, and independent space.

Or, consider this issue from a different angle. Any large city is a product of influences operating transregionally and transnationally. Chicago, as William Cronon brilliantly demonstrated, owed its rise to second-city status to the flow of goods and capital between it and the larger midwestern region and also back to the East and, specifically, New York City.[48] Whatever self-determination Chicago enjoyed was more than counterbalanced by the ways in which local forces and conditions were affected by or connected to urbanization's relational web. To offer one city as the basis of urban theory is to negate these interactive and scalar possibilities and to circumscribe inadvisably the space of urban theory. Are we to believe that Los Angeles, New York, or Chicago is autogenetic, its own creation? This seriously strains theoretical and empirical plausibility. I think these scholars would agree. Yet, they act as if this were true.

My fourth and last point has more to do with a reaction to the growth of city-based urban theories than with the theories themselves. One could argue that when scholars develop schools, they focus attention and create debate. Scrutiny encourages research and disagreement leads to new knowledge. Consequently, such theories should not be suppressed. Pluralism, though, is not what I suspect many of the proponents of these schools have in mind.

Intellectual pluralism is hardly an unassailable ideal. A commitment to scholarship requires skepticism. Just because city-based urban theories exist does not make them innocent and just because they spark debate does not make them net contributors to our understanding of cities. Are we to allow a Miami School of urban theory, an Amsterdam School, a Skokie School? Unlikely. In fact, scholars generally resist theoretical pluralism; already-established schools are wary of competitors and monopoly is the endgame.

Displacement and dominance infuse the debate. In addition, by fueling radical uniqueness, a proliferation of city-based theories diminishes what cities have in common and often denies that an "ordinary" city can add value to urban theory.[49] Instead, the claim is that some cities have theoretical value and other cities do not. The latter receive theory; the former create it. Thus, what is needed is not an acceptance of city-based urban theories but a critical spirit that fosters skepticism.

Conclusion

I am skeptical of city-based urban theories and, as a result, opposed to them. They are theoretically problematic: flirting with a fictional radical uniqueness, embracing an unreflective naturalism, undermining inclusivity, distorting space and place, and abetting an uncritical theoretical pluralism even as they resist it. Too many cities, too many different types of cities, are omitted from such formulations. In fact, the whole approach has an exclusive quality that divides cities and theorists into those who live and write about "significant" places and those who do not. That these theories have emerged from the largest cities of the country—the three largest, in fact—and some of the country's major academic institutions reinforces these hierarchical and elitist tendencies. Like theories of globalization that draw knowledge and perspective from the global north,[50] such theories narrow rather than expand our vision.

Undoubtedly, any urban theory has to specify the space to which it refers; it has to be grounded in some way. And, while a single city can be quite real compared to a category of cities, it is no more natural. All concepts and categories are deficient in this way. One solution is to retreat to ordinary cities as do Ash Amin, Stephen Graham, and Jennifer Robinson. For them, urban theory should be about, and be derived from, what cities have in common. The problem with this approach is that it too easily drifts into the realm of general theory in which all cities are the same, constitutes the whole world as urban, such that urban theory becomes social theory, or retreats to an implicit and debunked urban-rural dichotomy. The attention to ordinary cities is laudable, but if it elides differentiation among cities, it too is problematic. Other urban scholars believe that global cities are different from those on the margins of the circuits of capitalism, that Southeast Asian cities are different from Scandinavian ones, and that megacities belong in a different category from medium-size regional centers. All of this suggests that urban theorists need to avoid city-based theories as well as general theory. Where they should be located in the theoretical space bounded by these restrictions cannot be determined in advance of the theoretical work itself.

In negotiating this urban and theoretical terrain, the best advice is to always remember that categories and distinctions are unnatural, socially constructed, and thus useful in some instances and detrimental in others. There is no escape. Moreover, they contain assumptions, biases, and inclinations that have significant implications for how theory is formulated and understood. Leaving them implicit and unquestioned is the theoretical sin. The only defense against capitulation to a natural world where the obvious becomes necessary and what is "real" becomes what is "true" is a critical, and social, interrogation of categories. The point of theory is to protect scholars from the seduction of reality.

Notes

1. Larry S. Bourne, "On Schools of Thought, Comparative Research, and Inclusiveness: A Commentary," *Urban Geography* 29, no. 2 (2008): 178.

2. Richard Weinstein, "The First American City," in Allen J. Scott and Edward W. Soja, eds., *The City: Los Angeles and Urban Theory at the End of the Twentieth Century* (Berkeley: University of California Press, 1996), 22.

3. In contrast, and for London, see Doreen Massey, *World City* (Cambridge: Polity Press, 2007), 29–53.

4. Robert A. M. Stern, Thomas Mellins, and David Fishman, *New York 1960: Architecture and Urbanism between the Second World War and the Bicentennial* (New York: The Monacelli Press, 1995), 8.

5. Robert A. M. Stern, G. Gilmartin, and Thomas Mellins, *New York 1930: Architecture and Urbanism between the Two World Wars* (New York: Rizzoli, 1987), 18.

6. See Andrew Sayer, *Method in Social Science* (London: Routledge, 1992), 45–84; Eviatar Zerubavel, *The Fine Line: Making Distinctions in Everyday Life* (New York: The Free Press, 1991).

7. Immanuel Wallerstein, *The Uncertainties of Knowledge* (Philadelphia: Temple University Press, 2004).

8. Mike Savage and Alan Warde, *Urban Sociology, Capitalism and Modernity* (New York: Continuum Publishing, 1993), 2.

9. Phil Hubbard, *City* (London: Routledge, 2006), 1.

10. Andrew Barry, Georgina Brown, and Gisa Weszkalnys, "Logics of Interdisciplinarity," *Economy and Society* 37, no. 1 (2008): 20–49.

11. Andrew Sayer, "Realisms through Thick and Thin," *Environment and Planning A* 36, no. 1 (2004): 1777–89.

12. Edward A. Tiryakian, "The Significance of Schools in the Development of Sociology," in W.E. Snizek, E.R. Furman, and M.K. Miller, eds., *Contemporary Issues in Theory and Research* (Westport, Conn.: Greenwood Press, 1979), 211–33.

13. Robert A. Beauregard, "City of Superlatives," *City and Community* 2, no. 3 (2003): 183–99.

14. Jeffrey N. Wasserstrom, "Comparing 'Incomparable' Cities: Postmodern L.A. and Old Shanghai," *Contention* 5, no. 3 (1996): 78.

15. Michael J. Dear and Steven Flusty, "The Resistible Rise of the L.A. School," in M.J. Dear, ed., *From Chicago to L.A.: Making Sense of Urban Theory* (Thousand Oaks, Calif.: Sage Publications, 2002) 3–16.

16. Michael J. Dear and Steven Flusty, "Postmodern Urbanism," *Annals of the American Association of Geographers* 88, no. 1 (1998): 52.

17. See Michael J. Dear, *The Postmodern Urban Condition* (Oxford: Blackwell, 2000); Edward Soja, *Postmodern Geographies* (London: Verso, 1989).

18. Daphne Spain, "What Happened to Gender Relations on the Way from Chicago to Los Angeles?" *City and Community* 1, no. 2 (2002): 155–67.

19. M. J. Borer, "The Location of Culture," *City and Community* 5, no. 2 (2006): 179.

20. Soja, *Postmodern Geographies*, 191.

21. Thomas S. Kuhn, *The Structure of Scientific Revolutions* (1962; Chicago: University of Chicago Press, 2nd ed., 1970).

22. Michael J. Dear, "The Los Angeles School of Urbanism: An Intellectual History," *Urban Geography* 24, no. 6 (2003): 493–509; Michael J. Dear, "The L.A. School: A Personal Introduction," in Dear, *From Chicago to L.A.*, 423–26.

23. Robert A. Beauregard, "Break Dancing on Santa Monica Boulevard," *Urban Geography* 20, no. 5 (1999): 396–99.

24. Michael Dear et al., "Critical Responses to the Los Angeles School of Urbanism," *Urban Geography* 29, no. 2 (2008): 101–112.

25. Dear, *From Chicago to L.A.*, ix.

26. Ibid., xi.

27. Ibid., viii.

28. Ibid., x.

29. Ibid., ix.

30. Ibid., x.

31. Ibid., 3, my emphasis.

32. Jan Nijman, "The Paradigmatic City," *Annals of the Association of American Geographers* 90, no. 1 (2000): 135–45.

33. David Halle, "The New York and Los Angeles Schools," in David Halle, ed., *New York and Los Angeles* (Chicago: University of Chicago Press, 2003), 1–46.

34. Ibid., 15–23.

35. David Halle, "Who Wears Jane Jacobs's Mantle in Today's New York City?" *City and Community* 5, no. 3 (2006): 237–41.

36. My discussion of the conference is based on personal notes.

37. Terry Clark, "Amenities Drive Urban Growth," *Journal of Urban Affairs* 24, no. 5 (2002): 493–515.

38. Andrew Abbott, *Department and Discipline: Chicago Sociology at One Hundred* (Chicago: University of Chicago Press, 1999).

39. Manuel Castells, *The Urban Question* (Cambridge, Mass.: MIT Press, 1977); David Harvey, *Social Justice and the City* (Baltimore: The Johns Hopkins University Press, 1973).

40. See Ann Markusen, Yang-Song Lee, and Sean D. DiGiovanna, eds., *Second Tier Cities* (Minneapolis: University of Minnesota Press, 1999); Jennifer Robinson, *Ordinary Cities: Between Modernity and Development* (London: Routledge, 2006); Saskia Sassen, *The Global City: New York, London, Tokyo* (Princeton, N.J.: Princeton University Press, 1991).

41. Wasserstrom, "Comparing 'Incomparable' Cities."

42. See, for example, James Amelang, "Comparing Cities: A Barcelona Model?" *Urban History* 34, no. 2 (2007): 173–89.

43. Robinson, *Ordinary Cities.*

44. Sayer, *Method in Social Science,* 138–40.

45. Andrew Sayer, "Explanation in Economic Geography," *Progress in Human Geography* 6, no. 1 (1982): 68–88.

46. Doreen Massey, *For Space* (London: SAGE Publications, 2005).

47. See, for example, Janet Abu-Lughod, *New York, Chicago, Los Angeles: America's Global Cities* (Minneapolis: University of Minnesota Press, 1999).

48. William Cronon, *Nature's Metropolis: Chicago and the Great West* (New York: W.W. Norton, 1991).

49. Ash Amin and Stephen Graham, "The Ordinary City," *Transactions of the Institute of British Geographers* 22 (1997): 411–29; Robinson, *Ordinary Cities.*

50. Raewyn Connell, "The Northern Theory of Globalization," *Sociological Theory* 25, no. 4 (2007): 368–85.

Part IV

The View from Chicago

10

The New Chicago School of Urbanism and the New Daley Machine

▪ Dick Simpson and Tom Kelly

The Old Chicago School

At the beginning of the twentieth century, social scientists at the University of Chicago sought "scientifically" to capture the city of Chicago.[1] They framed their direct observations around ecological images such as rings of growth, like the growth rings of trees; racial patterns of settlement like the patterns of plant ecology; immigration patterns of expansion along radial lines; and an organic machine politics. They varied between the unique, textured, direct accounts of participant observation of real slums, gangs, politics, and other Chicago phenomena and the universal, scientific, abstract social science models they created.[2]

Collectively they created the Chicago School of urban studies, which so swept the social sciences that it provided the reigning paradigms of knowledge in urban sociology, politics, geography, and economics, for eighty years. However well these models fit when they were developed, these paradigms no longer fit our cities in the twenty-first century, not even in Chicago where they were created. Global cities and urban life today demand new descriptions and paradigms if we are to understand where we (and more of half of humanity) live.[3]

Chicago gave birth to the most famous image of the old Chicago School, the concentric rings of growth. It was modeled on Chicago at the turn of the twentieth century. There was a downtown, called in Chicago The Loop, after the original loop of the Chicago River and later the Chicago elevated tracks. Factories and slums surrounded this downtown. Farther out were the working-class neighborhoods, residential, and commuters zones.

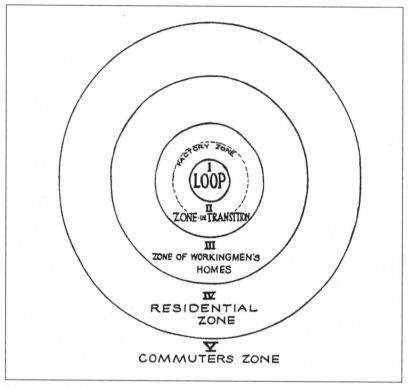

Figure 10.1 The Chicago Loop.

This concentric ring model was never a perfect fit. The Near South Side, especially along Prairie Ave., had houses of rich Chicagoans, such as the Palmers and the Armours. In the early twentieth century, Chicago had African American slums as well that stretched beyond the original rings of poverty in the diagram. The rich Gold Coast on the Near North Side also did not fit within the appropriate ring of development. However, it is much more significant that the concentric ring pattern clearly does not hold today. A modern twenty-first century city Loop does exist in Chicago, but it is no longer a shopping mecca. That role has been taken over by the Magnificent Mile along North Michigan Avenue and by shopping malls in the far-flung suburbs. Map 10.1 clearly demonstrates that high- and low-income communities do not fall primarily within their proper zones as they should according to the concentric rings model.

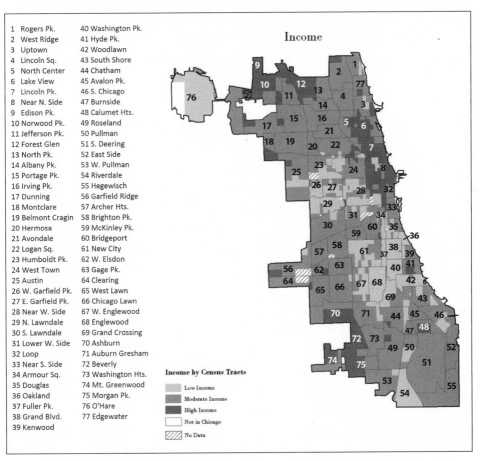

Figure 10.2 Chicago income by census tracts. Courtesy of the Institute for Housing Studies, DePaul University, August 2009.

As early as the 1960s, demographer Pierre de Vise and sociologist William Julius Wilson studied the connection between race and poverty in Chicago.[4] DeVise found that the ten poorest communities were all in the inner city and all black. The ten richest were all suburban, mostly north suburban, and all white.

The patterns of poverty in households below the poverty level published by Wilson showed that the poverty areas remained unchanged by 1980. Updating Wilson's work to the 2000 census shows poverty moving farther south and west and becoming slightly less concentrated. Still today, the patterns of poverty and wealth in the city of Chicago remain essentially the same as when de Vise and Wilson studied them. And because these are racial patterns as well, they affect economics and politics directly.

The New Chicago Reality

Not only is the concentric-rings-of-growth model outdated, its scale is incorrect. Chicago is no longer the compact urban area of the early twentieth century but a metropolitan region of as many as 12 million people, spanning three states. The Chicago area sprawls in networks of towns and governments unimagined even a few decades ago. As any twenty-first century map of economic wealth in the Chicago metropolitan region would demonstrate, poverty is no longer confined to the inner city. Communities such as the southern suburbs of Harvey and Markham, the western suburbs of Maywood and Aurora, and neighboring Gary, Indiana, have high poverty rates. Again demonstrating the correlation between race and poverty in the metropolitan area, many of the poorest communities surrounding Chicago have substantial African American populations.

There are no longer neat concentric rings of growth like rings on a tree, but a complicated system more like a human body with a heart and brain still in the Loop, but networks of arteries, veins, nerves, and appendages stretching for many miles. The broader map of the region using low tax capacity as a measure for community poverty shows that there are not only patterns of poverty in the city but in the suburban region, with the poorest communities in the south suburbs and the richest in the north. Poverty and race are now correlated throughout the entire metropolitan region.

Chicago scholars for the last ninety years have studied racial segregation. The original pattern of ethnic neighborhoods in Chicago has been supplanted by large racial regions of the city and suburbs. However, the racial patterns in twenty-first century Chicago have changed. Race is no longer just a stark division between black and white. Chicago has become more or less one-third African American, one-third white, and one-third Latino, interspersed with immigrants from the Middle East and Asia. Blacks, Latinos and whites are still segregated into different

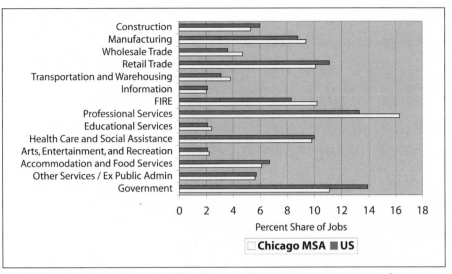

Figure 10.3 Industry share of total employment, Chicago, 2004. Source: Bureau of Economic Analysis.

communities but now those communities are suburban as well as inner-city communities.

Chicagoans speak every language on the globe, and its citizens have family ties overseas. While Chicago has yet to eliminate the vestiges of racial discrimination, it has become multicultural, multiracial, and multiethnic. These new racial realities are reshaping the society, economy, and the politics of the new Chicago metropolitan region. Instead of an Irish Richard Daley or an African American Harold Washington, the new political face of Chicago is the multiracial face of President Barack Obama.

Of course, underlying the social and political changes in Chicago are fundamental economic changes. Over a century and a half, the city has transformed from a trading post on the frontier to a mercantile and manufacturing city. From a manufacturing economy, it evolved into a service economy. It is now the Midwest capital of the global economy.

As shown by Figure 10.3, today in metropolitan Chicago, less than 29 percent of the jobs are in the manufacturing, trade, and construction sectors; nearly 40 percent are in the service sector; and 30 percent are probably linked to the increasingly globalized international economy, or global sector. Particularly importantly, Chicago had more than the national average of jobs in the finance, insurance, real estate, and professional service sectors, which lead the global economy. As Chicago is no longer just a black and white society, it is not just a manufacturing, mercantile, service, or global economy, but all four merged together in the special mix of a new global city.

As a global city, Chicago is a tourist and convention destination. It has more than ten million visits a year at cultural sites like Navy Pier, the Art Institute, and various museums, and thousands attend Chicago sporting events at ballparks, football fields, and the United Center. People from the metropolitan region, the nation, and the world come to Chicago for knowledge, entertainment, shopping, and vacations. Given the transformations in the new Chicago, it is reasonable to believe that Chicago politics have also changed in spite of the fact that a Mayor Daley has led the city for more than forty of the last fifty-one years.

The New Chicago Machine

Chicago machine politics was correctly described by Chicago School political scientists Charles Merriam and Howard Gosnell seventy years ago and updated by Mike Royko and Milton Rakove thirty years ago.[5] Originally there were multiple political machines, both Democratic and Republican in Chicago, governed by patronage and corruption. The City Council of Grey Wolves was run by cliques of machine aldermen in a constant struggle with reformers. Then in 1931, Anton Cermak created a single Democratic machine, continued after his death by Mayor Ed Kelly and party boss Pat Nash. After a brief interlude under Mayor Martin Kennedy, Richard J. Daley came to power and perfected the Democratic Party machine.

The Richard J. Daley machine had a distinctive set of features, which refined the machine politics that had governed most of the larger East Coast and Midwest cities from the last half of the nineteenth century until the late twentieth century. It was an economic exchange within the framework of the political party and an economic growth machine that married that political party to big businesses in a public-private partnership.

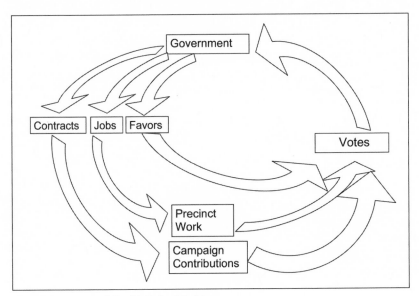

Figure 10.4 Mayor Richard J. Daley Machine.

Patronage jobs at city hall begat patronage precinct captains who contacted voters and persuaded them to trade favors or city services for votes for the party's candidates. Government contracts from city hall convinced otherwise Republican businessmen to give the campaign contributions necessary to fund campaign literature, walk-around money, and bribes. These contributions of precinct work, money, and votes won elections for the Daley machine, which then controlled the government so that the mayor could distribute the spoils that kept the machine running. Mayor Richard M. Daley continues some of the practices of his father, but he has once again modernized Chicago politics and government.

As shown in Figure 10.5, in the Richard M. Daley Machine, old style patronage and corruption now coexist with multimillion-dollar campaign contributions from global corporations, high-tech public opinion polling, and media manipulation. The ward organizations, and especially Daley organizations like the Hispanic Democratic Organization (HDO), still work the precincts. City contractors and construction labor unions still contribute money to the mayor's campaigns and to campaigns he specifies. But now rich individuals and global businesses, law firms, and financial institutions

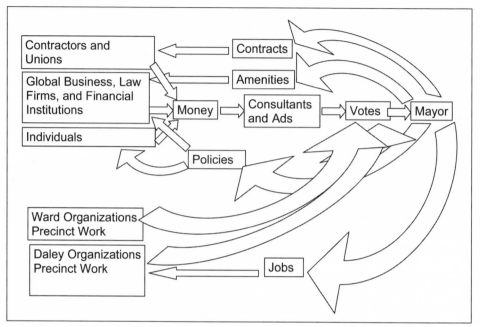

Figure 10.5 Mayor Richard M. Daley Machine.

contribute the millions of dollars necessary to hire national political consultants like David Axelrod to do public opinion polling, direct mail, and slick TV ads. The payoffs in the new Daley machine are also different. There are still patronage jobs given to precinct workers and contracts to contributing businessmen, just like under the Richard J. Daley machine. But now there are the amenities like flowers in the parkway, wrought iron fences, Millennium Park, and, most importantly, a tax structure favorable to the new global economy.[6]

The New Machine vs. the Old Machine

Despite superficial similarities, such as having a Mayor Daley in charge of the city of Chicago, several aspects of the new machine differ greatly from the machine of the past. Patronage/precinct organizations are now supplemented with media-based, synthetic campaigns. Campaigns are centered on the candidate more than the party and ward organizations are supplanted

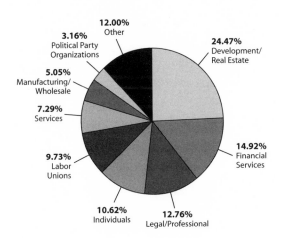

Figure 10.6
Sources of campaign
contributions to
Chicago Mayor
Daley in 2003 by
percent of total.

by special Daley political organizations. The rubber-stamp city council no longer has a significant opposition faction to oppose the mayor. Instead of being segregated into submachines or excluded entirely, minorities and other potential opposition groups are co-opted and rewarded with jobs and contracts for working within the system. Public policies are reoriented toward the global economy and no longer solely focused on local development interests.

Evidence of these assertions comes in various forms. The empirical data that define the contours of the new Daley machine and the new Chicago politics include: 1) election results, 2) campaign contribution data, 3) city council voting data, 4) proffers of evidence and court case findings in corruption and patronage cases, 5) city jobs and contract data from EEOC filings, and 6) demographic data.

In political campaigns, money is equivalent to power, influence, and access. Therefore, power players in the new machine can be partially tracked by examining the major sources of campaign revenue. As Figure 10.6 reveals, in 2003 Daley raised 27 percent of his campaign funds from financial services and law firms. He raised another 11 percent from wealthy individuals. Most of these are in the global economy sector. He raised only 10 percent from labor unions and 25 percent from developers and real estate. So, a little more than one-third of his money came from the global economy, one-third from

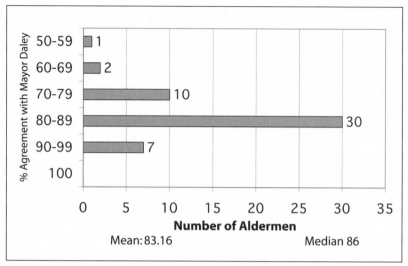

Figure 10.7 Aldermanic agreement with floor leader for 49 divided roll call votes in the Chicago City Council, May 7, 2003–November 15, 2006, Mayor Richard M. Daley.

the old economy, and one-third from smaller sections. Notice especially, that only 3 percent came from political party organizations.

The biggest change in the 2007 elections is that labor unions contributed over a million dollars to the mayor's aldermanic opponents and refused to endorse Daley's reelection. On the other side, global firms like Wal-Mart and Target, fighting against Chicago's Big Box ordinances that would have mandated higher wages and health benefits, supported the mayor's aldermanic allies and the mayor with several hundred thousand dollars in contributions. Global business firms, local businesses, and labor unions are the main contributors to Mayor Daley. The Democratic Party and its ward organizations contribute precinct work, but little money.

The Chicago City Council since the late 1990s has again become a rubber stamp and almost completely so after the 2003 elections. Figure 10.7 shows that from 2003 to 2006, in three and a half years, there were only 49 divided roll-call votes in the council instead of the 100 a year, which is more the norm for the Chicago City Council historically. However, some change has begun. The council became less controlled in 2006. The mayor lost four key council votes in 2006–2007 and had to use the mayoral veto

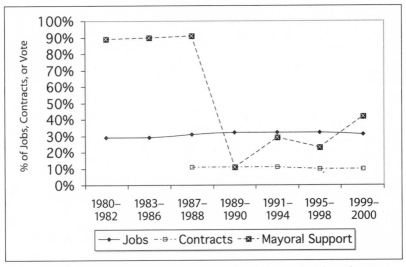

Figure 10.8 Black voter support for Chicago mayor in relation to city jobs and contracts awarded to blacks.

for the first time in his or his father's mayoralty. The new city council that took office in May 2007 is a weaker rubber stamp than past councils for the mayor because nine new aldermen were elected, most with the backing of unions and neighborhood organizations over pro-Daley incumbents. But the pattern of autocratic mayoral control and a weak council has character-ized twenty-first century Chicago under Richard M. Daley and continues to do so despite recently contentious votes on issues like moving the Children's Museum to Millennium Park, locating in the city Wal-Mart stores, which do not pay a living wage or benefits, and sale of the city's parking meters to a private firm.

Finally, it is important to track payoffs to racial groups that support and oppose mayors. Black voters originally opposed Mayor Daley and sup-ported black candidates instead. In his first election, less than 10 percent of black voters voted for him. In 2003, the mayor's support rose dramatically to over half of the black voters and it remained above 50 percent in 2007. But as Figure 10.8 shows, increasing support for the mayor has not yielded an increase in jobs and contracts. On the other hand, Daley did not punish the black community. They retained about the same number of jobs and

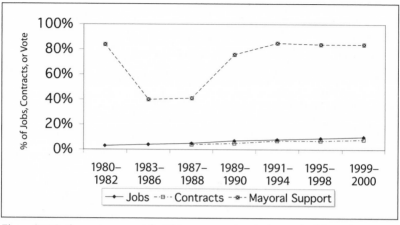

Figure 10.9 Latino voter support for Chicago mayor in relation to city jobs and contracts awarded to Latinos.

contracts as they had under Chicago's first black mayor, Harold Washington, who held office from 1983 to 1987.

The new Daley machine is fundamentally a coalition between whites and Latinos. Latinos have, in essence, calculated that there is more to be gained by supporting a white mayor than a black mayor, and Figure 10.9 supports this view.

While they gave less than a majority of their votes to Harold Washington in 1983 and 1987, the Latino vote was sufficient to elect him, and Washington gave them jobs and contracts in return. Their share of jobs and contracts has risen exponentially and today they have more city contracts than blacks and an ever-increasing share of jobs while blacks have barely kept what they had in jobs and contracts at city hall. In return, Latinos gave at first 70 percent and later more than 80 percent of their votes to Daley and that remained true in 2007.

Conclusion

The old Chicago School with its paradigms of concentric rings of development, radial racial expansion, black/white segregation, and the old Daley machine model is inadequate in the twenty-first century even in Chicago.

The old ecological image of cities is better replaced with the metaphor of the human body or the body politic. The heart and brain are in the political machine downtown and the public-private partnership called the "growth machine" or regime. The rest of the body politic is made up of networks stretching throughout the metropolitan region.

Since 2001, some two dozen urban scholars from a number of colleges and universities in the Chicago metropolitan region have banded together to found a new Chicago school of urbanism.[7] Its premise is that globalization has changed Chicago, but that Chicago has not automatically copied other global cities like New York, Los Angeles, London, Tokyo, or Paris. In Chicago, politics and government have remained central forces even in the face of globalization and metropolitanization. Thus, the new Daley machine is a central focus of the new paradigms developed by the new Chicago School. At the same time, Chicago scholars have studied social, economic, and cultural changes including a growth in conventions and tourism, which brings about fifty million tourists to the city each year with a corresponding demand for amenities like Navy Pier, museums, Millennium Park, new convention halls, and new sports stadiums. The city also aggressively sought to host the 2016 Olympics to further extend its global image. Although it lost in the final selection process, it remains a global city. The new Chicago School asserts that history and politics shape modern metropolitan life and mediates the impact of large-scale structural changes and impersonal economic forces like globalization.

This has forced the new Chicago School to study closely the new Daley machine, which is characterized by several trends. A compliant city council rubber-stamps most of the mayor's proposals, even if it recently has shown slightly more independence. The growing electoral power of the mayor has deterred viable opponents. A white-Latino coalition has emerged and now governs Chicago, replacing the black-white coalition of Richard J. Daley. The dynamic of minority groups being alienated by racist policies has largely disappeared.

Nonetheless, strong candidates are expected to run for mayor in 2011 or 2015. Cook County remains a Democratic Party bastion for the time being but metropolitan governance remains weak. Mayors in suburban municipalities have come together on some issues and have even begun to cooperate with Mayor Daley, but there is no regional government, and planning coordination remains on a volunteer basis despite the existence of a central planning agency, the Chicago Metropolitan Agency for Planning.

Richard M. Daley does not enjoy the same degree of power as his father. This Daley does not have the power to influence elections for higher office in the way the old one did. There are fewer patronage workers and weaker party organizations, so this Daley is not a kingmaker. However, campaign contributions indicate the reorientation of the machine toward the global economy, as do the resulting policies of the Daley administration. This has resulted in several major public-private partnerships including the creation of Millennium Park and launching the bid for the 2016 Olympics.

The old Chicago School theories are being completely revised by current Chicago urban scholars. Central to these revisions is the model of the new Daley machine. Clearly new paradigms, theories, and models will have to be developed if we are to better understand the new metropolitan regions in which we live in our global era. We must make sense of the social, economic, political, and governmental transformations. In Chicago, scholars have begun to go beyond simple description to develop a set of models and paradigms that may have relevance in other places.

Those of us studying Chicago recognize that a city like New York differs from us in being a hegemonic metropole like London, Paris, and Tokyo. We agree with New York scholars that the center is critical even as there is growth on the metropolitan periphery, that public services are a core organizing element in such a global city, and that politics remain important. While we differ in some ways with Los Angeles scholars, we concur that we must study the greater metropolitan region, take account of decentralization, and pay close attention to cultural changes. However, we disagree with the Los Angeles School that the center does not hold and that keno capitalism and postmodernism best describe our urban reality.

Each major U.S. global city is an exemplar for the developing patterns in other U.S. and international cities. In our study of Chicago, we believe that a careful historical analysis, attention to political phenomena, social and economic changes, and empirical data gathered on these elements provide the best way to understand the changes we are experiencing.

The studies of Chicago, Los Angeles, and New York suggest that we should be able to determine the range of variation in global cities and to understand how their history, politics, and circumstance cause them to follow both similar and different trajectories. The data collected in Chicago, such as demographic patterns, election results, campaign contributions, and city council voting patterns, can be collected in other cities. They would allow for a much more careful comparison of city politics and governance.

Notes

1. Robert E. Park, Ernest Burgess, and Roderick D. McKenzie, *The City: Suggestions for Investigation of Human Behavior in the Urban Environment* (Chicago: University of Chicago Press, 1925; reprint, 1967).

2. Thomas F. Gieryn, "City as Truth-Spot: Laboratories and Field-Sites in Urban Studies," *Social Studies of Science* 36, no. 1 (February 2006): 5–38.

3. Robin Hambleton and Jill Gross, *Governing Cities in a Global Era* (New York: Palgrave Macmillan, 2007).

4. Pierre de Vise, *Chicago's Widening Color Gap* (Chicago: Interuniversity Social Research Committee Report, 1967, reprint in Dick Simpson, ed., *Chicago's Future in a Time of Change* (Champaign, Ill.: Stipes Publishing, 1993); William Julius Wilson, *The Truly Disadvantaged: The Inner City, the Underclass, and Public Policy* (Chicago: University of Chicago Press, 1987).

5. Charles Edward Merriam, *Chicago: A More Intimate View of Urban Politics* (Chicago: University of Chicago Press, 1929); Harold Foote Gosnell, *Machine Politics: Chicago Model* (Chicago: University of Chicago Press, 1937); Mike Royko, *Boss: Richard J. Daley of Chicago* (New York: E. F. Dutton, 1971); Milton Rakove, *Don't Make No Waves, Don't Back No Losers: An Insider's Analysis of the Daley Machine* (Bloomington: Indiana University Press, 1975).

6. Dick Simpson, *Rogues, Rebels, and Rubber Stamps: The Politics of the Chicago City Council from 1863 to the Present* (Boulder, Colo.: Westview, 2001); Dick Simpson and Tom Kelly, "Chicago's City Council's Increasing Independence: Chicago City Council Report May 7, 2003–November 25, 2006" (Chicago: University of Illinois at Chicago, 2006), http://www.uic.edu/depts/pols/chicagopolitics; Dick Simpson and Tom Kelly, digital videotape of presentations by scholars of the Chicago, New York, and Los Angeles schools of urban studies at Urban Scholars Conference, University of Illinois at Chicago, April 10–11, 2007, http://www.uic.edu/depts/pols/chicagopolitics.

7. John P. Koval et al., eds., *The New Chicago: A Social and Cultural Analysis* (Philadelphia: Temple University Press, 2006); Simpson, "Chicago's City Council's Increasing Independence."

11

The New Chicago School
Notes toward a Theory

■ Terry Nichols Clark

Every city is unique. Cities partially shape their residents, sensitizing them to some concerns, while discouraging others. This chapter explores how the city of Chicago has encouraged a distinct flavor in the research and theorizing about cities by persons who have done time in Chicago's environs. The last section considers how these ideas may be joined together as components of a new Chicago School. It should be noted at the outset that the participants in the Chicago Not-Yet-a-School of urban politics—also known among themselves, tongue-in-cheek, as the Chicago Preschool—differ on the question of whether a new Chicago school has taken form.[1]

The reflections in this chapter are sparked by recent discussions of the L.A. and New York schools, which have substantially defined themselves in opposition to an old Chicago model—of Ernest Burgess, Homer Hoyt, and others. We agree with critics who maintain that core aspects of the older Chicago paradigms are inadequate.[2] We need new and better theorizing—especially about cities and urban phenomena. We reflect on these issues as the critics and flag-wavers on each coast seem not only to have misunderstood Chicago and Chicago-based theorizing, but also to have constructed foundations too limited for themselves and others to build on. Reflecting on Chicago can potentially enrich our theorizing about cities and societies around the world.

Chicago has long illustrated such diverse and openly conflictual politics that it draws in visitors like Max Weber (who wrote that Chicago was like a man with his skin cut off, so you could see the working organs exposed) and led Saul Bellow[3] to do graduate work in anthropology (which directly inspired his *Henderson the Rain King* and more). Chicago visitors have long been aghast by Chicago's politics and culture, yet these inspired many to dig deeper. Doing time around Chicago politics is like doing fieldwork among the Australian aborigines for a young anthropologist. It teaches cultural relativism. It shakes up the standard political labels, categories, and solutions that come from most European and American politics.

Chicago, I suggest, is a distinctly important world city because its core political dynamics were long those of clientelism or patronage—which in recent years have been reframed as bribery and corruption. This clientelism Chicago shares with Taipei, Naples, Bogotá, Lagos, and indeed most cities the world over. To confront this past openly, and consider how this legacy has changed and can change, is the most salient issue on the policy agenda of governments today—at national, regional, and local levels. It stands prior to and is definitional in conceptualizing development in its multiple possible forms. Chicago offers answers to these general queries.

We explore Chicago as a case, pointing out traits that are found elsewhere. That is, we strive to generalize by exploring the core, deeper structures that drive Chicago. If every city is unique, it is because general processes combine in unique ways in each location. But we can understand a single city better, and offer more lessons for others, by attending to the general processes as well as to how they combine to generate uniqueness.

Chicago's Uniqueness

Several factors make Chicago unique, and therefore capable of producing new ways of analyzing cities. These factors include the following:

1. Chicago is the largest major U.S. city with a strong tradition of Catholicism; white Protestants accounted for less than 20 percent of the population through the twentieth century. Chicago's Catholic tradition was drastically shaken in the 1984 election of Harold Washington, who first mobilized African-American Chicagoans for serious political engagement. The continual flow of immigrants from across the world has filled specific neighborhoods with new character, but

ethnically and culturally distinct neighborhoods remain stronger and more politically legitimate in this city than most U.S. locales.

2. Catholicism, by stressing concrete personal relations, helped legitimate Chicago's parishes, schools, and neighborhoods. The precinct captains have long been distinctly powerful; ethnic politics, clientelism/patronage, and material allocation of incentives were the key resources. Chicago is rife with the Wagnerian leitmotifs, the Levi-Straussian deep structures: Don't make no waves, don't back no losers. We don't want nobody nobody sent. Chicago ain't ready for reform. (The first two are titles of books by Milton Rakove; the third is a slogan once shouted at political rallies and on the floor of city hall, and now emblazoned on T-shirts.)

3. The strong neighborhoods and personal relations have led Chicago to be racially and ethnically segregated: in housing location and in politics, with ethnic slating of candidates, parades, and jealously guarded neighborhood autonomy. Aldermen made zoning decisions for their wards, granting or withholding building permits, sometimes indefinitely—unthinkable in a city with an at-large, good-government ethos.

4. Chicago was settled on the frontier, and grew so rapidly that it had weak elite culture, emboldening the common man. A "big-shouldered" acceptance of grit and crassness thus built on a snub-the-proper-folks attitude and encouraged creation of such popular labels as Hinky Dink Kenna, Bathhouse John, and Fast Eddy Vrdolyak—names used to refer to three powerful aldermen/bosses. This is epitomized in the speeches of Mayors Daley I and II. They were proud to speak Chicago Public School English, as are many Chicago Public School teachers. Chicagoans who speak what is elsewhere called General American are often asked, "Where are you from?" implying that their dialect is somehow alien. This dialect was often satirized by the late John Belushi (Chicago's Second City comedy theater supplied many Saturday Night Live actors). SNL spoofed it in a series of "Da Bears, Da Bulls" sketches. Chicago residents who considered themselves more cultured sometimes protested, as in an article in the upscale *Chicago Magazine* when

it ran a profile on "Da Mayor," citing his diction and pronunciation as evidence that he was as politically corrupt as his father.[4]

5. Often, the political norms of state and national governments have been regarded as alien and irrelevant. Seniority as a principle of political slating could lead to sixty-year-olds being sent to Washington as freshmen congressmen. This reverses the normal view that local government is lowly, but follows logically from the sanctity of personal relations, neighborhoods, and distinct policies. Seniority and waiting your turn are principles inculcated in Catholic schools, which have institutionalized practices such as choosing students for the minor roles, and slowly advancing them to major roles in Christmas pageants. Leading black politicians in Chicago long attended Catholic schools and sometimes practiced Catholicism. Even black Protestant ministers, traditional allies of the Chicago Democratic Party, generally accepted these principles.

6. Chicago has a culture of popular cosmopolitanism built on nostalgic old-world linkages. The main traditions in Chicago are not original, but hark back to County Cork or Kraków and are creatively reconstructed on a regular basis. Restaurants and churches, neighborhood schools, bars, and precinct captains carry on these distinct traditions. Commercial signs in Chicago proclaim "Ethnic Flags For Sale," in almost every permutation found in the United States: Polish, Mexican, Lithuanian, Swedish; the list is long.

7. Strong individualism, or at least neighborhood distinctiveness in temperament, meant little focus on public taste, or aesthetics, weak planning, and minimal government (although nongovernmental civic leaders long fought over the issues). Greed and unbridled individualism were the labels of those who did not look more deeply—probed by Steffens's *The Shame of the Cities,* Brecht's *Saint Joan of the Stockyards* and *Arturo Ui,* or Dreiser's novels. This inattention was dramatically reversed in the mid-1990s, when public art and aesthetics were embraced with a dynamism impossible most elsewhere, at least in the United States. (I date the embrace of culture and aesthetics by city hall

from 1995, after the blockbuster success of the Art Institute's Monet show, ostensibly the largest in the world.)

8. Openness and strong innovation—the lack of an established elite and Chicago's early frontier character made it a place where you could, and had to, make it on your own. Chicago was less tinged by tradition than "back East," or Europe, Asia, or even Latin America, which had much stronger, entrenched elites. Similarly in architecture: the skyscraper was invented in Chicago. The classic names in twentieth-century architecture were based in Chicago—Frank Lloyd Wright; Burnham and his plans; Mies van der Rohe; Skidmore, Owings and Merrill. They redefined the image of Chicago and other world cities. You can see the best and worst architecture on the same block in Chicago, as planning and holistic aesthetics were weaker than individual ambition. In other areas: Hugh Hefner's *Playboy* magazine, Playboy Clubs, Playboy Towers, exporting Chicago's bawdy tradition globally. Chicago, New York and L.A. all rank high on patents issued.

9. The political machine and the culture it nurtured long inspired the ambitions of gangs, big corporations, real estate developers, options traders, and mayors to Make No Small Plans. Most U.S. cities have far more fragmented political and social systems—Chicago, in this sense, most closely mirrors non-U.S. locations. Thus China today is a paradise for visionary architects and planners, who build unfettered by citizen protest and zoning found in Europe. Chicago developer Sam Zell, visiting Israel, told the *Jerusalem Times*[5] there was so much red tape that he refused to work in Israel.

10. Neighborhood distinctiveness, strong social ties, and a limited social vision legitimate decentralization to the neighborhood and precinct. The ideals of reform have been very weakly expressed, if at all.[6] Individualism is tempered by strong neighborhood/community/ethnic solidarity. This is embedded in a nonideological Catholicism, distinct from the moralistic utopianism of some Protestants and Jews in New York (especially the unions following David Dubinsky and the ILGWU or *The New York Times*), or the personal and less civic or politically

conscious individualism of L.A., of which Arnold Schwarzenegger is a dramatic manifestation.

11. Just as tremendous population growth and foreign immigration in the nineteenth century gave Chicago a dynamic ethos, so has globalization brought dramatic challenges in the twenty-first century. Chicago's culture of strong mayoral leadership has permitted powerful policy adaptations. For example: dramatic neighborhood renovation, new parks, new public space, buildings and public art designed by internationally renowned architects, roses and trees planted by the thousands (more trees planted "by" Mayor Daley than any other mayor in the world, city hall boasts). Miles of lakefront and marinas have been rebuilt, along with dozens of miles of new bicycle paths. Mayor Daley has made an extraordinary commitment to an economy of culture and entertainment. Entertainment is now Chicago's leading industry.

12. Chicago's reinvention as a global city and a city of culture and entertainment has led to deep contradictions and social conflicts. The term *yuppie* was a Chicago invention meant to label this cultural/ethnic type as a clashing insult to Chicago's blue-collar traditions, whereas in Washington, or even New York, yuppies were part of the normal establishment. The idea that less-articulate, blue-collar citizens had distinct values and preferences (preferences that would not necessarily disappear with political reform, education, or Americanization) legitimated a distinct, explicit focus on ethnicity as interpenetrating all aspects of life and politics. No yuppies in my bar!

13. Class was suppressed by the rise of ethnic groups, and this fact has long influenced intellectuals who lived in the city. The scholarship conducted at the University of Chicago illustrates this point. Arthur Bentley defined interests, and David Truman defined group politics, in nonclass terms. Edward Shils, Edward Banfield, James Q. Wilson, Daniel Elazar, Gabriel Almond, and Clifford Geertz laid the foundations for studying political culture, in national and global perspective, building on their Chicago experiences with ethnicity and neighborhood culture. This everyday acceptance of ethnic/national/cultural

distinctiveness led more to an anthropological cultural relativism and mutual tolerance—"You deliver your precinct, and I'll deliver mine"—that does not support the revolutionary-moralistic aspirations of New England abolitionists, or Dubinsky's Russian union organizers in New York City, or Caesar Chavez's Mexican farm workers in Southern California.

It should be emphasized that the characteristics I have identified are not immune to change, though they still prevail. The nonideological, traditional Catholic style of governance was changed to some degree by the mayoral tenure of Harold Washington from 1984 to 1987. His attempts to institute reform brought the traditional machine to its knees. It redefined the core of Chicago politics and laid a foundation for new rules of the game. The past was nonideological, personalistic exchange. Since Harold Washington, politics and policy have become more explicit and sometimes even ideological. But pragmatism remains a leitmotif: John Dewey and practicality have long been Chicago hallmarks. The persistence of the old political culture has provided the basis for Mayor Richard M. Daley's political authority since 1989. The old machine has pretty much died, but he has been able to build a new political organization based on the same traditional values. Nevertheless, the public norms have been transformed. Daley I, when asked why he gave a city contract to his son's insurance firm, famously replied, "It's a father's duty to help his sons." Daley II would answer, like Harold Washington: any corruption found in city hall will be prosecuted.

A New York School?

As America's largest city, New York provides a vast array of styles and subcultures. But if we ask what its core contributions to social science theory, political commentary, and urban research are, some main themes emerge, and these clearly differ from Chicago's.

Who settled New York? In the nineteenth century, one aphorism holds, the urban Jews left Russia and Poland for New York, while the rural Catholics went to Chicago. New York also had a stronger WASP elite, which in the late nineteenth century imposed strict legal measures on local government, dividing power among the five boroughs as well as the mayor, council, comptroller, and others.[7] Many WASPs moved to the suburbs, a migration assisted by new commuter railroads. The ethnic divisions were such that the Irish and Italian Catholics dominated the Democratic Party, while politically ambitious Jews preferred the unions and media. With legal powers more fragmented than in Chicago, politics was decentralized: the mayor and Democratic Party were continually attacked by the press and competing officials (especially the elected comptroller, who policed the incumbent mayor); civic-group initiated lawsuits were common.

In this context, intellectuals, political commentators, and journalists played a far greater role than in Chicago, and their moralistic reform politics had deeper impact. The culture of passionate, intelligent debate as a central aspect of public life was prized from the ancient prophets, as in Max Weber's *Ancient Judaism* to the CCNY alcoves 1 (Stalinist) and 2 (anti-Stalinist) of the 1930s. A remarkable, sensitive treatment of these issues is *Arguing the World* (film and book),[8] which explores four New York public intellectuals: Daniel Bell, Irving Howe, Nathan Glazer, and Irving Kristol. They illustrate the best of intellectual work, as citizens of the world.

Marxism and the reactions to it are pivotal, the foundation on which much else was built over the twentieth century, from David Dubinsky's 1930s and 1940s union leadership, to the 1950s anti-McCarthy mobilization, the 1960s student movement, to one version of the 1990s postmodernism. Marxism was attacked in its orthodox ("Stalinist") form from the 1930s onward, in the *Partisan Review* and later *Commentary* and *The Public Interest*, little magazines with big impact, led by New York intellectuals.

The ethnic bases of the two cities offer one obvious distinction, with Jews and reform Protestants more numerous in New York. Their religious traditions resonated more deeply with Marxist themes. A divinely inspired journey toward abstract, universal justice was a leitmotif. It was simultaneously an attack on competing subcultures, such as the strident individualism of the Wall Street market or the selfish pawnbroker. Ideological debates were heightened by the weakness of government and political parties and broadcast more by the many national media and publishing firms concentrated there. *The New York Times* is the most obvious illustration and carrier of this outlook to New York-centric locations across the United States, linked in turn to other media (CNN, *Time*, Internet sites, and the like). As New Yorkers rose to prominence in many professions, especially within universities, journalism, the media, and law, these views spread to locations like Washington, Cambridge, Berkeley, and Los Angeles and confronted older (New England moralist) Protestant traditions, which they reinvigorated and transformed in a more activist, intellectualized direction, especially after the 1960s. This style now dominates much of American academic life and professions far more than it did a few decades earlier.[9] Chicago and the University of Chicago, in particular, are often seen as the foil for such New York intellectual moralism.

Chicago is often labeled conservative and New York liberal or left, but this is too simple an analysis. There are subcultures in every city and region. One finds New York subculture in Chicago's artistic and bohemian enclaves, just as powerful Catholic/clientelist traditions persist in parts of Brooklyn and Queens and especially Staten Island.[10] The Jewish/Irish Catholic traditions are foundational sources of these two cultures. Although both are decreasingly linked to their original ethnic sources, they mesh with many allies and are ever changing.

In a more "secular Marxism," a label Seymour Lipset applied to his own work,[11] class analysis is used in a broader, looser sense, such as showing concern for the poor and for inequality. New Yorkers, especially those closest to intellectual life and the academy (not Wall Street or Madison Avenue denizens) are generally critical of the well-established themes of American culture, especially as expressed in suburban Protestant themes and Western unbridled individualism, as typified by cowboy images). New York's heroes are the culturally critical, the bohemian, the artists as social gadflies, with the gay and artist subculture of Greenwich Village and *Village Voice* quintessential examples. These themes join with humor and one-liners in characters like Alvy Singer (Woody Allen) in *Annie Hall*, TV talk shows, and stand-up comedians. This critique of the establishment leads to support for the disadvantaged and minorities, for women, the underclass, and for others disadvantaged by the workings of the political system. A brilliant intermediary type is the superhero (Superman, Batman, Spiderman, and the like) created by New York comic book writers, published by Marvel in the 1930s—co nceived by some as a means to lead the American cowboy to fight the European Fascists.

But note that these disadvantaged groups are often identified with—quite in the abstract—as fellow subjects of discrimination, past or present, by a capitalist/Protestant/upper status/suburban elite. This New York perspective contrasts with the Chicago ethnic/neighborhood diversity, which encourages deeper ethnographic exploration. Rather, this New York style is more deductive, operating from abstract principles that seek more universal applicability. Economic and class explanations are stressed, while culture, ethnicity, and politics are played down, at least as compared to the work of Chicago analysts. The state is invoked as the main policy solution (rather than the market or civic groups or individual initiative).

An L.A. Perspective, If Not a School?

The City of Angels has been deeply reshaped by its continuing immigration, first by a white protestant majority of military men, ranchers, and cowboy-like entrepreneurs who drove out the Mexicans in the mid-nineteenth century. When California entered the Union, progressive reform was the national mood, energized by white Protestants like Teddy Roosevelt. The reformers set a tone of can-do, individualistic heroism, continued from Horatio Alger to The Lone Ranger cowboy (cowboy culture, it should be noted, was consciously adapted for political purposes by Ronald Reagan and George W. Bush).[12] In this reform spirit, California's constitution required nonpartisan elections by local governments; distinctively important in California have been planners and city managers, overseen by low-key business and professional leaders.

Fundamental change came in the 1960s, when city managers and traditional nonpartisan councils were confronted by citizen activists demanding more council representation and staff hiring of women, blacks, and Hispanics. In 1986 I taught at UCLA and met with many local officials. One theme I floated from 1960s research was the finding that many council members served just one term, elections were often uncontested, and it was hard to interest candidates to run for office.[13] By the 1980s, I was told, this was ancient history because of the huge increase in women candidates, who worked long hours, had no other jobs, and drove out the part-timers of earlier years. A handful of localities refused to change in the late 1960s and sought to continue their nonpartisan style, but most changed, and drastically. The traditional city managers were ousted in city after city, and new leaders like Dianne Feinstein transformed government across the state. The city of Los Angeles saw dramatic increases in Mexican migration, compounded by out-migration of whites, and movement of many Asians to suburban areas like Orange and Ventura counties. Many older WASPs, who had supported the nonpartisan, "good government" style, withdrew from public life or moved to places like Montana. They left politics to a more aggressive crowd that passed voter initiatives like the infamous Proposition 13 (which cut property taxes by half) and later propositions that limited public services to illegal immigrants and abolished affirmative action in the University of California system. Turf battles toughened in the O. J. Simpson trial, which became the L.A. Police Department trial, election of a toy company magnate as Republican Mayor of L.A., state energy/financial scandals, recall of the Democratic governor, and his replacement in a special election by Governor Arnold Schwarzenegger.

This nasty battling over turf, and segregation via immigration and differentiation among localities, is stressed by Michel Dear and others. They label it fragmentation. The image is of the haves versus the have-nots, and not much more. The question of who lives where remains vague and abstract in their writings. This characterization builds on a popular reaction against the California dream, a feeling of being robbed, somehow, that the dream is hypocritical, that L.A.'s vast wealth, garishly displayed by film stars and executives in their homes, parties, and private jets, is selfishly denied to the poor. In Mike Davis's *City of Quartz,* the noir concept is as ubiquitous as Californians' shades. Like the New Yorkers, these L.A. writers play down politics and culture and yet often emphatically introduce their personal ideologies, moral outrage, and critique of capitalism, fragmentation or suburbanization, and gated communities as signs of class warfare where rich battle poor.

The image of Southern California as the most golden of American opportunities, with the best climate, the most beautiful people, the nicest beaches, and the tallest trees has long been reiterated by Hollywood and popular media, travel agents, and political leaders. The muscular surfer next to the blond beauty in their convertible on the Pacific Coast Highway is a classic image recognizable the world over. But the power of this Eden image generated critics, from the would-be actress who can find work only as a waitress, to John Steinbeck's *Grapes of Wrath,* featuring Oklahoma migrants to California who can find work only in lowly jobs and whose feelings ferment in a wine vat of wrath, to those whose anger with despoiled beaches or culture creates labels like Californication or Mexifornia.

Two contrasting subcultures are now in deep conflict across California, heightened by out-migration of more established people from Los Angeles, termination of affirmative action at the University of California, and referenda on immigration: the older, strong individualism and a new subculture, strengthened by immigration and closer to Chicago's Catholic collectivism. In the past, young people in L.A. would make the scene in their convertibles on Saturday night and demonstrate prowess by street racing. This ritual, an offering to the individualistic macho totem, was a socialization rite for newcomers (it is interesting that political scientist J. Q. Wilson and movie star James Dean both raced Porsches as adults).

This subculture contrasts with the Mexican (Catholic, more collectivist) gangs of Los Angeles and other locations, whose rumbles are collectivist rituals to an *anti*-individualistic totem. What happens after the Mexican kids get their cars? Does that weaken their ties to the collectivity? Daniel Bell[14] suggested that the Model T helped undermine small-town, middle-class morality and reinforce the individualism (or the coupleism) of the young, especially young women across America. This individualistic car culture was recounted as central for personal identity by a young Irish Catholic growing up in L.A. in the 1950s, with virtually no reference to neighborhoods or ethnicity as in Chicago or later in L.A.[15] The individualism of Los

Angeles is documented powerfully by Robert Putnam in new measures of trust in leaders, trust in friends, trust in family and social capital—on all of which L.A. falls near the lowest of the forty-eight U.S. cities surveyed by Putnam and his colleagues.[16]

Some West L.A. intellectuals elaborated the critical L.A. subculture in neo-Marxist urban studies. These include J. Allen Whitt's L.A. history *Urban Elites and Mass Transportation*, which stresses downtown business and the lack of public transit, Mike Davis's *City of Quartz*, Roger Friedland's work on business domination of American cities, John Logan and Harvey Molotch on developers and land value in *Urban Fortunes*, Mark Gottdiener's theorizing of capital as driving Disney-like commodification of our consumption world, John Friedmann's writings on globalization stressing capitalist exploitation and the rise of urban inequalities, and the popular versions of these themes, like Michael Moore's best-selling books and films like *Roger and Me*, pitting the auto industry against public transit.

Complementing this economic line, the subjective/individualist subculture was deepened when the UCLA Sociology Department added the ethnomethodology of Howard Garfinkel in the 1960s. He pushed inquiry back inside the head of each person and questioned the very grounds of any scientific observation in his close conversational analyses. More popular was the anthropology/philosophy/religious worldview of Carlos Castaneda, who brought a dreamy, drug-inspired subjectivism from the Mexican deserts to L.A. In the heady late 1960s, when drugs/sex/rock and revolution were national passions, Herbert Marcuse moved to California, bringing the Frankfort Marxist tradition, joining Marx with Freud, and these themes fortified the discourse of student activists at UCLA, Berkeley, and nationally. Timothy Leary left Harvard to experiment with LSD in California. These were national, indeed global trends, but these well-publicized leaders chose California.

Strong individualism encourages the postmodern withdrawal to inside one's own mind and body. Decades of immersion in film, L.A.'s main industry, can convince one that nothing is real except the image—the edited, screened, stunt-enacted effect. This postmodern temper privileged a strong, individualistic subjectivism. For instance: "What is distinct about postmodern envy is that the envied subjectivity of the Other is itself likely to be a commodified fantasy, a simulacra of selfhood no more substantial than that of the envier. Or, commonly, the envied is a character of media or the manufactured star of the 'unreality industry' who plays him or her."[17]

These themes combined in the postmodern outlook that Michael Dear, Mike Davis, and others termed the L.A. School: neo- or pseudo-Marxist economic determinism (including Groucho-like keno capitalism), highly subjectivist individualism, deliberately semiarticulate statements that blend the language and mood of high-on-dope dreams and scenes (space cadet, cool, and more argot), and an antiscience pose that snubs serious research as a bore. An often-sneering dismissal of Amerika and Kapitalism blends irony and humor in a tone resonant of film stars on talk shows.

This version of the L.A. School has missed some critical developments that have remade L.A. and its region. Mark Baldassare taught for some two decades in the Social Ecology program at the University of California, Irvine, and directed its Survey Research Center. His center conducted massive surveys of citizens, plus the mayors and council members in every municipal government in Orange County, year after year.[18] This close mapping of changes is not only one of the most rich and detailed for any set of citizens and local governments anywhere in the world, but it tells a dramatic story with important implications that redefine the L.A. School story. Dear and other scholars of the L.A. School stress the fragmentation of subpopulations, citing suburbanization as a key example, but do not explore what the values and attitudes are of actual suburbanites. They are assumed to be fiscally conservative, antiminority folks, traditional Republicans. And in a more distant past, Orange County was closer to this characterization.

This traditional heartland of Republicanism—supporting Ronald Reagan, Disneyland, and naming its airport after John Wayne—remade itself in the 1970s and 1980s, as revealed by the surveys. Women became more involved in politics, as did participants in other social issues from the late 1960s (women, the environment, gay and lesbian rights). All were increasingly supported by Orange County residents and their elected officials. A strong example is Irvine Mayor Larry Aigran, who personally locked arms with hundreds of citizens, blocking car traffic on the freeways at rush hour to protest in favor of mass transit and environmental sensitivity. Yet many citizens remained fiscally conservative, pressing leaders to do more with less.

The most dramatic example was the Orange County bankruptcy, generated by a financial manager who invested so aggressively that when interest rates shifted, the county suffered the largest public default in U.S. history.[19]

Why are these points theoretically important? The rise of social issues, pursued by political leaders appealing directly to citizens, combined with fiscal conservatism, do not register in the normal analytical lenses of Marxism or more generally the Left-Right party configurations that dominated most of the twentieth century in Europe and the United States. *The New York Times* and *Los Angeles Times* accounts of these developments and of leaders like Dianne Feinstein or Larry Aigran frame them as weird and idiosyncratic. Scenes like Orange County or events like Proposition 13 are invoked as products of gluttony and greed. These have become the new shade of noir, L.A. style.

Baldassare, in his rich surveys,[20] provides a deeper, more subtle, and far more empirically informed characterization of the specific values, cultural concerns, and political views of L.A.-area residents than do Michael Dear and Mike Davis, who mainly offer personal hunches and anecdotes on these topics. As his research shows, Orange County reinvented its politics in the last decades of the twentieth century. A new political culture emerged, with leaders stressing social issues like women's rights and the environment, combined with fiscal conservatism, populist appeal to citizens, criticism of traditional groups like parties, unions, and civil service bureaucrats, which then used the media and direct, personal, appeal to citizens to advance their issues.

Citizens' views are not homogenous, and they shift with business cycles as well as over longer time periods. One key point is that they do not move toward social exclusion; on the contrary, they are moving toward greater social tolerance of minorities and nonestablished values, Baldassare shows. This fits with many national studies of the same issues.[21] On issues such as advancing air pollution controls and public transit, there is both wide and deep support. But there are also strong concerns for costs and taxes. The question thus becomes how to advance a progressive social agenda without straining budgets. This is largely a political and administrative challenge that seeks to improve productivity. Here contracting out, negotiating contracts with staffs, and other policy questions loom large. They are by no means simple. They are, however, decidedly different from pursuing a policy of "lock me in behind my gated community," as described by Dear and other L.A. writers. The L.A. School omits serious political analysis.

The changing political culture of L.A. conforms to a global trend. What I have previously identified as the New Political Culture (NPC) has transformed the rules of politics across much of the world.[22] The NPC began to take shape locally in the United States in the 1970s,[23] championed by leaders like Dianne Feinstein as mayor of San Francisco, who adopted fiscally conservative but socially liberal policies. A dramatic convert was Governor Jerry Brown, whose father, Pat, built the freeways and University of California campuses as governor and continued New Deal Democratic traditions. Son Jerry campaigned against Prop. 13, but the day after it passed in 1978, he went on television and promised to implement it with such vigor that after a few weeks he seemed to be a born-again fiscal conservative. This was the opening salvo of the worldwide taxpayer's revolt.

NPC issues rose to national prominence when Bill Clinton transformed the Democratic Party in this same direction. François Mitterrand, Tony Blair, and Gerhard Schroeder did the same inside their Left parties, creating new programs that broke old rules.

These points are important for urban processes as they redefine the cleavages and demand shifts in past theories. In particular, the fact that citizens and leaders want to limit government does not imply that they are racist or antisocial—although the classic lenses of traditional Left-Right politics denies this since they cannot focus on the new cultural configuration. Nevertheless, many observers began to recognize change after national figures like Bill Clinton articulated these issues; the surprise is that some still seem not to have noted what has happened, or have not reflected on how these lessons challenge their paradigm. The NPC has come to Chicago, too, but the drastically different political cultures that existed in L.A. and Chicago have generated very different reactions, as I have noted.

Talking Points of a New Chicago School

As I have stated, I have found political culture to be an essential feature both for devising general urban theories and identifying the unique features of individual cities. Cities have distinct cultures inherited from the past. Globalization has not replaced traditional cultures but has inserted a new, more universal culture that may exist in tension with the old, or, in some cases, replace traditional values. My perspective about this process has been shaped by my participation with an international group of scholars for some years in mapping the global spread of the new political culture. In discussions at conferences of the Fiscal Austerity and Urban Innovation (FAUI) project, involving some 750 scholars from thirty-five countries, and the numerous publications of scholars in this project, our studies confirm the spread of a globalized set of political values as well as the persistence of distinctive local variations.

Based on this rich outpouring of research, as well as my own studies of Chicago and other cities, I offer the following eight axial points for research in Chicago and beyond.

First, *conceptualize the city as pluralistic, diverse, and filled with competing subcultures.* I see the world more as a gesellschaft, an ecosystem of games and scenes. Multiple subcultures map onto particular neighborhoods with distinct rules and rich subtleties, including civic groups and politics. All of these forces have long been recognized for the central roles they play in Chicago.

Second, though common patterns can be identified, it is important to *recognize that no city represents the nation or the world.* There is no Middle-town. Disputing Michael Dear's claim that L.A. is "the city of the future," our more culturally relativistic perspective suggests instead: No one city is The Future.

Third, *recognize that culturally strong neighborhoods remain separate from the workplace.* Chicago's remarkably rich neighborhoods differ from the European social democratic tradition, where workers would reside in homes built near their factories, and where social life was more driven by production. In many U.S. locations like Chicago, the proud, initially non-English–speaking immigrants naturally lived in neighborhoods where they could talk, eat, relax, and worship with persons of similar national/linguistic/cultural background. They would commute even to distant factory jobs to preserve this neighborhood-cultural-ethnic heritage. This created a more sharply distinct sphere of consumption, where different themes could surface, than if persons who worked together also lived together—as in

Germany initially, or, following the socialist tradition, Russia or China over the twentieth century.

Fourth, *use multiple research methods*—in-depth cases, oral history, ethnography, content analysis, archival history, voting behavior, elite interviews of leaders, and a combination of qualitative and quantitative approaches. As the original Chicago School demonstrated, and as the Chicago context drives home, this is the only way to capture the complexity of urban life.

Fifth, *include the entire metropolitan area*. The Chicago metro model is cooperative, voluntary, built from specific agreements among local governments and private contracting groups for distinct services. L.A. stressed the Lakewood Plan, privatization with contracting out, from the mid-twentieth century on. This has now become generalized, and new agreements are characteristic of suburban and intergovernmental organizations globally. This is important in international perspective; metro areas worldwide are moving away from metro-unified governments in this same direction. The lesson is that decentralization does not equal fragmentation in a one-to-one relationship. What the Europeans term *governance* is essentially pluralistic metro politics.

Sixth, *feature consumption*. W. Lloyd Warner defined the distinctive "American class structure" in the 1930s. He redefined social stratification as grounded not in jobs and workplace, but in consumption.[24] Today we build on this consumption focus,[25] with tourism and quality of life and amenities as key concerns of urban citizens. Current work by Spirou stresses amenities, as does Judd's on tourism,[26] Spirou and Bennett on sports stadiums,[27] and my own work on entertainment and scenes. This is not a unique or new theme to American cities but distinct in Chicago in its powerful implementation. It joins my themes and those of Richard Florida and Edward Glaeser in *The City as an Entertainment Machine*.

Seventh, *recognize that race and ethnicity and subcultural conflicts are normal dimensions of urban life, and they are mediated through political processes*. Chicago has always illustrated how central political processes are to managing social conflict. The Chicago case may be clearer than most, but it is not unique. For example, new forms of political agreements and intergovernmental arrangements among suburbs and neighborhoods are the norm everywhere. This directly contradicts the L.A. School's rather dismal and static portrayal of high levels of nearly unmanageable social antagonism and racial conflict.

Eighth, *recognize that globalization is a source of change in many urban dynamics.* These changes are expressed not only in economic and demographic trends, but also in cultural trends. Globalization has brought about new policy responses to important social problems. Chicago was one of the most self-consciously localistic big cities in the United States only a decade or two ago, and some neighborhoods still are. But top civic and government leaders and their consultants in Chicago are highly sensitive to policy initiatives undertaken in China, Paris, and other global forces. In 2005, Mayor Daley, in a speech to urban officials from across the United States, lamented that it takes ten years to add a runway to O'Hare, while the Chinese build six entire airports in the same decade. Many Chinese are learning English, so as a small step, he added, sixteen Chinese were brought to the Chicago public schools to teach Mandarin.

Conclusion: Beyond Schoolism

Each of the three perspectives considered in this chapter has distinctive contributions to offer. Reasonable urban researchers in all three cities, and in others around the world, can learn from the histories of these distinct perspectives and link them to their unique locales. Paris and much of Latin America, for instance, share a neo-Marxist past with New York intellectuals. But as John Mollenkopf's contribution to this volume makes explicit, there are many New York urbanists who are minimally linked to past Marxist themes. Since the fall of the Wall (in 1989) and heightened globalization, one finds all manner of striking transformations and convergences. Leaders are often smart urbanists who earlier stressed Marxist themes—Manuel Castells, Harvey Molotch, John Logan, perhaps John Mollenkopf—but in more recent work have moved toward new creative syntheses. Of course we are mostly following cities and their leaders in noting these transformations. But it is refreshing to see that as cities change, urban analysts can too, albeit with a bit of a lag. These paradigm changes are not, of course, unique to urban scholars. Political party leaders, journalists, civic leaders, and thoughtful citizens all have to rethink what is happening and why.

Although I label the eight axial points a program for a new Chicago School, it is clear that the points incorporate critical factors driving urban processes globally. They thus seek to go beyond schoolism. They are a set of suggestions for urban analysts to consider in seeking to probe the workings of local governments, big and small, the world over. This is by no means to suggest that all cities are similar or that convergence is the main process. When and where there are systematic differences, such as in who governs, one can interpret a city by careful comparison with others along general variables. This has been the focus of our FAUI Project for more than twenty-five years (see www.faui.org). Still it is critical to detail how and where the general variables combine in a unique manner in each location across the globe. These are the challenges of future urban analysis.

The goal of the eight axial points is to offer a framework for general urban analysis, transcending any single city or theory. How? First, by explicitly comparing the analytical frameworks of writers on New York, Chicago, and L.A. Second, by showing how each is embedded in its locale. Third, by joining each to broader perspectives in general social science theories—Marxist, individualist-postmodernist, and postindustrialist. Fourth, by indicating that these perspectives can combine, since their core processes interpenetrate each other in any empirical city (e.g., in different neighborhoods or times of day). Thus an analyst of a city like Berlin might ask how parts of Berlin are individualist, others show class conflict, while postindustrial processes are salient elsewhere—in distinct neighborhoods or issue areas (e.g., museums vs. pothole repair). Tensions among these elements are central dynamics of cities. Analysts that self-consciously distinguish such interpenetrations can transcend single-theory and single-city parochialisms. The new Chicago School thus illustrates how to transcend schoolism.[28]

Notes

1. Whether we are, or seek to be, identified with or avoid the "school" label changes with who is in the room. Though my comments cannot lay to rest this issue, identifying the ways that Chicago research has put into question the major tenets of the L.A. and New York

schools may help point to useful new directions in urban theory.

2. Brian J. L. Berry and Frank E. Horton, *Geographic Perspectives on Urban Systems* (Englewood Cliffs, N.J.: Prentice Hall, 1970).

3. Saul Bellow, "Writers and Literature in America,"in Terry Nichols Clark and Joseph Ben-David, eds., *Culture and Its Creators: Essays in Honor of Edward Shils* (Chicago: The University of Chicago Press, 1977), 172–96.

4. Jonathan Eig, "Da Rules," *Chicago* 48, no. 11 (November 1999): 115–17, 136–44.

5. *Jerusalem Times* (2004).

6. Terry Nichols Clark, "The Irish Ethic and the Spirit of Patronage," *Ethnicity* 2 (1975): 305–59.

7. Gabriel A. Almond, *Politics and Plutocracy in New York City* (Boulder, Colo.: Westview Urban Policy Challenges Series, 1998).

8. Joseph Dorman, *Arguing the World* (Chicago: University of Chicago Press, 2001).

9. Steven Brint, William L. Cunningham, and Rebecca S. K. Li, "The Politics of Professionals in Five Advanced Industrial Societies," in Terry Nichols Clark and Michael Rempel, eds., *The Politics of Post-Industrial Societies* (Boulder, Colo.: Westview Press, 1997), 113–42; Clem Brooks and Jeff Manza, "Partisan Alignments of the 'Old' and 'New' Middle Classes in Post-Industrial America," in Clark and Rempel, *The Politics of Post-Industrial Societies*, 143–60; Seymour Martin Lipset, *American Exceptionalism* (New York: W.W. Norton, 1996).

10. Jonathan Rieder, *Canarsie: The Jews and Italians of Brooklyn against Liberalism* (Cambridge, Mass.: Harvard University Press, 1985); Chris McNickle, *To Be Mayor of New York* (New York: Columbia University Press, 1993).

11. Seymour Martin Lipset, *Political Man* (Baltimore: Johns Hopkins University Press, second ed., 1981).

12. Daniel J. Elazar, *Covenant and Civil Society: The Constitutional Matrix of Modern Democracy—The Covenant Tradition in Politics*, vol. 4 (New Brunswick, N.J.: Transaction Publishers, 1998); William W. Savage Jr., *The Cowboy Hero: His Image in American History and Culture* (Norman: University of Oklahoma Press, 1979); Holiday Dmitri, "Frontier Justice: Cowboy Ethics and the Bush Doctrine of Preemption" (MA thesis, University of Chicago, August 2003).

13. Heinz Eulau and Kenneth Prewitt, *Labyrinths of Democracy* (Indianapolis, Ind.: Bobbs-Merrill, 1973).

14. Daniel Bell, *The Cultural Contradictions of Capitalism* (New York: HarperCollins, 1996).

15. James Q. Wilson, "A Guide to Reagan Country: The Political Culture of Southern California," *Commentary*, May 1967.

16. Robert Putnam et al., paper presented to the American Political Science Association, Chicago, 2004; R. E. Deleon and K. C. Naff, "Identity Politics and Local Political Culture: Some Comparative Results from the Social Capital Benchmark Survey," *Urban Affairs Review* 39, no. 6 (2004): 689–719.

17. Lauren Langman, "Neon Cages" (unpublished book, 2004). Langman, professor of sociology at Loyola University, is a Chicago self-labeled Marxist of the Frankfort school, whom .I cite to illustrate diversity.

18. Mark Baldassare, "Citizen Preferences for Local Growth Controls," in Terry Nichols Clark and Vincent Hoffmann-Martinot, eds., *The New Political Culture* (Boulder, Colo.: Westview Press, 1998), 261–77; Mark Baldassare, *A California State of Mind* (Berkeley: University of California Press, 2002).

19. Mark Baldassare, *When Government Fails: The Orange County Bankruptcy* (Berkeley: University of California Press, 1998).

20. Baldassare, "Citizen Preferences for Local Growth Controls."

21. Clark, *The Politics of Post-Industrial Societies;* Ronald Inglehart, *Modernization and Postmodernization; Cultural, Economic, and Political Change in 43 Societies* (Princeton, N.J.: Princeton University Press, 1997); Joseph Yi, "God and Karate on the Southside: American Culture and Civic Participation in a Global Era" (PhD diss., University of Chicago, 2004).

22. Terry Nichols Clark and Seymour Martin Lipset, eds., *The Breakdown of Class Politics: A Debate on Post-Industrial Stratification* (Baltimore: Johns Hopkins University Press, 2001); Clark, *The New Political Culture.*

23. Terry Nichols Clark and Lorna C. Ferguson, *City Money* (New York: Columbia University Press, 1983).

24. Clark, *The Breakdown of Class Politics.*

25. Terry Nichols Clark, ed., *The City as an Entertainment Machine: Research in Urban Policy* 9 (Oxford: JAI Press/Elsevier, 2004).

26. Dennis Judd and Susan Fainstein, *The Tourist City* (New Haven: Yale University Press, 1999).

27. Costas Spirou and Larry Bennett, *It's Hardly Sportin': Stadiums, Neighborhood Development, and the New Chicago* (DeKalb: Northern Illinois University Press, 2003).

28. Space considerations required deletion of elements of this chapter: 1. More linkages to broader social, political, and urban theories with many references and noted differences; 2. Contrasts between the sociology of knowledge and empirical analysis; 3. Analysis of quantitative data for the three cities, which showed that L.A. had more migration, but neighborhood effects were important within each of the three cities. Mapping neighborhoods showed Staten Island to be like Catholic Chicago, while Chicago's North Side increasingly resembles national patterns. The longer version of the paper may be found at www.tnc-newsletter.blogspot.com/.

12

The Mayor among His Peers
Interpreting Richard M. Daley

■ Larry Bennett

In the first chapter of this volume, Dennis Judd sketches brief accounts of the Chicago, L.A., and New York schools of urban studies. In the case of the Chicago School, the more typical characterization of Robert Park, Ernest Burgess, Louis Wirth, et al., specifies a Chicago School of *sociology*.[1] Nevertheless, in the early to mid-twentieth century there was a group of notable political scientists engaged in Chicago research, that is, research on Chicago. These included Harold F. Gosnell, Edward C. Banfield, and James Q. Wilson. What is less frequently noted is that there was, in that period, a clear theoretical connection between key features of the political machine—notably, as specified by Gosnell—and the urban ecology of the Chicago School sociologists. As interpreted by the Chicago School *political scientists,* the machine's leadership, incentive system, and geographic structure made it the crucial arbiter among the city's numerous and often warring ethnic populations.[2]

Since the 1950s, deindustrialization, suburbanization, and processes of immigrant assimilation have substantially altered Chicago's ethnic and neighborhood map. Seemingly venerable designations such as Greektown, in fact, refer to ethnic-themed commercial districts; newer designations such as Boystown specify something akin to the "urban village," except in this case the villagers share a lifestyle rather than a European regional lineage. Coincidentally, the once hegemonic urban sociology of Robert Park and his followers was challenged by an array of alternative interpretive frameworks.[3] Yet on the ground, in Chicago, the politics of the machine were more durable. Mayor Richard J. Daley dominated Chicago's public affairs from the mid-1950s until the mid-1970s, during these two decades substantially centralizing Cook County Democratic Party operations. At the peak of his power in the mid-1960s—and at a time when urban political machines across the country were in decline—the Daley machine appeared to be invulnerable.

By the latter years of Richard J. Daley's mayoralty, scholars' interpretation of Chicago politics had undergone a subtle and possibly unconscious shift. The city's retention of this iconic form of campaigning, government coordination, and activist recruitment was sui generis.[4] And for some commentators on Chicago politics—including political scientist Milton Rakove, but also journalists such as Mike Royko—the Democratic machine's idiosyncrasies and subterranean dealings had become a source of perverse civic pride.[5] From an analytical standpoint, commentators on Chicago's politics increasingly described a "closed system": emerging trends in Chicago politics were invariably outgrowths of previous local developments. The machine's fixity and influence on local political culture were so profound that external influences—or for that matter, any radical departure from past practice—was impossible.

This view of Chicago politics was certainly unsettled by the Harold Washington movement and mayoralty. Not only did Washington pose a profound threat to the inheritors of the Daley machine; the Washington administration's "urban populism" was aligned with insurgent, typically neighborhood-based political movements in several U.S. cities.[6] However, following Harold Washington's death in 1987 and the subsequent political ascendance of Richard M. Daley, various features of the "default view" of Chicago politics have returned: Richard M. Daley is loyally carrying through the agenda of his father; Chicago is governed by a permanently entrenched political machine (albeit a political machine lacking strong ward organizations and with a limited capacity to deliver large numbers of voters to the polls); as political boss of Chicago, Richard M. Daley's power is unchallengeable.[7]

This chapter is an exercise in interpreting Richard M. Daley's now two-decade-long mayoralty without recourse to the default perspective. How Daley has led Chicago is discussed against the context of evolving mayoral practice across the United States. Contemporary Chicago's self-promotion as a global city is also examined, with the particular aims of identifying how this policy vision emerged, the salient features of Richard M. Daley's administration's engagement with globalization, and the local effects of implementing the policies that advance this vision.[8] The discussion of Chicago particulars is further connected to a framework for interpreting mayoral initiatives across the field of U.S. cities. Most assuredly, contemporary trends in Chicago cannot be understood without harboring a healthy respect for the undead hand of the local past. But just as surely, the defining assumption of so much political commentary on this city—that Chicago is a machine city, and always will be—narrows understanding through its insistence that all Chicago politics is local, that the present is an undeviating, straight-line extrapolation from the local past.

A Short History of Mayoring

In the minds of most Americans, the office of mayor is undoubtedly likened to the U.S. presidency, though of course the scope of authority exercised by the municipal chief executive is much more limited than the president's executive reach. What most rank-and-file citizens do not realize is that just as the actual influence exercised by presidents—as a class of governmental officeholder—has flowed and ebbed over time, so have the political stature and influence of mayors—as a group—fluctuated. However, unlike the layperson's history of the United States, whose early decades are punctuated by the exploits of presumably strong chief executives—Washington, Jefferson, Madison, Jackson—there are very few remembered mayors before 1900. In the words of urban historian Jon Teaford: "In 1800 a visitor to Philadelphia or New York City would have discovered municipal power concentrated in the city council, or board of aldermen; the municipal legislature was virtually the government of these cities."[9]

The era of memorable mayors began at the end of the nineteenth century, when urban reform advocates—seeking among other things to more clearly specify accountability in municipal administration and increase day-to-day efficiency of operations—sought the reallocation of authority in city government. As a result of city charter revision, the large and sometimes bicameral legislative branch of city governments shrank in size, while executive powers and the duration of mayoral terms were increased. In reference to executive powers, mayors often became the dominant figure shaping the municipal budget, and as well, they were usually able to exercise some degree of agency oversight through expanded powers of appointment. The details of charter revision and enhanced mayoral power varied from city to city, but as Martin Schiesl, in his history of late nineteenth-century municipal reform, *The Politics of Efficiency*, emphasizes, growing executive power was also a function of more ambitious individuals seeking the office of mayor. Schiesl's account of "strengthening the executive" combines two elements: structural reforms giving mayors the opportunity to exercise broader governmental influence and mayors such as Carter Harrison I (Chicago), Seth Low (Brooklyn), and Hazen Pingree (Detroit) determined to use mayoral authority to transform municipal governance.[10]

The emergence of empowered mayors around 1900 did not guarantee that individuals holding the office would be either wise or effective, and the annals of many American cities were subsequently checkered by the misadventures of "scoundrel mayors" such as Boston's James Michael Curley, New York's "Beau James" Walker—that rarity among failed mayors, who actually fled the country before his second four-year term was completed—and Chicago's own William Hale Thompson.[11] However, the Great Depression also yielded a cohort of heroic mayors, figures such as Detroit's Frank Murphy and New York's Fiorello La Guardia, who are widely viewed as instrumental in their cities' safely navigating the economic crisis of the 1930s.[12]

During the first two decades following World War II, American cities were buffeted by a complex cycle of social and public policy change. The postwar economic boom, middle-class Americans' linked infatuations with physical mobility, the car, and the single-family home, and federal policy unleashed the pent-up rush to the suburbs that had been postponed during the crisis years of the 1930s and 1940s. Within central cities, neighborhood deterioration seemed to accelerate even as racial transition clearly occurred, but coincidentally, the federal urban renewal and interstate highway programs offered the opportunity to stem neighborhood deterioration and modernize core area infrastructure. Big-city mayors were typically at the center of such efforts. Writing in 1964, political scientist Robert Salisbury described a "new convergence" of political power in cities:

> It is headed, and sometimes led, by the elected chief executive of the city, the mayor. Included in the coalition are two principal active groupings, locally oriented economic interests and the professional workers in technical city-related programs. Both these groupings are sources of initiative for programs that involve major allocations of resources, both public and private. Associated with the coalition, also, are whatever groups constitute the popular vote-base of the mayor's electoral success.[13]

The presumed centrality of mayoral leadership in the execution of post–World War II urban redevelopment is reflected in this depiction of New Haven, Connecticut's, urban renewal effort, as offered by Jeanne R. Lowe in her widely read 1967 book, *Cities in a Race with Time:* "Richard C. Lee is the first Mayor in the country to have made urban renewal the cornerstone of his city's administration as well as of his political career. Under Lee, New Haven has done things that many other cities have just talked about or dabbled in."[14] In effect, the salvation of New Haven rested on the shoulders of the federal urban renewal program, whose success, in turn, rested on the shoulders of Mayor Lee. Recalling this era, and citing Richard Lee among his roster of "prototype mayors" of the time, political scientist Peter Eisinger adds: "They excelled in grantsmanship, and they understood how to use city hall as a bully pulpit in their efforts to bridge racial and class divisions."[15] Yes, Lee excelled at winning federal aid for New Haven, and John Lindsay of New York famously used the mayoralty as a progressive bully pulpit, but as a group, this generation of postwar activist mayors has been judged a failure. Within a few years of his departure from Gracie Mansion, John Lindsay's city had fallen into fiscal default. In a study of the comparative performance of American mayors, historian Melvin Holli offers this terse review of a pair of Lindsay's contemporaries, Detroit's Jerome Cavanagh and Cleveland's Carl Stokes: "two promising political high-flyers who were grounded by grim and ugly urban riots."[16] Even the achievements of the widely praised and repeatedly reelected Richard C. Lee have, with time, been downgraded. In his compendious account of New Haven's decline across the twentieth century, *City: Urbanism and Its End,* a sympathetic Douglas Rae charges Lee with noble overreaching: "By setting out to re-create a region in which firms and families pressed inward on the central city, seeking out opportunities to produce, sell, and live in the middle of New Haven, Dick Lee had set himself against history . . . Lee had addressed a project of social engineering that no government on any scale to my knowledge has managed to fulfill."[17]

The consensus view of the activist post–World War II mayors is that their ambitions soared beyond the capacity of their municipal administrations, their grasp of day-to-day governmental operations was often weak, and in most cases, they were blindsided by the intensified racial polarization of the late 1960s. Moreover, mayors such as Cavanagh, Lee, Lindsay, and Stokes presided over cities that were also badly punished by deindustrialization and the associated geographic and economic restructurings of the 1970s and 1980s. Yet in the face of the declining fortunes of East Coast and Midwest industrial centers, a new vision of municipal governance and mayoral craft began to form. By the late 1970s, a former Lindsay administration official, E. S. Savas, emerged as a persistent advocate of public service privatization, a strategy that Savas argued would contribute both to governmental cost-saving and improvement in the quality of service delivery.[18] Although Savas initially seemed like a voice in the wilderness—and various municipalities' early experiments in privatization produced limited results—by the late 1980s a more broadly framed reinterpretation of municipal governance problems and prospects coalesced. In 1992, a journalist, David Osborne, and former municipal administrator, Ted Gaebler—who pointedly asserted that "we believe deeply in government"—published their highly influential *Reinventing Government.* Their book is thick with examples of municipal innovation, but its essential arguments can be discerned in this introductory summary:

> Most entrepreneurial governments promote *competition* between service providers. They *empower* citizens by pushing control out of the bureaucracy, into the community. They measure the performance of their agencies,

focusing not on inputs but on *outcomes*. They are driven by their goals—their *missions*—not by their rules and regulations. They define their clients as *customers,* and offer them choices—between schools, between training programs, between housing options . . . And they focus not simply on providing public services, but on *catalyzing* all sectors—public, private, and voluntary—into action to solve their community's problems.[19]

During the 1990s, Osborne and Gaebler's gospel of restructured service delivery, close attention to performance measures, and citizen-focused action was vigorously and persistently reasserted in the pages of *Governing* magazine, one of Congressional Quarterly, Inc.'s publications, which regularly ran articles by David Osborne. Many issues of *Governing* featured profiles of new-style mayors such as John Norquist of Milwaukee, Stephen Goldsmith of Indianapolis, and Dennis Archer of Detroit, and these articles invariably praised initiatives aimed at simplifying bureaucratic regulations, reorganizing welfare services, or otherwise enhancing the local business climate.[20]

The 1990s also coincided with the comebacks of many central cities, which in some cases—such as Chicago—added population for the first time in decades, while in other urban centers, notable quality of life improvements were achieved. Among the latter, New York City's remarkable downturn in murders, as well as reported criminal activity in general, was exemplary.[21] Quite a debate could be generated by the following paradox: did the comebacks of major cities "make" successful mayors, or did effective mayors play a significant role in improving their cities? Judged by the proliferation of books by these mayors—or those chronicling their achievements—one has to suppose that the latter contention has the wider endorsement.[22] Among the mayor-authored books published in the 1990s, Stephen Goldsmith's *The Twenty-First Century City* and John Norquist's *The Wealth of Cities* are especially suggestive. Goldsmith, a Republican who led Indianapolis's government from 1992 to 2000, devotes much of his book to discussing how "marketization" of municipal services can improve cities. Yet linked to this emphasis on improving governmental efficiency is a distinctly moralistic cast of mind:

> The family is the fundamental unit of every successful society. But for the past thirty-plus years, government has consistently undermined this source of public virtue. Government has taken money away from families through ever-increasing taxes and then perversely used some of the revenues on programs that actively discourage poor Americans from forming families. [23]

Goldsmith thus presents himself as an unusual variety of municipal chief executive, on the one hand a "policy wonk" determined to cut city government costs, yet on the other, a crusader for rank-and-file Indianapolis families.

In contrast to the apocalyptic undercurrent discernible in *The Twenty-first Century City*—at one point Goldsmith discusses neighborhood conflicts pitting property owners against "superpredators"—Norquist, in *The Wealth of Cities*, writes as an enthusiastic, cosmopolitan student of cities.[24] Many of his arguments directly parallel Goldsmith's: federal fiscal aid has often harmed cities; service privatization can improve performance; a healthy local economy is the prerequisite for achieving a commodious city. Yet as Norquist wraps up his narrative, *The Wealth of Cities* takes on a theme, urban design, that is nowhere to be found in Goldsmith's book. Norquist is a proponent of new urbanism, and even of one of new urbanism's most controversial projects, the Disney Corporation–founded Celebration, Florida: "Celebration . . . features a traditional main street, with three-story commercial buildings close to the street, and residential areas, with houses built close together and trees for shade. Celebration is so popular that homeowners are being chosen from a waiting list via lottery." Norquist, by espousing the return to "real neighborhoods" and "real cities," without directly criticizing predecessors such as Richard Lee and John Lindsay, underlines another divide separating the mayors of the 1960s and 1990s.[25] While the earlier generation unquestioningly accepted the proclaimed benefits of revitalization through urban renewal—and as such, the modernist reworking of the city fabric—new-style mayors such as John Norquist, as well as Richard M. Daley, are more likely to prefer traditionalist architectural and public space planning strategies.

In this account of resurgent cities and resurgent mayoring in the 1990s, I so far have not directly noted some of the figures who most evidently were Richard M. Daley's peers: Rudolph Giuliani of New York, Ed Rendell of Philadelphia, and Richard Riordan of Los Angeles. These mayors, in addition to the leaders of smaller cities including Goldsmith and Norquist, all participated in national organizations such as the U.S. Conference of Mayors, and in various ways they engaged in on-the-job insight-sharing. For example, Giuliani biographer Fred Siegel notes that Ed Rendell was invited to address a transition workshop for New York City agency heads in the weeks following Giuliani's election as mayor in 1993.[26] The mayoring challenges of very large cities, such as New York, Philadelphia, Los Angeles, and Chicago, are distinctive, and it is in reference to these particular challenges that I think the most interesting commonality linking Giuliani, Rendell, Riordan, and Daley can be identified.

Each of these individuals straddled conventional political boundaries during their careers, most especially during their terms as mayor. Even as he adopted a highly moralistic attitude in reference to crime control and welfare reform, Giuliani was sympathetic to pro-choice and gay rights advocacy. Giuliani also consulted Democratic Party–affiliated political advisors and, in 1994, even endorsed the Democratic Party candidate for New York governor, Mario Cuomo. In many ways Ed Rendell has more closely fit the profile of loyal party advocate, but probably his greatest political triumph as Democratic mayor of Philadelphia was holding the line on salaries and fringe benefits for city workers, a heavily Democratic constituent group. Like Giuliani, Republican Richard Riordan depended on a number of political operatives drawn from the ranks of the Democratic Party. Political scientist Raphael Sonenshein further notes that Riordan "had little affection for the municipal government, whether its elected officials or its permanent employees. He wanted the sway that a CEO might have in a corporation . . . His real feeling of being an outsider at city hall hurt him when it was time to get something done, but was well received by the public."[27] Interestingly, although each of these mayors—like Richard M. Daley—regularly asserted his nonpartisanship, they were rarely noncontentious. Siegel's description of Giuliani as an "immoderate centrist" provides a useful insight. Giuliani,

Rendell, and Riordan often won political victories by outflanking municipal bureaucracies and surprising political opponents. Their policy positions sometimes defied conventional expectations, and their successes were often a function of redefining what the public expected from municipal government.

Chicago's Second Mayor Daley

Richard M. Daley was nearing his thirteenth birthday when Richard J. Daley defeated Robert Merriam in the mayoral election of April 5, 1955. The younger Richard Daley grew up in the Bridgeport neighborhood, home of his parents for the entirety of their lives. Richard M. left Chicago to attend Providence College, but he soon returned, completing his bachelor's degree at DePaul University. He also earned a law degree from DePaul. The younger Daley won his first elective office in 1969, when he was chosen as a delegate to the convention writing a new state constitution for Illinois.[28] For most of the 1970s, Daley served as a senator in the Illinois General Assembly. As a state legislator, Daley was not universally admired. In 1977, *Chicago* magazine published an article—based on a survey of twenty state capitol insiders—identifying the ten best and worst members of the general assembly. Richard M. Daley was ranked among the latter, described as "shrewd" but also "shark-like."[29]

Mayor Richard M. Daley regularly asserts his nonpartisanship, so it is of some interest that he served as 11th ward Democratic Party committeeman for a few years following his father's death. However, by 1980 Daley found himself in the unlikely position of running against the Democratic Party's endorsed candidate in the primary election for Cook County state's attorney. In this race, Chicago Mayor Jane Byrne had backed another young politician with deep family roots in the Democratic Party, 14th ward alderman Ed Burke. Daley defeated Burke, won the general election, and was reelected state's attorney in 1984 and 1988. During the 1980s, Daley also experienced the only electoral defeat of his political career, finishing a close third in the three-way Democratic mayoral primary of 1983 that was won by Harold Washington. Yet Daley did achieve a kind of victory in 1983. Campaigning as a "moderate, good government reformer," he won the endorsement of several prominent Democrats who had previously opposed his father.[30] Even more important, he distanced himself from the racially polarizing rhetoric of the more vociferous anti-Washington Democrats.

In 1989 Daley defeated the incumbent mayor, Eugene Sawyer—selected by the city council to serve as interim mayor following Harold Washington's sudden death in late 1987—in the special election primary, then triumphed over Ed Vrdolyak (until recently a Democrat, running as the Republican Party nominee) and Timothy Evans (qualifying for the election as the standard-bearer of the short-lived Harold Washington Party) in the general election. Daley has been reelected mayor five times, in 1991, 1995, 1999, 2003, and 2007. His original voting base was a "white/brown" coalition of working-class Democratic Party loyalists and Latinos. Until the mid-1990s there were recurring efforts by African-American activists to rejuvenate the "Harold Washington coalition" and unite behind an African-American candidate for mayor.[31] In fact, over the span of Daley's five reelection campaigns he has substantially increased his support among black voters. Until the emergence in 2004 of the series of corruption scandals that have substantially tarnished his administration, the one sign of Richard M. Daley political weakness has been his declining ability to mobilize the electorate.[32] Like his father, Richard M. Daley has been an incumbent whose reelection victories have combined impressive winning percentages and diminished voter turnouts. In the younger Daley's "landslide" election of 2007, he drew 250,000 fewer votes than in his special election victory of 1989.

Richard M. Daley—by all accounts—has been a very successful political leader. Apart from his string of election victories, he has reasserted mayoral control over what had been, in the 1980s, a very fractious city council. Moreover, he has extended mayoral control and generated visible results from various of the city's nonmunicipal, independent agencies, including the Chicago Public Schools, the Chicago Housing Authority, and the Chicago Park District. The national press has frequently and favorably commented on his record, and a variety of governmental, civic, and environmental groups have honored him. The latter have included the U.S. Conference of Mayors, the National Trust for Historic Preservation, and the National Arbor Day Foundation. In designating Daley as a Public Official of the Year for 1997, *Governing* editor Alan Ehrenhalt commented: "He has been patient and skillful in mastering the details of local government, and remarkably creative in devising pragmatic solutions to the most complex problems."[33] As such, Richard M. Daley fits comfortably among the prototype post–federal era mayors described by Peter Eisinger.

Though Eisinger's characterization of new-style mayors—which is of a piece with *Governing's* paean to Richard M. Daley—links their "mastering the details" to a withdrawal from the "bully pulpit," the Richard M. Daley administration, over time, has advanced a discernible and far from timid mayoral program. The three fundamental components of this program include promotion of Chicago as a global city, the reorganization of a variety of municipal and independent agency service functions, and social inclusivity at the elite level.

The Daley administration's promotion of Chicago as a global or world-class city is in no way a striking or innovative policy preference. One only needs to recall the bright-eyed Flint, Michigan, officials who were interviewed by Michael Moore in *Roger and Me* (1989) to recognize that the dream of postindustrial transcendence to the friendly skies of mass tourism and the leisure economy is an impulse driving many municipal leaders. The Daley administration, nevertheless, has pursued this goal in a plausibly strategic fashion. On the one hand, efforts to expand both O'Hare Airport and the downtown McCormick Place convention complex seek to build on demonstrated Chicago assets: geographic and transportation network centrality and extensive facilities to support trade shows and conventions. Likewise, the Daley administration's redevelopment of Navy Pier at the northeastern end of the downtown area, and the creation of the Millennium Park complex, have forged two powerful tourist magnets. Chicago's unsuccessful campaign to host the 2016 Olympic Games nonetheless served to reinforce the city's image as a primary global node.[34]

Less dramatically, but possibly more consequentially, Richard M. Daley city planners have implemented numerous small-scale infrastructure and beautification improvements, sped up approval processes, and reimagined local neighborhood identities in such a fashion so as to add momentum to the ongoing industrial to commercial/residential transformation of the city's Near West and Near South Sides. So far, the gentrification of these areas has engendered relatively little neighborhood resistance. From the standpoint of Chicago's image as a global city, this expanded cityscape of "upscale boutiques and stylish restaurants" represents both a talent-drawing amenity and a marker of Chicago's progressive, postindustrial character.[35]

Richard M. Daley has also been an aggressive reorganizer of local government bureaucracies. In 1995, he won state legislation enabling him to replace the school board and top administration at the Chicago Public Schools (CPS). Daley selected his budget director, Paul Vallas, to assume the new post as CEO of the schools. Vallas pulled back authority from the parent-dominated Local School Councils (elected to govern each Chicago public school), moved to standardize the curriculum, and pushed hard for improvement in student performance on academic achievement tests. Mayor Daley, in turn, poured immense resources into a program of school construction and rehabilitation. Since the mid-1990s, Chicago school system standardized test performance has generally moved upward, though slowly and unevenly across grades and testing fields. In June 2004, Daley and then-CPS CEO Arne Duncan (appointed to replace Vallas in 2001) announced Renaissance 2010, a proposal to close poorly performing schools and to replace them with one hundred new schools. Many of the latter are independent charter schools.[36]

No less sweeping has been Daley's makeover of the Chicago Housing Authority (CHA). Following the U.S. Department of Housing and Urban Development's takeover of the CHA between 1995 and 1999, Daley appointees initiated an agency restructuring called the Plan for Transformation. This plan aims to reduce the number of local public housing units from approximately 40,000 to 25,000 (with 10,000 units reserved for senior citizens), rehabilitate or build anew each of those 25,000 units, turn over day-to-day property management and social service provision to private vendors, and site most public housing in mixed-income developments. As a rule, these mixed-income developments adhere to a one-third/one-third/one-third proportioning of public housing, affordable housing (mainly rental, some for sale), and market-rate housing.[37]

The CHA's track record in implementing the Plan for Transformation has been very mixed. At some developments, resident acceptance of the new CHA vision has been forthcoming, at other developments—including the famous Cabrini-Green complex on the Near North Side—there has been substantial resident resistance. One of the most significant process challenges involved in a planning effort of this magnitude is resident relocation, both temporary moves as developments are rebuilt and permanent relocations from public housing. On both counts, the CHA's performance has been poor. At developments such as the ABLA Homes on the Near West Side, planning and project execution spanned more than a decade, during which time the inconveniences visited upon residents were extraordinary. For former public housing residents across the city, CHA-contracted relocation services have been spotty. The findings of researchers who have examined where former CHA residents have found new places to live are disturbingly uniform: in overwhelmingly African-American neighborhoods nearly as poor as the public housing communities from which they departed.[38]

Richard M. Daley's other major public service reorganization has been within the city government. In 1994 the police department implemented a citywide program of community policing known as the Chicago Alternative Policing Strategy (CAPS). The CAPS initiative has put more patrol officers onto Chicago's sidewalks, and via nearly three hundred monthly "beat" meetings brings together police personnel and community residents to discuss local, crime-related issues. During the later 1990s and into the current decade, Chicago's crime rate has paralleled the pattern of decline achieved in many cities. The Daley administration has not hesitated to attribute the local decline to the effective implementation of CAPS.[39]

The third component of the Daley program is elite social inclusivity. As mayor, Richard M. Daley has routinely filled important administrative positions with Latinos, African Americans, and women. Although his 1989 voting base included few African Americans, since that time Daley has worked hard to solidify his relationship with leading black political figures such as the late John Stroger, president of the Cook County Board of Commissioners from 1994 until 2006. Daley has also cultivated the city's business and civic leadership, which, for its part, has been warmly grateful to the mayor for Chicago's resurgent reputation. And not least, in a stunning departure from his father's politics, Richard M. Daley has courted formerly marginal constituencies such as gay rights and environmental activists. Richard M. Daley most strikingly distinguishes himself from his father—in terms of worldview, his sense of the city, and his coalition-building inclinations—through his appearances at the annual Gay Pride Parade.

Nevertheless, the current Mayor Daley's approach to social inclusivity is a matter of communication and consultation at the elite level. In a 1999 assessment of Daley's record, journalist David Moberg observed: "The mayor has done everything he could to discourage any popular involvement in civic affairs that would compromise his hold on power. Despite preserving many of the reforms that emerged during Harold Washington's brief tenure, he has largely rejected Washington's belief in community participation in planning and implementing public policy."[40] Daley planners, in effect, dictated the terms of public housing redevelopment, and since the mayor's asserting his control of the Chicago Public Schools in 1995, there has been a substantial erosion of influence exercised by the neighborhood-based, elected local school councils. Even the mayor's admirers agree that he is a reclusive decision maker who relies on the advice of a handful of close advisors. In short, Daley promotes Chicago as a prospective home and workplace for all, though as the chief executive he has depended on a very narrow stream of local information gathering, expertise, and counsel.

The preceding review of the basic features of the Richard M. Daley program has, in its retrospectiveness and thematization of particular intiatives, also tended to exaggerate the program's coherence and the degree of rationalistic forethought that shaped it. Daley's candidacy in 1989 was described as a "cautious, scripted campaign," and his April 1989 inaugural address was brief though richly platitudinous:

> Our common opponents are crime and ignorance, waste and fraud, poverty and disease, hatred and discrimination. And we either rise up as one city and make the special effort required to meet these challenges, or sit back and watch Chicago decline. As one who loves Chicago, I'm ready

to make that special effort—and to ask everyone in our city to do the same. Business as usual is a prescription for failure. The old ways of doing things simply aren't adequate to cope with the new challenges we face. In times of limited resources, government must be more creative and productive than ever before. We must do a better job with the resources we have.[41]

In a subsequent passage—which was also the only section of the speech addressing a specific local government function—Daley turned to Chicago's public schools. Education reform, of course, has become a signature Richard M. Daley initiative, but his crucial move in this policy area—which was to seek state government approval for reorganizing the Chicago Public Schools—would wait for another six years, following his reelection to a second four-year term as mayor. In the pages to follow, I attempt to explain how Richard M. Daley's program emerged, and in so doing, link his mayoralty to recent trends in American mayoral practice and specify some of its more individualistic sources.

Richard M. Daley Reconsidered

A generation ago, political scientist John W. Kingdon published a book entitled *Agendas, Alternatives, and Public Policies,* in which he offered a "loose, messy" decision-making model as a more realistic alternative to "the tight, orderly process that a rational approach specifies." Even my unadorned summary of Richard M. Daley's main initiatives *suggests* a degree of rationality in policy selection that is at odds with reality. In this reconsideration of Daley's program, I propose an interpretive framework that is loosely drawn from Kingdon's triad of public agenda sources: "problems, policies, and politics."[42]

The Richard M. Daley administration's approach to governing Chicago bears the mark of five shaping forces. These forces are a mixed bag, but also represent a constellation of influences structuring the action of any big-city mayor: broad-scale economic and social conditions; the mayor's personal inclinations as a municipal leader; opportunities presented by emerging situations or trends in public policy; the laundry list of prospective projects (usually, physical projects) circulating among local elites and begging the mayor's attention; and what I term "politically usable policies" that emerge as priorities due to their strategic constituent appeal. As we walk through this funhouse of potential action, I believe we can begin to understand more readily both the coherence and incoherences of the Daley program, even as we also gain a deeper sense of why his particular program emerged.

In terms of understanding the main threads of Richard M. Daley programmatic action, the simplest of the five shaping forces to identify are the pair of basic structural conditions that in 1989 loomed over both Chicago and his nascent mayoralty. The first of these was the massive economic restructuring that had undermined Chicago's industrial economy since the 1960s. The second was carryover racial polarization, initially produced by the city's wrenching neighborhood transitions and the politics of civil rights activism and resistance in the 1960s, then reignited during the election of 1983 and the subsequent Harold Washington mayoralty.

In reference to economic restructuring, with the exception of Harold Washington—an outlier not just among the ranks of Chicago chief executives—the dream of every Chicago mayor running back to Richard J. Daley has been the transformation of central Chicago into a more formidable corporate management district and upscale residential enclave. This reworking of the central city's physical environment has been promoted both to compensate for the decline of the manufacturing economy and to boost the Loop and its environs as generators of tax revenue. In effect, local leaders since the 1950s have sought what is literally unspeakable in the proud city of Chicago, the Manhattanization of the Loop and the adjoining Near North, West, and South Sides. Richard M. Daley's contribution to the achievement of this dream—apart from holding the mayoralty at a time when the real estate market was moving very briskly along a parallel course—has been to skillfully use public works to environmentally enhance central Chicago and deploy an array of planning tools intended to lubricate private investment. Mayor Daley's efforts to expand O'Hare Airport and the McCormick Place convention complex, likewise, have sought to boost Chicago advantages as a transportation node and tourist/trade show destination.

Traditional infrastructure and central city development initiatives have not been Richard M. Daley's only gambit to economically reposition Chicago. In the early 2000s, his CivicNet initiative sought to build a citywide fiber optic network, and although the city government was unable to find a private-sector partner for CivicNet, the Daley administration has continued its efforts to enhance telecommunications access across Chicago.[43] Daley's city government has also sought to protect viable portions of the city's residual industrial economy.[44] Nevertheless, in terms of resources committed and publicity generated, not just the rebuilding, but more grandly, the reimagining of central Chicago, has grown out of Richard M. Daley's particular approach to his city's long arc of economic transformation running back to the 1960s.

Also attuned to conditions originating in the 1960s has been Richard M. Daley's commitment to elite social inclusivity. Richard M. Daley is neither a political natural—in the sense of embracing crowds and seizing the opportunity to speak from the stump—nor is he a philosophical populist. Yet recognizing the racially divided electorate of the 1980s—and more fundamentally, Chicago's unresolved social conflicts dating from the 1960s—Daley has moved to co-opt key figures representing various dissident constituencies, notably African Americans and anti-Richard J. Daley "independent" Democrats. He has also reached out to the city's corporate and civic leadership while cultivating new constituencies such as gays and environmentalists. Daley is not a warm politician in the style of a Harold Washington or Fiorello La Guardia, but through high-level consultation and careful observance of the city's civic protocols he has projected the image of a publicly attentive, if not personally accessible chief executive.

Then there are Richard M. Daley's personal inclinations as mayor, which admittedly constitute an amorphous subject for analysis. Nevertheless, various of the mayor's biographical details do permit a plausible explanation of one of his administration's most persistent commitments, its diversified campaign of civic beautification. My cautiously offered explanation of this Daley inclination begins by noting his coming of age during the 1960s, and more pertinently, during the latter half of his father's administration. During that period, the Chicago cityscape was badly damaged: by civil unrest that destroyed scores of buildings along major South Side and West Side commercial corridors; by fires, housing abandonment, and demolitions in many residential areas; by deferred maintenance of public structures such as schools, transit stations, and, most notably, public housing developments.[45]

Given the proprietorial mindset that Richard M. Daley does seem to share with his late father, his persistence in repairing—or rebuilding more grandly—basic infrastructure such as roadways, bridges, schools, libraries, and parks buildings brings to mind the heir to a once great estate who aspires to restore its past glory. Moreover, Daley has determined that there is an economic payoff to urban beautification. The following comment drawn from his address to the Urban Parks Institute's "Great Parks/Great Cities" conference in 2001 makes the point quite succinctly: "The nice thing is, if you improve the quality of life for the people who live in your city, you will end up attracting new people and new employers."[46] Other factors that surely have stoked Daley's commitment to physically restore Chicago include his mingling with the likes of John Norquist at U.S. Conference of Mayors events, as well as his extensive international travels. Unlike his father, the younger Mayor Daley is a geographic and urban cosmopolitan.

Among the striking elements of the Richard M. Daley beautification campaign is the multitude of small-scale physical improvements one observes across Chicago. Much press coverage has been devoted to Daley's big projects such as Millennium Park, but for rank-and-file Chicagoans, the mayor's most lasting contribution to physical Chicago has been the installation of hundreds of sidewalk bicycle racks, the planting of perennial flowers and shrubs in previously neglected traffic islands, the rebuilding of neighborhood public libraries, and the like. Daley's urban design inclinations, typically street-level in their focus, have clearly been influenced by the thinking of celebrated urbanist Jane Jacobs. They are the sorts of microscale physical improvements that may often spring to Mayor Daley's mind as his chauffeur-driven automobile navigates Chicago's streets .

Richard M. Daley has also been an opportunistic mayoral leader, responding in imaginative ways to unforeseen situations or even programmatic setbacks. Political scientist Joel Rast has proposed that the Daley administration's reengagement with a previously dismissed policy option—neighborhood economic development, which was initially viewed as too closely associated with Harold Washington's administration—was just such an opportunistic policy selection. Having experienced the political undoing of several large-scale public works proposals, notably a South Side airport plan and a near-Loop casino project, and having suffered through the embarrassing "Loop flood" of 1992 (when tunnels running beneath downtown office towers filled with water escaping from the main channel of the Chicago River), Daley and his planners determined that basic infrastructure improvements should be given greater attention.[47]

Between 2004 and 2008, the Daley administration signed long-term leasing agreements with private vendors to operate several city-owned facilities and physical assets: the Chicago Skyway, a South Side toll highway; municipal parking garages and parking meters; and Midway Airport. In the face of a growing city budget deficit, these lease agreements promised to generate more than five billion dollars in immediate revenues. In turn, the firms operating the skyway and the city's parking meter network announced plans to substantially increase user fees. In the long run, it is both uncertain how responsibly these properties will be managed and physically maintained, as well as how the Daley administration will use the cash generated by these deals. Also noteworthy was the lack of either public discussion or city council involvement as these leasing arrangements were worked out.[48]

Though community policing in Chicago is repeatedly invoked as a mayoral initiative, it was, in fact, a grassroots movement—the Chicago Alliance for Neighborhood Safety—that initially promoted intensified street-patrolling and closer cooperation between the police department and neighborhood residents.[49] The Daley administration has certainly been a leader in promoting public school and public housing restructuring, but these are also policy areas in which there had been years of national debate preceding the advent of local action.[50] Once more, it bears mentioning that Richard M. Daley has been an active participant in national organizations whose agendas have, in part, been directed to discussion of just such policy innovations.

In years to come, Chicago's many visitors will principally celebrate Richard M. Daley's accomplishments as an urban builder. In central Chicago, his term in office has coincided, most notably, with the redevelopment of Navy Pier as a tourist/entertainment attraction, the reconstruction of Wacker Drive paralleling the main and south branches of the Chicago River, the development of Millennium Park, the rerouting of Lake Shore Drive (which permits uninterrupted pedestrian movement between the Field Museum, Shedd Aquarium, and Adler Planetarium, the area now known as the Museum Campus), the rebuilding of Soldier Field, and several expansions of McCormick Place. The Daley administration has won much praise for seeing these projects through to completion, but the roots of several of these initiatives precede Daley's mayoralty. Plans to convert the then-derelict Navy Pier into a public promenade date from the 1980s.[51] From about the same time, the Chicago Bears National Football League franchise, Soldier Field's principal tenant, had lobbied for a stadium upgrade.[52] Historian Timothy Gilfoyle, in his account of the creation of Millennium Park, notes that even this public works extravaganza—which is so closely identified with Richard M. Daley—grew out of preceding efforts by several of Chicago's civic notables to create a "Lakefront Gardens" performing arts complex.[53]

There is, however, an overriding logic that has yielded this clustering of public works initiatives, and which is attributable to Richard M. Daley. In a fashion that mimics the approach to civic enhancement—if not invariably the classically inspired architectural monumentality—associated with the early twentieth-century City Beautiful Movement, Daley has devoted billions of dollars to dignifying those portions of his city most accessible to visitors, but which might also be considered a civic common ground for Chicagoans. And judging by the popularity of these sites, this effort to create a memorable civic gathering place for all Chicago has been successful. For Richard M. Daley—personally speaking—there is good reason to suppose that this mammoth program of civic refurbishment is also a satisfying exercise in erasing physical reminders of Chicago's sad decline in the 1960s and 1970s.

In short, Richard M. Daley, the urban builder, has pursued a course of action that has general sources—the dreams of nearly all ambitious mayors include large-scale public works accomplishments—but is also reflective of his proprietorial view of Chicago, and as well, persistent opportunism. Practically speaking, the Daley public works program has involved picking a group of projects—several of which were already in the civic/municipal pipeline—and bringing them to fruition. This taking on and completing initiatives that antedate one's administration is a characteristic feature of successful public works execution, but it is a form of action not limited to infrastructure and public buildings. Richard M. Daley's movement into public school reform, from the standpoints of political action and policy choice, has followed an analogous course. Toward the end of Harold Washington's mayoralty, parent groups, a civic/business alliance known as Chicago United, and members of the mayor's administration began to promote an overhaul of the Chicago Public Schools. Ironically, the fruit of their work was state legislation passed in 1989 that dramatically decentralized CPS operations by vesting new powers in the local school councils. Daley's "takeover" of the CPS in 1995, in one sense, carried on reform efforts that had begun in the previous decade, even as, in another sense, these reforms were reversed by Paul Vallas's recentralization of CPS decision making.[54]

If Rudolph Giuliani can be characterized as an immoderate centrist, the equivalent designation for Richard M. Daley might be eccentric relativist. Among Daley's arsenal of politically usable policy stances has been a bewildering series of moral issue endorsements: neighborhood referenda to de-license "problem" taverns, official recognition of same-sex marriages, online identification of sex offenders.[55] There appears to be little philosophical coherence to Daley's expressed commitments on these matters, but there is a discernible political logic. Over his two-decade mayoralty, Daley has persistently sought to broaden his initially white/brown electoral (and racially/ethnically inflected) coalition. This strategy has involved reaching out to African-American ministers, who are often vigorous proponents of strict moral standards, and it has also involved catering to Chicago's substantial gay population. It is a strategy that clearly incorporates some of the mayor's particular inclinations, especially his support of urban bicycling and various green measures such as rooftop gardens. Each of these constituencies—socially conservative African Americans, gays and lesbians, outdoors enthusiasts and environmentalists—represents a relatively small increment of support, but conjoined they have allowed Richard M. Daley to expand his base of support well beyond his initial voting coalition.

The most encompassing of Richard M. Daley's politically usable policies has been his personal identification with managerial innovation. Apart from the real policy reorientations evident in the Chicago Public Schools, Chicago Housing Authority, and the police department, Daley has steadfastly presented himself as a mayor above politics. As he explained to a reporter in 1994: "If I had to worry about my election, I'd never make a decision here and my role is to make decisions. I don't consume this political stuff . . . I'm not a political junkie. [Working in government] is where you get things done."[56] It has been many years since Daley served as 11th ward Democratic committeeman, and as a rule, he has adopted a neutral pose in the face of internecine Democratic Party disputes. Yet it is also evident that Daley's posture as manager rather than politician has served a useful political purpose. Until the spate of corruption scandals rocked his administration in 2004, Daley routinely deflected criticism by asserting that efficiency and calculation of the public good were his first—and only— executive considerations. The following is his response to criticism that had been directed at the Chicago Public Schools in early 2006:

> There is nothing wrong with people giving me their ideas, whether Congressman [Luis] Gutierrez or you or anyone else . . . That is what you do as a public official. You listen. You take their criticism, you take their evaluation . . . I had the vision, I had the will and I had the character to do it, and the courage . . . I said we are going to make a difference, and there has been a difference. I am the only mayor in the United States who would take that political responsibility. Every other mayor ran out left and right.[57]

In this representation by Daley of his own aims and means, executive wisdom and courage are contrasted with the small-minded carping that is the presumed stock-in-trade of politicians such as Congressman Gutierrez.

Richard M. Daley and Municipal Neoliberalism

Despite holding Chicago's mayoralty for two decades, Richard M. Daley remains a surprisingly enigmatic figure, the object of widely varying appraisals. For some commentators, the scope of his local political dominance combines with certain of his personal attributes—notably his colossal temper and maladroit public speaking—to establish a direct link to his father. The result is an interpretative stance presenting Richard M. Daley as the most recent in Chicago's long line of political bosses. Almost perfectly at odds with Daley-the-boss is another widely circulated image, Richard M. Daley the nuts-and-bolts manager and administrative innovator. A variant of the latter image is the view of Daley accepted by many of Chicago's corporate leaders, "The CEO of City Hall."[58]

The contention that Richard M. Daley is a contemporary political boss typically does not come to terms with two fundamental features of Chicago's early twenty-first century political landscape: the decline of most of the Democratic Party ward organizations as voter mobilizers; the rise of media-directed, fund-raising–dependent local campaigning. Richard M. Daley has been a tremendously effective fund-raiser and has used his campaign war chest to win the loyalty of many subordinate elected officials (notably city council members).[59] Just as crucially, Daley triumphs in municipal elections attracting fewer than 40 percent of the registered voters and in which there is no cohesive opposition party. The much-vaunted Cook County Democratic machine, these days, is a paper tiger, but riding astride this ghost of machines past is a mayor who has achieved a powerful personal hold on the local electorate and government.

In the wake of the overlapping city hall patronage and "Hired Truck" contracting scandals between 2004 and 2006, Mayor Daley has himself backed off from his previous self-presentation as the ultravigilant manager: "I wish I could be on top of every detail. I'm aware that the prevailing perception is that I am. Obviously, in an organization as large and multi-layered as city government, that's impossible."[60] Ultimately, Daley's success as Chicago's administrator-in-chief does not appear to be a function of anything particularly distinctive in his management style, nor even of an uncanny knowledge of municipal arcana. The mayor has elicited strong performance from many subordinates due to some currently unfashionable executive strengths: his stranglehold on reelection, which produces the widely held presumption that the man at the top will be in charge so long as he wishes to be, and ruthlessness in punishing subordinates in the wake of publicized performance breakdowns. Even the Daley administration's recent spate of privatization activity—contracting out Chicago Skyway, parking garage, parking meter, and Midway Airport operations (the latter agreement was subsequently withdrawn)—appears to be an impromptu escape from deficit ambush as opposed to a studied reordering of municipal priorities.

It is noteworthy that Richard M. Daley's approach to managing city services has also been the source of some of the most pointed criticisms of his administration. Sociologist Eric Klinenberg's study of the mid-1995 Chicago temperature spike and its deadly aftermath, Heat Wave, identifies Daley administration-implemented social service privatization and police and fire department emergency services reorganization as amplifiers of the temperature-induced health crisis.[61] Fellow sociologist David Pellow, in *Garbage Wars*, his examination of Chicago's since-terminated "blue-bag" recycling program, reaches conclusions that are directly analogous to Klinenberg's. Chicago's recycling rate stalled at well below 10 percent, and the private firm in charge of the blue-bag program from its initiation in 1995, Waste Management, Inc., was poorly regarded both in terms of its environmental record and labor/management practices. In effect, quite like the municipal government's privatization of social services, favorable publicity for presumably cutting-edge management practice—that is, contracting with private vendors—masked underlying performance deficiencies.[62]

Though Richard M. Daley's considerable ego does not allow for much acknowledgement of influences, he is a mayor who has learned from the practice of peers such as Rudolph Giuliani, Ed Rendell, and John Norquist. Whereas Daley's father by the late 1960s had become the self-conscious defender of an older urban order—a Chicago in which family and community allegiances were presumed to be fundamental sources of identity, the city of journalist Mike Royko's primal, ethnic "nation states"—the second mayor Daley is self-consciously an innovator, catching the wave of new trends in city management and planning (even if the latter, like new urbanism, are themselves explicitly traditionalist). Of particular significance—for Chicago, and as an exemplar of the new form of urban governance that has taken shape across the United Since in the last two decades—is how Richard M. Daley's administration has recast the aims of municipal administration. No longer the direct provider of the full slate of essential local services and with no aspiration whatsoever to equalizing individual and family opportunity through redistributive means, Daley's municipal government *facilitates* economic entrepreneurship, neighborhood redevelopment, and privately devised policy innovation (for example, charter schools). This redirection of municipal policy has not produced an appreciably smaller city government—public works are expensive and over the years the Daley administration payroll has dipped only slightly—but it has substantially narrowed its aims. In effect, municipal government in Chicago has become the collaborator with major firms and key investors in advancing *their agendas,* promoter of the city's overall image (and in particular instances, the fortunes of promising neighborhoods), and the provider of a residue of traditional services such as police and fire protection, sanitation, and basic physical infrastructure.

By shedding redistributive functions while emphasizing physical enhancements, stripped-down municipal custodianship, and attention-garnering mega-events, Richard M. Daley has turned Chicago's municipal government into a public sector agent in support of corporate investment, upscale residential development, and associated arts, entertainment, and leisure-sector functions. This basic policy emphasis has been developed while on the job, both as a result of local lessons learned and via the shared experience of peer mayors and their cities. Given the widespread admiration of Richard M. Daley's mayoralty, and the similarly widespread perception of Chicago as a city that has successfully made the industrial-to-postindustrial transition, Daley-style mayoring is likely to be carried to other cities in the coming years. Yet at root, Daley-style mayoring operates within a political economic framework—neoliberalism—whose sources transcend the local milieu: "urban policy [that] . . . shift[s] away from an explicit concern with social and spatial equity, full employment and welfare programmes and toward initiatives aimed at promoting workforce flexibility and the economic competitiveness of the private sector."[63] Richard M. Daley is certainly the product of a particular place, but his approach to municipal governance is very much a function of his time and the globalized capitalism that shapes prevailing understandings of what can and cannot be accomplished by even the most efficacious of municipal chief executives.

Notes

1. Fred Matthews, *The Quest for an American Sociology: Robert E. Park and the Chicago School* (Montreal: McGill–Queen's University Press, 1997); Martin Bulmer, *The Chicago School of Sociology* (Chicago: University of Chicago Press, 1984).

2. In particular, see Harold F. Gosnell, *Machine Politics: Chicago Model* (1937; Chicago: University of Chicago Press, 1977), chapters 2–4.

3. Mark Gottdiener, *The New Urban Sociology* (New York: McGraw-Hill, 1994).

4. See the essays included in Samuel K. Gove and Louis H. Masotti, eds., *After Daley: Chicago Politics in Transition* (Urbana: University of Illinois Press, 1982).

5. Milton L. Rakove, *Don't Make No Waves—Don't Back No Losers: An Insider's Analysis of the Daley Machine* (Bloomington: Indiana University Press, 1975); Mike Royko, *Boss: Richard J. Daley of Chicago* (New York: Plume, 1988); Alan Ehrenhalt, *The Lost City: The Forgotten Virtues of Community in America* (New York: Basic Books, 1995), 35. The 1988 edition of *Boss* includes as an introduction Royko's column written just following Richard J. Daley's death. Ehrenhalt characterizes low-level bribery during the Richard J. Daley years as a "civic tradition."

6. Pierre Clavel and Wim Wiewel, eds., *Harold Washington and the Neighborhoods* (New Brunswick, N.J.: Rutgers University Press), in particular, Clavel and Wiewel's introduction.

7. Recent work by Terry Nichols Clark represents a notable exception to this framing of Richard M. Daley. See Clark, "Amenities Drive Urban Growth," *Journal of Urban Affairs* 24, no. 5 (2002), especially 503–11.

8. Also, see the essays in John P. Koval et al., eds., *The New Chicago: A Social and Cultural Analysis* (Philadelphia: Temple University Press, 2006).

9. Jon C. Teaford, *The Unheralded Triumph: City Government in America, 1870–1900* (Baltimore: Johns Hopkins University Press, 1984), 15.

10. Martin J. Schiesl, *The Politics of Efficiency* (Berkeley: University of California Press, 1980), 46–67.

11. Jack Beatty, *The Rascal King* (Reading, Mass.: Addison-Wesley, 1993); Robert Caro, *The Power Broker* (New York: Vintage, 1975), 324–28; Douglas Bukowski, *Big Bill Thompson, Chicago, and The Politics of Image* (Urbana: University of Illinois Press, 1998).

12. Mark I. Gelfand, *A Nation of Cities* (New York: Oxford University Press, 1975), 30–39, 52–54; Sidney Fine, *Frank Murphy: The Detroit Years* (Ann Arbor: University of

Michigan Press, 1975); Caro, *The Power Broker,* 444–57; Thomas Kessner, *Fiorello H. La Guardia and The Making of Modern New York* (New York: McGraw-Hill, 1989).

13. R. H. Salisbury, "Urban Politics: The New Convergence of Power," in Murray Stewart, ed., *The City: Problems of Planning* (Harmondsworth, Middlesex, UK: Penguin, 1972), 395. Salisbury's essay originally appeared in the *Journal of Politics* 26 (1964): 775–97.

14. Jeanne R. Lowe, *Cities in a Race with Time* (New York: Random House, 1967), 405.

15. Peter Eisinger, "City Politics in an Era of Federal Policy Devolution," *Urban Affairs Review* 33, no. 3 (Jan. 1998): 320.

16. Melvin G. Holli, *The American Mayor: The Best and Worst Big-City Leaders* (University Park: Pennsylvania State University Press, 1999), 19.

17. Douglas W. Rae, *City: Urbanism and Its End* (New Haven, Conn.: Yale University Press, 2003), 360.

18. E. S. Savas, *Privatization: The Key to Better Government* (Chatham, N.J.: Chatham House, 1987). In their 1983 book, *City Money,* Terry Nichols Clark and Lorna Crowley Ferguson described the emergence of "new fiscal conservatives," mayors such as Peter Flaherty of Pittsburgh, Edward Koch of New York, and Dianne Feinstein of San Francisco, who combined social-issues liberalism and conservative municipal finance practices. In the longer run, fiscal conservatism linked to social liberalism was not especially characteristic of the new-wave mayoral practice in the 1990s. See Clark and Ferguson, *City Money: Political Processes, Fiscal Strain, and Retrenchment* (New York: Columbia University Press, 1983), 173–203.

19. David Osborne and Ted Gaebler, *Reinventing Government* (New York: Penguin, 1993), xviii, 19–20. Italics appear in the original text.

20. David Osborne, "John Norquist and the Milwaukee Experiment," *Governing,* November 1992, 63; Rob Gurwitt, "Indianapolis and the Republican Future," *Governing,* February 1994, 24–28; Rob Gurwitt, "Detroit Dresses for Business," *Governing,* April 1996, 38–42.

21. James Lardner, "Can You Believe the New York Miracle?" *New York Review of Books,* August 14, 1997, 54–58.

22. Philadelphia's Ed Rendell is the subject of Buzz Bissinger's *A Prayer for the City* (New York: Random House, 1997). Rudolph Giuliani has been profiled by many journalists and scholars. Fred Siegel's *The Prince of the City* (San Francisco: Encounter Books, 2005) is both detailed and admiring. Giuliani's book, *Leadership* (New York: Hyperion, 2002), far more than the Goldsmith and Norquist books discussed below, can be considered an advertisement for himself. For a more critical view of Giuliani, see Wayne Barrett, *Rudy!: An Investigative Biography of Rudolph Giuliani* (New York: Basic Books, 2000).

23. Stephen Goldsmith, *The Twenty-first Century City* (Lanham, Md.: Rowman and Littlefield, 1999), 173.

24. Ibid., 146.

25. John O. Norquist, *The Wealth of Cities* (Reading, Mass.: Addison-Wesley, 1998), 194, 206. Following his resignation as Milwaukee's mayor, Norquist became president of the Chicago-based Congress for the New Urbanism.

26. Siegel, *The Prince of the City,* 108. Another speaker at this event: David Osborne.

27. Raphael J. Sonenshein, *The City at Stake: Secession, Reform, and the Battle for Los Angeles* (Princeton, N.J.: Princeton University Press, 2004), 65, 70.

28. A biographical essay on Richard M. Daley, a list of his honorary citations, and various of his public statements can be accessed at the City of Chicago Web site: http://www.ci.chi. il.us/city/webportal/home.do. Other profiles of Richard M. Daley include Thomas Hardy, "His Goal: Make His Own Name," *Chicago Tribune*, April 5, 1989, sec. 2; James Atlas, "The Daleys of Chicago," *New York Times Magazine*, August 25, 1996, 37–39, 52, 56–58; Evan Osnos, "The Daley Show," *The New Yorker*, March 8, 2010, 38–51.

29. Henry Hansen, "Ten to Keep Around, Ten to Kick Around," *Chicago*, November 1977, 146–47.

30. David Moberg, "Can You Find the Reformer in This Group?" *The Reader* (Chicago), February 18, 1983.

31. Thomas Byrne Edsall, "Black vs. White in Chicago," *New York Review of Books*, April 13, 1989, 21–23.

32. Shane Tritsch, "The Mystery of Mayor Daley," *Chicago*, July 2004, 58–63, 88–93; Gary Washburn and Ray Long, "Daley Will Kill Scandal-Torn Hired Truck," *Chicago Tribune*, Feb. 9, 2005; Rudolph Bush and Dan Mihalopoulos, "Daley Jobs Chief Guilty," *Chicago Tribune*, July 7, 2006.

33. Alan Ehrenhalt, "Master of the Detail," *Governing*, December 1997, 22.

34. Larry Bennett, Michael Bennett, and Stephen Alexander, "Chicago and the 2016 Olympics: Why Host the Games? How Should We Host the Games? What Should We Accomplish by Hosting the Games?" (research report, Egan Urban Center, DePaul University, Chicago, November 2008).

35. Saskia Sassen, "A Global City," in Charles Madigan, ed., *Global Chicago* (Urbana: University of Illinois Press, 2004), 29. At a presentation by Sassen a number of years ago, she referred to these gentrifying areas of Chicago as the city's "glamour zone."

36. Anthony S. Bryk, David Kerbow, and Sharon Rollow, "Chicago School Reform," in Diane Ravitch and Joseph Viteritti, eds., *New Schools for a New Century* (New Haven: Yale University Press, 1997), 164–200; Tracy Dell'Angela and Gary Washburn, "Daley Set to Remake Troubled Schools," *Chicago Tribune*, June 25, 2004; Tracy Dell'Angela, "12 Years In, School Reforms Mixed," *Chicago Tribune*, February 5, 2007, sec. 2.

37. Chicago Housing Authority, "Plan for Transformation," Chicago, January 6, 2000; Larry Bennett, Janet S. Smith, and Patricia A. Wright, eds., *Where Are Poor People to Live? Transforming Public Housing* (Armonk, N.Y.: M.E. Sharpe, 2006).

38. Paul Fischer, "Section 8 and the Public Housing Revolution: Where Will the Families Go?" (Chicago: The Woods Fund, September 4, 2001); Paul Fischer, "Where Are the Public Housing Families Going? An Update" (unpublished paper, January 2003); Susan Popkin and Mary K. Cunningham, "CHA Relocation Counseling Assessment," (Washington, D.C., The Urban Institute, July 2002); Thomas P. Sullivan, "Independent Monitor's Report No. 5 to the Chicago Housing Authority and the Central Advisory Council," Chicago, January 8, 2003. Sullivan writes on CHA relocation activities in summer and early fall of 2002: "In July, August and September 2002, the large number of HCV [housing choice voucher]-eligible families still in the CHA buildings, coupled with imminent building-empty dates, and the relatively small number of relocation counselors, caused a rush to place families in rental units. This in turn

led inevitably to placing families hurriedly, and to relocating families into racially segregated areas already overwhelmingly populated by low-income families. Housing quality was overlooked or given little attention," 22; also see Dan A. Lewis and Vandna Sinha, "Moving Up and Moving Out?: Economic and Residential Mobility of Low-Income Chicago Families," *Urban Affairs Review* 43, no. 2 (Nov. 2007): 139–70.

39. Wesley G. Skogan and Susan M. Hartnett, *Community Policing, Chicago Style* (New York: Oxford University Press, 1997); Wesley G. Skogan et al., "Taking Stock: Community Policing in Chicago," (Washington, D.C.: National Institute of Justice, July 2002).

40. David Moberg, "How Does Richie Rate?" *The Reader* (Chicago), February 19, 1999.

41. The characterization of the 1989 Daley campaign appeared in Hardy, "His Goal: Make His Own Name"; Richard M. Daley, "Inaugural Address," Chicago, April 24, 1989, http://www.chipublib.org/cplbooksmovies/cplarchive/mayors/rm_daley_inaug01.php (accessed 6 September 2010).

42. John W. Kingdon, *Agendas, Alternatives, and Public Policies* (Boston: Little, Brown, 1984), 83, 93. Although his subject is mayoral leadership rather than the sources of mayoral programmatic action, my argument also parallels the main lines of Richard Flanagan's analysis in "Opportunities and Constraints in Mayoral Behavior: A Historical-Institutional Approach," *Journal of Urban Affairs* 26, no. 1 (2004): 43–65.

43. Paul Merrion, "City's Internet Project Becomes a Daley Double," *Crain's Chicago Business*, Jan. 14, 2002, 9; Jon Van, "Broadband Picture Not Finished," *Chicago Tribune*, Sept. 9, 2007, sec. 3; Report of the Mayor's Advisory Council on Closing the Digital Divide, "The City that Networks: Transforming Society and Economy Through Digital Excellence," Chicago, May 2007.

44. Joel Rast, *Remaking Chicago: The Political Origins of Urban Industrial Change* (DeKalb: Northern Illinois University Press, 1999), 132–57.

45. Amanda Seligman, *Block by Block: Neighborhoods and Public Policy on Chicago's West Side* (Chicago: University of Chicago Press, 2005), 63. By the mid-1960s, some local civic activists began to express the view that the aggressiveness of city government-initiated building demolition activity itself posed a threat to neighborhood stability.

46. Richard M. Daley, "Revitalizing Chicago through Parks and Public Spaces," July 31, 2001, http://www/pps.org/daleyspeech/ (accessed 6 September 2010).

47. Rast, *Remaking Chicago*, 149–50.

48. Dan Mihalopoulos, "Group Pays for Skyway Lease," *Chicago Tribune*, Jan. 25, 2005, sec. 2; Ben Joravsky, "Easy Money," *Chicago Reader*, October 16, 2008; Dan Mihalopoulos and Hal Dardick, "Pain in the Meter," *Chicago Tribune*, Dec. 3, 2008; Dan Mihalopoulos and Hal Dardick, "Parking Meter Deal Okd; Rates Going Up," *Chicago Tribune*, Dec. 5, 2008.

49. Skogan, *Community Policing, Chicago Style*, 138.

50. Clarence N. Stone et al., *Building Civic Capacity: The Politics of Reforming Urban Schools* (Lawrence: University Press of Kansas, 2001); Janet L. Smith, "Public Housing Transformation: Evolving National Policy," and Yan Zhang and Gretchen Weismann, "Public Housing's Cinderella: Policy Dynamics of HOPE VI in the Mid-1990s," in Bennett, Smith, and Wright, *Where Are Poor People to Live?*, 19–67.

51. James M. Smith, "Special-Purpose Governance in Chicago: Institutional Independence and Political Interdependence at the Municipal Pier and Exposition Authority" (paper presented at the annual meeting of the Urban Affairs Association, Montreal, April 2006) 9–10.

52. Robert A. Baade and Allen R. Sanderson, "Bearing Down on Chicago," in Roger G. Noll and Andrew Zimbalist, eds., *Sports, Jobs, and Taxes: The Economic Impact of Sports Teams and Stadiums* (Washington, D.C.: Brookings Institution Press, 1997), 324–54.

53. Timothy J. Gilfoyle, *Millennium Park: Creating a Chicago Landmark* (Chicago: University of Chicago Press, 2006), 63–76.

54. Jeffrey Mirel, "School Reform, Chicago Style: Educational Innovation in a Changing Urban Context, 1976–1991," *Urban Education* 28, no. 2 (July 1993): 116–149; Dorothy Shipps, *School Reform, Corporate Style: Chicago, 1880–2000* (Lawrence: University Press of Kansas, 2006), 130–69.

55. Gary Washburn and John Chase, "Daley Puts on a Press for Liquor Proposals," *Chicago Tribune,* Oct. 22, 1998, sec. 2; Kathryn Masterson, "Gay-marriage Backers Get Daley's Signature," *Chicago Tribune,* Oct. 29, 2004, sec. 2. John Chase, "City to Put List of Sex Offenders On-line," *Chicago Tribune,* Nov. 23, 1998, sec. 2.

56. David H. Roeder, "Mayor Daley as Conciliator," *Illinois Issues,* April 1994, 23. The brackets appear in Roeder's text.

57. Gary Washburn, "Daley Quick to Defend His Record," *Chicago Tribune,* May 10, 2006, sec. 2.

58. See Joseph Weber, "The CEO of City Hall," *BW Chicago,* premier issue, 2007.

59. Anthony Gierzynski, Paul Kleppner, and James Lewis, "The Price of Democracy: Financing Chicago's 1995 City Elections" (Chicago: Chicago Urban League and the Office for Social Policy Research, Northern Illinois University, September 1996).

60. Tritsch, "The Mystery of Mayor Daley," 63.

61. Eric Klinenberg, *Heat Wave: A Social Autopsy of Disaster in Chicago* (Chicago: University of Chicago Press, 2003), 129–64.

62. David Naguib Pellow, *Garbage Wars: The Struggle for Environmental Justice in Chicago* (Cambridge, Mass.: MIT Press, 2002); also see Dan Mihalopoulos and Gary Washburn, "City to Wave White Flag on Blue Bags," *Chicago Tribune,* Oct. 25, 2006.

63. Joe Painter, "Regulation Theory, Post-Fordism, and Urban Politics," in David Judge, Gerry Stoker, and Harold Wolman, eds., *Theories of Urban Politics* (Thousand Oaks, Calif.: SAGE Publications, 1995), 286–87; Peter Eisinger, "The Politics of Bread and Circuses: Building the City for the Visitor Class," *Urban Affairs Review* 35, no. 3 (Jan. 2000): 316–33; Neil Brenner and Nik Theodore, eds., *Spaces of Neoliberalism: Urban Restructuring in North America and Western Europe* (Malden, Mass: Blackwell, 2002); David Harvey, *A Brief History of Neoliberalism* (New York: Oxford University Press, 2005); Jason Hackworth, *The Neoliberal City: Governance, Ideology, and Development in American Urbanism* (Ithaca, N.Y.: Cornell University Press, 2007).

13

Both Center and Periphery
Chicago's Metropolitan Expansion and the New Downtowns

▪ Costas Spirou

William Cronon in his classic *Nature's Metropolis* documents Chicago's emergence during the nineteenth century by focusing on the distinct role of ecologic and economic changes that aided the city's ascendance. Utilizing an environmental perspective on historical development, Cronon shows the dynamism and the powerful influence of Chicago in facilitating the westward expansion and in the process transforming American culture. But this unparalleled growth was also fueled by the city's dominance and control over the surrounding region and beyond. In reality, the region was subjugated to Chicago's economic interests, further aiding its unprecedented change. This dominance reveals the importance of "the center" in understanding the urban development processes.

While late nineteenth- and early twentieth-century downtown Chicago had become economically and culturally vibrant, a similar trend can be also observed in other cities of the metropolitan area. Nearby satellite, industrial cities of the region: Aurora (2006 pop. 170,617), Elgin (2006 pop. 101,903), Joliet (2006 pop. 142,702), and Waukegan (2006 pop. 92,066) form part of a half-circle and are located between 35 and 40 miles from Chicago's Loop. All of these have had a long history, dating back to the 1850s. Each grew rapidly, benefiting from their industrial/manufacturing activities, their proximity to Chicago's robust economic environment, and their location on key transportation routes of regional and national importance.

This chapter focuses on the reemergence of the center in urban development and stands in contrast to contemporary arguments advanced in recent urban scholarship that have identified an urban landscape devoid of a core, guided by sprawl, and characterized by fragmentation, hopelessness, and a general disconnect. Based on their observations about the spatial dynamics of Los Angeles, scholars associated with the L.A. School have asserted the inevitable decline of the downtown. This chapter argues that this assertion is geographically and historically limited, and it does not appear to describe twenty-first century metropolitan patterns of development.

The four midsized peripheral cities covered in this essay benefited by supporting Chicago's economic centrality. That dependency persisted following deindustrialization; as Chicago's economy declined, so did these satellite communities. By the 1990s, Chicago began a remarkable recovery based partially on policies to promote culture and tourism. This strategy was mirrored by the four cities in this study since their local governments explored entertainment-driven modes of redevelopment, aiming to bring back their once-dominant downtowns. The result is a strengthening of both the urban core and poles of development in the suburbs, a finding that directly challenges the theories of the L.A. School.

Centerlessness in Metropolitan Development

Urban scholars have asserted in recent years that a distinct movement has occurred in metropolitan areas, away from modern urbanism—exemplified by the perspectives and writings of the Chicago School—to postmodern urbanism, advanced by the intellectual contributions of the L.A. School. My goal here is not to account for the various differences and all the arguments that have come to describe these two broad frameworks. Rather, I am interested in the treatment of "the center" by L.A. School social scientists in informing contemporary urban development patterns.

It is clear that for L.A. School advocates, the center has a diminishing importance, and this lack of centrality is reflected in the physical morphology of Los Angeles. Edward Soja argues that the old metropolitan forms with dominating downtowns do not hold true anymore as these have been fundamentally deconstructed, giving rise to new formats that are unpredictable and are hard to characterize since they have taken numerous forms and functions. According to Soja:

Some have called these amorphous implosions of archaic suburbia "Outer Cities" or "Edge Cities"; others dub them "Technopoles," "Technoburbs," "Silicon Landscapes," "Postsuburbia," "Metroplex." I will name them, collectively, *Exopolis*, the city without, to stress their oxymoronic ambiguity, their city-full non-cityness.[1]

This highly decentralized environment clearly describes Los Angeles's recent pattern of development. It is appropriately argued that the L.A. region has grown without possessing a dominant central city and has evolved into a distinct state, beyond the post–World War II period of mass suburbanization. Edward Soja and Allen J. Scott refer to this new form as "mass regional urbanization."[2]

This pattern of development lacks coherence and is fragmented; as a result, it is also without agency. Michael Dear and Steven Flusty provide the following description of the development dynamics that result in the construction of a centerless mode of metropolitan development. They argue that

> the relationship between development of one parcel and nondevelopment of another is a disjointed, seemingly unrelated affair. While not truly a random process, it is evident that the traditional, center-driven agglomeration economics that have guided urban development in the past, no longer apply. Conventional city form, Chicago-style, is sacrificed in favor of a noncontiguous collage of parcelized, consumption-oriented landscapes, devoid of conventional centers.[3]

The outcome of this centerless, decentralized process is the "exopolis," which lacks purpose in its development. Consequently, fragmentation leads to intensified social inequality expressed by gated communities, generating despair due to fortified landscapes that are uninviting and keep people out, especially racial and ethnic minorities, women, and the poor.[4]

The absence of the core is thus a key feature of this postmodern condition found in Los Angeles, which, according to the L.A. School, emerges as the paradigmatic city. As such, this prototypical city reflects not only the current patterns but also the future direction of urban development. According to Soja, "We are predicting that other cities will undergo changes and restructuring like Los Angeles,"[5] and Dear and Flusty note that "Los Angeles may be a mature form of this postmodern metropolis."[6]

There are two key questions regarding the role of the center in twenty-first century patterns of urban development. The first concerns its standing and function. Specifically, is the center outmoded, a thing of the past? Is it irrelevant, unattended to, and left behind? Secondly, is centerlessness the future form of urban development and an appropriate archetypical predictor of future settlement patterns? L.A. School researchers have affirmatively responded to these questions. Yet, as I will show, downtowns are actively supported by local governments, business interests, and civic organizations that, for various reasons, are committed to seeing a revitalized and reenergized core.

The Return of the Center

The L.A. analysis is problematic in that it is historically and geographically limited. Specifically, while Los Angeles serves as an appropriate backdrop of the assertions offered, its descriptions are indigenous to its historical development processes. Simply put, not all cities are evolving in a similar manner. The endless sprawling settings observed in Los Angeles adequately offer an advanced state of decentralization, but during the last two decades we can observe that downtowns are becoming repopulated with the rebuilding of significant infrastructures, signaling new ways of experiencing urban life. Cities across the country are refashioning themselves, utilizing culture, leisure, entertainment, and tourism around which they are developing a new economy, fueling residential growth.

As Table 13.1 shows, only four of twenty-two downtowns with a population of at least 10,000 residents experienced population decline from 1990 to 2000. From 1970 to 1980, sixteen of these recorded population decreases. This makes the Los Angeles assertions historically limited, as the sprawl is largely the outcome of post–World War II conditions of American cities.

Globalization, decentralization, economic restructuring, and new policies of federalism in the 1980s forced cities to aggressively pursue new approaches to economic development by becoming active providers of

	1990	2000	1970–1980	1990–2000
EAST				
Baltimore	28,597	30,067	-13.9%	5.1%
Boston	77,253	80,903	- 3.0%	4.7%
Lower Manhattan	84,539	97,752	17.8%	15.6%
Midtown Manhattan	69,388	71,668	14.9%	3.3%
Philadelphia	74,686	78,349	-8.8%	4.9%
Washington, D.C.	26,597	27,667	-18.7%	4.0%
SOUTH				
Atlanta	19,763	24,931	-21.9%	26.1%
Chattanooga	12,601	13,529	-6.3%	7.4%
Dallas	18,104	22,469	-27.7%	24.1%
Miami	15,143	19,927	-41.1%	31.6%
Orlando	14,275	12,621	-24.7%	-11.6%
San Antonio	19,603	19,236	-21.6%	-1.9%
MIDWEST				
Chicago	56,048	72,843	-3.1%	30.0%
Detroit	38,116	36,871	-32.4%	-3.3%
Indianapolis	14,894	17,907	21.5%	20.2%
Milwaukee	14,458	16,359	-11.6%	13.1%
Minneapolis	36,334	30,299	- 7.0%	-16.6%
WEST				
Los Angeles	34,655	36,630	46.7%	5.7%
Portland	9,528	12,902	- 2.5%	35.4%
San Diego	15,417	17,894	2.2%	16.1%
San Francisco	32,906	43,531	-19.1%	32.3%
Seattle	12,292	21,745	2.7%	76.9%

Source: Eugenie L. Birch, Who Lives Downtown *(The Brookings Institution, November 2005), 5.*

Table 13.1 Downtown population change in metropolitan areas with 10,000 minimum residents, 1990–2000.

services. The commodification of leisure, increases in disposable income, and the overall restructuring of the travel industry, among many other forces, offered new economic avenues as cities searched for growth.

The realization of this direction also requires the creation of an infrastructure to serve as part of a new production process. Dennis Judd and Susan Fainstein document how a new political economy of urban tourism has contributed to revisiting local economic development strategies within a complex, highly evolving structure of global influences.[7] Infrastructural investments in convention centers, festivals, museums, parks, stadiums, and outdoor events have resulted in the reorganization of space, in the process remaking the urban landscape.[8] The creation of "tourism bubbles" and the evolution of tourism districts exemplify the value placed on maintaining these locales as engines of urban economic growth.[9]

Interestingly, even downtown Los Angeles has experienced considerable investment in the last few years. The Staples Center, constructed in 1999 for $375 million provides numerous entertainment opportunities and Frank Gehry's Walt Disney Concert Hall opened in downtown Los Angeles for $274 million. The Cathedral of Our Lady of the Angels underwent a $200 million renovation in 2002, a year after Los Angeles City Hall received a $300 million refurbishment. In 2007, to support a robust population growth, a new supermarket opened in downtown Los Angeles, the first of its kind in decades.

The local government is also committed to seeing the rebirth of the downtown area. In 1999, the Los Angeles City Council approved an adoptive reuse ordinance that helped the redevelopment of buildings into residential loft living and office conversion. In 2007, the council passed new zoning regulations that, over time, will fundamentally restructure the downtown area by expanding the core and by aiding dense residential development.[10]

Those downtown developments are dwarfed by current plans, which under the L.A. Live initiative will introduce an entirely new entertainment destination. At a cost of $2.5 billion, this public-private partnership will refashion 27 acres into an entertainment campus. According to L.A. Live, the project:

> will provide Los Angeles' residents, commuters . . . a "content campus" and THE event center for Southern California . . . L.A. LIVE will expand the entertainment content in downtown Los Angeles' South Park neighborhood

with complementing venues, fully functioning broadcast studios, restaurants, cafes, cinemas, bowling lanes, music clubs and a cultural museum . . . [This will be] a major mechanism in rejuvenating the downtown core, [and] will invigorate an emerging high-density urban residential neighborhood and pedestrian district."[11]

The first phase of this ambitious project opened in October 2007 and included the 7,100-seat NOKIA Theater, the NOKIA Plaza, and 1,500 parking spaces. In October 2008, 12 restaurants, the NOKIA Club, a bowling facility, a Grammy Museum, ESPN headquarters, and 2,000 additional parking spaces were completed. The final phase scheduled for 2010 includes a J.W. Marriott and Ritz-Carlton Hotel, residences, ballrooms, and a major cinema.[12]

In addition to the L.A. Live activities, another government-backed initiative, the Grand Avenue Project, will help "transform the civic and cultural districts of downtown Los Angeles into a vibrant new regional center which will showcase entertainment venues, restaurants, and retail mixed with a hotel and up to 2,600 new housing units." Headlined as "Creating a Center for Los Angeles," this massive $3 billion investment will include impressive public spaces and will be managed by the Los Angeles Grand Avenue Authority, a county/city unit established in 2003 focusing on regional growth.[13]

It is ironic that Los Angeles, the highly celebrated fragmented, centerless city is undergoing monumental planning at its core. From 2005 to 2008 there has been a 42 percent increase in the downtown population, and, according to city estimates, a 20 percent increase from 2000 to 2006, well above the 8 percent overall growth across L.A. According to Carol E. Schatz, president of the Central City Association, a downtown business advocacy group, "We have created a desirable place to live. As the whole region comes out of the downturn, we will speed ahead. There's no other place you can go to the opera, a Lakers game or a world-class concert."[14]

But the story of downtown Los Angeles is not unique, as similar patterns can be observed in cities across America. Investment in downtown infrastructure, residential growth of the core, culture, tourism, and entertainment are becoming focal points of economic development agendas and pro-growth policies aiming to reinvent and refashion city centers. In the following pages, I present the case of the Chicago metropolitan area by noting how Chicago, Joliet, Waukegan, Aurora, and Elgin (see Figure 13.1) have embraced an active redevelopment agenda focusing on their downtowns, while attracting visitors to their locales and expanding opportunities for economic growth through leisure and urban tourism.

Chicago's New Downtown along the Lakefront

Like many other American cities, Chicago was subjected to considerable changes following World War II. Extensive economic restructuring in the 1970s and 1980s meant manufacturing decline and population loss. The decentralization movement that followed significantly expanded the metropolitan area, substantially increasing the region's population outside Chicago's borders. Since 1950, the city's population successively declined from 3.6 million (1950) to 2.8 million (1990). The 2000 census revealed, for the first time, a reversal of this trend when Chicago experienced about a 113,000 population increase to 2.9 million.

The accompanying urban crisis also resulted in considerable social problems including unemployment, challenges in managing an increasingly deteriorating and ineffective educational system, housing decay, crime, and a general decline of the neighborhoods. Chicago's civic, corporate, and political leaders attempted to develop strategies to deal with the negative consequences of these developments. As mayor, Richard J. Daley (1956–1976) focused on protecting the Loop by supporting an aggressive office construction program downtown. New residential developments like Marina Towers and Dearborn Park were aimed at retaining existing residents and attracting new ones, while the creation of the Water Tower Place on Michigan Avenue in 1975 was intended to offer an array of new shopping opportunities.

While succeeding mayors attempted to meet various urban needs, it was Richard M. Daley (1989–present) who advanced a new vision for

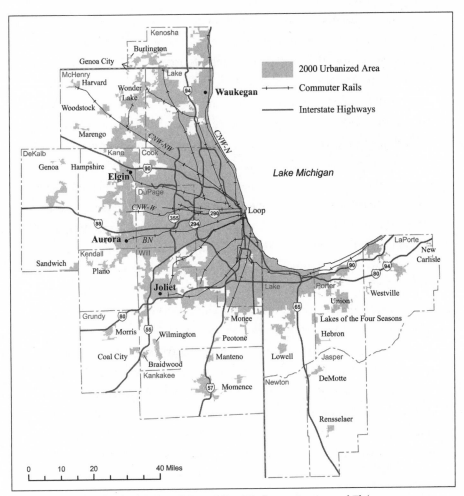

Figure 13.1 Redevelopment in Chicago, Joliet, Waukegan, Aurora, and Elgin.
Courtesy of Richard Greene and Lenny Walther, Department of Geography, Northern
Illinois University.

Chicago. Daley focused on the city's core, investing more than $5 billion
on infrastructural development and millions more on urban beautification,
summer festivals, and year-round events. Navy Pier, Museum Campus, two
large expansions of the McCormick Place convention center costing nearly
$2 billion, Soldier Field, Meigs Field, and the half-billion-dollar Millennium
Park development fundamentally restructured the downtown and their
presence reimaged the city.

One of the first projects the new mayor tackled was Navy Pier. The 3,300-foot structure was revamped in 1995 for over $200 million. Attractions now include the Chicago Children's Museum, a 32,000-square-foot indoor botanical garden, a fifteen-story Ferris wheel, street entertainment areas with outdoor stages, an IMAX theater, retail concessions, restaurants, food courts, a skyline stage, a festival hall, a huge ballroom, and fifty acres of parks and promenades. Over the years, the district has become the most popular attraction in the city. According to the Chicago Office of Tourism and the Chicago Convention and Tourism Bureau, 3.5 million visited the site when it first opened to the public in 1995. The attendance exceeded 7 million in 1997. In 2003, 8.7 million visited the pier, generating $45.8 million. In 2004, 2005, and 2006, attendance was maintained at around 8.7 million, slightly behind the 9 million-visitor peak attendance achieved during 2000.[15] The initial boom of the project was so impressive that public officials viewed Navy Pier as having a positive effect on the revitalization of nearby housing in the Streeterville community.[16]

But as with other types of tourism districts, Navy Pier officials recognized the need to unveil plans for additional changes. The goal is to boost attendance and revenues, and according to former McPier CEO Leticia Peralta Davis, the government agency that operates the site, "Navy Pier is a great success today, but we need to make sure that success continues . . . We hope to see a framework of what Navy Pier might look like in the next 10 years. We want to keep things very fresh. An entertainment venue like Navy Pier needs to keep things fresh."[17] Plans for this more than $1 billion expansion project include additional parking structures, a new 900-seat venue for the Chicago Shakespeare Theater, a new hotel, a monorail system that will aid visitors' experience of the pier, and a larger Ferris wheel that could be used year round, equipped with access to food and drinks during the rides. The most ambitious portion of the plan includes an 80,000-square-foot, Great Lakes-themed, family-oriented water park, the second largest of its type in the world. In addition, an indoor park with rides and a new marina that could provide 250 boat slips would be added to the complex.

In the early part of the 1990s, Daley's focus centered on the south end of Grant Park, the location where the successful Century of Progress Exposition was held some sixty years earlier. Committed to advancing a culturally driven redevelopment agenda, the city would focus on four major projects: the creation of the Museum Campus, the conversion of Meigs Field, the redevelopment of Soldier Field, and a massive addition, McCormick Place West, to the already expansive convention center. The vision to join the grounds of the Field Museum of Natural History, the Shedd Aquarium, and the Adler Planetarium created a unique cultural setting. At a cost of more than $120 million, the Metropolitan Pier and Exposition Authority carried out the project with city and state financial resources, adding more than fifty-seven acres of green space on the lakefront, advancing the image of Chicago as a city of culture.[18]

The mayor then focused on adjacent Meigs Field, a small airport used by business leaders on Northerly Island next to the museums and downtown. The goal to transform the space into a public park met with intense resistance from then Governor Edgar of Illinois and the corporate community of Chicago. According to the mayoral proposal, the space would be altered to create a ninety-one-acre park at a projected cost of $27.2 million. The plan would link the park to the Museum Campus and would include botanical gardens, playgrounds, wetlands, a nature center, and a sensory garden for the visually and hearing impaired. According to city projections the "superpark" would generate over $30 million a year in revenues from parking, concessions, souvenirs, and other fees and it would draw more than 350,000 visitors annually.[19]

In March 2003, discouraged by delays, Mayor Daley stepped in and in the middle of the night ended the controversy over the future of Meigs Field. City equipment quickly carved X's in the airport's runway and ended the transportation function of the lakefront space, setting the stage for its conversion to a park. While the action created a public outcry, some influential civic leaders including the president of the Grant Park Advisory Council praised the mayor by noting his "courage and progressive leadership . . . in closing Meigs Field."[20]

In the summer of 2005, the city organized the opening of the Charter One Pavilion on Northerly Island. The 7,500-seat venue offers outdoor concerts and live entertainment to music fans.[21] The new space has been widely embraced by Chicagoans and quickly evolved into a destination spot, receiving praise as critics declared, "It's hard to argue with a venue where a view of the Chicago skyline serves as the backdrop. Lake Michigan provides air conditioning."[22]

The construction of nearby Soldier Field in 2003 for $680 million included about $200 million in nearby investments. Extensive underground parking has been added and surface parking areas to the south of the stadium were landscaped, adding more than fifteen acres of green space. Overall, 1,300 trees of forty-five different species were planted, a sledding hill was configured, and a children's garden has been created.[23] The new facility is in concert with the city's larger vision of keeping Soldier Field as part of the lakefront, positioning it as an additional piece to the available entertainment venues along Chicago's front yard.

Yet, it is the construction of the Millennium Park on the north edge of Grant Park that would become a signature project of the new Chicago. Initially conceived in 1998 at a cost of $150 million, this initiative would rely on corporate sponsors and private donations contributing $30 million of the total cost. A year later, the Chicago Department of Transportation announced an expansion of the previous plan. New additions to this plan included a warming house and a restaurant for an ice-skating rink; an increase of the planned indoor theater seating, from a 500- to a 1,500-seat auditorium; a commuter bicycle center; a glass greenhouse pavilion; and an improved music pavilion design with good sight lines. The size of the park also increased to 24.6 acres.

One of Millennium Park's central projects was the Frank Gehry band shell design of the music pavilion. His signature massive steel trellis, unveiled in 1999, was built over a seating area for 11,000 spectators, the new home of the Grant Park Symphony Orchestra. Employing similar architectural principles, Gehry contributed the design of a nearby bridge connecting the Jay Pritzker Pavilion with the Daley Bicentennial Park to the east and across Columbus Drive. Over $200 million was raised from ninety-one donors to make this twenty-first century, half-billion-dollar park.[24] A few years after the unveiling of the park, Crown Fountain and the Cloud Gate sculpture have become key attractions for tourists and locals.

The park draws about 3.5 million visitors annually. In addition, it has had an impact on the surrounding real estate activities: a study commissioned by the city revealed in 2005 that $1.4 billion in residential development was attributed to the presence of Millennium Park. Moreover, an increase by $100 per square foot in area residential real estate values was connected to the new park.[25]

Chicago's downtown has been restructured in the last fifteen years. Extraordinary residential development has populated once again the south and west sides, and even downtown has experienced a population boom. Tourism has increased despite being briefly interrupted by the September 11, 2001, terrorist attacks. The extraordinary infrastructure along the lakefront catapulted Chicago into the global arena as one of the four final cities that competed to host the 2016 Olympic Games.

Joliet: Downtown Revival through Entertainment

The City of Joliet is located forty miles southwest of Chicago, and in recent years the city boundaries have grown in a rapidly developing Will County to also occupy parts of adjacent Kendall County. The city has historically relied on its transportation function, which supported its economic growth and population expansion. The location of a downtown core along the Des Plaines River allowed Joliet an opportunity to create a significant business center, as its connection to the Illinois and Michigan Canal offered significant growth potential. By the late 1850s, a number of railroad lines passed through the city, including the Elgin, Joliet and Eastern, the Santa Fe, and the Rock Island, making this an important southwest hub for Chicago.

During the second half of the nineteenth century, Joliet relied on manufacturing, housing the Joliet Steel Mill, which became Illinois Steel and, by 1901, the merged and renamed United Steel South Works. During their heights, these steel mills employed as many as two thousand workers. Like other industrial midwestern cities, Joliet experienced a significant decline, clearly reflected in demographic trends. U.S. Census data show that the city experienced a population increase from 66,780 (1960) to 78,827 (1970). The population remained almost constant for the next twenty years at 77,956 (1980) and 76,836 (1990). In 1982, only sixteen homes were built within the city limits.[26]

The city explored a variety of ways to bring Joliet back and in the early part of the 1990s, under the Joliet City Center Development Plan, they embraced a revival program that focused on the redevelopment of the downtown.[27] An integral part of this plan was the integration of the Des Plaines River, which was viewed as having enormous potential. According to Donald J. Fisher, Joliet planning director, "We're working very hard to promote some of the recreational-type activities that we would like to see happen on the river and banks. The river then would be a magnet for other types of development, such as housing, commercial, retail, etc. It would become a focal point for the rest of the city."[28]

Numerous projects can be attributed to the Joliet City Center Development Plan, all concerned with the revival of the downtrodden core. Specifically, sports and entertainment have been a key strategy of this regeneration effort, helping convert Joliet into a tourism destination spot. Construction of the $27 million Silver Cross Field (6,650 spectator capacity), home to the minor league baseball Joliet JackHammers of the Northern League, was completed in 2002. The city provided $25 million of the total construction cost. The JackHammers's rivals in the league include the nearby Schaumburg Flyers and the Gary Southshore Railcats, whose fans help fuel downtown activity during home games.

Another significant addition to transforming Joliet into a destination has been the Chicagoland Speedway. The developers completed the $130 million project in 2000 and chose Joliet over other west suburban locations because "the surging city jumped at the chance to build the speed palace."[29] The city annexed over 1,300 acres for the project, which includes seating for 75,000 as well as for an additional 20,000 fans watching from the D-shaped track infield. Notable auto racing events include the NASCAR Winston Cup Series, NASCAR Busch Series, and the IRL IndyCar Series, among others. Additionally, the Route 66 Raceway, constructed nearby in 1998, accommodates 35,000 fans with thirty-eight luxury skyboxes.[30]

But it is the riverboat gaming industry that has been credited with the turnaround of downtown Joliet, the recipient of two gaming licenses by the state, the Empress River Casino in 1992 and Harrah's Casino in 1993, located on the Des Plaines River in the city center. Bob Herrick of the Joliet/ Will County Center for Economic Development notes that "when riverboat gaming came along, it was a perfect match for the [downtown redevelopment] plan."[31]

Concurrently, the city attempted to refashion its downtown into a continuous entertainment hub by focusing on the addition of high-end dance clubs, converted department stores, comedy clubs, ethnic restaurants, theater, symphony, and a dizzying array of indoor and outdoor activities, many of them staged along the riverfront. According to Tom Mahalik, vice president of City Center Marketing:

> After many years and lots of effort in developing the downtown, we are delighted our goal of establishing a downtown entertainment center is successful. We have worked very hard and with the introduction of four new restaurants and entertainment venues over the last year, we are proud to make downtown the place to be.[32]

These activities have brought additional visitors to the city, as reflected by the growth in the construction of hotel rooms and subsequent revenues. Specifically, in 1990 the hotel gross receipts were $7.941 million and the available guest rooms numbered 1,050. In 2003, sales increased to $19.621 million (an increase of 147 percent), with 2,255 hotel rooms (an increase of 114.76 percent).[33] In 2002, the U.S. Census Bureau identified Joliet as the tenth fastest-growing city in the United States, a position that Joliet has maintained in recent reports (fifteenth in 2005).[34]With a headline titled "If it's fun . . . it's in downtown Joliet," Mayor Arthur Schultz proclaimed in a recent city publication:

> Joliet has gone through a lot of changes during my time as mayor and we are definitely moving forward. We have welcomed NASCAR, IRL and NHRA racing, the Joliet JackHammers professional baseball club, Harrah's

and Empress Casinos, a new AutoBahn Country Club, Challenge Park Extreme, Splash Station Water Park, the Joliet Area Historical Museum and the new west side branch of the Joliet Public Library . . . Baseball games, concerts, races, festivals and other special events are the theme as we head from spring into summer.[35]

The city's home page echoes this sentiment, noting "You don't have to drive to Chicago for quality entertainment, with Joliet's new entertainment destination . . . It's right in your own backyard . . . There's no need to travel anywhere else!"[36] While it is not clear how the next phase of Joliet's revival will fare, it is certain that the city's future is strongly connected to its culture/tourism-based development efforts strongly aided by a committed local government. As one observer declared: "You have [in Joliet] a pro-growth City Council,"[37] making the rise of downtown Joliet very impressive, since more than $128 million in property valuation has been added to the core.[38]

Waukegan: Rebuilding the Core along the Lakefront

The city of Waukegan, located about thirty-six miles north of Chicago, has benefited from its position on Lake Michigan and its function as a commercial port. The trade/shipping opportunities offered by the city's location on Lake Michigan would attract large numbers of immigrants, helping the city's population grow from 9,426 in 1900 to 33,499 in 1930.

The effect of deindustrialization in the 1970s and 1980s became most visible during the 1990s. The Johns-Manville Corporation, a major Waukegan employer, closed its industrial facility in 1990. The Outboard Marine Corporation declared bankruptcy in 2000 and the subsequent owner, Bombardier, moved the manufacturing jobs to Wisconsin. Together, these companies occupied more than 500 acres of lakefront space.[39] The presence of manufacturing industries had also helped develop Waukegan into an ethnically and racially diverse community. In 2000, the city's population boasted 19.2 percent African American and 44.8 percent Hispanic residents.

During the latter part of the 1990s, the city focused its energies in revitalizing the downtown, though the factory-marred adjacent lakefront would create numerous challenges. Much of the discussion at that time focused on an ambitious redevelopment plan that included a performing arts center, hundreds of condominiums, and a hotel and a convention center. In 1998, the city created a tax increment financing (TIF) district, encompassing much of the lakefront area occupied by empty factories.[40]

In August 2003, the Waukegan City Council unanimously approved the Waukegan Lakefront–Downtown Master Plan, an ambitious vision aimed at reviving the city's depressed core. While the focal part of the plan was the downtown area, the design guidelines included extensive planning for three additional districts: the South Lakefront, the Harborfront, and the North Harbor. These nearby locales would complement the city center, recasting a new urban image following the decline that characterized the lakefront in recent decades.

The city's poor economic standing and subsequent disinvestment had not only resulted in expansive tracks of unused lakefront property, but the deteriorating downtown made the waterfront areas increasingly inaccessible. Recognizing the need for action, in the early part of 2000, late Mayor Dan Drew and city leaders called for a process that would revive the community by refocusing on its location on Lake Michigan. The Urban Land Institute (ULI) was retained to provide guidance on how to ensure effective redevelopment outcomes. Led by panel chair William J. Hudnut, former mayor of Indianapolis, the ULI considered market potential, planning rationales, as well as development and implementation strategies. The overall community feedback to the plan proved quite positive and as one resident noted: "I've lived here for sixty-one years, and this was a real town at one time. These are good ideas. Maybe it can be a real town again."[41] Then Waukegan Mayor Richard Hyde echoed the sentiment: "This is one of the most exciting times in Waukegan. All these plans have revived the city."[42]

With the assistance of the noted Chicago-based firm Skidmore, Owings and Merrill, the Waukegan Lakefront–Downtown Master Plan moved forward to completely refashion 400 acres of downtown area and 3.5 miles of lakefront. The redevelopment transformed the space from its existing industrial composition to one formulated around residential, cultural, recreational, and entertainment districts. The plan included the construction of 3,752 new residential units on 125 acres, most of those (1,058) located in the downtown district. The report conveys this vision: "Downtown uses will include a mix of commercial and retail activity in addition to unique opportunities such as the historic Genesee Theater. Waukegan's downtown will build on its history and its lakefront location, providing a lively and attractive district with diverse uses and users. A significant amount of new residential use in the downtown will be balanced by retail, office, entertainment, education and culture areas."[43]

The massive size of the Waukegan downtown-lakefront redevelopment plan is reflected in its estimated cost of $1.2 billion. The city will finance the project by attracting $950 million in private investment, with the remaining deriving from city, county, state, and federal sources. Tax-increment financing would contribute an additional $111.3 million.[44]

While the $23 million restoration of the Genesee Theater in 2004 was welcomed as the first substantial sign of Waukegan's rejuvenation, ensuing development has been sluggish. The much-needed public-private partnerships, which would help fuel the activities, proved slow to materialize. The Waukegan Lakefront Corporation, a private development partnership, has expressed interest in building a hotel and a 900 housing-unit complex called Harbor Place Condominiums along the city's marina. Land acquisition issues with its public partner, the Waukegan Port District, have delayed the project. Similarly, while a few new restaurants and other small businesses have surfaced in the last few years, the expected residential influx has not materialized. New housing units were priced before the current recession at a minimum of $300,000.

Issues related to the polluted environment brought many of the planned development activities along Waukegan's lakefront to a standstill. The city currently plans to expend $35 million (including $23 million in federal funds) to clean up PCBs from the area. The project is expected to take years to complete. According to a 2003 study by the Northeast-Midwest Institute in Washington, D.C., when completed, a clean harbor would increase the residential property values of Waukegan by $500 million. This will be a welcome change as the city tries to negotiate more than $94 million in outstanding bond debt.[45] Notwithstanding the numerous challenges facing Waukegan, it is clear that the city is attempting to reposition itself within the new conditions of a postindustrial economy by focusing on remaking its core.

Aurora: Riverboat Gaming and a New Downtown

The City of Aurora, located about thirty-five miles west of downtown Chicago, has had a rich history dating back to the early 1830s. Strategically located along the Fox River, the city utilized its position to develop businesses and attract laborers. Following its incorporation in 1845, Aurora slowly evolved into a manufacturing center. In the mid-1850s, the Chicago, Burlington, and Quincy Railroad Company, which operated from 1849–1970, placed its railcar factory and maintenance facilities within Aurora's borders. The facility closed in 1974, largely due to the development of the Eisenhower Expressway, which allowed the automobile to provide easy access from the western suburbs to the Loop.[46]

The recession of the 1970s further hurt the local economy, forcing many of the factories and businesses to shut down. Nearby, large suburban malls sprang up, attracting many shoppers and furthering the dilapidating condition of downtown Aurora. For example, the 1975 development of the Fox Valley Center, adjacent to the city's eastern Naperville border, introduced a sea of trendy, new stores. A bit further east, the self-enclosed Oakbrook Center opened in 1962. The Oakbrook megamall complex saw successive expansions in 1973 and in 1981, affecting the economic future of many western suburban downtowns.

During the late 1980s, the Aurora City Council recognized that resurrecting its core was vital if the community was to rebound from its economic decline. Three redevelopment plans were initially pursued. Two of those focused on addressing visibly abandoned structures with the intent of converting them into usable spaces that could attract visitors to the area. A new ordinance encouraged light manufacturing and residential occupancies to be integrated above first-floor uses. With this policy agenda in place, the core of a new downtown district could be created while also encouraging increased pedestrian traffic.[47]

The other key step taken by the local government was the creation of a TIF aimed at providing developers with financial assistance. Initiated for the first time in 1986, some of the programs under that effort included exterior restoration, interior rehabilitation, and architectural grants. The city also maintained an ongoing commitment to visually enhancing the area by expending considerable funds on streetscape beautification programs and related infrastructural improvements. In addition, an intense program of festivals, outdoor street performances, and seasonal entertainment venues called Downtown Alive! has been continually expanded. Karen Christensen, Aurora's downtown Riverwalk administrator asserted:

> We went through what happened to every [other city] in Illinois: People started running to the mall and a lot of local employers were hurt and had to move to other places. Things are [improving] now because 15 years ago folks sat down and said, "We've got to do something to save our city and its architectural history and uniqueness.'" We didn't want to turn into a cookie cutter of every other place. Aurora is a city in its own right, and I think we are on our way back, big time.[48]

However, many credit Aurora's revival to riverboat gambling and the casino that located in downtown in 1993. Secured by the leadership of the Aurora Civic Center Authority, Hollywood Casino, with more than 1,500 employees (the largest employer in downtown Aurora), generates $13.6 million in local tax revenue.[49] In the context of the ongoing cost/benefits debate related to gambling, the Illinois Casino and Gaming Association singled out Mayor David L. Stover, who commented:

> Riverboat gaming in Aurora has accomplished just what the state legislature intended. Hollywood Casino-Aurora brings hundreds of thousands of people to downtown Aurora. The local share of the gaming tax allows us to do significant capital improvements projects throughout the city that we could not otherwise afford.[50]

Downtown historic preservation has also received special attention in Aurora. The Paramount Arts Center underwent a $5.6 million update as part of a TIF designation.[51] Facade restoration of existing historic structures and concern with the architectural detail of new developments gained extensive support. Between 1999 and 2004, more than 500 projects came under review and sixty building owners utilized special finance opportunities provided by the city to aid in the rehabilitation of the city center. Similarly, the commercial value of building permits issued in the area during that period surpassed $50 million. In 2003, the first Downtown Heritage Tour and Cell-Phone Guided Walking Tour formally marketed the history of downtown Aurora to tourists. That same year, the Midwest Literary Festival was introduced, and the Blues on the Fox and Rock on the Fox have proved popular events, drawing thousands to downtown.[52]

Parades and children's activities, musicals and theater productions, outdoor performances, a popular Farmers Market, and street vendors have focused Aurora on a strategy that utilizes its developing downtown identity as a magnet to also entice businesses. A promotional flyer by the Aurora Economic Development Commission declares the attractiveness of the location by noting the presence of over 130,000 annual visitors to Paramount Theater, more than 2 million annual visitors to Hollywood Casino, 52,000 annual visitors to the SciTech Hands-On Museum, and 80,000 visitors to the highly successful Downtown Alive! summer entertainment programs.[53] Many of the city's recent promotional materials reference the downtown area as a "neighborhood" and broadly describe the city as "the Midwest's Newest Urban Lifestyle Community."

The addition of specialty restaurants and attention to formal gathering spaces like the Millennium Plaza, Rotary Park, Tivoli Plaza, and the Sesquicentennial Park have helped attract a housing development program that is expected to further fuel the vibrancy of the core. For example, the newly constructed River Street Plaza Lifestyle Condominiums are a popular housing option in the downtown area. Occupied in 2007 and 2008, this 5.6 acre mixed-use redevelopment provides 200 new units and more than 80,000 square feet of space. It includes cafes and upscale and casual dining along the riverfront. Additionally, a fourteen-story hotel and an adjacent

100,000-square-foot convention center by the $100 million Fox River Plaza complex have been proposed. The center will host trade shows, concerts, and sporting events. The structure includes one of the largest green roofs in the country, covering more than a 150,000-square-foot area.[54]

The City of Aurora has embraced a strategy centered on the belief that visitors will be attracted to the downtown of the community to work, live, and play. In its 2003/2004 report, the Aurora Economic Development Commission declared:

> [Our] City planners continue to look at the opportunities near the Fox River for home ownership. Opportunities include upscale residential town homes and specialty retail development . . . More residents are discovering the Central City when they come to enjoy the summer festivals such as Downtown Alive! and patronize the Paramount Theatre as well as downtown art galleries and historical venues.[55]

In an effort to resist the negative consequences of deindustrialization and the mega-malls that have sprung up on its outskirts, Aurora envisioned its future according to the motto of its celebrated son and local icon, Bud Meyer, a business leader and philanthropist, who often publicly explained that "The image of the city is its downtown."[56]

Elgin: Downtown Leisure and Residential Development

Developed along the Fox River, Elgin, Illinois, is located approximately thirty-six miles northwest of downtown Chicago. The city relied on its position as a transportation center by not only connecting to north/south routes along the river, but also by evolving into a key stop between Chicago to the east and Galena to the west. By the middle of the nineteenth century, Galena had become a major commercial center near the Mississippi River and the effort to develop the Galena and Chicago Union Railroad reached Elgin. Elgin's railroad status would prove critical as Chicago's economic prominence was elevated in the latter part of the nineteenth and early part of the twentieth centuries.

The city continued to take advantage of its railroad center location, eventually playing a major role in interurban metropolitan travel. Any trip from the far western suburbs to Chicago necessitated travel to the Loop through Elgin. A number of manufacturing companies thrived in Elgin, among them the Elgin National Watch Company and the Elgin Sweeper Corporation. These and other factories drew large numbers of Hispanic residents, who found work in the city's robust economic environment.

The post–World War II experience of downtown Elgin mirrored that of Aurora. Just as the west suburban Oakbrook Mall pulled visitors away from that city's core, the massive Woodfield Mall, built in Schaumburg in 1971, had a similar effect on Elgin's downtown. Just twelve miles east of the downtown, the new northwestern shopping center was identified during its unveiling as the largest enclosed shopping structure in the world. The development of additional strip malls in the outskirts of Elgin in the 1970s and 1980s to support new housing subdivisions would further deteriorate the center, reducing its commercial function. The early 1980s sealed the fate of Elgin's downtown. In 1980, Sears moved to nearby Spring Hill Mall, the Woolworth Company store closed in 1983, and in 1984 the J.C. Penney Company facility moved to Spring Hill. According to a city senior planner, "We are not looking at the downtown area as the retail core anymore."[57]

The city would make downtown development a priority in 1999, when Mayor Schock announced a new master plan for the core. On that occasion, he reflected on the historic importance of the city center by noting that in 1945 the local leadership wanted to transform the riverfront into the "jewel of the Fox Valley." According to the mayor, "[they] had a vision. But the execution has languished for fifty years."[58]

Recourses for the advancement of the downtown derived from the gaming industry. Like Joliet and Aurora, Elgin pursued the opportunity to locate a riverboat casino along the shore of the Fox River. The Grand Victoria Riverboat Casino began operation in 1994 and has since become an entertainment option for thousands across the Chicago metropolitan region. With more than 1,200 gaming positions, this $100 million investment is the fifth most popular tourist destination in Illinois, attracting 2.3 million visitors annually. Understandably, Elgin led the opposition in downstate Springfield when Chicago recently expressed interest in an additional gaming license. A Chicago casino would take business away from Elgin, whose revenues from gaming in 2007 reached $24.3 million.[59]

In May 2000, the Elgin City Council approved the Riverfront/Center City Master Plan: City of Elgin, Illinois. The plan outlined numerous goals including recreational opportunities along the Fox River, support for mixed-use spaces, civic and cultural activities, historic preservation, as well as the creation of a sustainable economic base in downtown. Two of the key goals were to promote a twenty-four-hour urban living atmosphere and identify ways to develop residential projects that would enhance the core. In 2001, the downtown plan received the Planning Award by the Illinois chapter of the American Planning Association.

The city strategically reached out to developers to expand investment in the downtown, not only by pointing out the benefits of the Fox River setting but also by expending resources on public infrastructure to produce downtown amenities. Recent plans include Water Tower Place, a $53 million proposal that will introduce luxury units adjacent to new retail facilities, offering shopping opportunities and waterfront restaurants. Fountain Square on the River Project is another mixed-use riverfront development adding expanded housing and retail space. River Park Place, a $30 million mixed-use project will contribute 200 more residential units. A promotional brochure offers the key advantages of this initiative by noting the opportunity to "imagine living within the redeveloped streets of historic downtown Elgin . . . feel the energy of a revitalized downtown Elgin."[60]

The plan has been ambitious, since more than $250 million has been invested in the downtown during the last ten years. More than 1,000 new units will be added in Elgin's center, supported by a recently completed array of infrastructural projects, including a $41 million recreation center, a $30 million public library center, and a $10 million redevelopment and expansion of the Metra station, providing main suburban commuter rail service to Chicago. An $11.5 million Festival Park near the river has become a focal point of the revitalization efforts, with year-round parades, festivals, and celebrations.

The goal of the City of Elgin is clear–by focusing on culture and entertainment, revive the core once again to its vibrant past. According to a city official, "The downtown is really the heart of the area and we want to maintain that."[61] Cherie Murphy, marketing officer for the City of Elgin, captures the direction of the city and the importance of its downtown:

> Elgin is positioning itself as the "City in the Suburbs" and attracting new homebuyers with the wide variety of things we offer for any lifestyle. This includes a great park system and cultural arts for all ages, including the Youth Symphony, Elgin Children's Choir and more. The downtown offers an urban lifestyle at an affordable price, with access to all the amenities of the suburbs close at hand.[62]

Conclusion

The cases presented in this analysis contradict the position of L.A. School scholars that metropolitan development is evolving devoid of downtowns and identifiable centers. Chicago's dominance in the late nineteenth and early twentieth centuries as an industrial powerhouse helped these peripheral cities grow their economies. This essay shows that the depressed Chicagoland downtowns left behind following deindustrialization and decentralization are rebounding once again. They are reemerging as viable, sought-after spaces for living, working, and playing.

The recent revitalization of Chicago's downtown as a city of leisure, tourism, and entertainment is emulated by its satellite cities, which have embraced similar strategies. It is within this framework that two observations can be made regarding the relationship of the center to twenty-first century patterns of urban change. The first concerns the presence of agency and the second the overall value and role of the core as it relates to metropolitan growth. The amorphous development asserted by the L.A. School signals a lack of action, focus, and intent. Yet, the cases examined in this chapter show that agency is of paramount importance in determining the redevelopment efforts. Strong mayors, entrepreneurial business leaders, attentive city councils, committed civic groups, and ordinary citizens all converge in a common mission to create city-center revitalization. The downtown, arts, and entertainment-oriented initiatives are produced within distinct municipal backdrops and the outcomes vary because of this agency.

At the same time, the revival of these urban cores offers some unique opportunities. A well-coordinated planning action can result in a multi-centered development, a clear departure from the unstructured format presented by the L.A. school. Political scientist Larry Bennett suggests that Chicago's policymakers can "pursue a politics of regional and intergovern-mental collaboration" as a way to engage in effective planning practices.[63] As residential expansion enters the exurbs, these new developing down-towns can serve as cultural and entertainment hubs, providing more livable environments in settings that otherwise would have been characterized by sprawl. It will be interesting to see how these grand plans fare in the cur-rent economic recession. In Chicago and the suburbs highlighted here, it appears that while their growth may slow, as it did in the downtown after 2001, the rebuilding of the downtown core will succeed in creating a multi-nuclei pattern of metropolitan development.

Notes

1. Edward Soja, *Thirdspace: Journeys to Los Angeles and Other Real-and-Imagined Places* (Oxford: Blackwell, 1996), 238.

2. Edward W. Soja and Allen J. Scott, "Introduction to Los Angeles, City and Region," in Allen J. Scott and Edward W. Soja, eds., *The City: Los Angeles and Urban Theory at the End of the Twentieth Century* (Berkeley: University of California Press, 1996), 11.

3. Michael Dear and Steven Flusty, "Postmodern Urbanism," *Annals of the Association of American Geographers* 88, no. 1 (March 1998): 66.

4. Edward W. Soja, "Los Angeles, 1965–1992: From Crisis-Generated Restructuring to Restructuring-Generated Crisis," in Allen J. Scott and Edward W. Soja, eds., *The City: Los Ange-les and Urban Theory at the End of the Twentieth Century* (Berkeley: University of California Press, 1996), 433–48; Mike Davis, *City of Quartz* (New York: Verso, 1990).

5. D. W. Miller, "The New Urban Studies," *Chronicle of Higher Education*, August 18, 2000, A15.

6. Dear, "Postmodern Urbanism."

7. Dennis Judd and Susan Fainstein, *The Tourist City* (New Haven: Yale University Press, 1999).

8. Dennis Judd, *The Infrastructure of Play: Building the Tourist City* (Armonk, N. Y.:

M.E. Sharpe, 2003); Terry Nichols Clark, ed,. *The City as an Entertainment Machine,* Research in Urban Policy 9 (Boston, Mass.: Elsevier/JAI, 2003); Costas Spirou and Larry Bennett, *It's Hardly Sportin': Stadiums, Neighborhoods, and the New Chicago* (DeKalb: Northern Illinois University Press, 2003).

9. D. R. Judd, "Constructing the Tourist Bubble," in D. R. Judd and S. S. Fainstein, eds., *The Tourist City* (New Haven: Yale University Press, 1999), 35–53; Costas Spirou, "The Evolution of the Tourism Precinct," in Bruce Hayllar, Tony Griffin, and Deborah Edwards, eds., *City Spaces-Tourist Places: Urban Tourism Precincts* (Oxford: Butterworth-Heinemann, 2008), 19–38.

10. Sharon Bernstein and David Pierson, "L.A. Moves Toward More N.Y.-Style Downtown," *Los Angeles Times,* Aug. 8, 2007.

11. http://www.lalive.com/ (accessed March 10, 2008).

12. Ibid.

13. http://www.grandavenuecommittee.org/ (accessed March 14, 2008).

14. Peter Y. Hong, "Downtown Not the Center of It All, *Los Angeles Times,* March 13, 2008.

15. Chicago Convention and Visitors Bureau Home Page (2006). Available at: www.choosechicago.com (accessed April 2008).

16. David Bernstein, "Just a Quiet Night at Home," *Crain's Chicago Business,* May 3, 2004, 13.

17. Kathy Ryan, "Navy Pier Unveils Plans for Sweeping Makeover," *Crain's Chicago Business,* January 13, 2006, 32.

18. "Lake Shore Drive," *Planning* 61, issue 2 (Feb., 1995): 42.

19. James Hill and Daniel Borsky, "City Lifts Veil on Hopes for Meigs Wetlands, Botanical Gardens Are Included," *Chicago Tribune,* July 2, 1996, sec. 5.

20. Bob O'Neill, "Daley's Magnificent Moment," *Chicago Tribune,* April 4, 2003.

21. G. Kot, "Stunning Skyline," *Chicago Tribune,* June 27, 2005.

22. Bob Gendron, "Rating Summer Sheds," *Chicago Tribune,* July 20, 2007.

23. L. Ford, "Soldier Field Landscaping Takes Shape," *Chicago Tribune,* April 26, 2004, sec. 2.

24. Fred A. Bernstein, "Big Shoulders, Big Donors, Big Art," *New York Times,* July 18, 2004.

25. Robert Sharoff, "How a Park Changed a Chicago Neighborhood," *New York Times,* June 4, 2006, sec. 11.

26. Ken O'Brien, "Joliet Rising," *Illinois Issues,* June 2001, 20–23.

27. David Elsner, "Joliet's Hopes Ride on the River Waterfront Key to City's Plan to Revitalize Downtown," *Chicago Tribune,* July 15, 1990.

28. Jim Sulski, "Des Plaines River Vital to City's Future: Stream Seen as Key to Development," *Chicago Tribune,* August 23, 1989.

29. Chicagoland Speedway, "Track Showcase History," http://www.chicagolandspeedway.com/ (retrieved April 26, 2008).

30. Brian McCormick, "New Track Gearing up for Nascar: Chicago Is Latest Urban Spot for Fast-Growing Sport," *Crain's Chicago Business,* June 11, 2001, 21.

31. O'Brien, "Joliet Rising."

32. "Joliet City Center Eyes Another Big Year," *The Herald News Online,* Feb. 20, 2005, http://www.suburbanchicagonews.com/heraldnews/aboutus/progress/2005/j20joliet.htm (retrieved May 29, 2008).

33. *Annual Report, Aurora Economic Development Commission, 2003–2004,* City of Joliet, 34.

34. Stephen Ohlemacher, "Joliet Joins List of Fastest-Growing Cities: Southwest Suburb One of Few Booming Cold-Weather Areas," *Chicago Sun-Times,* June 21, 2006.

35. Arthur Schultz, "If It's fun. . . . It's in Downtown Joliet," *Joliet Journal,* Spring, 2004.

36. City of Joliet Home Page, http://www.jolietdowntown.com/ (retrieved Nov 20, 2007).

37. O'Brien, "Joliet Rising."

38. Ken O'Brien, "Joliet's Downtown Seeing Some Evidence of a Revival," *Chicago Tribune,* July 10, 2004.

39. James Evans, "Waukegan Trying to Retool Its Image," *Crain's Chicago Business,* Oct. 8, 2001, 4.

40. Kevin Knapp, "Waukegan Tests Another Revival Plan," *Crain's Chicago Business,* Aug. 2, 1999, 3.

41. John Flink, "Waukegan Lakefront Plan Bows in Public," *Chicago Tribune,* March 13, 2002, metro sec.

42. Marcia Sagendorph, "Waukegan Poised to Remake Lakefront—Applicants Offer Downtown Plans," *Chicago Tribune,* Sept. 1, 2002, metro sec.

43. Skidmore, Owings and Merrill, *Design Guidelines: Waukegan Lakefront Master Plan* (March 2005).

44. Bob Tita, "Shore Restore," *Crain's Chicago Business,* Jan. 5, 2004, 21.

45. Andrew Wang, "Harbor Cleanup Outlined—Waukegan Officials Say Effort Is Worth $35 Million Price Tag," *Chicago Tribune,* April 20, 2006, metro sec.

46. City of Aurora, *Aldermen's Information Guide* (June 2005), 19.

47. Katherine Seigenthaler, "Three Paths Converge on Aurora's Downtown," Chicago Tribune, Feb. 26, 1987.

48. Warren Moulds, "Bragging Rights: Wheaton and Aurora Provide Two Examples of Towns That Take Pride in Reviving Downtowns," *Chicago Tribune,* March 18, 2001," West Suburban Outlook.

49. City of Aurora, *Comprehensive Annual Financial Report* (2005).

50. Illinois Casino and Gaming Association. 2006. Hollywood Casino-Aurora. http://www.illinoiscasinogaming.org/impact_files/hollywood.htm (Retrieved October 10, 2007).

51. Amy Roth-Fischer, "Theater Expansion Delayed until June," *Chicago Tribune,* April 21, 2005.

52. Annual Report, *Aurora Economic Development Commission 2003–2004.*

53. *Restaurant Site Opportunity, Downtown Aurora, Illinois,* Aurora Economic Development Commission (2006).

54. David Garbe, "Hotel, Convention Center in Works for Aurora," *Chicago Sun-Times,* July 7, 2006.

55. *Annual Report, Aurora Economic Development Commission, 2003–2004,* 4.

56. Karen Christensen, *Downtown Aurora Newsletter,* May 1, 2003.

57. E. C. Alft, *Elgin: An American History, 1835–1985* (Elgin, Ill.: Crossroads Communications, 1984), 314.

58. Rob Smith, "Elgin Brainstorm Session Gathers Downtown Ideas," *Chicago Tribune,* Nov. 12, 1999).

59. Bob Tita and Greg Hinz, "Casino Cash No Jackpot: $1-Bil. Revenue Would Net City $150 Mil., But Slots Could Save CTA," *Crain's Chicago Business,* Oct. 22, 2007.

60. *River Park Place: A New Neighborhood for Downtown Elgin* (Elgin, Ill: River Park Place).

61. Jim Sulski, "Three Towns Garner Loyalty—Elgin, East and West Dundee Enjoy Small-Town Feel," *Chicago Tribune,* April 3, 2002.

62. *River Park Place: A New Neighborhood for Downtown Elgin.*

63. Larry Bennett, "Chicago's New Politics of Growth," in J. Koval et al., *The New Chicago: A Social and Cultural Analysis* (Philadelphia: Temple University Press, 2006), 53.

Part V

**The Utility of
U.S. Urban Theory**

14

The City and Its Politics
Informal and Contested

■ Frank Gaffikin, David C. Perry, and Ratoola Kundu

The primary collaborator in the study of the city is the city itself. The essays here suggest that the cities of New York, Chicago, and Los Angeles have been, and continue to be, instrumental to our understanding of the forces and conditions of contemporary urbanism. The key word here is *continue* because they have been driving centers of modernist urbanism for most of the past two centuries. As such centers, or what Connell[1] calls *"metropoles,"* of the modernist-colonial production of the city's key economic role, it is unsurprising that they are considered integral to scholarship that addresses the primacy of global capital and the cities formed by such logic. However, in the new century, the most dramatic growth of modern urbanism is evident in the developing world.[2] In the early part of this new century, for the first time in the history of the human species, more of us found ourselves living in urban settlements than in rural.[3] While some of this change certainly has occurred in major cities like Los Angeles and New York, most of it has occurred in the urban centers of the global south, leading in its most expansive form to the phenomenon of "mega-cities"—whereby urban development extends into city-regions or peri-urban metropolitan entities[4] rather than remaining contained inside tightly drawn city boundaries.[5] Overall, it is estimated that up to 95 percent of all new urban settlers will be lodged in these city-regions, such that by 2030, the developing world will hold just under 80 percent of the world's urban population.[6] Therefore, describing this century as a metropolitan one is certainly apt—but the notion of metropolitan, in the context of the developing world's dramatic demographics and new relations of urbanism, will require a recasting of our urban "collaborators" with which to produce both the empirics and theory of urban study in the metropolitan century.

Of course, contemporary urban research should not eschew, as a starting point, first world cities and the conditions that inform them. However, in this new century, since many of the most pronounced conditions of urban sociospatial, political, and economic change are occurring in the city-regions of the global south, modern urban theory is better informed when the patterns of such urbanism are central to urban scholarship in both the first and third worlds. This argument derives in part from Connell,[7] who, in arguing for a "southern theory" of social science, suggests that the study of the cities of the global south should be predicated on what can be learned *from* the native erudition and experience in such cities, not on what can be learned *about* them. Conversely, Connell suggests that if we continue to *begin* our study of modern (urban) society from the perspective of the dominant sociospatial and political features of the first world's global cities, our work will be decidedly limited—prone to a flawed theoretical "fit" to the intensive urbanization in societies registering the greatest development in the contemporary world. However, notwithstanding its limited capacity to appreciate this extraordinary urbanism, the explanatory power of conventional urban theory is not without heuristic value. Like Connell, we suggest a social-science synthetic, whereby the urban of the global south is appropriately studied and linked with the theories of the metropole. In this way, both urban and global orders are placed in relevant, albeit clearly differentiated, relations. Chatterjee finds such relations not ones of "copresence" of formal developed world and informal developing world, but rather "new products" of the encounter between informal communities and the formal institutions of state and market[8]—relations that are certainly the stuff of a deeply contested politics.

Here we suggest that a notable condition of urbanism in the developing world—informality—holds resonance not only for our understanding of places registering the greatest amount of urban change, but also for ways in which such conditions find contested expression in first world cities.[9] In discussing the conditions of the "informal city," we will apply empirical examples from a diverse set of urban arenas: in the global south (Kolkata,

India, Cape Town, South Africa, and Michoacán, Mexico) and in the first world (from the global yet hypersegregated city of Chicago to the deindustrial and nationalist-contested city of Belfast).

The City: Informal

The standard notion of the developing world includes a telling condition of urbanism: a large share of all urban growth in the new century will, for the foreseeable future, be contained in slums, squatter settlements, and other communities of urban "informality." This concept of informality is certainly not new. Varied approaches to the term have been offered in the international development literature, describing sectors of the workforce,[10] housing,[11] and residents' legal status[12] as sources of *exclusion* from, or *exception* by, the formal regularized relations of market and state.[13] Since the urban transformation of humanity in this century is going on disproportionately both in the global south and in an informalized version of urban human settlement, the informal cannot be considered as some kind of marginal category. While those who endure such disadvantage are marginal in the sense of their social exclusion, this should not be confused with their central significance to new urban form.

With more than 50 percent of all humans now living in cities, the prognosis is that by 2030, the world's urban population, as a proportion of total population, will get to approximately 60 percent, and a probable 75 percent by the middle of this metropolitan century.[14] Such intensified urbanization ensures that between 2001 and 2030, the lion's share of all global population growth will occur in urban areas, and thereby the world's slum inhabitants will double to around 2 billion, escalating from 32 percent to 41 percent of the world's urban population in the process.[15] This entails a remarkable transformation, given that in 1975, only 27 percent of the developing world's population was urban. By 2030, it is estimated to be 56 percent.[16] Over a longer time frame, from 2007 to 2050, the world's urban population will likely increase almost double, from 3.3 billion to 6.4 billion, surpassing the anticipated rise of total world population during this time, and incorporating extensive migration from rural to urban settlement.[17] Mostly, the newcomers live "in houses and neighborhoods which have been developed illegally. In most cities, 70 to 95 percent of all new housing is built illegally."[18] In short, as expressed by one observer, "the urban future lies neither in Chicago nor Los Angeles, it lies in hyper-dense mega 'Third World' cities like Rio de Janeiro, Mumbai and Hong Kong."[19]

And further, such demographics suggest that this "third world urbanism" is overwhelmingly defined by informality—comprised of illegal squatter settlements beyond the "asphalt world" of the formal planning process and statutory recognition,[20] yet constituting a major model of contemporary human settlement.[21] Mike Davis refers to this profusion of precarious habitat as a "planet of slums," a maze of spatially concentrated impoverishment. Unlike predecessor urban forms that were attached to processes of industrialization and modernization, these disenfranchised townscapes struggle for sustainability often without a similar economic lifeline. But, even within the global south, there remain marked asymmetries in deprivation levels. An estimate in 2005 indicated that almost three-quarters of the urban populace in the least developed nations were slum dwellers.[22]

Yet, because there is still a tendency to view these places through the traditional urban lens, the paradigm for effective intervention in their plight is typically misguided. As expressed by Burdett and Rode:[23]

> In many ways, the emerging Urban Age agenda – in favor of the compact, mixed-use, well-connected, complex and democratic city . . . . runs contrary to what is happening on the ground in the vast majority of urban areas. They are larger than anything we have seen before, and are growing at a faster pace, but the shape and the language of the emerging urban landscapes are somewhat familiar. They are, in effect, by-products of outdated western planning models predicated on separation rather than inclusion, propounding single-function zones, elevated motorways and gated communities as the answers to rapid urbanization. Despite the increasingly mature pro-city debate in the economically advanced countries of the world, we seem to have dumped these models on to the fragile urban conditions of the exploding cities of the Global south.

Expressed differently, our argument is that urban study in the metropolitan century must theorize the city in *both* the developed and developing world as *both* formal and informal. Rather than being considered a
marginal category of population, market, or land in the city, this notion of
informality needs to be understood as a *mode* of urbanization, "an organizing logic, a system of norms that governs the process of urban transformation itself."[24] As such, those who live in the city under informal conditions
are fundamental to contemporary urbanism, their existence representing
an import going well beyond their place as contingent or day labor, or their
residential location in marginalized shantytowns. Their significance rests
in their pivotal urban role in a "series of transactions that connect different
economies and spaces to one another."[25] Indeed, the demographics of modern urban growth provide evidence of these "series of transactions" through
which the informal city is produced via the importance, first, of *migrants* to
cities, especially of the developing world; second, of *immigrants* to cities in
both developing and developed worlds; and third, of the ways minorities
in both places are prone to be relegated to stigmatized territories or zones
of advanced urban marginality.[26] Each of these groups of urbanites constitutes, by their very presence and the sociospatial, economic, and political relations of their daily lives, both collectively and individually, *the* city.[27]
The character of the informal city varies in different geopolitical parts in
the world. In the global south particularly, and the developing world more
generally, the in-migration and birthrates of new urban dwellers have created what Martine calls "massive urban growth,"[28] or what Hall and Pfieffer
call "informal hypergrowth."[29] Whatever the characterization, informality
remains the single most important ingredient in the *rate* of urbanization.
As described by Davis, "the exploding cities of the developing world are . . .
weaving extraordinary new urban networks, corridors and hierarchies."[30]
One ingredient seems to drive the networks and relations of squatters and
it does not begin with land ownership.[31] Rather, the city people of Brazil,
Kenya, India, or Turkey, for example, do not "go through the tremendous
struggles of building and improving their homes to liberate their dead
capital. They (go) through incredible privation and deprivation for one

simple reason: because they (need) a secure, stable, decent and inexpensive home . . . and title deeds—so natural to those of us who live in the developed world—can actually jeopardize this sense of security by bringing in speculators, planners, tax men and lots of red tape and regulations . . . When squatters feel secure in their homes, they build, invest, and prosper—and they don't need a title deed to do so."[32]

The Informal City and Migrants

But, the scale of this informal operation—the rising numbers of rural migrant squatters and their illegal presence in land, housing, and public services—changes the political relations between the formal and the informal city and induces an entanglement between the two, in what Chatterjee calls the "imbrication between elite and subaltern politics."[33] Kolkata, India, is an exemplar of such politics. Long known as the dying city, its decline has been attributed to the mix of massive deindustrialization and sustained influx of population from rural hinterlands and Bangladesh into the city that together have burdened the existing physical and social infrastructure. Since the British colonial era, the city has been afflicted with intractable poverty and congestion. The high-density core city accommodates almost five million residents, of whom one-third live in informal settlements of two types: (1) the recognized *Bastis,* which are more formalized, regulated, protected, and serviced and (2) the unrecognized, spontaneously created squatter settlements. These latter unrecognized habitats can be found along rail yards or even between roads and walkways, but they have become especially a feature of spontaneous invasions of vacant public and private land, found mostly in the peri-urban reaches.[34] Clearly important here is the fact that, at both the core and the peri-urban, rural in-migration and their informal squatter development, recognized or not, have been central to the historical urban development of one of India's and the world's largest metropolitan regions. For example, Kolkata's City Development Plan 2006 actually describes its peri-urban fringe as a "twilight zone," referring to the range of the largely informal or "extra-legal" land ownership and local development strategies that are key not only to squatter development but also to the practices of the people and state that constitute middle-class new town development.

Most of the several hundred thousand residents of this peri-urban region do not view their place as a twilight zone nor their extralegal development as an ephemeral state of living. To them, the practice of creating illegal squatter settlements and subsequent appropriation of utilities in extralegal ways is simply a normal part of urban life. To accomplish much of this, squatter residents are organized into associations, which often act as intermediaries between slum dwellers and government in welfare administration. This entanglement of the informal with the formal—of informal settlements with internal formal organization, of land rights with rights to the city—creates a contested *politics* of capital (mainly in the form of land ownership) and identity. However, these associations, generated by the slum dwellers' deprivation, are more than intermediaries. Though they are not recognized agencies of government or civic/formal society, they "spring from a collective violation of property laws and civic regulations."[35] While the state cannot recognize them as having the same legitimacy as formal associations pursuing legal objectives, the squatters also admit that their occupation of public land is both illegal and contrary to accepted civic/legal life. But they make a claim to habitation and a livelihood as a matter of right and deploy their associations as the principal collective instrument to advance that entitlement. In a Kolkata slum first studied by Asok Sen, a settlement of southern Bengali and East Pakistani migrants was established along railways, on peri-urban railroad land.[36] For several decades, beginning in the late 1940s, the slum was led by an owner of several hundred of the shacks in a recurring politics of both resistance to, and collaboration with, government leaders to avoid the slum dwellers' eviction by the formal land occupier—the railroad. In the 1980s, a squatters' welfare association attracted support for services to the slum—from health care to utilities—all for slum residents bereft of land ownership claims and the requisite material assets to legitimately acquire such services. Representing refugees, landless people, day laborers, all below the poverty line, the informal association was deeply enmeshed in contested space, since its claims could "only be made on a *political terrain,* where rules may be bent or stretched, and not on the terrain of established law or administrative procedure."[37] Between 1980 and 1996, the association established everything from governmental child care services in the association offices to individual shanty electricity hookups and potable water and public toilet facilities—all "on illegally occupied public land barely three or four feet away from the railway lines."[38] This form of urban politics illustrates how state laws and policies obtain, at some times, while at other times, they are "stretched or broken," when both "opposition" and "engagement" with the dominant forces of the state are practiced by informal urban communities.[39] Geographers Sophie Oldfield and Kristian Stooke maintain that this politics of the informal city occupies a very narrow political space.[40] In their South African example, this space rests precariously between the polarized binary of neoliberal policy and rhetoric and the antistate opposition dominated by post-Marxist scholars and activists. Describing a new *politics of contestation* between the neoliberal formalization of state services and the informalized demands of Cape Town slum communities and townships, Oldfield and Stooke produce an account of "political society" not dissimilar to that of Chatterjee's informal centers of urbanization in Kolkata. The contestation mobilized by Cape Town's informal, low-income housing communities is embodied in an umbrella organization offering political identity and an image of collective resistance among twenty-five different and often internally contested community groups, demanding housing, fighting against evictions and displacement and for connections of water, electricity, and other services. With each community requiring a different mix of services and articulating different demands, this politics of the informal is, like the peri-urban slum in Kolkata, very localized. A case in point is the slum's United Front Civic Association's organization of Cape Town's Valhalla Park community, whose successes were built equally on protesting against, and engaging, the formal state to stretch policies to attain services that otherwise would not be formally offered to the community.

This successful politics of informal urbanism is a product of a strategic mixture of engagement and resistance that has been honed over two decades of everyday relations between the government and the civic front. The lesson of constant vigilance—to the point that whenever a government operative enters Valhalla Park, residents immediately alert the civic front—coupled with long-term personal connections between the civic front and the government, creates platforms for resistance and service. For example, constant surveillance of the electric or water service personnel keeps the civic front able to maintain services to the slum. As Oldfield and Stooke report, the relations between the police and the civic front are so close that crimes are often first reported to the association before the police.[41] Alongside this example of the role of rural migrants in reshaping the urban, there is the growing presence of immigrants, particularly in the developed world, creating more multiethnic cities, and, in the process, bringing very visible manifestations of globalization to first world urbanism.

The Transnational City and Immigrants

While the future growth of developed world cities is estimated at no more than 5 percent of the overall growth rate of urbanization, such cities are experiencing an increasing transnationalization of their citizens. This pattern of ethnically, religiously, and even illegally new urban residents contributes another informalization through the "operation of social networks 'from below' through the mechanisms of transnational migration and political mobilization."[42] Transnational in-migration challenges the city as a distinct territory[43] and as a site of differentiated political identity[44] and legal citizenship, "such that it has the potential to render the city, or parts of it, ungovernable."[45] The diverse realities of the lived space of transnational refugees, migrants, exiles, and diasporas accord a more complex meaning to the city, challenge the discursive role of the state in relation to these "others," and ultimately reinforce the political space and meaning of informality and contestedness.

In this transnational zone of the informal city, daily practices of the newcomers are at once full of new possibility and yet layered with formal political, economic, and cultural exclusions. Informing the identity of these urbanites is the fragile, and perhaps transitory, state of their citizenship and residence, reflecting either a politics of return or an illegal state of border-crosser (with no public space of legitimacy), or a more permanent state of cultural and ethnonationalist ambiguity. Each of these precarious states of urban existence requires a "reprocessing of identity by those who once saw their lives as more or less predictably constrained by the givenness of established orders."[46] The givenness of identity and belonging in one's home state is transformed by the exigencies of everyday life of a very different order in the new, receiving state, which often casts the increasing numbers of immigrants crossing its borders as threats to its sovereignty. In turn, this perception can be presented as the basis of stigmatizing labels such as "cultural aliens," "illegals," "undocumented workers," or the like, and thereby *explanation* of chauvinism can readily become *legitimation* of exclusionary practice. In response, the deterritorialized transmigrants are prompted to redefine themselves. For instance, the "politics of return" for those who have been thus set adrift can be differentially processed—either as an imagined place of home that one dreams of as a place of return, or it can become a feature of the city—a site that turns dominant cultural stigma into transnational reterritorialization, whereby the informal city (of transnational otherness) becomes "Little Saigon" or "Korean Town" or "Little San Juan."[47]

Moving between their natural home city and their city of new residence, transmigrants often find themselves transforming their identities at both ends of their translocal circuit.[48] Robert Smith,[49] in a study of Mexican rural immigrants, found that the transnationals needed to re-create a localized identity for themselves to overcome cultural and racist denigration in New York, while they resisted local power structures and created new modes of community organization and grassroots politics when they returned home. In short, the translocal identity required that they produce new urban relations of accommodation in New York and resistance as a form of relegitimation in their home state. At a different level, Marcia Farr studied, for decades, the circuit of ranchero migration from Michoacán Mexico to Chicago—finding that transnationals from Mexico to the United States did not see their identity as either "minority," "racialized," or even Latino, but rather as deeply tied to both their places of origin and the Chicago communities in which they resided. Thus, the circuit of transmigration reprocessed its very own language and set of political and sociocultural activities carried out both in the Michoacán villages and the Chicago neighborhoods—best captured in the linguistic identity of "Chicagoacan" and the parallel village festivals, mayoral leaders, and celebrations in village-dominant neighborhoods of both Chicago and Michoacán. That Mexico now recognizes such reprocessed identities, to the point where political and fiscal transfers of votes and monies are now commonly accepted, exemplifies this transnationalization of the urban.

In May 2006, some 400,000 people, over 90 percent of whom were Latino and, by every estimate, most of whom were illegal or undocumented, marched in Chicago. Quietly supported by their churches, employers, and even their schools, they heard the Chicago mayor proclaim that "we are all immigrants" in America. Recasting the notion of America, one participant in these protests later explained in a YouTube video: "We are American. We are fighting for our rights. We want to work. We want to pay taxes. We are American too, because America is a continent. It is not just a state or a country."[50] The emergence of these new transnational voices in cities produces not only new politics of formal and informal resistance, but also, as evident from the avowal of employers, schools, churches, and even the Chicago mayor, new responses by the regularized city institutions, that at once recognize the exceptional change generated by transnational urbanites and also seek to control and regularize it. In such interactions and circuits, the transmigrants of the informal city come to inform a new urban politics in both developed and developing worlds.

The Hyperghetto and Stigmatized Informality in U.S. Cities: Chicago

Another variation of the informal city finds expression in the new ways some ethnic groups remain trapped in segregated enclaves that serve to deepen both their social exclusion and the challenge to urban cohesion, whatever the formal political claims about equal opportunity and equality before the law. This form of the informalization of the city derives from the socio-spatial relegation of historically segmented, communally ghettoized people (of color): from "the communal ghetto of the Fordist-Keynesian era" to territorially stigmatized "lawless zones," such as the notorious "outlaw estates" of the dispossessed residents of first world Paris's banlieue or Chicago's "hyperghettos."[51] The epitome of such Chicago ghettos were the massive public housing projects, whose residents endured poverty rates exceeding 60 percent and unemployment rates as high as 90 percent, with almost as many having lived in public housing for at least a decade, and two-thirds not having finished high school. In short, they constituted part of the nine poorest census tracts in the United States.[52]

Yet, the projects did not start out that way. The history of Chicago's public housing and of that in many large U.S. cities is one of institutional relegation of racial minorities to distressed (ultimately stigmatized) conditions of urban informality—public housing deteriorated beyond rehabilitation; social conditions of segregation and racialized poverty so acute as to be beyond the capacity of the immediate community to redeem; and rising threats of gang violence and drug trafficking, uncontainable through normal policing:

> Once a place is publicly labeled a "lawless zone" or an "outlaw estate" ... it is easy for the authorities to justify special measures, deviating from both law and custom, which can have for effect—if not for intention—to destabilize and further marginalize their occupants, and to submit them to the dictates of the deregulated labour market, render them invisible, or drive them out of coveted space. [53]

Importantly, this sociospatial stigmatization is a complex cultural, legal, and political process, whereby the very features of territorial ignominy are not simply meant to be an "object of state regulation, but rather are produced by the state itself."[54] As such, the city, along with the ghetto dweller, contributes to the production of informal spaces, and the state accentuates the process by casting such places and their people as spaces or states of exception. In essence, the state joins with the surrounding dominant culture to produce planning and legal practices in the ghetto that are, at the same time, "outside and inside the juridical order. If the sovereign is truly the one to whom the juridical order grants the power of proclaiming a state of exception, and therefore, of suspending the order's own validity, then the sovereign stands outside the juridical order and nevertheless belongs to it. "[55] This state of the state, being both inside and outside the law, is certainly central to Dumper's concept of "central paradox"[56] in identifying the state's role in the production and sustenance of the informal—the territorially stigmatized slums and squatter settlements of the developing world and the banlieue or hyperghettos of first world cities. They are, by the poverty, ethnoracial identity, and socioeconomic practices of their residents, and the increasing state relegation of these life practices as deviant, defined, by both culture and state, as urban territories of sociocultural exclusion and stigma—or what Wacquant calls "advanced marginality."

Crucial to this designation is a concept of the state/or government as not only the agency of law and formality, but also as an institutional source of the definition of informality itself. Informality, and the territories of distress in which it thrives, are not the "chaos that precedes order, but rather the situation that results from its suspension."[57] Such a construction of the informal or advanced marginal conditions of slums in cities everywhere is linked to the state's policy, planning, and legal structures, which can help "to determine what is informal and what is not, and to determine which forms of informality will thrive and which will disappear."[58]

To examine this contention, it is useful to trace the history of U.S. public housing, which started as a multigoal program—from replacing unsafe and unsanitary slums with a supply of sound, low-income housing to supporting the housing industry during the Depression and later the postwar period. Most early units were low-rise walk-ups and only after 1945 did government concede to the building design movement's penchant for dense high-rise buildings that currently typify popular perception of this tenure form. Two preeminent examples of this new high-rise construction were Pruitt-Igoe in St. Louis and a two-mile strip of tower blocks along Chicago's State and Federal Streets that included the nation's largest project—the Robert Taylor Homes, comprising twenty-eight buildings and over 4,300 units.

For much of this era, the public housing programs were "generally segregated and primarily housed white, working–class tenants" transitioning from downtown rental to suburban ownership housing.[59] The combination of the high-rise era and civil rights legislation designed to combat racial seg-regation opened up public housing to extremely low-income residents, who had either been displaced by other public programs, such as urban renewal, or had no market recourse. Inadvertently, this accelerated the concentration of very poor, minority tenants in large-city public housing developments. Thus, while public housing started out as a place of transition, a pathway to home self-sufficiency, it quickly transformed into housing of last resort. "Tenant incomes dropped steadily after 1974. By 1991, nearly 20 percent of public housing tenants had incomes that were less than 10 per cent of the local median. The majority of households received public assistance, and approximately two-thirds were headed by single females."[60] Even more important was the fact that once such families secured public housing, the material distress of their lives virtually guaranteed they were doomed to stay—not only was public housing a "last resort," it was becoming increas-ingly a final destination. Thus, the U.S. narrative of public housing accords with Dumper's "central paradox,"—even as such developments were pro-duced to engage residents' circumstance, no matter what program or level of investment was offered, conditions for the most distressed urban minor-ity families seemed to degenerate rather than regenerate.

With this shift in tenants' material poverty, the federal government attempted to cap the fiscal strain on residents by a formula that required no more than 30 percent of adjusted income—whether the source was earned or welfare shelter. Since rental income was nowhere near what local housing authorities needed to maintain the housing, federal funds were essential to fill the fiscal gap. However, for over two decades, no funds were forthcoming for significant modernization,[61] until the 1980 Comprehensive Grant Pro-gram set a formula for supporting repair costs. But, since it never factored in the full upgrading costs for what were, by this stage, severely distressed, large public housing units, the sector suffered high vacancy levels along-side long tenant waiting lists and increasingly severe management issues, from accounting to security. Meanwhile, dense, poorly designed high-rise developments like Pruitt-Igoe in St. Louis and Chicago's Cabrini Green had become national symbols of crumbling buildings, evidencing dangerous, often violent environments, controlled as much by gangs as by the local public housing authority serving families distressed as much by their housing as by their socioeconomic conditions.

Unsurprisingly, the implosion of Pruitt-Igoe proved to be one of the nation's most-watched television events of 1972. The event's popularity prefigured the current public policy approach favoring complete dissolution of this urban form. The U.S. government, following its fiscal, programmatic, and administrative failures to modernize public housing and return it to a tradition of socioeconomic transition, created its own version of housing demolition. Not a criminal destruction like that of gang leaders or a maintenance failure like that of public housing managers, this was a publicly approved decade-long demolition program of the large, disintegrating public housing units that had come to be recognized more for their sociospatial segregation and rat-infested, unhealthy, and crime-ridden conditions than as beacons of a responsive welfare state. To accomplish what HUD would call "a comprehensive revitalization of severely distressed public housing developments by a simultaneous investment in sites, buildings and people,"[62] the federal government offered a Home Opportunity for People Everywhere (HOPE VI) program—specially designed for thirty-two of the nation's largest urban public housing authorities—who managed 37 percent of the country's public housing units and served 71 percent of all families in pre-1960 developments of more than 300 units (i.e., almost all high-rise large urban units suffering the most physical decline and the highest rates of poverty and family distress).

Integral to this program's success in most instances were federal-city-private sector plans to demolish a substantial share of public housing and relocate large numbers of residents to other city communities. No city contained more of these aging, distressed units in large developments than Chicago. The final Plan of Transformation in Chicago called for the demolition of all fifty-three high-rise and most mid-rise buildings, containing almost 21,000 of the city's 39,000 units of public housing, 40 percent of which were "legally vacant," even though 55,000 people were waiting for housing. Located almost exclusively in the most racially segregated and poorest city neighborhoods, estranged from the rest of the city by highways, and so mired in poverty and its most destructive impacts, the vast majority of units were considered by Chicago's housing authority (CHA), in agreement with the federal government, to be beyond rehabilitation. With demolition came a plan to relocate residents, if they chose, by granting them Housing Opportunity Certificates (or Section 8 vouchers) to be used to enter the rental market, in what was hoped would be new mixed-income, stable neighborhoods. If they qualified, and also chose, ultimately all residents could return to a rehabilitated or new unit in the mixed-income housing scheduled to be built on the site of the demolished units.

According to the CHA's Plan for Transformation (2000),[63] all this would be accomplished by 2009—when a total of 25,000 new and rehabbed units would be constructed to more than match the 16,000 units legally occupied at the time of the old units' demolition. Ironically, these figures exclude the 16,000-plus vacant units that management and maintenance limitations and fiscal shortfall in modernization funds found impossible to keep habitable. Since 2000, thousands of public housing families have used Section 8 vouchers to move to new neighborhoods, or have been resettled in new public housing units, either on-site or elsewhere. Others, seniors, have been moved to senior units—comprising the greatest share of finished rehab housing.

One study of residents, following their relocation, shows that while they move to marginally less racially segregated and economically depressed areas that are safer (for women), they find their new neighbors disproportionately unsupportive and the overall neighborhoods are still poor and filled with multiple housing challenges.[64] In short, five years through the transformation, the one general conclusion most studies of displacement and relocation show is "that poor black people stay in struggling black communities."[65] However mixed the outcomes of the move for those public housing residents who can claim a voucher or a spot in a rehabbed unit, including ongoing segregation, poverty, and relatively higher levels of crime than comparable city neighborhoods, they stand in stark contrast to what the future portends for those who cannot move.[66] What observers of this process find is that those who can get a housing voucher and leave the project do so, even if they end up moving into struggling communities. By contrast, the predicament of the remaining, and not insignificant number, of "hard-to-house" public housing residents is bleak. This category includes: large extended-family units with nontraditional custodial adults, squatters in vacant units, lease-uncompliant residents with multiple financial problems, the poorly educated, victims and perpetrators of domestic violence, ex-felons, drug users, the chronically unemployed, jailed or newly released prisoners with no housing placement, and the mentally and physically disabled. Any one of these conditions could be grounds for a lease violation and cause for eviction under the "one-strike" requirement for public housing lease compliance.

Finding adequate housing for special-needs families, especially those with a nontraditional or informal family history, is difficult. For example, while households with a single elderly adult as the primary caregiver may have been common in the informal community of public housing in the past, today the regulations for senior housing do not accommodate custodial nontraditional grandparents.[67] Large households remain common, but four-bedroom units are not. Thus, a substantial share of the informal, or what some call the nontraditional, everyday life of public housing residents is challenged if not excluded from the requirements for residents returning to their homes or even qualifying for a unit. One study estimates that no more than 11.4 percent of all residents will be eligible to return to their housing, even though it has been reported that 75 percent of residents report that they would like to return.[68] However, the state's ability to "except," or otherwise exclude, a family is substantial. One housing specialist working with Cabrini Green tenants observes that "if the CHA is so inclined, it can find a reason to except 100 percent of the residents."[69] But this is certainly not the way either the CHA or housing activists prefer to see public housing parsed out. Through first what it called the "social connector" program, and later on, through the support of the MacArthur Foundation and its LISC-based (Local Communities Support Corporation) intermediary, the New Communities Program, the CHA and community groups, the city and housing activists are working diligently to create the social, educational, job training, and housing counseling programs to make public housing residents successful in their foray into the rental housing market through vouchers. The successes of such connector or social-service programs have been marginal, in part because the housing goal is in some ways the easiest part of the picture. The long-term structural conditions of ill health, drug dependency, criminalized street economies, and poor educational and training opportunities have produced the cultural stigma of "advanced marginality." This, in turn, has relieved the state of fully engaging its foremost obligations to maintain and manage the housing of the city's racially segregated residents (but also of criminally, economically, and socially marginal sectors) in the same way that the housing of the dominant classes is maintained and managed.

Another way of characterizing this larger institutional dilemma raised by large-scale urban public housing policy is that the HOPE VI interventions generate conflict and ambivalence among all the stakeholders involved, including the poorest tenants. In a recent ethnographic study of the politics of race and class in Chicago, Mary Pattillo is skeptical about the entire "mixed-income route" to redressing the compounded social problems associated with the spatial concentration of race and poverty, arguing that its assumed efficacy is really "because it is consonant with urban elites' interests in recapturing the middle class for the city's tax base." Nevertheless, she notes the complicated feelings involved.[70]

> Poor residents . . . both favor income mixing and desire more low-income rental housing; they don't like the vacant lots but worry about getting pushed out once those lots are all filled up, and they have mixed opinions on the question of having neighbors with lifestyles similar to their own.

Understandably, such assorted views generate a conflicted and confusing politics, particularly among the most socially marginalized, who have limited options with which to negotiate their urban condition. Thus, such processes have produced a paradox of politics—whereby the informal city is relegated, by dint of its outcast status to a state of exception and the urban politics that frames policy and planning is meant as much to relieve the challenges faced by a fiscally limited state as it is to fully address the stigmatized conditions of the hyperghetto.[71] The challenges of housing and lease compliance are tied to exigencies that stem from lack of access to living-wage jobs. Without them, the ranks of the hard-to-house will swell and the potential for evictions or loss of right to return will also escalate. These tasks are burdensome. They have not been solved anywhere in the system. To expect that the CHA and its social connectors can readily achieve them is unrealistic. In the formidable task of building new communities, public housing administrators act less like formal observant members of the lease-compliance requirements and more like what Lipsky has called practitioners of street-level bureaucracy. In Chicago today, very few, if any, former public housing residents are being turned away—not from housing, and especially not from the counseling, training, and requisite work development. Like Chatterjee's examples of the state in the "political society," or Oldfield and Stooke's analysis of the "politics of engagement/resistance" in Cape Town, or Smith's consideration of transnational urbanism, the CHA and public housing residents agree to engage—even if regulations must be stretched. For everyone involved, too much is riding on the transformation of Chicago's public housing for anyone to eschew flexible and informal routes to that policy objective.

Linking the Informal to City Contestedness

The politics of resistance can arise from those who either defy exceptional status and the role of the state in marginalizing or delegitimating their lives, or produce an identity out of such exceptionality within which reside rights to the city and its services—rights based on their ethnicity, race, class, slum status, economic practice, and most importantly, their very presence in the city as urbanites.

Dumper, as we have suggested earlier, argues that when the state engages in the differentiated production of services for those who, by dint of their legal status or identity, are living in an urban state of exception, this is prone to create the central paradox of government.[72] In essence, this means that public policy inadvertently exacerbates rather than ameliorates the problem it is designed to remedy. Applying this concept, he evidenced the role of the modern practices of the Israeli state, whose macro agenda to maintain Jewish demographic security has left Palestinians living in the country effectively demoted into a state of exception. So, even when the state formally set out to redress some adversities experienced by Israeli Arabs, its nationalist priorities compromised this intervention. Thus, conditions for those in this state of exception actually deteriorated, even as certain economic and housing conditions were materially altered. This partisan role of the state in using legal and planning instruments to subjugate its political opponents has been characterized as "ethnocracy."[73] In cities like Belfast, the concept of ethnocracy in these terms has little explanatory power. Here, the state's declared role in shaping the city throughout the "Troubles" has veered between claims for even-handed neutrality,[74] via a technocratic apolitical planning system, and a limited compensatory model of positive discrimination, informed by values of equity and diversity. Yet, the state's republican and loyalist opponents have at times challenged the accuracy of this formal characterization of the state as referee between the two tribes while champion of the disadvantaged. But, on the ground, space and territory have been central to the dispute, typical of turf wars in conflict about land.[75] The spark for the Civil Rights Movement, which immediately preceded this period of conflict, was housing allocation, and the distribution of housing settlement remains at the heart of the divide. In Belfast, overall patterns of demographic decline—a reduction of one-third in the two decades since 1971—have overarched shifts in sectarian geography, whereby the Catholic share of the population has risen and the Protestant share has declined, to a point where a city that was once two-thirds/one-third in favor of Protestant residents is now close to fifty/fifty. As this pattern becomes reflected in the political composition of city government, the extent to which these demographic changes are voluntary or enforced becomes a central part of the ongoing contest about "whose Belfast?" It is a contest that has been marked as much by informal street politics as by traditional political exchange.[76]

An example of this pattern is to be found in the relationship of West Belfast to the rest of the city over recent decades. This republican heartland operated for much of the Troubles as a state within a state, developing informally a set of initiatives designed to challenge government as an alien British state and to prefigure an alternative nationalist polity and culture. Thus, following a decision to curtail formal public transport service in the area in response to the intensity of regular rioting, a local community form of transport, known as the Black Taxis, was developed. Flexible and affordable, this provision offered itself as a superior model of public transport, relative to the standard service, whose reduced public subsidy at the time compromised its capacity for reliability and economy. Initially, government cast the organization as illegal, operating without proper insurance and registration. However, over time, its durability and popularity compelled the authorities to retreat from outright opposition. Ultimately, the informal community service was incorporated into the city's transport system, an arrangement negotiated with the Black Taxi Association, prepared to engage around issues such as insurance. The outcome has contributed to a reconceptualization of transport in the city and a more diverse service.

In similar vein, in response to persistent high unemployment in the area, local groups developed a range of social economy projects that sought to link local redundant skills to unmet social need. From such grassroots enterprise in such communities, a third economic sector has evolved in Northern Ireland, between the orthodox private and public sectors.[77] Of course, since these schemes in West Belfast were largely associated with a political project to subvert the British state in Northern Ireland, there were notable linguistic and cultural programs attached to them, such as the annual West Belfast Festival, geared to the promotion of Irish arts. Again, many of these dimensions, such as the creation of Irish Language Schools, where children would be taught through the medium of Gaelic, have since become formally endorsed and financially supported by government as part of a reshaped pluralist politics to respect diverse identities and cultures within a value framework of equity and interdependence.[78] Such patterns are typical of segregated spaces where conflictive identity formations, and the deliberate use of symbolism and idiom as cultural representation, significantly shape the urban polity.[79]

Violent conflict came to Belfast in the late 1960s at the exact same time as the city was undergoing comprehensive housing redevelopment. In this way, issues of space and territory became readily entangled with the ethnonationalist contest over land ownership and sovereignty. Specifically, the republican insurrection against the state and its alter ego in the shape of loyalist paramilitarism provided a backdrop in certain working-class communities to forms of "insurgency" planning, whereby local broad-based organizations would resist the "bulldozer" form of demolition and population displacement. From such informal campaigns materialized greater recognition on the part of the state for the legitimacy of inclusive participatory planning.[80] In short, many of these initiatives that started out as informal and antistatist were adapted and, in reconfigured form, validated by government. Interestingly, this ingenuity was emanating from the kind of urban communities that by the 1980s were being characterized in terms of a dependency culture. Of course, this is not a simple binary narrative of dispossessed informal community versus powerful formal state. For one thing, places like West Belfast contained many local agencies that were sustained by community development grants and official urban programs. For another, the state has responded flexibly and informally at times amid the exigency of violent upheaval and the complexity of sharing in a divided city. Thus, it exemplifies again the hybridities and latency that derive from a combination of resistance and engagement.[81]

Conclusion

In recent decades, urban theory has seen a retreat from both the positivism of spatial science and the overdeterminism of Marxist structuralism. Dominating the debate since the 1980s has been a set of ideas such as structuration and poststructuralism, which accord human consciousness a more central role, while acknowledging that the scope for human agency is circumscribed by both structural context and social contingency. Since the 1990s, the cultural turn has elucidated the politics of identity and the ways identity is constructed through performativity, while the continued elaboration of a postmodern urbanism has offered cities like Los Angeles as prefigurative arenas of emergent urban forms and virtual spaces, characterized by diffuseness, fluidity, heterogeneity, and fragmentation. This greater recognition of plurality, differentiation, and complexity is to be welcomed in a circumstance where the extent, volume, and velocity of global interaction have been increasing. Nevertheless, while the insights of such intellectual lineage remain relevant, it is argued here that a credible theory of the contemporary urban should start by forsaking the skewed cultural lens of Western-centrism and its habitual exclusion of "massive urban change" cities in the developing world. Given the demographic impetus in the cities of the global south, the genesis of an alternative urban praxis should be sought there. And there we find, as *normal*, conditions of informality and differentiated citizenship that provide the basis for urban resilience amid acute sociospa-tial exclusion. In doing so, we need not devalorize the formal as fictional any more than we need be dismissive of the informal as a chaotic, even anarchic, set of random and incongruent interventions by a marginal public. Indeed, reductive and determinist explanations that conflate the informal with insurgence of a victim population miss the point, since such populations contain both passivity and defiance. Equally, restricted focus on *resistance*, rooted in an oppositional politics of identity or reaction to a status of excep-tion, misses the dimension of *engagement* with the formal state. Thus, the multispaces of the city have to be recognized, and it is the intersections of the formal and informal—embodying orthodox and tacit knowledge, modernity, and tradition, manifest and oblique power, inclusion and exclu-sion—that transmute, often inadvertently, into the interesting hybridities and continual reconfigurations that compose the city.

Examples of urban relations have been introduced here to emphasize the dominance of these both conflictual and unofficial components of normal everyday city life. The resourcefulness and resilience nurtured by the informal city provide at least a modest balance in this uneven power encounter. Thus, perhaps, something significant can be learned about suc-cessful urban outcomes by examining, for example, the politics of infor-mality in Cape Town and Kolkata, Chicago and Belfast—revealing ways that produce direct services to squatters, townships and hyperghettos, not because these parts of the city are illegal or nontraditional or lawless or sites of urban outcasts, but because life in these settlements is urban life, and engaging this life, in a direct politics based on the right to the city[82] that derives from that life, creates not only practical urban policy, but also a theory of urban politics that brings into higher definition the city's informal and contested dimensions.

Notes

1. R. Connell, *Southern Theory: The Global Dynamics of Knowledge in Social Science* (Malden, Mass.: Polity, 2007).

2. G. Martine, "Preparing for Massive Urban Growth: A Win/Win Approach" (paper presented at the Richard J. Daley Urban Forum, Chicago, 2008); R. Neuwirth, *Shadow Cities: A Billion Squatters, A New World* (New York: Routledge, 2006).

3. Michael Davis, *Planet of Slums* (New York: Verso, 2007); Martine, "Preparing for Massive Urban Growth"; D. Clark, *Urban World/Global City* (2nd ed., New York: Routledge, 2002).

4. P. Chatterjee, "The Rights of the Governed," *Identity, Culture and Politics* 3, no. 2 (2002): 51–72.

5. Neuwirth, *Shadow Cities;* Clark, *Urban World.*

6. Martine, "Preparing for Massive Urban Growth."

7. Connell, *Southern Theory.*

8. Chatterjee, "The Rights of the Governed," 53.

9. H. Lietner, J. Peck, and E.S. Sheppard, eds., *Contesting NeoLiberalism: Urban Frontiers* (New York: Guilford Press, 2007); F. Gaffikin and M. Morrissey, *Northern Ireland: The Thatcher Years* (London: Zed Publishing, 1990).

10. H. DeSoto, *The Mystery of Capital: Why Capitalism Triumphs in the West and Fails Everywhere Else* (New York: Basic Books, 2000).

11. J. Hordoy and D. Satterthwaite, *Squatter Citizen: Life in the Urban Third World* (London: Earthscan Publications, 1989).

12. P. Hall and U. Pfeiffer, *Urban Future 21: The Global Agenda for Twenty-First Century Cities* (London: E. and F.N. Spon, 2000).

13. G. Agamben, *Homo Sacer: Sovereign Power and Bare Life* (Palo Alto, Calif.: Stanford University Press, 1998); Ananya Roy, "Urban Informality: Towards an Epistemology of Planning," *Journal of the American Planning Association* 71, no. 2 (2005): 147–56.

14. R. Burdett and D. Sudjic, eds., *The Endless City* (London: Phaidon, 2008).

15. A. K. Tibaijuka, "Divided Cities, Caught between Hope and Despair: Meeting the Challenge of Rapid and Chaotic Urbanisation in the Face of Climate Change" (Betty Memorial Lecture, McGill University, Toronto; Nairobi, Kenya: UN-Habitat, October 2007).

16. D. Hinrichsen, R. Salem, and R. Blackburn, *Meeting the Urban Challenge: Population Reports* ser. M, no. 16 (Baltimore: Population Information Program, Center for Communication Programs, The John Hopkins Bloomberg School of Public Health, Fall 2002).

17. UN Population Division, *Population Newsletter* no. 84 (New York: United Nations, Dec. 2007).

18. Hordoy and Satterthwaite, *Squatter Citizen,* 12.

19. From remarks by Douglas Massey at a plenary session of the American Sociological Association meeting in Atlanta, Georgia, 2001, as quoted in Roy, "Urban Informality."

20. Neuwirth, *Shadow Cities.*

21. Global Urban Observatory, *Slums of the World: The Face of Urban Poverty in the New Millennium* (Nairobi, Kenya: UN-Habitat, 2003); Davis, Planet of Slums.

22. UN Population Division.

23. Burdett and Rode, 22–23.

24. Roy, "Urban Informality."

25. Ibid., 148.

26. Loïc Wacquant, *Urban Outcasts: A Comparative Sociology of Advanced Marginality* (Malden, Mass.: Polity Press, 2008).

27. N. Al Sayyad, "Urban Informality as a 'New' Way of Life," in N. Al Sayyad and A. Roy, eds., *Urban Informality: Transnational Perspectives from the Middle East, Latin America, and South Asia* (Lanham, Md.: Lexington Books, 2004), 7–30; Hordoy and Satterthwaite, Squatter Citizen; Chatterjee, "The Rights of the Governed."

28. Martine, "Preparing for Massive Urban Growth."

29. Hall and Pfeiffer, *Urban Future 21.*

30. Davis, *Planet of Slums,* 5.

31. Hordoy and Satterthwaite, *Squatter Citizen;* Roy, "Urban Informality"; Neuwirth, *Shadow Cities;* Chatterjee, "The Rights of the Governed"; Connell, *Southern Theory.*

32. Neuwirth, *Shadow Cities,* 20–21.

33. Chatterjee, "The Rights of the Governed,"62.

34. Chatterjee, "The Rights of the Governed."

35. Ibid., 62.

36. Asok Sen, "Life and Labour in a Squatter's Colony," Occasional Paper 138, Center for Studies in Social Sciences, Calcutta, October, 1992.

37. Chatterjee, "The Rights of the Governed," 66.

38. Ibid., 64.

39. Ibid.; Lietner, Peck, and Sheppard, *Contesting NeoLiberalism.*

40. Sophie Oldfield and Kristian Stooke, "Political Polemics and Local Practices of Community Organizing and NeoLiberal Politics in South Africa," in Lietner, Peck, and Sheppard, *Contesting NeoLiberalism,* 149.

41. Ibid.

42. M. P. Smith, *Transnational Urbanism: Locating Globalization* (Malden, Mass.: Blackwell Publishing, 2001), 5.

43. Saskia Sassen, *Territory, Authority, Rights: From Medieval to Global Assemblages* (Princeton, N.J.: Princeton University Press, 2006).

44. Engin F. Isin, *Democracy, Citizenship and the Global City* (New York: Routledge, 2000).

45. Roy, "Urban Informality," 148.

46. Smith, *Transnational Urbanism,* 164.

47. Ibid., 152.

48. R. Rouse, "Mexican Migration and the Social Space of Postmodernism," *Diaspora* 1, no. 1 (1991): 8–23; Marcia Farr, *Rancheros in Chicagoacán: Language and Identity in a Transnational Community* (Austin: University of Texas Press, 2006).

49. R. Smith, "Transnational Localities: Community, Technology and the Politics of Membership within the Context of Mexico and U.S. Migration," in M. P. Smith and

L. E. Guarnizo, eds., *Transnationalism from Below* (New Brunswick N.J.: Transaction, 1998).

50. Fred Hickle, *Immigration Rights March Chicago, May 1, 2008,* YouTube (Chicago: CIMC, 2008), 7 min., 16 sec. video. Chicago indymedia.org.

51. Wacquant, *Urban Outcasts.*

52. S. Popkin and M. K. Cunningham, "Beyond the Projects: Lessons from Public Housing Transformation in Chicago," in X. de Souza Briggs, ed., *The Geography of Opportunity: Race and Housing Choice in Metropolitan America* (Washington, D.C.: Brookings Institution, 2005), 187.

53. Wacquant, *Urban Outcasts,* 204.

54. Roy, "Urban Informality," 149.

55. Agamben, *Homo Sacer,* 15.

56. M. Dumper, *The Politics of Jerusalem Since 1967* (New York: Columbia University Press, 1997).

57. Agamben, *Homo Sacer,* 18.

58. Roy, "Urban Informality," 149.

59. U.S. Department of Housing and Urban Development (HUD), *An Historical and Baseline Assessment of HOPE VI: Volume 1, Cross-Site Report* (prepared by Abt Associates), 2007, I-3.

60. Ibid., I-4.

61. Ibid., I-5.

62. Ibid., I-8.

63. Chicago Housing Authority, Plan for Transformation (2000).

64. D. Lewis and C. A. Ward, *The Plan for Transformations and the Residential Movements of Public Housing Residents* (Northwestern University, Institute for Policy Research, n.d.).

65. Ibid.

66. Popkin and Cunningham, "Beyond the Projects," 176–96.

67. S. J. Popkin, M. K. Cunningham, and W. T. Woodley, "Residents at Risk: A Profile of Ida B. Wells and Madden Park" (Washington D.C.: The Urban Institute, 2003).

68. Popkin and Cunningham, "Beyond the Projects."

69. Y. Zalalem, conversation with David Perry, 2008.

70. Mary Pattillo, *Black on the Block: The Politics of Race and Class in the City* (Chicago: University of Chicago Press, 2007), 107, 109.

71. Wacquant, *Urban Outcasts.*

72. Dumper, *The Politics of Jerusalem.*

73. O. Yiftachel, *Ethnocracy: Land and Identity Politics in Israel/Palestine* (Philadelphia: University of Pennsylvania Press, 2006).

74. S. A. Bollens, *Urban Peace Building in Divided Societies: Belfast and Johannesburg* (Albany: State University of New York Press, 1999); S. A. Bollens, Cities, *Nationalism and Democratization* (New York: Routledge, 2007).

75. J. Sack, *Human Territoriality: Its Theory and History* (Cambridge: Cambridge University Press, 1986); D. Delaney, *Territory: A Short Introduction* (Oxford: Blackwell Publishing,

2005); G. Modan, *Turf Wars: Discourse, Diversity and the Politics of Place* (Oxford: Blackwell Press, 2007).

76. Gaffikin and Morrissey, *Northern Ireland.*

77. M. Morrissey and F. Gaffikin, "Northern Ireland: Democratizing for Development," *Local Economy* 16, no 1 (2001): 2–13.

78. M. Morrissey and F. Gaffikin, "Planning for Peace in Contested Space," *International Journal of Urban and Regional Research* 30, no. 4 (2006), 873–93.

79. M. Waters, *Ethnic Option: Choosing Identities in America* (Cambridge, Mass.: Harvard University Press, 1990); S. Musterd, "Segregation and Integration: A Contested Relationship, *Journal of Ethnic and Migration Studies* 29, no. 4 (2003): 623–41; L. Purbrick, "Introduction: Sites, Representations, Histories," in L. Purbrick, J. Aulich, and G. Dawson, eds., *Contested Spaces: Sites, Representations and Histories of Conflict* (Basingstoke, UK: Palgrave, 2007).

80. Gaffikin and Morrissey, *Northern Ireland;* W. Neill, *Urban Planning and Cultural Identity* (London: Routledge, 2004); P. Shirlow and B. Murtagh, *Belfast: Segregation, Violence and the City* (London: Pluto Press, 2006).

81. Y. Jabareen, "Space of Risk: The Contribution of Planning Policies to Conflicts in Cities: Lessons from Nazareth," *Planning Theory and Practice* 7, issue 3 (2006): 305–23; H. Anheier and Raj Y. Isar, eds., *Conflicts and Tensions* (London: SAGE Publications, 2007).

82. H. Lefebvre, *Writings on the City,* trans. Eleonore Kofman and Elizabeth Lebas (New York: Wiley-Blackwell, 1996).

15

Understanding Deep Urban Change
Patterns of Residential Segregation in Latin American Cities

■ Francisco Sabatini and Rodrigo Salcedo

Residential Segregation in Latin American Cities

Statistical and empirical research in Chilean cities, as well as clues from (the scarce) available data and studies of other cities in Latin America, lead us to think that, though varying in speed, composition, and intensity, the traditional patterns of residential segregation are undergoing a consistent and radical shift throughout urban Latin America: there have been decreases in the scale of segregation even while social inequality remains very high. The spatial dispersion of the Latin American urban elites from the "affluent cone," where they had gradually concentrated along most of the twentieth century, toward different sections of the urban periphery, including those where low-income classes had tended to agglomerate, is perhaps the most salient change. The building of private housing complexes of unprecedented size for the affluent, mainly gated communities located amid low-income settlements, and served by freeways connecting to nearby shopping and the distant downtown and other centralities, is perhaps the image that best summarizes the changing city.

The forces behind such spatial inflection have been, most importantly, the reform and liberalization of land markets—and of the national economies as a whole—and the ever-increasing concentration of real estate capital. Two contextual variables helping these changes are, on the one hand, public works in roads and communications at a large regional scale, aimed at adding competitiveness to cities, and, on the other hand, economic growth that fuels dynamism to the real estate sector.

For all these trends, Santiago seems to be the city that has made the earliest and farthest-reaching progress in the region. At present, Santiago's pattern of residential segregation departs from what we still see in most cities in the subcontinent. Yet, at the same time, Santiago shows in a neat way the transforming power of the structural forces that neoliberal capitalism has unveiled in cities across Latin America. That Santiago and urban Chile exhibit traits that perhaps will hardly, if ever, materialize in other cities of the continent—like the very low percentage of illegal occupation of land—does not mean that the city is not, at the same time, representative of the structural forces shaping contemporary cities, forces that indeed are having influence beyond Latin America.

These structural transformations tend to generate two contradictory and complex outcomes:

1. On the one hand, the gentrification of tracts of the popular urban periphery by higher-income residential compounds and shopping and office complexes has given rise to new venues for social integration (mainly, economic and symbolic) between social groups at the edges of the social ladder. This is a fairly new trend clearer only in some cities and (still) absent from many others, depending on the advancement of economic reform and liberalization of land markets in specific countries and cities. Some tracts of the Santiago gentrified "popular" periphery seem to show an increasing level of social integration.[1] More work is required to determine if this pattern is appearing elsewhere. Conceivably, proximity would not prompt social integration of any sort in cities where crime and violence are much higher than in Santiago. This is an open question, but an important one.

2. On the other hand, and at the same time, most Latin American cities are witnessing the emergence of urban ghettos, a reality that was unfamiliar to urban Latin America before the 1980s neoliberal economic reform. Ghettos of despair and crime are taking form both in the legal, paved, serviced, and adjusted-to-land-use-norm neighborhoods produced by "social housing" policies in Santiago[2] as well as in the typical shantytowns that abound in most Latin American cities, which land

markets and public policy still structurally tend to produce in all of these cities, Santiago included.

Data for Santiago we are currently analyzing show the spatial dispersion of the elite and upper-middle-income groups (specifically, a decrease in segregation as measured by dissimilarity and isolation indexes), and the ghettoization of low-income neighborhoods.[3] Figures 15.1 to 15.6 show the decrease in segregation in the period between the two last censuses (conducted in 1992 and 2002). Table 15.1 summarizes Santiago's social stratification and its variation. "Popular" groups correspond to strata D and E, which represent almost 45 percent of the poorest households in the city. Group E approximates the poverty level (10.8 percent of Santiago households were in poverty as of 2003, according to a nationwide survey conducted by the Ministry of Planning). Tables 15.2 and 15.3 show significant correlations between segregation (spatial isolation) and selected social problems among popular households of Santiago, mainly unemployment and youth inactivity—the latter being a precursor of crime and youth imprisonment, according to police statistics.

We believe that the generalized processes of gentrification—and thus the fragmentation of the elite urban space—that we observe in Santiago

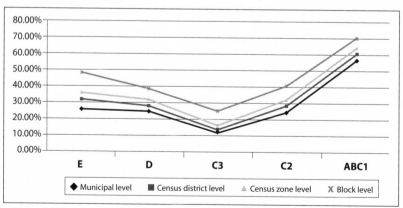

Figure 15.1 Residential segregation in Santiago 1992 (Dimension 1) for different socio-economic groups, following Duncan's index, at different spatial scales. Note: ABC1 corresponds to the elites (10% of the population); C2 and C3 to middle classes (20% and 25% of the population), D and E to the popular sectors (35% and 10% of the population).

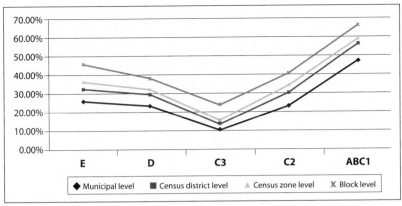

Figure 15.2 Residential segregation in Santiago 2002 (Dimension 1) for different socioeconomic groups, following Duncan's index, at different spatial scales.

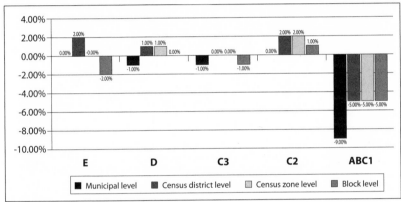

Figure 15.3 Change in residential segregation in Santiago 1992–2002 (Dimension 1) for different socioeconomic groups, following Duncan's index, at different spatial scales.

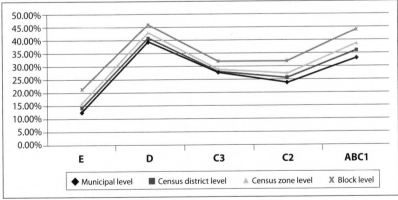

Figure 15.4 Residential segregation in Santiago 1992 (Dimension 2) for different socioeconomic groups, using the isolation index, at different spatial scales.

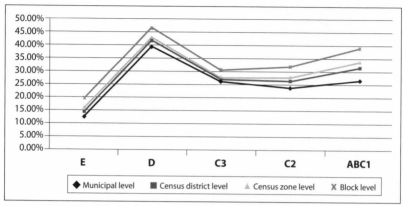

Figure 15.5 Residential segregation in Santiago 2002 (Dimension 2) for different
socioeconomic groups, using the isolation index, at different spatial scales.

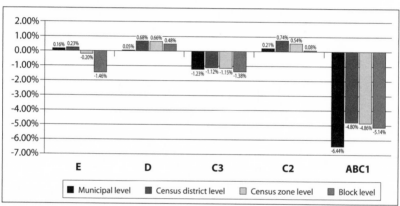

Figure 15.6 Change in residential segregation in Santiago 1992–2002 (Dimension 2)
for different socioeconomic groups, using the isolation index, at different spatial scales.

Level	E	D	C3	C2	ABC1	Total	N
1992	12%	33%	24%	21%	10%	100%	1245812
2002	9%	34%	26%	20%	11%	100%	1428010
1992–2002 %	-12,85	20,21	20,71	13,43	17,12	14,62	

Table 15.1 Distribution of socioeconomic groups, Santiago, Chile, 1992 and 2002.

Correlation between percentage of D and E households at each spatial scale with:	Municipal level	Census district level	Census zone level
Juvenile inactivity E+D (15-24 years) *	0.902	0.722	0.567
Juvenile unemployment E+D (15-24 years) *	0.57	0.284	0.177
Head of household unemployment E+D *	0.79	0.847	0.626
Teenage pregnancy E+D (15-19)	0.017	0.033	-0.011

Significant at 0,01.

Table 15.2 Simple correlations between social problems and residential segregation, Santiago, Chile, 2002. Segregation dimension 2 at different spatial scales. Two-tailed Pearson correlation.

Correlation between percentage of D and E households at each spatial scale with:	Municipal level	Census district level	Census zone level
Juvenile inactivity E+D (15-24 years) *	0.911	0.831	0.734
Juvenile unemployment E+D (15-24 years) *	0.703	0.589	0.374
Head of household unemployment E+D *	0.792	0,0.674	0.555
Teenage pregnancy E+D (15-19) **	0.214	0.131	0.095

*Significant at 0,01; ** Significant at 0,05.*

Table 15.3 Simple correlations between social problems and residential segregation, Santiago, Chile, 1992. Segregation dimension 2 at different spatial scales. Two-tailed Pearson correlation.

is also occurring in other Latin American big cities (see, for example, the gentrification of the southern zones of Buenos Aires's metro area). In today's Santiago, gentrification is generalized; it is occurring in many different zones and functionally encompasses commercial and office uses and not only residential markets. It is spreading down the social ladder and includes the poor and the middle class at the periphery. The Americo Vespucio, a seventy-kilometer-long beltway the state has gradually built since the early 1960s, once attracted almost only social housing compounds and politically organized massive land seizures, but it is now hosting middle- and high-income residential developments, large supermarkets and shopping malls, office complexes, university campuses and other modern facilities and developments, such as private graveyards and sporting clubs.[4]

The gentrification of Chilean cities is different from the phenomena described by that term in the United States. The expulsion or replacement of the poor, a typical component of gentrification is, for the most part, not taking place with regard to residential uses of land. The high demographic coverage of social housing programs, where dwellings are privately owned by low-income families—not rented as in Europe or the United States— makes up for most of the difference. According to the 2002 Census, 73 percent of Chilean households occupied a dwelling that was their own, a percentage that we estimate to be higher, close to 80 percent, for popular groups.

In such circumstances, it is difficult for an investor to buy all of the properties in a given site so as to replace them with a (gated) complex of houses for families of higher social standing. For gentrification to be profitable, new complexes in the popular periphery must be of a sizable scale. Buyers seek houses in homogenous complexes, and these cannot be small. It is improbable that affluent families would be willing to move to a small residential development in popular areas. Size of complexes and walled designs give feasibility to such a sociospatial shift. One owner unwilling to sell his/her property makes it impossible to assemble large blocks of land. This urban and juridical hindrance to social replacement explains why most gentrifying gated communities are built on vacant land close to, or surrounded by, popular neighborhoods.

It might be supposed that the social segregation of space could be decreasing in Santiago only because its scale is shrinking, with no social mixing taking place at the microlevel scale. Yet, what research and census data for Santiago show is that even the last process is materializing.[5] As shown in Figure 15.5, isolation shows a decrease at every single scale, even including at a block level. For other big Latin American cities where economic growth, reduction of poverty, social housing programs, and economic reform have not been as strong as in Santiago, it appears that the reduction in the scale of segregation, which seems quite widespread, is not coming from a market-driven gentrification of the urban periphery, but mainly from the penetration of elite zones by those in despair and economic insecurity, due to high levels of unemployment and the prevalence of unprotected and unstable jobs.

While Santiago is experiencing a generalized and fragmented gentrification, other big cities in Latin America are undergoing an illegal, irregular arm of the same process—one we could recognize as the structural tendency of the unprotected poor to improve their geography of opportunity. These marginalized groups tend to move their residences even to risky, illegal spots in the interstices of the formal city. In the last inter-census period, the favelas that grew the most in Rio de Janeiro were not those where more space was available, but those that were very dense, closer to the beaches, the urban center, and near middle- or upper-income neighborhoods. A similar trend was observed in Buenos Aires, whose three-million-people city area (out of a thirteen-million-person megacity) shrank by almost 7 percent between 1991 and 2001 (last two censuses), while the population in *villas miseria* in the city area more than doubled (a 105 percent increase).[6]

Both kinds of gentrification are important elements in the structural processes reshaping Latin American cities. They combine in peculiar, unrepeatable ways that create unique patterns in different cities. This observation probably applies outside of Latin America, too. The reduction in the scale of segregation due to gentrification processes seems to be not only a Latin American phenomenon, but something that is gaining weight in urban development in cities in other countries as well, like the United States, where the degree of residential segregation has also declined, both in racial terms[7] and in the spatial agglomeration of poor households.[8]

The L.A. School

Awareness of the social malaise that the restructuring of late capitalism has brought about in cities, as well as a sociogeographical description of its specific forms (fragmentation of space, decentering of cities at the expense of powerful suburbanization processes, disintegration of urban life into socially circumscribed layers, increase in violence and fear, and so forth), can be seen as the main contributions of the scholars associated (often loosely) with the L.A. School. Economic forces, represented by globalization and a post-Fordist regime of production and accumulation, have indeed contributed to transform Latin American and other regions' cities. Urban form is subjected to extensive reshaping by real estate markets, and a fragmentary urban landscape results. Traditional spatial "ecological" models, like those proposed by the old Chicago School, do not any longer describe the spatial patterns of today's cities or of the urban dynamics we are witnessing. The new arguments are more accurate: the "urban periphery organizes the center in the context of a globalizing capitalism."[9]

As we have noted, in Latin America, traditional upper- and middle-income areas are penetrated by the urban poor looking for better employment and life opportunities, while the periphery is colonized by the wealthy, geographically creating the "wealthy islands in the sea of decay"described by Mike Davis.[10] In addition, the security measures employed to protect the areas recently colonized by the elite, represented in gated communities and shopping malls, tend to generate in postmodern cities the kind of "vigilante paranoia" described by Davis and by Dear and Flusty.[11] In fact, while crime has remained stable in Santiago in the last few years, fear of crime and crime coverage in the news have skyrocketed. Moreover, urban ghettos have mushroomed in cities where they were once unknown. The increase in ghetto violence in most cities, most notably Sao Paulo and Rio de Janeiro, corroborates the negative consequences of the neoliberal transformation that the L.A. School describes so well.

Writers identified with the L.A. School emphasize that economic restructuring and globalization overwhelmingly influence the way different cities are developing; thus, they conclude, our primary attention should be drawn to the structural conditions of that restructuring: the seamlessness of the global economy, new structures of production, changes in the labor force and labor conditions, and the like.[12] These structural conditions seem to represent the common scenario of every city, and Los Angeles, which seems to exist at the height of these transformations, necessarily becomes a referent to be scrutinized.

Another important contribution of the L.A. School is its capacity to engage people in a debate about cities and their future. The overtly pessimistic tone in the literature of the L.A. School, with its focus on a capitalist "urban dystopia," engages students and scholars in a discussion about the urban future and the (negative) consequences of globalization and economic restructuring. As Judd argues, the L.A. School derives much of its power from its sweeping and often dramatically bleak interpretation of urban life.[13] Thus, for example, at the beginning of a class we sometimes read paragraphs of Mike Davis's *Fortress L.A.* ("Welcome to post-liberal L.A., where the defense of luxury lifestyles is translated in a proliferation of new repressions in space and movement, undergirded by the ubiquitous armed response"[14]) or Dear and Flusty's "Postmodern Urbanism." These readings guarantee attention and discussion, especially since all students can relate their arguments to their day-to-day experiences. They just need to translate East L.A. into Rio's Rosinha, Santiago's La Legua, or Buenos Aires's Fuerte Apache, and U.S. gated communities into *barrios privados* or *condominios,* and look at the appearance of shopping malls and highways, to see the transnational character of the phenomena they are witnessing on a daily basis. The Angeleno nightmare seems to be approaching their cities and neighborhoods.[15]

The tone of the L.A. literature appeals beyond the confines of the classroom, too. In the academic and policy environments of Latin America, the books and articles based on the premises of the L.A. School—for example, Teresa Caldeira's dramatic portrayal of Sao Paulo in *City of Walls*—have generated an almost unified critical consciousness about the modernizing process cities are currently experiencing. The structural similarities across many contexts explain the popularity of this discourse.

However, as noted earlier, empirical research reveals shortcomings in the L.A. perspective. The L.A. School's description of global processes and their impacts are close-grained enough to sustain a full understanding of urban processes, especially as these play out in particular cities. Despite the fact that L.A. School writers, particularly Dear, claim that they have a non-dogmatic approach and comprise, in any case, a loosely associated group of researchers,[16] the school's emphasis on structurally and economically deterministic factors is obvious. The idea that global economic forces determine the way cities are developing leads to a tendency to dismiss outcomes that do not fit the (theoretically) expectable outcome as anomalies unworthy of being studied—a sort of "empirical noise."

The deterministic approach in L.A. School texts represents, for those of us in Latin America, a new version of the tradition initiated in our subcontinent by the deterministic dependency theory of the 1960s and 1970s.[17] The world systems theory of the 1980s[18] can be considered a bridge to the L.A. School. The notions of (a) a world (global) capitalist system that moves through phases, whose determining forces and trends are pervasive and expansive; (b) new economic structures and social divisions that emerge "deductively" at the national, local, and urban levels; (c) new problems and social divisions that are deeper and more desolating than those in the previous phases of world capitalism;[19] and (d) new economic and social realities that give rise to new spatial forms: all of these are the main elements of the type of analysis that became popular in Latin America in the wake of dependency theory. This chain of arguments still provides the foundation for the understanding of many scholars and students in the urban field in Latin America. Today, we could name it the "globalization deterministic chain."

Let us comment on some of the parallels between the dependency theory of the 1960s and today's L.A. School. The assertion that "marginal masses" of Latin American cities do not perform the reserve and salary functions that Marx assigned in the "industrial reserve army" was one of the cornerstones of the marginality theory built by scholars in the shade of the dependency theory.[20] While Marx's army was part of the competitive early phases of capitalism, irreversible marginality (social exclusion, in today's terminology) was part of monopolistic capitalism, especially in its dependency phase (Latin American economies under imperialistic domination). The idea that absolute trends of social exclusion prevail today has turned into a sort of uncontested truth. Arguing that things could be more open or dynamic may put one at risk of misinterpretation or, bluntly, of being accused of ideological laxity or confusion.[21]

The contention that new spatial forms follow directly from the new social structures and social divisions is also an important parallel between dependency theory and the L.A. School perspective. The contention that new social forms correspond to the new spatial structures and social divides that economic globalization is bringing about is the last of the parallels we make. "Global cities" (a notion that raises theoretical and empirical doubts) become defined, in part, as "dual cities." This is perhaps one of the most pervasive and persistent ideas in the whole structuralist approach of Latin American cities that the L.A. School has contributed—knowingly or not—to "aggiornate" in the last decades.

The idea that spatial forms correspond directly with phases of capitalist development has been promoted prominently by Manuel Castells, who lived in Latin America in the late 1960s. In his seminal 1971 work *Imperialism and Urbanization in Latin America,* he was the first to present the "chain argument" linking world capitalism trends, dependency, urbanization, and marginality.[22] Yet, almost every empirical study carried out since then in the popular tracts in the periphery of Latin American cities has questioned the dual-city insight. It turns out that marginals were not really marginals. Despite being exploited, discriminated against, segregated into shantytowns, politically repressed, or poor, no small number have shown specific forms of integration into the system (defined by these scholars as the one built around corporate capitalism). Considerable percentages of dwellers were employed in big industries, were unionized, and were politically active or integrated into neighborhood organizations. The notion of marginality did not fit with what could be observed.[23]

Scholars got around this inconvenient fact by contesting reality itself: The "current overlapping between reserve army and marginality," Anibal Quijano argued back in those days, will be cleaned up in the near future by the inexorable march of monopolistic capitalism.[24] This type of reasoning, which is common among adherents of globalization determinism, has important epistemological flaws. It is reductionist, in the sense that reality is adjusted to fit theoretical and ideological preconceptions. Consistent with these problems is the fact that scientific empirical research—meaning that hypotheses are risked to empirical refutation—is not usual among these scholars. For example, those few studying residential segregation tend to select those pieces of reality that demonstrate their hypotheses (or preestablished conclusions).[25] Much of the reasoning is tautological: What better proof that globalization and growing inequalities necessarily fuel residential segregation than gated communities?

The postmodern urban dogma, therefore, conforms to a long entrenched structuralist intellectual tradition in Latin America. Post-Fordist (global) capitalism is said to bring inequality, violence, and segregation to any city in any given circumstance. This sweeping homogenization has a material, physical expression to it in the multiplication of certain urban artifacts, such as gated communities, shopping malls, and electronic cashiers. Common to every city, they are presumed to be destroying public spaces and local identities.[26]

One important difference between dependency discourse and the current L.A. School approach is that while the first was connected to political optimism, the second, as we have noted, is deeply pessimistic. The writers of the 1960s thought that growing contradictions would undermine capitalism and lead to socialist transformation. In contrast, today, the assertion that the powers of global capitalism penetrate every single dimension of economic and social life and urban process has metamorphosed into a sort of admiration. Criticism can combine or give way in awkward ways with subtle tones of respect, and the possibilities for social struggles and change are reduced merely to personal or small groups' acts of resistance, such as protest by neighborhoods, minorities, and the like. Such reformulation and reiteration of the same old schematic notions gives us little help in understanding the urban processes of particular cities.

Summing up, many Latin American scholars[27] make use of the writings of the L.A. School to persevere in, and upgrade, their old ways of interpreting urban phenomena. The causal chain linking economic globalization, which causes social inequality, which causes sociospatial segregation has been reinstated as an interpretation of today's urban reality. Since the first two (globalization and inequality) are uncontested facts, the increase in segregation is taken for granted, and this way it biases research, directing attention to supposedly growing segregation, material ostentation, and the privileged lives of the gated rich. Garay takes the argument one step further and states that social inequality derived from the conditions of the new economy has a physical reflection manifested in the social segregation of Latin American urban space. This is an elegant idea. Its straightforward, almost mechanistic quality illustrates why Latin American scholars who have grown up with dependency theory are so attracted to the theories that march under the banners of post-Fordist urbanism and the L.A. School.

Insights from Chicago

In the current urban academic map of Chicago, we may distinguish two different traditions: one coming from the discipline of planning—concerned with public housing, poverty, and community development—the other coming from political science or sociology, and focusing on the effect of culture, social movements, and, especially, local politics in shaping the way cities are developed. The first group is represented by academics working at the College of Planning and Public Policy Administration at the University of Illinois at Chicago, such as Janet Smith, John Betancour, and David Perry, while the second is spread throughout the Chicago area at several universities, and several are contributors to this book. Even considering the differences in the interests and approaches of the many scholars involved, they share enough similarities to make us think that there may be a protoschool of urban studies incubating.

The main commonality in their research is their stress on human agency, as expressed in organizational and neighborhood politics and political action. The city is seen as a pluralistic and diverse space[28] in which different social or ethnic groups attempt to negotiate their differences while at the same time maintaining their own identities. The idea that economic or structural factors do not overwhelm all else is helpful in understanding complex urban phenomena and in supporting research approaches similar to those of the old Chicago School. It also provides a basis for analyzing particular cities and their deviations from what might be considered "normal" effects of economic restructuring and globalization processes. As Clark argues, "if every city is unique, it is because general processes combine in unique ways in each location. But we can understand a single city better, and offer more lessons for others, by attending to the general processes as well as how they combine to generate uniqueness."[29]

Of course there are significant differences in the perspectives of the Chicago scholars. For Clark, culture is the most important variable distinguishing different cities. Making the case for the importance of culture, Clark argues that the fact that Chicago is mostly a Catholic city has contributed to the maintenance of community ties at a neighborhood level and a decentralized local political system in which different ethnic groups can keep their traditions as well as some of their political power. The influence of Catholicism seems particularly relevant in the context of Latin American cities, where (social or cultural) tolerance for difference appears as a virtue that is not observed in many U.S. cities, and where the homogeneously wealthy suburb is a less common phenomenon than in the United States.[30] Thus, for example, a religious culture that is more open to difference may explain why the mere spatial closeness between the poor and the wealthy is enough to generate some social integration for the poor, as we have found in the city of Santiago,[31] and has not been enough in many U.S. cities, with their public housing projects located as "islands of decay in a sea of wealth."

The work of other scholars (Judd; Bennett, Smith and Wright;[32] Bennett; and Simpson)[33] has considered the way that local political systems work in negotiating the differences among interest groups and social and ethnic movements. Most of this research has focused on Chicago, but not all. Judd, for example, makes the case, using St. Louis as a case study, that residential segregation of the African American population is not only an economic structural phenomenon but also has been reinforced by the actions or omissions of different layers of government.[34] This argument also resonates in different Latin American cities, where the national state, in order to solve the housing deficit for the poor, buys land in the outskirts of the cities, where it is cheap, and concentrates the poor population there. In this same vein, Bennett argues that public policies have helped Chicago combat the structural decay brought about by deindustrialization, and that these reflect the influence of a broad range of institutional players in the public and private sectors, including community organizations.[35]

Insights from New York

Discussing the subject of a real or imagined New York School is a difficult task because it is almost impossible to clearly distinguish what ideas they share from the ideas that represent only the concerns of certain scholars.

Accordingly, it is far easier to analyze individual authors than to characterize a distinctive school of thought.

David Halle calls Jane Jacobs the "doyenne" of the New York School.[36] Jacobs has been valued by leftist intellectuals for her analysis of the street as a place where there is an overlapping of different activities and a rich network of interactions.[37] For Jacobs, this diversity of the street is the cornerstone of urban social life, a street that is not completely determined or appropriated by any user or activity. Jacobs's analysis, however, has been reified and conservatively interpreted by different scholars. What is important for these scholars is the preservation of the modern diverse street, rather than Jacobs's theoretical contribution, which contributes not only to an understanding of the street, but also of the whole city, as a space where there is a certain degree of indeterminacy arising from the complex interaction of different actors, forces, and land uses. Another New Yorker, Richard Sennett, has promoted a similar idea. He states that disorder, and to a certain degree, anarchy, are necessary elements in a mature city, a city whose identity and the identity of its inhabitants are not threatened by the encounter and conflicting interests with a different other.[38] A preoccupation with indeterminacy and disorder has been updated by a third New Yorker, the software guru Steven Johnson. For Johnson, a system of different relatively simple elements may organize spontaneously and without explicit laws and generate a complex and intelligent system, such as a neighborhood. This is what he calls "emergence."[39]

Our earlier discussion should make it clear that indeterminacy and emergence help to explain the late capitalist cities in which we are living; cities in which capital, developers, and the restructuring of the economy interact with political power, social resistance, culture, and geographical conditions to create spaces that are both similar (given the structural conditions) and different, depending on the particular conditions of a place and the social struggles that occur there.

Other New York authors who provide insights relevant to the current Latin American city are Susan Fainstein[40] and Sharon Zukin.[41] Both have described, although from different perspectives, the ways in which developers and the real estate markets shape the geographies of urban space. In these authors' work, gentrification and city redevelopments are not simple consequences of globalization and economic restructuring, as the L.A. School may argue, but instead reflect profound changes both in the real estate market (Fainstein) and in the way people construct their cultural identities (Zukin). Thus, for example, the development of lofts in urban areas represents a new form of living related to certain segments of the upper middle class who have acquired a sensibility for culture, aesthetics, and lifestyle.[42]

In spite of these important arguments, we believe that the analysis that emerges from the particularities of New York must necessarily deemphasize certain aspects that are central to the understanding of Latin American cities—specifically, sprawl, suburbanization, and the changes in economies that were never fully industrialized. These metropolitan conurbations are transitioning from an incomplete and unequal industrial modernization to the service and post-Fordist economy. Accordingly, their spatial development shows tendencies both toward more activity at the center and greater decentralization.

Conclusion

Urban dynamics are complex; to understand them, we must take structural factors, human agency, and the indeterminacy and contingency of urban processes into account. Economic structures materialize in different cities in specific forms of interaction that play out in politics, culture, and movements of social participation and resistance. Urban dynamics occur on a relatively open and contested ground, as can be seen in the Latin American context, which promotes social integration and the worst possible ghetto scenarios at the same time. The connection between social differentiation and spatial segregation is not only dynamic (it has a time dimension that is at least as important as its spatial dimension) but is also mediated by forces, mechanisms, and processes that define a more open outcome than what is usually assumed to prevail, whether the theory stresses structure, agency, or urban culture. The idea that social inequality is reproduced on urban space in some photographic process is simplistic and misguided.

As an example of these complex dynamics, the city of Santiago shows that, at least in some cases, and through the gentrification of the poor periphery, private sector developers have helped to reduce residential segregation, and the result has sometimes also been an increase in social interaction between the classes. The state has also shaped spatial patterns in unexpected and unintended—and often in contradictory—ways. On one hand, since the recovery of democracy in 1989, left-of-center governments, constrained by skyrocketing land prices and by the need to build enormous numbers of housing units for the poor, have tended to concentrate public housing complexes in the outskirts of the city, where land is cheaper, or in spaces left behind by market forces because of a concentration of poor people or relative inaccessibility. Ghettoization is thus breaking down, but it is also occurring in segregated public housing complexes rather than in the remnants of shantytowns, according to the preliminary findings of our own fieldwork.[43] Thus, while the state may have solved the problem of the shantytown and of illegal settlements by providing housing, sewage facilities, drinking water, and some minimal infrastructure for the poor, it has contributed to the kind of ghetto problematic that is common in developed countries.

Moreover, shantytown dwellers living in municipalities that are undergoing gentrification have struggled to remain in those spaces, even if it means rejecting new housing units located at the periphery. In the case of "la toma de Penalolen," the last important land seizure in Santiago (in 1999), located in a traditionally poor and now gentrifying area, its inhabitants organized and fought government attempts to move them out. Finally, they cut a deal with authorities, obtaining new housing units in the same municipality they were living in. This story makes it clear that one theoretical size does not fit all.

The way the poor are locating in Santiago highlights some of the important intermediate factors that need to be incorporated into a theoretical framework that might explain future developments in Latin American cities. Among them we stress the following dimensions:

> • *Juridical:* Latin American cities show a high level of home ownership of state-produced or subsidized dwellings (social housing instead of the U.S. public housing). Private ownership of housing units may help the ralentization of social displacement that follows gentrification; and thus,

planners might be able to stabilize socially mixed areas for long periods of time, even decades, even in places being gentrified by aggressive real estate capitalism.

- *Economic:* The popular periphery as well as middle-income neighborhoods, and suburban as well as urban areas, represent a huge booty for real estate interests that could fuel a long-lasting real estate dynamic that reduces residential and social-class segregation. Thus, structural economic mechanisms may combine with agency to mediate the relationship between social differences and spatial restructuring of the city.

- *Social identities:* Latin American classist or uneven societies represent a sort of social capital for the possibility of reducing sociospatial segregation, at times when the latter seems to be pushing low-income neighborhoods into ghettoization. Since class divides are well defined and quite static (upward social mobility is not as strong as in the United States), there seems to be little need to resort to spatial segregation to build or defend those identities. As a consequence, the middle class is willing to live close by the poor.

- *Violence and fear:* Looking at different countries in Latin America, it is possible to argue that the degree of fear and social violence is related to the possibilities of generating social integration. While in Latin American countries the poor are trying to live closer to the wealthy, and the wealthy are colonizing traditionally poor enclaves, the social effects of this reduction in the scale of segregation are not uniform. Violence and fear are determinant factors. In this respect, the lessons of the L.A. School are very relevant.

It would be too easy and unfair to say that the L.A. School's theories of the city do not match contemporary realities. The assertion we have made that contemporary cities are more complex than the available theories should not be equated with an antiscientific, commonsense stance that is all too common.

The processes depicted by writers identified with the L.A. School are almost universal; accordingly, they provide crucial insights about cities almost everywhere. What is missing, however, is the other side of the story: the mediation of local forms of resistance and accommodation, the inherited material structure of cities, and cultural factors. The tendency to overlook these local differences in a deductivist, empirically insensitive way has weakened the social sciences, and especially urban research, in Latin America. While the geographical map the L.A. School draws of the postmodern city (fragmented, class-divided, and in constant sprawl) may, and in fact does fit, Latin American cities, the deterministic views of that map's emergence and its consequences seem limited. The complex and dynamic urban scenario in which political, cultural, social, and developers' motivations have an important role in the reshaping of urban space, does not match the dual-city images so popular among these scholars.

While we may agree with the L.A. School's general geographic description of the postmodern city, we believe the determinist (and pessimist) tendencies of the school do not describe the reality of the majority of cities in Latin America. Moreover, what the L.A. School sees as negative urban phenomena of late capitalism, such as fragmentation, may be interpreted in a completely different fashion. In Latin American cities, and in other cities of the world, local cultures, land markets, governmental policies, and local resistance have created cities that are similar—and thus global—but at the same time very different from one another. While capitalist restructuring may contribute to fragmenting the Latin American city, there are other processes, less structural in nature, that contribute to give any specific city its character, making cities more open and unpredictable. The peculiar, unedited combination of structural forces makes every city unique. The factors and processes that make up this uniqueness have been better covered in the works of both Chicago and New York scholars than by those of the L.A. School.

Notes

1. For examples collected in low-income neighborhoods in Santiago, see R. Salcedo and A. Torres, "Gated Communities in Santiago: Wall or Frontier?" *International Journal of Urban and Regional Research* 28, no. 1 (2004): 27–44; F. Sabatini and G. Cáceres, "Los barrios cerrados y la ruptura del patrón tradicional de segregación en las ciudades latinoamericanas: el caso de Santiago de Chile," in F. Sabatini and G. Cáceres, *Barrios cerrados en Santiago de Chile: Entre la exclusión y la integración residencial* (Santiago and Boston: Lincoln Institute of

Land Policy, 2004); F. Sabatini and R. Salcedo, "Gated Communities and the Poor: Functional and Symbolic Integration in a Context of Aggressive Capitalist Colonization," *Housing Policy Debate*, 18, no. 3; R. Salcedo, G. Fernández, and A. Torres, "Barrios cerrados y comunidades ideológicas," in R. Hidalgo, R. Trumper, and A. Borsdorf, eds., *Transformaciones urbanas y procesos territoriales: La nueva ciudad latinoamericana* (Santiago: Ediciones Pontificia Universidad Católica de Chile, 2005).

2. A. Rodríguez and A. Sugranyes, *Los con techo: Un desafío para la política de vivienda social* (Santiago: Ediciones SUR, 2005).

3. Data for other cities in Chile show similar tendencies after 1970—for Valparaiso and Concepcion, the second- and third-largest cities, see F. Sabatini, G. Cáceres, and J. Cerda, "Segregación residencial en las principales ciudades chilenas: endencias de las tres últimas décadas y posibles cursos de acción," EURE 27, no. 82 (2001): 21–42. With financing from the World Bank and the Chilean government, we are currently undertaking separate surveys and qualitative research in eight state-subsidized social housing compounds in three Chilean cities, including Santiago, to gain knowledge on the influence of residential segregation on individual, household, and collective progress and life opportunities.

4. Social heterogeneity has interesting political implications, like the empowerment it means for residents fighting against Locally Unwanted Land Uses (LULUs). Sabatini and Wormald compared the mobilizations that two landfill projects spurred in two tracts of the western periphery of Santiago with the success of the most heterogeneous group of protesters and the defeat of the group consisting almost entirely of popular residents. See F. Sabatini and G. Wormald, "La guerra de la basura de Santiago: Desde el derecho a la vivienda al derecho a la ciudad," EURE 30, no. 91 (2004): 67– 86.

5. See Salcedo and Torres, "Gated Communities in Santiago."

6. Statistical data for Buenos Aires was kindly provided by Mercedes di Virgilio from Universidad de Buenos Aires.

7. E. Glaeser, "Racial Segregation in the 2000 Census: Promising News" (Washington, D.C.: The Brookings Institution, 2001).

8. Paul A. Jargowsky, "Stunning Progress, Hidden Problems: The Dramatic Decline of Concentrated Poverty in the 1990s" (Washington, D.C.: The Brookings Institution, May 2003).

9. Michael Dear and Steven Flusty, "Los Angeles as Postmodern Urbanism," in Michael Dear, ed., *From Chicago to L.A.: Making Sense of Urban Theory* (Thousand Oaks, Calif.: SAGE Publications, 2002).

10. Mike Davis, *City of Quartz: Excavating the Future of Los Angeles* (New York: Verso, 1991).

11. See Dear and Flusty, "Los Angeles as Postmodern Urbanism," 67.

12. See especially the works of Allen Scott: *Metropolis: From the Division of Labor to Urban Form* (Berkeley and Los Angeles: University of California Press, 1988); *New Industrial Spaces: Flexible Production Organization and Regional Development in North America and Western Europe* (London: Pion, 1988); *Technopolis: High-Technology Industry and Regional Development in Southern California* (Berkeley and Los Angeles: University of California

Press, 1993); "Regional Push: Towards a Geography of Development and Growth in Low- and Middle-Income" Countries," *Third World Quarterly,* 23, no. 1 (Feb., 2002), 137–61.

13. D. Judd, "Stirrings of a Chicago School II: A New Approach to Urban Scholarship?" *Pragmatics: Journal of Community-Based Research* 8, no. 1 (2005): 4–8; see esp. 4.

14. See Davis, *City of Quartz.*

15. In an interview in *O Globo* (Rio de Janeiro), May 23, 2006, Carlo Marcola, leader of the criminal groups that in recent months almost took over Sao Paulo, argues, "We are not afraid of dying, you are scared to death. We are well armed, you just have the old thirty-eights. We are attacking, you are defending yourselves and your society. You have your humanism, we are cruel, with no mercy. You transformed us into criminal superstars."

16. See Dear and Flusty, "Los Angeles as Postmodern Urbanism," 13.

17. Andre Gunder Frank, *Latin America: Underdevelopment or Revolution* (New York: Monthly Review Press, 1969); F. H. Cardoso and E. Faletto, *Dependencia y desarrollo en América Latina: Ensayo de interpretación sociológica* (Ciudad de México: Siglo XXI, 1969); T. Dos Santos, *Dependencia y cambio social* (Santiago: Ediciones Universidad de Chile, 1970).

18. See Immanuel Wallerstein, *The Capitalist World-Economy* (Cambridge: Cambridge University Press, 1979); *The Modern World-System, vol. II: Mercantilism and the Consolidation of the European World-Economy, 1600–1750* (New York: Academic Press, 1980); with Terence K. Hopkins et al., *World-Systems Analysis: Theory and Methodology* (Beverly Hills, Calif.: SAGE Publications, 1982); with Samir Amin, Giovanni Arrighi, and Andre Gunder Frank, *Dynamics of Global Crisis* (London: Macmillan, 1982); *The Politics of the World-Economy: The States, the Movements and the Civilizations* (Cambridge: Cambridge University Press, 1984).

19. For a discussion of the myth of an open and democratic past in urban topics, see R. Salcedo, "El espacio public en el debate actual: Una reflexión crítica sobre el urbanismo post-moderno," EURE 28, no. 84 (2002): 5–19.

20. See, among others, J. Nun, "Superpoblación relativa, ejército industrial de reserva y masa marginal," *Revista Latinoamericana de Sociología,* 2 (1969): 174–236; A. Quijano, "Redefinición de dependencia y marginalización en América Latina" (working paper, CESO, Universidad de Chile, 1970).

21. On several occasions in academic environments we have been privately advised about being "inconvenient" or even "politically incorrect" after leveling criticism of the "globalization deterministic chain" and offering more open views of contemporary cities. That global capitalism could stimulate, let alone host, decreases in residential segregation or create new venues for social integration, even if these are depicted as partial, weak, or occasional, as we have argued, is something one can hardly mention without being accused of being a neo-liberal or a right-winger.

22. M. Castells, *Imperialismo y urbanización en América Latina* (Barcelona: Gustavo Gili, 1971).

23. For a more detailed discussion of these studies and their conclusions, see F. Sabatini, "La dimension ambiental de la pobreza urbana en las teorías latinoamericanas de la marginalidad," EURE 8, no. 23 (1981): 53–67.

24. A. Quijano, "Redefinición de dependencia y marginalización en América Latina."

25. See, for example, M. Svampa, *Los que ganaron: La vida en los countries y barrios cerrados* (Buenos Aires: Biblios, 2001); R. Hidalgo, "De los pequeños condominios a la ciudad vallada: Las urbanizaciones cerradas y la nueva geografía social en Santiago de Chile (1990–2000)," *EURE* 30, no. 91 (2004): 29–52.

26. See, among others, C. De Mattos, "Santiago de Chile, globalización y expansión metropolitana: Lo que existía sigue existiendo," *EURE* 25, no. 76 (1999): 29–56.

27. See, for example, A. Garay, "Dimensión local de lo territorial" (class notes from the graduate course "Local Development in Metropolitan Areas," Instituto del Conurbano de la Universidad Nacional de General Sarmiento de Argentina, e Instituto de Investigadores Sociales de la Universidad Nacional Autónoma de México, 2002); R. Segré, "Arquitectura y ciudad en América Latina: Centros y bordes en las urbes difusas," *Periferia (1998),* http://www.periferia.org/; C. de Mattos, "Santiago de Chile: Globalización y expansión metropolitana: Lo que existía sigue existiendo," *EURE* 25, no. 76 (1999): 29–56.

28. Terry Nichols Clark, "The New Chicago School: Notes Toward a Theory," chapter 11, this volume.

29. Ibid.

30. J. Vargas, "Aspectos de la vida privada de la clase alta de Valparaíso: la casa, la familia y el hogar entre 1830–1880," *HISTORIA,* no. 32 (1999). Vargas, making an historical analysis of elite private life in the city of Valparaíso, argues that while the traditional Catholic aristocracy remained along with the poor in the section of the city near the seaport, the immigrant elite (mainly British) colonized the hills, creating enclaves that were both 100 percent Protestant and wealthy.

31. Sabatini and Salcedo, "Gated Communities and the Poor in Santiago, Chile."

32. Larry Bennett, Janet S. Smith, and Patricia A. Wright, eds., *Where Are Poor People to Live? Transforming Public Housing Communities* (Armonk, New York: M.E. Sharpe, 2006).

33. Dick Simpson, *Rogues, Rebels, and Rubberstamps: The Story of Chicago City Council from the Civil War to the Third Millennium* (Boulder, Colo.: Westview Press, 2001).

34. D. Judd, "The Role of Governmental Policies in Promoting Residential Segregation in the Saint Louis Metropolitan Area," *Journal of Negro Education* 66, no. 3 (1997): 214–40.

35. L. Bennett, "Community Power Applied: Chicago's Engagement with Twenty-First Century Globalization," *Sociological Imagination* 42 (2006): 65–82.

36. David Halle, *New York and Los Angeles: Politics, Society and Culture: A Comparative View* (Chicago: University of Chicago Press, 2004).

37. Jane Jacobs, *The Death and Life of Great American Cities* (New York: Vintage, 1961).

38. R. Sennett, *The Uses of Disorder: Personal Identity and City Life* (New York: W.W Norton and Co., 1970).

39. S. Johnson, *The Connected Lives of Ants, Brains, Cities, and Software* (New York: Touchstone, 2001).

40. Susan Fainstein, *The City Builders* (Malden, Mass.: Blackwell, 1994).

41. S. Zukin, *Loft Living: Culture and Capital in Urban Change* (New Brunswick, N. J.: Rutgers University Press, 1989); S. Zukin, *Landscapes of Power: From Detroit to Walt Disney*

(Berkeley: University of California Press, 1991); S. Zukin, *The Culture of Cities* (Malden, Mass.: Blackwell, 1995).

42. See Zukin, *Loft Living*.

43. "Barrios exitosos y barrios en crisis producto de la vivienda social en Chile," CONICYT–World Bank (research project).

16

Studying Twenty-first Century Cities

■ Dick Simpson and Tom Kelly

Twentieth-century urban theory has proven inadequate to tackle urban issues of the twenty-first century. Even Chicago, home of the Chicago school of urban studies, no longer fits the paradigms of these earlier scholars. These older theories describe cities outside the United States even less well. Today's cities exhibit different patterns of development, economics, politics, culture, society, and government from the manufacturing-based city of the early twentieth century.

The essays in this book do not offer a single uncontested theory that fits all cities and metropolitan regions. There is no single paradigm capable of replacing the one created by the Chicago School. No single hegemonic theory of cities is sufficient for all modern metropolises.

The essays in this book demonstrate why the old paradigms are inadequate in the twenty-first century. Recent theories, whether they come under the label of "schools" or not, may help in understanding cities in Europe, Asia, and Latin America, but they are likely to fall short in some key respects. We can be confident that these paradigms are useful in helping us to understand important aspects of urban development in the United States; more than that it is difficult to say.

The Development of Urban Theory

We believe the essays and empirical evidence presented in this book have demonstrated that any adequate theory would account for the following characteristics:

1. *A metropolitan region in which the center still holds:* The twentieth-century city has metamorphosed into the twenty-first century metropolis. Within these metropolitan regions, both the forces of centralization and the forces of fragmentation are occurring at the same time. While central cities remain important, peripheral growth can be consistent with a vibrant center.

2. *Multiculturalism:* Heterogeneity compels interaction among unlike peoples. When race, poverty, and segregation are highly correlated, conflict is inevitable and governance becomes difficult. Alternatively, multiculturalism is a highly positive feature that confers major advantages in the global economy.

3. *Globalization:* Each region must be examined not only in relation to its place in the global system, but in terms of its local responses to global forces. The evolution of modern metropolitan regions reflects local constraints, choices, and history. New York, Chicago, and Los Angeles became cities in different historical periods, which is one of the reasons they differ. Accounting for these differences is a central task of urban theory.

4. *Comparative research:* Where possible, given resource and time limitations, we need to compare cities to fully understand them. Comparing cities allows us to identify both their common characteristics and profound differences. Only from comparisons can we develop and test useful social science theories and paradigms.

5. *Multiple theoretical lenses:* We begin this book by describing the theories developed by the scholars of the original Chicago School, then follow with the schools that have appeared more recently. As Janet Abu-Lughod urges in her essay, it is our task to test these theories against the empirical realities on the ground. Ultimately, the goal of our search is to find explanations for the urban processes taking place in many different contexts.

6. *Politics and governmental institutions:* Metropolitan regions are not formed solely by impersonal social and economic forces. Human agency, operating through established institutions and protest organizations like Janitors for Justice, which Amy Bridges describes in her

essay, helps determine urban policies and urban development. A key question, especially in the United States, is whether there is sufficient political and governmental capacity at the local level to provide adequate governance and leadership in the twenty-first century.

These categories are helpful because they emphasize an inclusive approach. In the past, urban theory has often been hampered by the tendency to regard a single city or metropolitan form as the archetype for all other places, and by an exclusive focus on cities in the United States. Comparative studies that include cities in the United States and in other countries are certain to make urban theory more robust and complete.

A Metropolitan Region in Which the Center Still Holds

From the perspective of the United States, it is obvious that the expansion beyond formal city boundaries makes it increasingly difficult for local governments to govern effectively. In every large metropolitan region there are hundreds of towns, villages, and special districts. Nonetheless, the center still holds. These metropolitan regions remain anchored by central cities geographically, economically, and politically. Just as our solar system of planets is organized around a single sun, metropolitan regions are organized around central cities. It may be true that there is an urban corridor from Boston to Philadelphia or from Los Angeles to the Mexican border, but even suburbanites recognize whether their center is Boston, New York, Los Angeles, or San Diego. This does not deny that the study of middle-sized cities and suburbs is also important. In fact, much more careful study of these places needs to be done in developing any adequate twenty-first century urban paradigm. Yet, as David Halle and Andrew Beveridge demonstrate in their essay, what New York and Los Angeles now have in common is population growth at the core. Even as centrifugal forces and decentralization continue, the center is becoming revitalized. Urban sociology, geography, economics, planning, and politics still focus on the central city because even after a century of decentralization the center helps to organize the metropolitan region. It is likely to continue to do so.

Multiculturalism

Heterogeneity, which makes personal interaction between unlike people compulsory, characterizes the multiracial, multicultural metropolitan regions of the twenty-first century. Older models of settlement patterns based on race have become inadequate. Some cities still experience stark segregation, but the division between black and white no longer describes urban development. The importance of embracing multicultural and multiracial perspectives becomes undeniable when cities are examined on a global scale, considering that some of the largest metropolitan regions in the world have populations that include only small numbers of either black or white people.

Beyond race, various ethnicities and religions that cut across racial categories are added to the multicultural mix. European and American regions are attracting increasing Muslim populations from Asian, Arab, and North African countries. Outside the United States, religion often overwhelms racial considerations. In Abuja, Nigeria, tensions exist between the Muslim and Christian residents. In Belfast, cultural and even physical barriers have been erected between Catholic Christians and Protestant Christians. Such divisions between differing racial, ethnic, or religious groups can readily be connected to patterns of wealth and poverty in metropolitan regions. On a metropolitan scale, we can follow these patterns of settlement, wealth, and poverty across municipal boundaries and study the causes and effects in suburbs that have heavy concentrations of specific races, ethnicities, or religions.

Complicating things still more, many residents of metropolitan areas in developing countries belong to no formal jurisdiction. This is increasingly important because already more than half of the world's population lives in cities. In the next few decades, millions more will live there, especially in cities of developing nations. By 2030 it is estimated that more than two billion people will live in informal shantytowns in the third world nations, usually without running water or electricity. Similar living arrangements exist in the slums and ghettos of the United States today, although they have been generally ignored by urban scholars. Models of formal city structure isolated from surrounding municipalities or models of metropolitan areas devoid of illegal or unregistered residents fail to reflect the modern urban reality. Several essays in this book focus at least partially on the "informal city" and the problems of the permanent underclass. They focus as well on often-overlooked events like race riots and their causes.

The increasingly complex structure of the modern metropolis, created through global networks, massive migration, incorporation of sprawling developments, and the rise of privatized city space, poses challenges for governance throughout the world. Concerns arise over the isolated poor, the disenfranchised informal residents, and the general lack of coordination for the public good under the hodgepodge of localities and authorities. Some cities outside the United States, such as Jerusalem, experience vicious struggles for physical space. Others in postwar countries like Freetown, Sierra Leone, face the daunting task of providing working electricity, clean water, proper sewage disposal, better education, and adequate health care with inadequate municipal budgets. A metropolitan framework that accounts for multicultural differences may provide insights into the struggles related to wealth distribution, physical space, and political legitimacy in cities in many different places.

Globalization

While the immediate pressures of global forces may differ from region to region, and while local responses to those pressures differ even more greatly, the twenty-first century reality is that major urban centers are linked through a global network of social and economic forces. If any further proof were needed, the experience of cities and metropolitan regions with the current recession demonstrates the downside of our global interconnectedness. Future urban theory must not only recognize these international forces but also include their effects on metropolitan regions inside and outside the United States.

Even if the Los Angeles, New York, and Chicago schools of thought could be effectively combined into a comprehensive paradigm, the new paradigm would still miss developments in the majority of the world's urban population. Even if a Beijing School, a Santiago School, and a Cairo School were included, naming a school of thought after a single city only makes sense if we use that name to categorize groups of scholars with similar theoretical perspectives. Proclaiming any single city to be an example of future city development is impractical. However, if we can understand the forces governing different metropolitan regions we may be able to develop theories that help us understand cities in widely varying contexts. Globalization is one of those forces, and future theory must account not only for the differences between regions due to globalization but also for the similarities that develop among them. It may be that Mexico City is most like Los Angeles, that Toronto is most like Chicago, and that London is most like New York City. If so, there is much that similar cities can learn from each other despite their differences in their national context, histories, and cultures. This may take the form of adopting what urban planners call "best practices," policies that seem to work in improving the urban condition.

Comparative Research

Any relevant urban theory must confront the diversity of cultures, histories, political structures and processes, geographies, and economic conditions. As Abu-Lughod writes, the purpose of theories is "to construct credible narratives about enormously complex ongoing processes in the real world." She goes on to say that theories become useless "words about words" when they are developed without observations from the real world. New urban theories must be founded on research on specific places to remain coherent and relevant to actual events. The focus on the "centerless" metropolis reflected the fractured metropolitan landscape of the Los Angeles region. This fact itself illustrates why theories derived from the study of a particular place must be partial and incomplete.

The rise of the Los Angeles School occurred because the old Chicago School proved unworkable and no other set of ideas was available to replace it. The incomplete nature of the L.A. School, coupled with its failure to predict revival of the urban core, opened the door for the ideas underpinning the New York School and the recent research on Chicago.

Several important developments in the urban world slipped through the theoretical cracks of all three schools. One is the understanding that extreme sprawl and fragmentation are mostly located in United States because of its decentralized urban policy. As the essay by Francisco Sabatini and Rodrigo Salcedo demonstrates, gated communities result in greater racial and economic segregation in the United States, but not in Latin America. Urban scholars did not anticipate the desire for a revived urban culture, which explains the resurgence of downtown populations mostly in the United States. Theories on globalization and the development of global cities reach beyond the borders of the United States but mostly fail to apply to the developing world, where the majority of urban residents live. In some Latin America cities, for instance, segregation has fallen at the same time that social inequality remains high. Differences like this explain how the best urban scholarship draws on nuanced comparative analyses across such metropolitan regions.

Multiple Theoretical Lens

Based on his studies of Los Angeles, Michael Dear maintains that five principal social dynamics underlie today's urbanism: globalization, network society, polarization between rich and poor, hybridization, and sustainability. These categories seem sufficiently broad to suggest that any theory of the urban must take them into account. The essays in this book have uncovered other social dynamics at work in the twenty-first century cities. Perhaps the two most important are: human agency and indeterminacy. These two principles suggest that urban processes are not solely determined by implacable economic and social forces. Any city is a dynamic place that develops from a clash of structural forces, institutions, and people. The outcomes cannot be fully predetermined. Only comparative analysis will allow us to determine how these dynamics interact to shape today's cities.

This observation may seem to suggest that schools are counterproductive. We do not believe that to be the case. Schools tend to evolve among scholars working in the same place because of the empirical facts on the ground arising from spatial form and local culture. Scholars look out of their home and office windows and share some common experiences. That means, of course, that the ideas advanced through these schools are bound to be limited. Our essays make it clear that past paradigms were never completely adequate. For example, the concentric rings of development proposed by Homer Hoyt do not describe today's realities in Chicago (and only approximately reflected yesterday's). Of course the facts on the ground themselves reflect different perspectives even of the same city. As Daphne Spain points out, Jane Addams and the settlement workers saw the city from a perspective at odds with the one held by most of the scholars at the University of Chicago. They documented "factors" that they personally observed and experienced, not the "forces" with which the scholars were most concerned. She and her colleagues were activists, but in the end they were, unavoidably, theorists.

However, we should not assume agreement even among people with shared experiences. If it is true that a school of thought develops a shared perspective, a common research agenda, a sense of membership in a school, and residence in the same metropolitan region, then none of the schools discussed in our book are completely solidified. This was as true of the original Chicago School as it is of the current schools. The L.A. School soon splintered, and the New York School has, by the account of Halle and Beveridge, disappeared. The scholars now working in Chicago cannot even agree on whether they have constituted a school or not. Even so, in all three cases a central set of ideas can be identified.

When the authors of the essays in this book convened at Hull House in Chicago several years ago, our debates made us reconsider carefully our assumptions and conclusions. Although our urban symposium revealed that a single paradigm of urban development does not exist, what our schools of thought do share is a commitment to empirically grounded research. As the two essays by Amy Bridges and by Steven Erie and Scott MacKenzie amply demonstrate, scholars studying Los Angeles are firmly rooted in an empirical tradition. The essay by David Halle and Andrew Beveridge is based on a great deal of statistical analysis that convincingly shows that recent patterns of demographic movement in New York and Los Angeles have converged. The recent scholarship on Chicago places a strong emphasis, as did the original Chicago School, on empirical evidence and participant observation. In the spirit of the Chicago School, some members of the recent group of Chicago scholars carry on the older reform tradition that entails the study of topics like political corruption and practical reform of city government, public schools, the police department, and the physical development of the metropolitan region.

Even when it reflects clear normative values, the Chicago scholarship is based on a rich trove of empirical evidence. The research is based on census data showing where racial groups cluster and where the rich and the poor live within the metropolitan region. Economic data provides information about the impact of the new global economy. Election results and patterns of campaign contributions provide information on politics. The voting pattern of the city council provides information on the government and the political clashes over policies that shape the region. Studies of the new economy are focused on tourism, infrastructure, and strategies of economic development.

Politics and Governmental Institutions

Human action, whether deliberate or unintentional, is a primary factor affecting metropolitan processes. Even in the global era, politics still matters. Residents of a single metropolitan area can do little to control the forces of macroeconomics, globalization, technological advancement, or immigration. They can neither control the decisions of higher levels of government, nor dictate where international firms will locate their businesses. They cannot prevent terrorist attacks nor avoid global economic recessions. Individual cities cannot make laws that have jurisdiction outside of their physical boundaries. And, of course, all metropolitan areas are subject to global forces, even if they are partially sheltered by national governments.

But the fortunes of a metropolis or an individual city are not outside the control of local politics. Local leaders respond to the forces of globalization differently. Each metropolitan region remains to some degree unique because of its unique history, development, and responses to these forces. Local actors shape the responses to forces outside their control. The Richard J. Daley machine that governed Chicago from 1955 to 1976 used local political muscle to shape the physical, social, and economic development of the city in the face of challenging circumstances. The titans of Wall Street and Mayors Giuliani and Bloomberg of New York help to shape their city and to recover from the September 11, 2001, attacks.

History and politics shape spatial and social dynamics of a city. Political considerations decide where public housing will be built, which neighborhoods will be razed for redevelopment, which groups will be marginalized, and how local government will ultimately adapt to forces beyond their control, such as cutbacks in federal assistance or a natural disaster. A fractured metropolis may result in the ability of residents to vote with their feet, but that does not preclude cooperation among localities for development, provision of services, or even tax sharing. Even the privatization of public space, such as the creation of gated communities, is the result of local decisions to surrender the costs of administering tracts of land while simultaneously collecting property taxes. As the literature on Los Angeles makes clear, the "spontaneous" development of the Los Angeles area was carefully planned and developed by local political forces.

The actions of governments at other levels matter too, even in the United States, which lacks a coherent urban policy. Recent events indicate that it is likely that national policy will become more important. In February 2009, the Obama administration announced that it was creating the White House Office of Urban Affairs. Later, in a speech to urban leaders, Vice President Joe Biden reaffirmed that the administration proposes to create a metropolitan agenda for urban regions, which house 80 percent of the U.S. population, provide two-thirds of the nation's jobs, and produce three-fourths of the gross national product.[1] As a first step, under the Obama administration, the American Recovery and Reinvestment Act poured billions of dollars into health care research, transportation projects, energy improvements, and higher education in our nation's cities.

The Future of Urban Theory

Directly or indirectly, urban scholars tend to agree on a singular principle: we study to advance the goal of a livable, just, and democratic city—or as Jane Addams put it, of a "socially just city." As this book goes to press, we are in the midst of a global recession greater than any since the Great Depression of the 1930s. But in many places in the world, urban conditions are so deep that they are scarcely touched by the global economic crisis.

A recent book on the challenges facing cities around the globe reports that "within three decades, one of every three human beings will live in near total squalor [mostly in cities]—lacking sanitation and clean water, fueling the spread of disease."[2] These realities make it imperative that urban theory be grounded, and relevant. A book like this cannot do much to map out the project of creating a livable, just, and democratic city, but it may help us to improve our understanding of the processes that have created the present urban condition and those that may point to a different future.

Notes

1. Vice President Joe Biden, speech at the Richard J. Daley Urban Forum at the University of Illinois at Chicago, April 27, 2009 (author's notes).

2. Neal R. Pierce and Curtis Johnson with Farley M. Peters, *Century of the City: No Time to Lose* (New York: The Rockefeller Foundation, 2008), 7.

Contributors

Janet Abu-Lughod is professor emerita from Northwestern University and the New School for Social Research. She has published thirteen books and more than one hundred articles on Middle Eastern cities, urban sociology, globalization, and urban riots. She is author of *New York, Chicago, Los Angeles: America's Global Cities* (Minnesota, 1991) and *Race, Space, and Riots in New York, Chicago, and Los Angeles*. In 1998 she was the recipient of the Robert and Helen Lynd Lifetime Career Award, Section on Community and Urban Sociology, American Sociological Association.

Robert A. Beauregard is professor of urban planning in the Graduate School of Architecture, Planning, and Preservation at Columbia University. He has written extensively on urban theory, urbanization, redevelopment policy, and planning theory. His most recent books include *Voices of Decline: The Postwar Fate of U.S. Cities* and *When America Became Suburban* (Minnesota, 2006).

Larry Bennett is professor of political science at DePaul University in Chicago. His most recent book is *The Third City: Chicago and American Urbanism*.

Andrew A. Beveridge, professor of sociology at Queens College and Graduate Center of CUNY, is working on a series of projects regarding long-term urban economic and racial change in the United States, including its impact on inequality. Recently, he began a study of the distribution and social effects of mortgage foreclosures with his colleague Elena Vesselinov. He is the creator of Social Explorer, a Web site for rapid visualization of demographic patterns and change from 1790 to the present in the United States. Since 1993 he has served as demographic consultant to the *New York Times*.

Amy Bridges is professor of political science at the University of California, San Diego. She has pioneered in research on the history of machine and reform politics. Her books include *A City in the Republic* and *Morning Glories*.

Terry Nichols Clark is professor of sociology at the University of Chicago. He has published thirty books, including *The New Political Culture* and *Urban Innovation*. He is the coordinator of the Fiscal Austerity and Urban Innovation Project, which has analyzed cities throughout the world.

Nicholas Dahmann is a PhD candidate in human geography at the University of Southern California. His work focuses on community mobilization and radical democratic practices against the gentrification of Skid Row in Downtown Los Angeles. Other ongoing research interests include the territorial and scalar politics of alliances and coalitions of community-based organizations.

Michael Dear is professor of city and regional planning at the University of California, Berkeley and honorary professor in the Bartlett School of Planning at University College London. His research interests are in urban theory and comparative urbanism, and his recent publications include *From Chicago to L.A.* and *The Postmodern Urban Condition.*

Steven P. Erie is a professor of political science and director of the urban studies and planning program at the University of California, San Diego. He has written on urban machines, ethnic and racial politics, social policy, infrastructure, bureaucracy and economic development, and public finance and governance. With Vladimir Kogan and Scott A. MacKenzie, he is completing *Paradise Plundered: Fiscal Crisis and Governance Challenges in San Diego.*

Frank Gaffikin is professor of spatial planning at the School of Planning, Architecture, and Civil Engineering, Queen's University of Belfast; the director of the Institute of Spatial and Environmental Planning; and a senior research fellow at the Great Cities Institute, University of Illinois at Chicago. He is involved in a major research project on contested cities and urban universities.

David Halle is professor of sociology at the University of California, Los Angeles. He has published on a variety of urban topics, including blue-collar workers, urban culture, and urban theory. His books include *New York and Los Angeles, Inside Culture,* and *America's Working Man.*

Dennis R. Judd is professor of political science and acting director of the Great Cities Institute, University of Illinois at Chicago. He has published extensively on urban economic development, urban tourism, and related topics. He is author of *City Politics,* coeditor of *The Tourist City, The Infrastructure of Play, Cities and Visitors,* and many other books, and is the former editor of the *Urban Affairs Review.* With Costas Spirou, he is working on a book on the cultural, tourism, and urban amenities strategy of urban redevelopment in Chicago.

Tom Kelly is a PhD candidate in the Department of Political Science at the University of Illinois at Chicago. He is currently at work on a dissertation on the politics of eminent domain in the United States.

Ratoola Kundu is a PhD student in the Department of Urban Planning and Policy, College of Urban Planning and Public Affairs at the University of Illinois at Chicago. She has researched extensively on urban issues in India and is a collaborator, with Frank Gaffikin and David Perry, on an ongoing research project on contested cities.

Scott A. MacKenzie is assistant professor of political science at the University of California, Davis. His current research examines national, state, and local political careers; the effects of electoral system institutions; and local economic development policies. He has written on economic development, infrastructure, public finance, and governance issues. With Steven P. Erie and Vladimir Kogan, he is completing *Paradise Plundered: Fiscal Crisis and Governance Challenges in San Diego.*

John Hull Mollenkopf is distinguished professor of political science and sociology at The Graduate Center of the City University of New York and directs its Center for Urban Research. He has authored fifteen books on immigration, urban politics, and urban policy, including *A Phoenix in the Ashes*, *The Contested City*, *Place Matters*, and *Inheriting the City*.

David C. Perry is director of the Great Cities Institute and professor of urban planning and policy at the University of Illinois at Chicago. He writes extensively in the areas of urban policy, urban infrastructure, institutional political economy, urban theory, and the role of place-based urban institutions in urban change. His most recent books include *The University as Urban Developer* and *Global Universities and Urban Development*.

Francisco Sabatini is professor at the Pontificia Universidad Católica de Chile, in Santiago. He has published extensively on urban studies and planning, residential segregation, and environmental conflicts. He combines his academic work with NGO-based research and action projects throughout Latin America.

Rodrigo Salcedo is assistant professor in the Institute of Urban and Territorial Studies, Pontificia Universidad Católica de Chile, in Santiago. In addition to his research on segregation, urban space, and related topics, he has been an advisor for the Ministry of Government and has headed the urban policy group of the Chilean Socialist Party.

Dick Simpson is professor and head of the Department of Political Science, University of Illinois at Chicago. He is the author of sixteen books and more than eighty professional articles and films. An expert on Chicago politics, he is author of a leading book on Chicago's party machine, *Rogues, Rebels, and Rubber Stamps*, and a reader on American urban politics, *Inside Urban Politics*.

Daphne Spain is James M. Page Professor, Department of Urban and Environmental Planning, in the School of Architecture, University of Virginia. Her most recent book is *How Women Saved the City* (Minnesota, 2001). She is conducting research on how social movements transform the use of urban space.

Costas Spirou is professor in the Department of Social and Behavioral Sciences at National-Louis University in Chicago and visiting fellow at the University of Notre Dame. He has published widely on culture policy, urban redevelopment, and urban tourism. He is author of *Urban Tourism and Urban Change: Cities in a Global Economy* and coauthor of *It's Hardly Sportin',* a book about stadium politics in Chicago. With Dennis Judd, he is working on a book on the cultural, tourism, and urban amenities strategy of urban redevelopment in Chicago.

Index

The following abbreviations are used in this index: "L.A." for Los Angeles and "NYC" for New York. The designations *f* and *t* after page numbers indicate figures and tables, respectively.

DATE DUE

FEB 1 0 2012	
APR 1 5 2012	
MAY 2 9 2013	
FEB 1 0 2014	
NOV 1 3 2 2 2014	
NOV 1 3 2014	